ECONOGUIDE® SERIES

ECONOGUIDE® CRUISES 2005

Cruising the Caribbean, Hawaii, New England, Alaska, and Europe

COREY SANDLER

The
Globe
Pequot
Press

GUILFORD, CONNECTICUT

To buy books in quantity for corporate use
or incentives, call **(800) 962–0973, ext. 4551,**
or e-mail **premiums@GlobePequot.com.**

Econoguide is a registered trademark of Word Association, Inc.

Text design by Lesley Weissman-Cook

ISBN 0-7627-3143-5
ISSN 1529-9015

Manufactured in the United States of America
Third Globe Pequot Press Edition/First Printing

To Janice, who keeps me on course

ACKNOWLEDGMENTS

AS ALWAYS, dozens of hardworking and creative people helped move my words from the keyboard to the book you hold in your hands.

Among the many to thank are Jeff Serena, Mary Luders Norris, and Liz Taylor of The Globe Pequot Press; we look forward to many years of partnership. Thanks, too, to the editorial and production staff at Globe Pequot, including Mimi Egan, Erin Joyce, and Melissa Evarts.

Gene Brissie has been a believer for a decade, and the feeling is mutual.

My appreciation extends to the cruise lines and public relations staffs who helped me assemble the massive stack of specifications, itineraries, and prices and wrangle them into manageable shape.

As always, thanks to Janice Keefe for running the office and putting up with me, a pair of major assignments.

And thanks to you for buying this book. We all hope you find it of value; please let us know how we can improve the book in future editions. (Enclose a stamped envelope if you'd like a reply; no phone calls, please.)

Corey Sandler
Econoguide Travel Books
P.O. Box 2779
Nantucket, MA 02584
You can send us e-mails at info@econoguide.com.

You can also consult our Web page at
www.econoguide.com

We hope you'll also consider the other books in the Econoguide series. You can find them at bookstores, or ask your bookseller to order them. All are written by Corey Sandler.

Econoguide Walt Disney World® 2005
Econoguide Disneyland® Resort, Universal Studios Hollywood® 2005
Econoguide Las Vegas 2005
Econoguide Buying or Leasing a Car
Econoguide Buying and Selling a Home

Also by Corey Sandler:
Watching Baseball: Discovering the Game within the Game, with Jerry Remy
Fix Your Own PC, Seventh Edition

CONTENTS

INTRODUCTION

WELCOME ABOARD for a cruise between the covers of the 2005 edition.

During the past few years, I've floated from one stunning horizon to the next on a series of journeys that have taken me from my home in one of the rugged harbors of New England to the iridescent waters of the Caribbean, the wild geological stew of geysers and glaciers in Iceland, the wondrous ice-carved canyons of Alaska's Inside Passage, the fire-born islands of Hawaii and the South Pacific, and through the man-made wonder of the Panama Canal. I crossed the "pond" from England to the New World, and I played tag with hurricanes. For two magical weeks we cruised from one magnificent Mediterranean port to another, and on another trip we circled the British Isles from Dover to Ireland to Scotland.

Some of the highlights of my recent career at sea:
- Sailing from New Zealand through the tumultuous Tasman Sea to Australia on a ship with luxuries Captain Cook could never have imagined.
- Joining the captain on the bridge in a predawn crossing of the Cape Cod Canal on a memorable cruise that sailed north to Canada to avoid a storm in the Bermuda Triangle.
- Cruising dramatically out of New York on a waterborne Restaurant Row several cuts above your basic lido buffet.
- Floating into history on a thoroughly modern sailing vessel.
- Ten days afloat from Iceland to New York in sybaritic luxury in a three-room suite on a ship where the champagne flowed like water.
- Living the pampered life aboard the world's largest private sailing yacht, while visiting some obscure corners of the Caribbean like Îles des Saintes, Carriacou, and Bequia.
- Enjoying culinary theater in a dining room decorated with century-old paneling from a classic liner, within a high-tech modern ship powered by jet turbines.
- Floating into Skagway, Alaska, to retrace the path of the Gold Rushers on the White Pass and Yukon Railroad.
- Watching the horizon at dawn as a distant Christmas tree slowly revealed itself to be an oil rig standing in the icy Atlantic a few hundred miles off the coast of Newfoundland, the first sign of human civilization other than our own ship after nearly a week on a transatlantic crossing from England to Boston, Massachusetts.
- Seeing the wonder in the eyes of a child on a nearly untouched South Pacific atoll where we had been deposited by a modern cruise ship; we felt like friendly visitors from another planet.
- Cruising between the hulls of a huge catamaran at anchor off the remote island of San Andrés, a northern outpost of Colombia in the Caribbean Sea. The pilot of our tender drove between the pontoons of the one-of-a-kind twin-hull luxury cruise ship, transporting us through a 400-foot-long white tunnel floating on an azure sea.

- Thrilling to a midnight fireworks salute offshore a Bahamian island as a cruise ship on her maiden voyage had a rendezvous with her twin sister.
- Seeing the unreal baby blue hues of South Sawyer Glacier at the end of Tracy Arm in Alaska, as a classic steamship made a slow turnabout in the deep pool at the face of the river of frozen water. We watched squads of seals pass by on ice floes and were in turn tailed by pods of whales in the Inside Passage.
- Passing by a gigantic megaship docked in New York City, looking, in the pre-dawn darkness, like a floating horizontal version of the Manhattan skyscrapers behind her.

Those were some of the places we went. And then there were the amazing sights onboard the cruise ships that took us there. Things such as:

- The jaw-dropping decadence of an all-chocolate midnight buffet.
- A full-scale musical production on a stage that had more technical facilities than many a Broadway theater. And we were moving at 23 knots, a hundred miles off the coast of Florida at the time!
- Day after day of gourmet food, presented with artistry and attentive service at breakfast, brunch, lunch, midafternoon snack, dinner, and midnight. My children, on the other hand, loved the all-hours room service, ice-cream stand, and pizza parlor.
- The incomparable beauty of a Caribbean sunset, glimpsed from a deck chair on the private veranda outside our stateroom.
- The unimaginable heat and bone-rattling rumble of the engine room of a cruise ship moving at full speed through the Pacific. Up above, guests were pampered in air-conditioning and elegant luxury, completely insulated and hidden from the stygian scene down below.
- The calming vista of endless sea, with no signs of land or life for nearly three days, while traveling south from Honolulu into the South Pacific.

DEAR READER: A CONFESSION

As a travel writer, I love the excitement of an expedition off the beaten track in an unusual place. I like nothing better than "going native" anywhere I visit: renting a car to drive on the wrong side of the road in the United Kingdom or Tortola; riding the subways of Seoul, Tokyo, or Barcelona; heading out with a guide across the top of a mountain in Vermont or Utah, and generally choosing my own schedule and itinerary.

Put another way, there is nothing I dislike more than a regimented trip where everything is arranged: when and where to eat, entertainment, and minute-by-minute calendars of activities. I want to know everything there is to know about the places I visit—before I go there—and then I want to wander off.

And so I fully expected that I would find cruising an intolerably confining and overorganized experience. What if I didn't like the ship? What if the cabin was unappealing? What if the food was awful? What if I didn't like the other people on the ship?

Well, with a bit of careful research before I booked passage, I was able to choose ships that ranged from well-kept old dowagers to a brand-new classic in the making. I knew more about the cabin I had booked than any travel agent did. I knew the details of the ship's cuisine in gourmet detail. And I found ways to shield myself from unwanted company when it suited me.

To my surprise, I found that I greatly enjoyed going on a cruise. During my seasons at sea, I learned the wonderful sense of peace and relaxation that comes from putting yourself in the hands of a capable cruise staff on a well-run cruise ship.

I discovered that I truly enjoyed staying put while the ship kept moving. My "hotel" traveled with me from port to port, along with a cabin steward and restaurant staff who, at least for the week or so I spent with them, treated me as if I were a combination of their benevolent employer and a best friend.

I found that, for a change, I enjoyed leaving the driving and the scheduling to someone else. I concentrated on relaxing.

Each day the ship arrived in a new port, I was among the first to clamber into the tender or charge down the gangplank. Based on research I had done before the trip, my wife and I took an occasional organized shore excursion, rented a car to head away from the tourist section of the port and explore for the day, or embarked on our own shore parties, far from the cruise crowd.

I always intend to do more than my share of off-the-cuff, unplanned travel at almost every opportunity. I will still chafe at any suggestion that someone else plan my trips, and I'll happily clamber aboard a cruise ship headed for unusual ports and high adventure.

WE ARE NOT ALONE

I suppose I should not have been surprised to find myself becoming a cruise convert. It turns out that I'm in very good company. In 1970 about half a million Americans took cruises; in 2003 more than 8.3 million North Americans took cruises, and the numbers for 2004 are estimated at nearly 9 million.

Here are some more cruise industry facts:
- Cruise lines aimed at North Americans booked about $10 billion in business in 2003.
- About 85 percent of U.S. adults have never cruised.
- The states producing the most cruise passengers are Florida, California, Texas, Massachusetts, New York, Pennsylvania, New Jersey, Illinois, Ohio, and Georgia.
- More than 90 percent of all cruise passengers book through travel agents, and cruise sales account for more than half of agents' vacation sales. At the same time, travelers are gaining more opportunities to do their own bookings or research online.
- Cruising has begun to shed its image as a vacation choice of seniors. Although millions of older persons enjoy the stress-free pampered life aboard ship, the average age of cruise passengers has dropped from fifty-six to fifty over the past decade.

- The biggest cruising headline of 2004 was the arrival of the massive, elegant *Queen Mary 2,* the new flagship of the Cunard fleet and for the moment, the longest, tallest, and largest passenger ship in the world.

Here are some of the other headlines of 2004:

- **Carnival** added *Carnival Valor* and *Carnival Miracle,* and prepared for the arrival of a third 110,000-ton sister ship *Carnival Liberty* in 2005. The much older, smaller *Jubilee* was sent to P&O Cruises Australia.
- **Costa** welcomed *CostaMagica,* its second Megaship and ordered an even larger cousin for 2006.
- **Holland America** added *Westerdam,* the third compass point of its Vista-class ships, and ordered a new *Noordam* to join the fleet in 2006. The older *Noordam* departed at the end of 2004 to sail for a British company under a new name.
- **Norwegian Cruise Line** shuffled its deck, introducing the *Norwegian Sky* under its new name *Pride of Aloha* in Hawaii as the first American flag cruise liner in decades. The line also added to the fleet the former *SuperStar Leo,* renamed as *Norwegian Spirit.* The new build *Pride of America* is due in 2005, after a delay caused by a mishap in the shipyard. And two more large ships are under construction and due in the fleet by 2006. Meanwhile, the classic *Norway* has apparently sailed its last cruise.
- **Princess Cruise Line** added three huge ships in 2004: *Caribbean Princess, Diamond Princess,* and *Sapphire Princess.* In the same year, the company traded ships with sister company P&O Cruises, bringing back the *Sea Princess* and transferring the older, smaller *Royal Princess.*
- **Royal Caribbean** added *Jewel of the Seas* in 2004, and ordered the first "Ultra-Voyager" ship, a vessel intended to take back the title of the largest cruise ship in the world when it arrives in 2006.
- The Caribbean continues as the leading destination for cruises. In the face of terror threats, there were declines in trips to the Mediterranean and increases in nearby waters of the Caribbean, Mexico, and Alaska.

Here are the Cruise Lines International Association estimates of the breakdown of passengers for 2002, the most recent data available:

- Caribbean, 42 percent
- Europe, 21 percent (Mediterranean, 10.2 percent; Northern Europe, 10.9 percent)
- Alaska, 8 percent
- Pacific Mexico, 5.3 percent
- Bahamas, 4.5 percent
- Panama Canal, 3.3 percent
- Hawaii, 3 percent
- South America, 2.2 percent
- Bermuda, 2 percent
- Canada and New England, 1.8 percent
- Transatlantic, 1.6 percent

- Orient, Southeast Asia, and Africa, 1.5 percent
- South Pacific, 1.3 percent
- Other areas, including Transpacific and Antarctica, 2 percent

Cruising continues as mainly an American product, with more than 70 percent of cruisegoers hailing from the United States. The next most popular market is the United Kingdom, representing approximately 10 percent of cruise passengers. The percentage of British and European travelers is expected to rise in coming years as some of the megaships expand their presence in the Mediterranean and Asian areas.

More huge new cruise ships are being built in shipyards around the world than ever before. As a result, cruise lines are becoming increasingly competitive. Although berths on holiday and peak-season sailings will remain at a premium, you can expect to see some fabulous deals at other times of the year from every major cruise line.

GONE FROM THE FLEET

One of the most difficult economic positions to sustain is to be a mid-sized company; the large companies have almost unlimited resources, while the small companies have the greatest flexibility. That was the situation for the Greek-owned Royal Olympia Cruises, which went into receivership in 2004. Its two newest ships, the speedy *Olympia Voyager* and *Olympia Explorer,* were sold off by creditors and most of its older classic ships were sent to the breakers for salvage.

Other events of recent years include Carnival's unfriendly takeover of Princess, breaking up a planned friendly merger between Princess and Royal Caribbean. Princess now operates as a semiautonomous company with its own ships, policies, and identity.

In late 2001 well-respected Renaissance Cruises fell victim to intense competition and changing economic conditions. The company's fleet of eight upscale destination-oriented ships were dispersed to other lines, including Princess Cruises and Swan Hellenic. A start-up company, Oceania Cruises now sails with three of the ships in a new line that closely resembles the former Renaissance operation.

World Explorer Cruises, which operated the venerable *Universe Explorer* in Alaska and Central America with a well-respected curriculum of lectures and enrichment activities, suspended operations in early 2003 when it lost the lease on its vessel. The company hopes to resume cruising in the future, although 2004 came and went without its return.

Regal Cruises went under in April 2003 when its entire fleet, the half-century-old *Regal Empress,* was attached by a creditor. The ship was purchased by Imperial Majesty Cruises.

ABOUT THIS BOOK

The main purpose of this book is to help you choose the right ship, the right itinerary, the right cabin, and even the right dining options. I'll also tell you how to find ways to be alone among a few thousand other passengers and how to pick and choose your activities to make the cruise ship meet your expectations, not the other way around.

My staff and I have collected information on the best cruises at any price, along with details of how to get the most for your money, no matter how much you spend, as well as advice on how to travel in economical style from coast to coast.

In the 2005 edition we cover every major cruise line marketing cruises to Americans and Canadians in U.S., Canadian, Caribbean, Mexican, and South Pacific waters. We also cover seasonal cruises in the Mediterranean, the Baltic, elsewhere in Europe, and transatlantic repositioning trips.

We offer a selection of money-saving coupons from travel providers. There is no connection between the information in this book and the coupons we publish, except that *everything* between the covers is intended to save you money.

Pardon us for saying so, but we think the cost-effectiveness of this book will speak for itself. With its assistance, you should easily be able to save many times its price while enjoying your cruise.

CHAPTER ONE

How to Choose a Cruise

THE FIRST DECISION is the easy one: Do you want to check into a fine hotel and sit back and relax as it floats from one fascinating place to another, all the while plying you with gourmet food and great entertainment? That's the basic offer from cruise lines large and small.

Now comes the slightly harder part—the *Econoguide* **top-ten questions for cruisegoers:**

- Would you prefer a gigantic floating city with a population of a few thousand strangers and dozens of dining and entertainment options? Or would you instead choose a well-equipped but small, intimate vessel that is more like a semi-private yacht?
- Do you want to laze your way through the blue Caribbean, be thrilled by the Inside Passage of Alaska, venture way out to sea on a transatlantic or transpacific crossing, explore the remains of the ancient civilizations of Central America, cruise the Mississippi on a paddle wheeler or a river barge, or join a growing number of travelers who use a cruise ship as their hotel between ports in the Mediterranean, Baltic Sea, Irish Sea, and the English Channel?
- Is the itinerary the most important factor in your decision, or do you want to choose a ship and ride her wherever she travels?
- Are you the sort of person who looks forward to a cruise that goes for a long haul with full days at sea? Or would you prefer a new port every morning: Go to sleep in Aruba and awake in Curaçao; lights out in Boston, daybreak in Nova Scotia; good night Saint Martin, good morning San Juan?
- Does the stateroom of your dreams include a sitting room, bedroom, private balcony with hot tub, and a butler? Or do you just need a place to store your stuff and lay your head when you're not out at the pool, in the dining room or the casino, or at the barbecue, the theater, or the midnight buffet?
- Are you a blue jeans and T-shirt kind of person, or are you looking for a place to break out the tuxedo or cocktail gown?
- Do you want familiar food and hometown customs, or would you like to sail on a ship with a bit of a foreign flavor: British, Dutch, German, Greek, or Italian-style cruising?

■ Do you enjoy being assigned a dining time and the company of six strangers for the duration of your cruise, or do you prefer a table for two in the corner, whenever you choose to use it?

■ Are you looking for particular sports and health club facilities, such as a golf simulator (or a miniature golf course), a luxurious spa, an indoor swimming pool, or (really!) an ice-skating rink and a rock climbing wall out at sea? Or are you more interested in the thickness of the cushions in the lounge?

■ For some people this is the killer question: How much are you willing to pay? Are you looking for a bargain price for good value, or is money no object to your pursuit of pleasure?

There are no right or wrong answers to any of these questions. The wide range of choices available to cruisegoers is a good thing. The purpose of this book is to help you find the perfect cruise for you. Before you sign on the bottom line for a seaborne vacation, make yourself an expert on the world of cruising.

In this book we'll explore ships from massive megaships that would have dwarfed the *Titanic* to luxurious superyachts and intimate adventure boats. We'll look at the latest and greatest, and we'll examine a few floating antiques, stylish reminders of the days of the great ocean liners.

THE LIST PRICE AND THE REAL PRICE

Cruise and new car brochures have a lot in common: gorgeous pictures of the hardware, photo spreads of handsome models having a great time in exotic places, and a price list that could stop a heart.

But for both cars and cruises, only a few unfortunate and generally uninformed people actually pay the sticker price. Let me put it another way: Those relative few who pay list price subsidize the rest of us who search out the best bargains.

In many instances, there's the list price and there's the real price. There are many ways to save. In fact, with some cruise lines, you may find it hard to pay the list price; there are sales to be found almost all the time. If you choose cruises and the time of year carefully, discounts of 50 percent or more off the brochure rate are quite ordinary.

Start out with a determination not to pay the prices you see quoted. Contact a cruise specialist or a travel agent who has some expertise in cruises, or check with the cruise line directly for special rates. Consult the Internet to research cruise lines, and use what you learn to obtain the very best prices—whether you book directly or through a travel agent.

Be direct and to the point: Ask the agent or reservationist to save you money off the published list price. This accomplishes two goals: First, it announces right at the start that you're aware the list price is often a starting point in a sales negotiation. It also puts the agent on notice that you expect a close eye on the bottom line.

DO YOU NEED TO USE A TRAVEL AGENT?

You do not *need* to work with a travel agent to book *most* cruises. You may, though, *want* to consult an expert for advice about ships, itineraries, and special deals.

You've got most of the basic information about cruises and cruise ships right here in this book, and every cruise line offers extensive information about its offerings in brochures, telephone help lines, and Internet Web sites. Although some cruise lines insist that you book your trip through a travel agent, most will also work directly with travelers by telephone or over the Internet.

Here's my advice: Spend a week or so collecting information from this book, Web sites, and other sources, and then contact cruise lines directly to find out about availability and special promotions.

Among cruise lines that take direct bookings over the Internet or by telephone are Royal Caribbean, Celebrity Cruises, Carnival Cruise Line, Holland America, Costa Cruises, Norwegian Cruise Line, and others. Most allow you to "reserve" a cruise for a few days without putting down a deposit; this is a good way to compare the best rate you can find for yourself with one that is arranged by a travel agent.

Then look for a knowledgeable travel agent; ask friends and acquaintances for recommendations. Be specific in your criteria: the type of cruise ship, itinerary, and cabin you're looking for.

Compare the suggestions of the travel agent with the results of your own research. If the agent can save you money or time or get you an upgrade, go ahead and lay down your credit card.

If the agent's prices are significantly higher than ones you can get on your own, or if he or she seems to be pushing a different cruise line or itinerary than the one you've identified, ask yourself—and the travel agent—if there is some ulterior motive here. The fact is that some travel agents receive additional commissions or special rebates from particular cruise lines; a handful of travel agents specialize in just one or two cruise lines for that reason.

If you're not convinced the agent is looking out for your interests first, or if you discover that you know more about the business than the supposed "expert," move on to another agent or do it yourself.

TRICKS TO GETTING THE BEST RATE

Here are some of the best ways to pay less than the list price:
- Book early.
- Book late.
- Cruise in the off-season.
- Choose a repositioning cruise.
- Cruise a new itinerary.

- Extend a cruise with back-to-back trips.
- Take advantage of special offers for frequent cruisers.
- Take advantage of special discounts.
- Buy from a cruise consolidator or major cruise travel agency able to negotiate special deals for its customers.
- Buy directly from a cruise line, grabbing last-minute deals or Internet-only specials.
- Be flexible on the ship's itinerary or date of departure.
- Upgrade your cabin onboard.

  Or, if you insist, here's how to end up paying top dollar for a cruise:
- Choose a hot new ship in its inaugural season.
- Insist on sailing during a holiday period.
- Be rigid in your sailing date or itinerary.
- Insist on a particular class of cabin.
- Require a particular bed configuration, especially for a cabin for more than two persons.

■ BOOK EARLY

Many cruise lines offer discounts of as much as 50 percent off bookings made six months to a year in advance. If you sign up for such a deal, be sure you understand your rights in case of an unexpected need to cancel; you might also want to include trip cancellation insurance in your purchase.

If you are planning a major celebration—a wedding or anniversary, for example—or hope to travel on a special occasion such as New Year's Eve or a solar eclipse, you might have no choice but to commit to a cruise six months to a year in advance.

■ BOOK LATE

If you are flexible on departure date and itinerary, you can really clean up with a last-minute deal. An unsold cabin is a loss that can never be recouped. Cruise lines just hate to sail with an unused cabin, and they'll carve deeply into list prices to fill those empty berths.

The downside is that in some cases, cruise lines will upgrade their customers who paid full- or near-full rates. This leaves last-minute cruisers the least attractive cabins, albeit at a deeply discounted rate.

In general, the first cabins to sell out on a cruise ship are those at each end of the spectrum: the lowest-priced staterooms and the most spectacular (and relatively scarce) suites.

Register with a cruise agency or, in some cases, directly with a cruise line, and indicate your willingness to take whatever is available on a particular date or itinerary, then be ready to make a last-minute dash to the port.

It is hard to predict when a cruise line will offer these deals. Sometimes the unsold cabins are on the most desirable cruises: Christmas and New Year's in the Caribbean, or the heart of summer in Alaska or the Mediterranean. At other times, the best deals are available on repositioning cruises and trips at the "shoulders" leading up to or out of peak season.

Disadvantages to last-minute booking: You may have to pay top dollar for last-minute air travel to the port unless it is within reasonable driving distance. Be sure to figure in airfare costs to see if the bottom line for a spur-of-the-moment cruise still makes sense. Also, the last-minute cabins are almost always the least desirable staterooms.

■ CRUISE IN THE OFF-SEASON

As with most everything you buy, you can expect a better price when there are more sellers than buyers.

In many cases, you'll find cruising in the off-season just as attractive as in the heart of the season; happily, you'll have less company and pay less for the privilege. You could, though, run into problems caused by the weather, such as late-season hurricanes or unusually rough seas. Do the research and know your preferences before you book off-season—or any other time of the year, for that matter.

Here are a few *off-season* times for cruising:

■ **Caribbean and Mexican Riviera.** After Labor Day to pre-Christmas, early January, and April through Memorial Day.

■ **Panama Canal.** January and February; repositioning cruises in spring and fall.

■ **Alaska.** Beginning and end of the season: May and September.

■ **Europe.** Beginning and end of the season: May and September.

■ **Bermuda.** Beginning and end of the season: May and September.

There are usually a few dead periods too, even in what might otherwise be considered prime season. In most markets, for example, the period between Thanksgiving and Christmas is relatively quiet, as is the period immediately after New Year's Day.

PRIME TRAVEL SEASONS

	Jan	Feb	Mar	Apr	May	Jun	Jul	Aug	Sep	Oct	Nov	Dec
Alaska						★★	★★★★	★★★★	★★★			
Bahamas	★★★★	★★★★	★★★★	★★★★	★★★★	★★★★	★★★☆	★★★☆	★★★☆	★★★	★★★	★★★★
Bermuda					★★★★	★★★★	★★★★	★★★★	★★★★	★★★★		
Caribbean	★★★★	★★★★	★★★★	★★★★	★★★★	★★★★	★★★☆	★★★☆	★★★☆	★★★☆	★★★☆	★★★★
Western U.S.	★★★★	★★★★	★★★★								★★★★	★★★★
Hawaii	★★★★	★★★★	★★★★	★★★	★★★	★★★	★★★★	★★★★	★★★★	★★★	★★★	★★★★
Mexico, Central America	★★★★	★★★★	★★★★	★★★	★★★	★★★	★★★	★★★	★★★☆	★★★☆	★★★☆	★★★★
New England									★★★	★★★★	★★★	
Canada							★★★	★★★★	★★★★	★★★		
Eastern U.S.					★★★★	★★★★	★★★★	★★★★	★★★★	★★★		
Europe						★★★★	★★★★	★★★★	★★★★			
Transatlantic reposition				★★★						★★★		
World cruise	★★★★	★★★★	★★★★	★★★★								★★★★

★★ Low   ★★★ Good   ★★★★ Prime   ★★★☆ Prime, but hurricane season

■ CHOOSE A REPOSITIONING CRUISE

There is nothing scarier to a cruise line bean counter than a $350 million ship with nowhere to go and no incoming payments to apply to the mortgage. The Caribbean is pretty much a year-round destination, but most other areas of the world are more seasonal in their draw.

One example of a seasonal schedule puts a ship in Alaska for the summer, then down the West Coast to the Panama Canal in the fall and through to the Caribbean for the winter. The process is reversed in late spring. The ship might also make a wide detour to Hawaii on its way south to the canal.

These repositioning cruises are sometimes less popular than regular itineraries for a particular ship or cruise line. They may call at unusual ports or spend several days out to sea instead of in port, but to some travelers, these are the very things that make repositioning cruises so attractive. You can expect significant discounts as well as cabin upgrades on many repositioning itineraries.

■ CRUISE A NEW ITINERARY

A careful shopper may be able to find a bargain fare on a cruise ship pioneering a new port or a new itinerary. In some cases, the cruise line might be testing the appeal of a new schedule, or the line may be just beginning to build its business in a new area. Sometimes the first few sailings from a new port are fully booked by those who seek out new and different ports, then there is a period of lower bookings while the cruise line markets its new offering.

Once again, try to take advantage of any situation in which there may be more cabins than passengers.

■ EXTEND A CRUISE WITH BACK-TO-BACK TRIPS

Many cruise lines will offer significant discounts to travelers who book more than one trip in a row. For example, many ships offer alternating east and west Caribbean itineraries and will reward passengers who book a cabin for both legs.

You could also receive a discount for booking multiple legs of a round-the-world cruise or other long-term cruises.

■ TAKE ADVANTAGE OF SPECIAL OFFERS FOR FREQUENT CRUISERS

Many cruise lines make special offers to members of their own clubs of former passengers. Companies might maintain a more formal "club" of passengers with newsletters and get-togethers, or they may merely send offers to former clients.

Typical offers range from discounts to upgrades. Some companies offer special discounts if you make a booking for another cruise while onboard ship.

■ TAKE ADVANTAGE OF SPECIAL DISCOUNTS

Keep your eyes open for special deals offered directly by the cruise line as well as those offered in conjunction with associations, credit card companies, and other groups.

For example, some cruise lines offer special rates to AARP or AAA members. I have often received discount coupons for cruise vacations with my monthly credit card bills.

Be on the lookout—and don't be afraid to ask—for special programs that offer reduced rates for third and fourth passengers in a room, for single passengers willing to be matched in a double cabin, and other such deals.

Some cruise lines also offer a "guaranteed outside cabin" deal, priced at or below the lowest specific outside cabin class. In other words, you won't be choosing a particular deck or type of room but are willing to accept whatever outside stateroom is available. You just might be lucky enough to get a better accommodation than you would receive by specifying a particular class.

■ BUY FROM A CRUISE CONSOLIDATOR OR MAJOR CRUISE TRAVEL AGENCY

Consolidators purchase large blocks of cabins on particular sailings at deep discounts and resell them to consumers. You'll sometimes find great deals here, but be sure to compare the agent's price with one you could obtain on your own. And don't let yourself be talked into a ship or cruise line that is not what you originally decided on. Look for consolidators at Internet Web sites.

■ BUY DIRECTLY FROM A CRUISE LINE

Some cruise lines are cautiously exploring selling trips directly to the consumer at a discount. I say cautiously because they do so at the risk of alienating their primary source of sales: travel agents. Look for the best price you can find online, and then ask a travel agent to beat it.

■ BE FLEXIBLE ON THE SHIP'S ITINERARY OR DATE OF DEPARTURE

If you can adjust your travel plans to take advantage of the best available offerings, you are sure to save money.

Let's say you are able to tell a travel agent or cruise line that you are interested in cruising sometime in February or March, are willing to consider a wide range of ports of embarkation and itineraries, and are willing to travel on any of a wide range of available ships.

In a way, you are putting your business out for sale to the lowest bidder. Of course, you do need to look closely at any offers, and your agent should be able to give you a full and honest answer about why a particular cruise is being discounted.

■ UPGRADE YOUR CABIN ONBOARD

Another strategy is to search for upgrades to cabins once you're onboard the ship. Visit the reception or purser's desk after the ship sets sail and ask about any available cabins. Nearly all cruise lines offer reduced rates on premium staterooms when there is no longer any chance of selling that cabin to a last-minute arrival. This scheme will not work, of course, if the ship is fully booked.

Matching Services for Singles

► **Connecting: Solo Travel Network.** www.cstn.org; (800) 557–1757. A fee-based listing service that helps singles find each other, the network also posts information on cruises and other travel packages, making special discount offers to single travelers.

► **Travel Companion Exchange.** www.travel companions.com; (631) 454–0880. This fee-based matching service requires participants to fill out a detailed information and preferences form.

► **Vacation Partners.** www.vacationpartners.com; (800) 810–8075. Vacation Partners is a fee-based matching service for cruises and other travel.

► **Travel Chums.** www.travelchums.com. A free bulletin board service, Travel Chums helps match single travelers, but performs no verification of the identity of members.

SINGLE CRUISERS

Like it or not, cruise lines base their fares on double occupancy, building in the costs of meals, entertainment, and other services. For that reason, single travelers face "premiums" or "supplements" of as much as 200 percent if they choose to reserve a cabin for themselves.

Some cruise lines are a bit more reasonable, charging only 110 to 150 percent of ordinary rates, and several lines offer special deals from time to time, selling double-occupancy cabins to singles at regular fare.

Here are some money-saving options:
■ Ask if the cruise line has a singles-matching program. The company will pair you with another single traveler of the same sex, and you will each pay the standard double-occupancy rate. In many cases, if the cruise line is unable to pair you with another single you will end up with a cabin to yourself at half the double rate. Some cruise lines offer to fill up a triple or quad cabin with singles, reducing the cost markedly for all travelers, albeit at some loss of privacy.
■ Look for a cruise line that offers cabins specifically designed for singles. Not all that many of these staterooms are available, and they are generally found on older ships. Single cabins are often the least impressive inside staterooms, but they do save travelers a bit of money. (Among the vessels with single cabins is the still-impressive *Queen Elizabeth 2.*)
■ If the cruise line is going to charge you as though you had a second person in your cabin and you don't want to travel with a stranger, why not invite a friend or relative to join you? For the cost of an airline ticket to the port, you'll have comfortable company.

You can also cautiously explore several services that promise to help match up singles to share rooms; my recommendation would be to arrange to meet with a potential roommate for a weekend trip before booking a cruise. Some single travelers use services to match up with a traveling companion for a cruise but still book separate single rooms for the trip.

COMPARING THE COST OF A CRUISE WITH ANOTHER VACATION

Cruises sound expensive, and, indeed, the most luxurious suites onboard a modern ship can cost hundreds of dollars per person per night. But the cost for a cabin in the middle range compares well with other types of vacations when you look at the entire picture.

Think of the cruise equation as:

Cruise Ticket = Transportation + Room + Meals + Entertainment + Sports Activities

Of course, the more cruise amenities you use, the better the deal. If you're planning to stay in your room and skip the sumptuous meals, the midnight buffet, and the nightly theatrical shows, perhaps you should stay in a room at a motel on the shore.

The following example is based on a middle-of-the-market, seven-day cruise in a midrange cabin on a premium carrier such as Holland America or Norwegian Cruise Line, compared with a week's stay at a good-quality resort in Florida or the Caribbean.

	On a Cruise	On a Land Vacation for Two
Cruise fare for two	$2,500	$0
Hotel room	Included	$875 (7 nights)
Transportation	Included	$400 (7 days car rental)
Entertainment	Included	$500 (7 nights)
Sports activities	Included	$280 (7 days)
Breakfast	Included	$200 (with gratuity)
Lunch	Included	$300 (with gratuity)
Dinner	Included	$600 (with gratuity)
Snacks	Included	$200 (with gratuity)
Drinks	$150	$150
Other gratuities	$210	$50
TOTAL	**$2,860**	**$3,555**

Not included in either package are airline transportation and airport transfers. Note that some cruise packages include air transportation.

CRUISERS' FREQUENTLY ASKED QUESTIONS

Won't I get seasick? Modern cruise ships are very comfortable in most seas; most include high-tech stabilizers that act like underwater wings to even out much of the side-to-side roll that upsets some travelers.

You can also pick your cruise itinerary to try to avoid rough seas. For example, Caribbean waters are generally calm except for short periods of time during hurricane season. Trips on the Inside Passage from Vancouver or Seattle to Alaska are usually smooth and offer many opportunities to get off the ship and onto land.

If you are prone to motion sickness, I would avoid trips with full days at sea, and especially transatlantic and transpacific crossings, during which you might not set foot on land for as much as a week at a time.

If you are concerned about sway, you can consider the location of your stateroom. The least rocky rooms are on lower decks, toward the center of the ship; on most ships these are also less expensive cabins.

Medication such as Dramamine tablets or doctor-prescribed long-term scopolamine patches work well for those particularly prone to problems; be sure to check with your physician if you have any special medical conditions. Other remedies that work for some travelers include acupressure bracelets or herbal treatments such as ginger.

In these troubled times, is it safe to go out on a cruise? Alas, it may be that no place in today's world is completely free of the threat of terrorism. That said, cruise lines have done a lot to improve security in recent years. Luggage and freight are routinely inspected, passengers are checked at embarkation and at each port, and crew members are closely screened.

In American waters and nearby, cruise lines work closely with the U.S. Coast Guard and local port authorities to guard ships in port.

Because many travelers are more concerned about flying from their home to the port, most cruise lines have increased their "homeland" itineraries, sailing from the United States and Canada. Passengers can drive to departure cities on the East or West Coast or the Gulf of Mexico, or fly in on domestic airlines.

Operations in foreign waters, especially in the Middle East and Asia, have been curtailed in recent years. Many cruise lines have also reduced the number of ships sailing in the Mediterranean and the Baltic.

The smart traveler does not throw caution to the wind on any vacation. Pay attention to the world situation; be on the lookout for suspicious persons or activities—you should do nothing less at home.

I heard about epidemics at sea. Will I get sick on a cruise? There is nothing particular about a cruise ship that causes epidemics, except that there are a lot of people in a relatively small enclosed space. Of course the same thing can be said about shoreside theaters, schools and universities, day care centers, and hospitals, as well as airports, planes, buses, and trains.

The best protection from disease at sea is common sense. Wash your hands frequently, especially before eating, and keep away from anyone who's visibly ill.

Will I go crazy being confined in a small place for a week? First of all, modern cruise ships hardly qualify as small places. The largest cruise ships afloat, classified in this book as a *Megaship, Colossus,* or *Gargantuan,* are more like midsize towns, with many restaurants and clubs, movie theaters, show rooms, gyms, jogging tracks, shops, and much more. A complete circuit of each deck on a

Maiden Voyages

Do you dream of being first to sleep in a new cabin, first to belly up to the buffet, and first to a new port? There'll be grand speeches, free-flowing champagne, and a sky filled with fireworks . . . kind of like the *Titanic,* presumably without the icebergs.

With a dozen or so major new cruise ships being launched each year, your chances of getting on a maiden voyage are better than ever. You'll find information about many of the upcoming launches in this book.

Many cruise lines will accept reservations for maiden voyages as much as a year ahead of scheduled dates; in some cases, first choice is offered to preferred customers.

The bad news, though, is that as ships become larger and more complex, the chances of delays in announced maiden voyage dates are also better than ever. If a cruise ship is not available for her scheduled maiden voyage, you might be offered a trip on another ship or a high-priority reservation on the actual first sailing. Some lines offer discounts or upgrades to soothe customers made unhappy by delays.

By the way, "maiden" voyages are not always the true first trip for a new ship. Modern cruise ships are generally built at yards in Europe or Scandinavia and go through several "shakedown" cruises near the yards before making a transoceanic crossing; some cruise lines schedule several weeks or months of trips before the formal start of service. Contact the cruise line to see if space is available on these pre–maiden voyages.

Gargantuan ship is nearly a half mile in length. In my experience, any ship with at least 20,000 tons of capacity is big enough to allow a few changes of scene.

You can also choose an itinerary with lots of port calls; many ships in Europe and the Caribbean sail by night and are in port every day.

Help! I want my privacy; I don't want to share my dinner with six strangers. Choose a cruise that offers free choice for dining, a growing trend. Let your travel agent or the cruise line know of your preference for a private table at the time of booking. If you're unable to confirm a table to your liking, head directly for the maître d' when you board the ship; on most crews, the dining room managers are available for changes to table assignments or seatings on the day of embarkation.

On most ships you will find that the early seating is more fully booked; you should have an easier time selecting a table if you're willing to eat later.

On ships with open seating, let the maître d' know of your preference early in the cruise, and keep your elbows out to protect your privacy. Find the best time to show up; on many ships you can have your pick of tables early or late in the evening.

Cruise Demographics

The passenger mix will vary across cruise lines and itineraries, but here's an example of one cruise on Holland America Line's *Veendam* in the Caribbean: Forty-two percent of passengers were age fifty-four and younger, and 58 percent were fifty-five and older. About 56 percent of the guests were female.

I hate the feeling that every waiter and cabin attendant looks at me as a walking gratuity. Is there another way? You're hardly alone; many lines have moved away from the awkward passing-of-the-envelope ceremony on the last night of the cruise. You might want to look for a cruise that includes tips in your fare or automatically adds them to your account. This system is becoming increasingly popular as cruises move away from assigned seatings for passengers.

Cruising is too expensive, isn't it? For many people, it is difficult to look past the bottom line on a cruise contract. There's one large figure, and it has to be paid for with a check or credit card. But as I've shown already, if you break it down and consider the cost of transportation, food, entertainment, and lodging, most cruise vacations turn out to be comparable with other types of travel.

You can also find ways to dramatically reduce the cost of a cruise. Look for trips at the start and end of a season, the so-called "shoulder seasons" when prices are often slashed. Some cruise lines commonly offer two-for-one deals to fill their ships.

Consider a repositioning cruise, when a ship is sent from one part of the world to another to prepare for the coming season. Sign up for notification of last-minute special offers.

Cruising is just for old folks. Won't I be the only one under seventy? Not anymore, if this ever was true. The biggest area of growth for many lines is among first-time cruisers and younger travelers. That's why they've added discos, rock climbing walls, skating rinks, and more.

All cruise lines welcome adult travelers of all ages, although a handful do not encourage or accept young children. Spend the time to learn a bit about the cruise line's policies and atmosphere.

The "party" lines, including Carnival and Royal Caribbean, may have a slightly younger crowd. The premium lines, including Norwegian Cruise Line, Celebrity, and Holland America Line, attract a slightly older audience, as do superluxury lines such as Crystal, Silversea, and Seabourn.

Cruising is just for young folks. Aren't I too old for this sort of thing? Not at all. A cruise ship is a wonderful way to travel for many people who want to take it easy. You'll check in once and unpack your bags for an extended period of time. Modern ships have ramps and elevators, making it easy to get about. Cruise lines are quite capable of dealing with guests in wheelchairs, with oxygen tanks, and with other special needs.

All major cruise lines have a medical clinic and doctor on board, and most lines will work with you and your doctor to accommodate special medical needs.

It's also possible to arrange for special dietary requirements. You can find out from the shore excursions staff about port trips that meet your needs.

I don't want to learn how to carve ice. What will I do all day? Not interested in napkin folding either? Many cruise lines have moved beyond some of the silly old standbys to offer much more substantial courses. I've sat through fascinating lectures on anthropology and geology on a cruise in Alaska, heard a maritime historian tell the inside story of the *Titanic* on a transatlantic cruise that passed very close to the spot where the ship went down, and sailed through the Caribbean on a jazz cruise with some of the best musicians in the world. And of course, some of us enjoy seven days of pampered indolence.

I don't want to take a bus tour in each port. How can an independent traveler enjoy a port call? There is no requirement that you take a guided bus tour when you arrive in port. Spend the time before you leave home to investigate renting a car, hiring a vehicle and driver, or traveling by local train on your own. Be sure to allow a comfortable cushion of at least an hour at the end of the day to make sure you don't miss the boat; the main advantage of taking a cruise line–endorsed shore excursion is a guarantee that the ship will wait for passengers on the tour.

Hiring a car and driver, especially for a group of four people, is almost always less expensive than traveling on a chartered bus. You can impress the rest of the ship when they clamber down the gangplank to their bus and see a driver holding a card bearing your name.

Do the research in advance of your trip. Know more about the ports than the shore excursion staff does. Make phone calls to tourist bureaus; hire guides by phone or over the Internet.

How long a cruise should I take? First-time cruisers might want to take a three- or four-day voyage, although the best values are usually for seven-day or longer trips. More important to some is the nature of the itinerary. Are there days at sea? Some inexperienced cruisers may find that prospect a bit anxiety-inducing, while some veterans seek out relaxing days beyond sight of land. Does the ship spend every day in a port? You'll see less of the ship and more of the shore, which may or may not be your goal, but cruisers with a fear of seasickness will be able to regain their footings every morning.

CHAPTER TWO

HOW BIG IS BIG?

HOW BIG IS BIG ENOUGH? Everyone has his or her own answer. Some people yearn for a floating city with theaters, nightclubs, ice rinks, rock climbing walls, shopping malls, and a different restaurant for each night of the cruise. Others prefer a small but safe and comfortable raft in the vastness of the open ocean, their entertainment coming from the ever-changing sea.

Today's biggest ships are rated as 100,000 or more tons in size, a Brobdingnagian stature that was considered unrealistic a few years ago.

The largest passenger vessel afloat is the *Queen Mary 2*, a massive vessel of more than 150,000 tons, 1,132 feet in length, and a beam of 135 feet. Only slightly smaller are the five ships in Royal Caribbean's Voyager class: *Voyager of the Seas, Explorer of the Seas, Adventurer of the Seas, Navigator of the Seas,* and *Mariner of the Seas,* each a Gargantuan 142,000 tons in capacity.

Royal Caribbean's *Voyager of the Seas* and her sisters are among the largest cruise ships now in service. *Courtesy of Royal Caribbean International*

Each of these modest little boats is three times the size of the *Titanic* and more than double the magnitude of one of the Megaships that were the harbingers of the cruising boom of the 1990s.

But wait: The space race for cruise ships shows no signs of ending. Royal Caribbean has announced the first order for an Ultra-Voyager ship, planned to be 160,000 gross tons and due in May 2006. The line took an option with a shipyard in Finland for a second ship for 2007. The Ultra-Voyager class would be about 1,112 feet in length and carry accommodations for 3,600 passengers and a crew of 1,400.

And Carnival Cruise Lines was reported to be considering an even larger vessel for the latest addition to its portfolio of lines, Princess Cruises; that new ship could be as large as 180,000 tons and carry as many as 4,000 passengers.

Many cruise lines have chosen to keep their ships within the "Panamax" specifications, the maximum width and length for a ship to be able to pass through the Panama Canal between the Atlantic and Pacific Oceans. The locks of the canal are 110 feet wide and 1,000 feet long; any ship wider or longer than that must go the long way around the tip of South America if she is to be repositioned from one ocean to another. Already the *Queen Mary 2*, the Royal Caribbean Voyager-class ships, and a few other whoppers are bigger than the locks at Panama.

And how big is too big? Some dreamers—and a few planners—envision a future floating resort that will be a palatial waterworld.

The concept of economy of scale pushes cruise ships to either end of the spectrum—to small, ultraluxury (and ultra-high-priced) vessels or to Gargantuan ships that have cabins for more than 2,000 guests. On the small luxury ships, cruise lines can charge very high rates per passenger; on huge ships the costs of the construction of the ship, fuel, show rooms, and other fixed expenses are spread over a large number of guests.

AN ECONOGUIDE TO SMALL, MEDIUM, LARGE, AND GARGANTUAN

Size does matter—in facilities, atmosphere, and the overall experience of a cruise. There are those who prefer citizenship in a city at sea and others who would rather be in a floating supper club.

I divide cruise ships into classes based on gross registered tons, a measure of capacity I'll define in a moment. Here are the *Econoguide* size classes:

Gargantuan	130,000 or more tons
Colossus	100,000 to 130,000 tons
Megaship	70,000 to 100,000 tons
Large	40,000 to 70,000 tons
Medium	10,000 to 40,000 tons
Small	Less than 10,000 tons

So, how big is big enough? If you have a large cabin, a comfortably uncrowded dining room, and more deck chairs than people, you might consider a Medium 20,000-ton ship big enough. If you're one of 3,000 guests on a 100,000-ton Colossus and find yourself standing in line for a half hour to get to the buffet table, you may decide that the ship is way too small.

(Cunard's Gargantuan *Queen Mary 2* carries a relatively small passenger load and offers an exceptionally large amount of public space, which leaves a lot of room to roam.)

Clipper Cruise Line's *Nantucket Clipper,* a small 102-passenger vessel, at dock in Halifax.
Photo by Corey Sandler

Any ship 70,000 tons or larger will have multiple restaurants, large clubs, and other indoor and outdoor facilities.

So let's look at two important measures of size: gross registered tons and passenger-space ratio. We'll also define another way to think about quality of service: the passenger-to-crew ratio.

■ GROSS REGISTERED TONS

First of all, it is important to understand that *tonnage* is not a measure of the weight of the ship. A ship of 100,000 tons does not weigh 200 million pounds. In nautical terms, a ton is actually derived from a French measure known as *tonneaux,* which referred to a particular size of wine cask.

The concept of gross registered tons (GRT) was developed as a means of taxing vessels based on their cargo-carrying capacity. GRT is a measurement of the total permanently enclosed spaces of the ship, excluding certain essential areas such as the bridge and galleys. In modern terms, one GRT is equal to 100 cubic feet of enclosed, revenue-generating space.

Here is another way to think of GRT: A typical four-door compact car occupies roughly 300 cubic feet, or three tons. A basic kitchen refrigerator is between 40 and 50 cubic feet in size, equivalent to four-tenths to one-half GRT.

So a 100,000-ton Megaship has revenue-generating space equivalent to about 33,333 compact cars or 250,000 kitchen refrigerators.

Some ships—freighters and smaller vessels among them—are measured in net tonnage, which is the gross tonnage minus certain additional spaces, such as crew and officer quarters and a calculated portion of the engine space.

▓ PASSENGER-SPACE RATIO

Another way to look at the size of a ship is to compare the gross tonnage with the number of passengers onboard. The passenger-space ratio, which you'll find listed in charts later in this book, divides gross tonnage by a ship's standard double-occupancy capacity. The higher the space ratio, the less likely you'll find a stranger in a bath towel in your personal space by the pool or be assigned a seat at a dinner table for twelve. In this book, the range of space ratios for cruise ships runs from about 19 to 57, with most ships in the mid-30s range.

Passenger-space ratios are very rough measures. Some ship designers make staterooms large at the expense of public spaces; other ships have sprawling casinos and magnificent open atriums but offer broom-closet cabins. As we'll discuss later, some guests are willing to accept a small sleeping room because they don't intend to spend much time behind its closed door.

The space ratio does not work very well when applied to small adventure ships and sailing vessels that have different designs, including small bridges, galleys, engine rooms, and multipurpose public rooms. This class of ship also typically makes use of open deck space for viewing and dining.

IS BIGGER BETTER?

If you're looking for a Broadway theater at sea, a waterborne ice-skating rink, or a choice of five restaurants for dinner, sometimes bigger is better. A bigger ship may also offer larger cabins with more amenities. However, sometimes smaller is better—if you're looking for more personalized service, easier embarkation and disembarkation, and calls at less often visited ports.

Following is a plus-and-minus comparison of large and small cruise ships.

▓ LARGE SHIPS

Plus

+ Large ships are generally more stable in rough seas, although roll may be more pronounced in certain conditions because of top-heavy construction.
+ More activities are offered: theaters, show rooms, casinos, ice-skating, and so on.
+ Passengers can take advantage of multiple dining choices.
+ Many newer large ships have more verandas, larger windows, and more cabin choices.
+ Shore excursion programs are larger and more diverse.

Minus

- Deeper draft may limit ports or require passengers to transfer to small boats (called tenders) to go ashore.
- A small city's worth of people can be accommodated in the show rooms.
- Large dining rooms may result in more institutional-style food and service.
- Large passenger capacity may result in long lines for embarkation, immigration clearance, and disembarkation.
- Thousands of guests will descend upon small ports at once, lessening the quality of your visit.

■ SMALL SHIPS

Plus

- + Shallower draft may allow visits to smaller ports and require less frequent use of tenders.
- + Public rooms are relatively intimate.
- + More personalized service is available from cabin and restaurant staff.
- + Less structured, sometimes open seating is available in the dining room.
- + Small ships may have water-level water sports platforms or internal docks.
- + There is less of an impact on ports of call from smaller passenger loads.
- + A smaller number of passengers allows for easier embarkation at the start of a cruise and disembarkation at the end.

Minus

- Smaller ships are generally less stable in rough seas.
- There are fewer choices for entertainment.
- Fewer verandas and categories of cabins are available.
- Few or no choices are offered for dining.

IS A NEW SHIP BETTER THAN AN OLD CLASSIC?

The only thing you can say for certain about a new ship versus an old one is that a modern ship is, well, newer. Some spectacular new vessels include amenities well beyond the dreams of the most luxurious queens of the sea. But some new ships also have sections akin to a shopping mall food court. Some older vessels are tired relics counting the days until the scrap yard. But other veteran ships are handsome classics, offering a sense of elegance and class not duplicated by new construction. A fine example is the *QE2,* which has given over her transatlantic liner duties to the new *Queen Mary 2* but will continue as a cruise ship, mostly in European waters.

A typical life for a new cruise ship in the hands of a major cruise line is approximately ten to fifteen years, after which the ships are pushed along to a succession of secondary cruise companies. That doesn't mean there is anything wrong with these older ships or with the cruise companies. It just means the ships might not match a line's current marketing plan.

There are some areas of concern: A handful of very old ships may not fully meet the current safety regulations, operating under temporary or permanent exemptions. For example, these include old riverboats, antique Tall Ships, and a few older cruise ships that are due for retrofitting with sprinklers and other safety systems. Older ships are also not likely to be very accommodating to persons in wheelchairs and to others who may require an elevator.

New ships include state-of-the-art propulsion, air-conditioning, television, telephone, theater, and other facilities. They also are constructed using the latest safety regulations and equipment. Cabins usually have internal hallway entrances, permitting portholes, windows, or verandas along the sea.

Many new ships have shallower drafts, which allow visits to smaller ports and less frequent use of tenders; bow and stern thrusters allow maneuvering in narrow ports. On the minus side, a shallower draft may mean less comfortable cruising in rough weather.

CHAPTER THREE

WHERE IN THE WORLD DO YOU WANT TO GO?

WHERE IN THE WORLD do you want to go? Well, let me refine that a bit: Where in the world's oceans and major rivers do you want to go?

The waters around the United States are the world's most popular for cruising. In this book we cover any ship that touches an American port or sails nearby. Under that definition we include New England, Canada, the East and West Coasts, the Caribbean, Bermuda, the Bahamas, the Mexican Riviera, Hawaii, and Alaska. And we add coverage of voyages in Europe and the Pacific offered by the same major cruise lines.

When the modern cruise boom got into full swing in the 1980s, the heart of the market was offering trips into the Caribbean, principally from Florida. Guests were expected to fly to the port to meet ships that were just a day's sail or less from the islands.

Today, though, cruise ships depart from nearly every deep water port that is within a few hours of a metropolitan area. The reasons for the change include the rapid expansion in the number of ships, limited space in traditional ports, faster cruising speeds, and, most recently, security concerns that have made flying less attractive for many travelers.

There has been a significant increase in departures from such domestic ports as Florida (Tampa, Port Canaveral, Fort Lauderdale, and Miami), New York, Boston, Philadelphia, Baltimore, Galveston, Houston, Los Angeles, and Seattle. Cruise industry officials point out that these domestic ports are within a half-day's drive of 40 percent of the households in North America.

Among today's fastest growing ports are New York (for trips that go as far as the Caribbean), Boston (for cruises to the Bahamas), and Seattle (for Alaska sailings). These ports take advantage of modern ships that can sail an extra 100 or so miles per day. Regional ports also make it more attractive for local residents to take three- or four-day cruises without the added expense of airfare.

In 2004 New York signed a long-term deal with Carnival Corporation and Norwegian Cruise Line that is expected to lead to the development of at least four new cruise piers in Manhattan and Brooklyn and the renovation of the existing Passenger Ship Terminal. Carnival and NCL will receive preferential use of the piers; between them the two companies are expected to bring at least 13 million passengers to New York in the next dozen years, paying the city at least $200 million in fees.

About the same time, Royal Caribbean Cruises announced that it would send two of its vessels, the 3,114-passenger *Voyager of the Seas* and the 2,020-passenger *Empress of the Seas* to a redeveloped pier in Bayonne, New Jersey, across the Hudson River from Manhattan's West Side.

Galveston continues to enjoy its renaissance as a cruise port; in 2004 seven cruise ships used it as a home port for parts of the year, embarking 384,000 passengers. Some 30 million people live within a 500-mile drive from the port; about 70 percent of guests drive to the port to meet their ship. The 40-foot-deep channel is capable of handling Megaships.

Hawaii is also seeing a boom in visitors, with the number of cruise-ship passengers there increasing by about 16 percent in 2004, compared to the year before. Much of that is due to the expanding role there of NCL and its American-flag brand NCL America.

In Alaska, Carnival moved the 2,124-passenger *Carnival Spirit*'s southbound home port to Whittier, saving guests ninety minutes travel time from the airport in Anchorage compared to the previous departure point of Seward.

Many cruise lines have sharply reduced or completely canceled sailings in Europe, the Middle East, and Asia due to security or health concerns. You can, though, still find a good selection of cruises in the Mediterranean, the British Isles, the Baltic, and Scandinavia on many lines.

Itineraries from East Coast ports include the Caribbean, the Bahamas, Bermuda, and Canada. From Gulf of Mexico and Florida ports, there are more cruises to the Western Caribbean, South America, and the Panama Canal than ever before. From West Coast ports ships head north to Alaska, west to Hawaii, and south to Mexico, South America, and the Panama Canal.

Travelers willing to fly to familiar nearby ports will also find increased service from Puerto Rico, Antigua, Aruba, and Honolulu.

I'll discuss many of the most popular cruising destinations a bit later in the chapter. First, though, let's explore the political and economic reasons behind most cruise itineraries.

OCEANS AWAY: INTERNATIONAL AFFAIRS

Cruising is one of the most international of businesses, and its operations are very much shaped by politics, economics, and protectionism.

I first wrote these words onboard a cruise liner built in Spain, registered in Panama, and leased from a Scandinavian holding company by Norwegian Cruise Line, a Norwegian corporation that had its headquarters in Miami. We were sailing through the American Hawaiian Islands with a 2,400-mile round-trip detour to stop at an undeveloped beach on Fanning Island in the South Pacific Republic of Kiribati.

Let's deconstruct that global stew.

Today's modern cruise ships are mostly built at a handful of giant shipyards in Italy, France, Germany, and Scandinavia. There is hardly any American shipbuilding industry left.

The ownership of cruise ships follows the financing; a new Gargantuan ship can cost upward of $400 million. The largest cruise lines—Carnival and Royal Caribbean among them—are huge multinational companies. Some of the smaller cruise companies, like Crystal and MSC Italian, are related to major freight shipping lines in Europe, Scandinavia, and Japan.

A ship's registry is for the most part a legal fiction. The great ships of old represented their nation's political and economic strengths, were proud to bear their country's flags, and, most important, abided by their home nation's laws, regulations, and customs. The Cunard Line's historic ships *Queen Mary* and *Queen Elizabeth,* for example, flew the Union Jack of Great Britain. From the stern of the *France* fluttered the Tricolor. Great American vessels such as the *United States* hoisted Old Glory. Each acted as a floating extension of its homeland.

Today, though, a new cruise ship is most likely to fly the flag of countries such as Panama, Liberia, or the Bahamas. They do so because the accountants and lawyers have determined that the cruise line can save money on construction costs, taxes, and operating expenses by doing so. In addition, if a ship is registered in the United States, labor and immigration laws require that crew members be American citizens or legal aliens.

Many of the vessels flying these exotic flags have never touched the waters of ports in those nations. These are "flags of convenience."

■ THE JONES ACT

Why does a ship sailing from New York on a cruise to New England have to make a port call in Canada? Why does a ship from Honolulu have to steam thousands of miles to Vancouver, Canada, or Ensenada, Mexico, or a tiny dot of a Pacific island nation before returning? Why can't you cruise up or down the California coast? Why do most Alaska cruises originate in Canada or make a stop in that country as they go to or come from the forty-ninth state?

The answer comes from a nearly two-century-old set of laws intended to protect U.S.-flagged vessels from unfair foreign competition.

The Jones Act requires that cargo moving between U.S. ports be carried in a vessel that was built and maintained in the United States and is at least 75 percent owned by American citizens or corporations. The Jones Act actually refers to Section 27 of the Merchant Marine Act of 1920; prior legislation to accomplish essentially the same thing has been in effect since 1817.

The act has actually done very little to preserve the U.S. shipping industry, of which there is not much left. The same applies for the American cruise industry, where the bill has had the unintended effect of boosting the economy of some otherwise obscure foreign ports whose main advantage is that they are within a reasonable cruising distance of a U.S. port. (Witness the Republic of Kiribati I mentioned earlier.)

Nearly fifty countries around the world have laws similar to the Jones Act. The United States is especially tough in its ban against flying an American flag on a foreign-built vessel; Canada permits importing ships but requires payment of a tariff equal to 25 percent of the vessel's value, which all but makes foreign vessels economically infeasible.

While the Jones Act applies to cargo, the Passenger Vessel Act of 1886 declares that "no foreign vessel shall transport passengers between ports or places in the United States." Cruise companies face a substantial fine for violating the law.

Railroads, airlines, bus lines, and trucking companies in the United States must follow similar rules of ownership and operation.

STRANGE ITINERARIES

Until and unless changes are made to the Jones Act, cruise vacationers have options like these:

- Take a cruise from a U.S. port in Florida or a Gulf of Mexico port (including New Orleans and Galveston) that makes a visit to a Caribbean nation or Mexico.
- Leave from a Canadian port on the East or West Coast and sail to an American destination such as Boston, New York, or Alaska, or the reverse.
- Follow an unusual itinerary on a repositioning cruise, such as a trip from Vancouver to Hawaii, Hawaii to Mexico, or Florida through the Panama Canal to California.

As more and more ships are launched, and more and more ports are opened to welcome their business, cruise lines are on the lookout for new places to visit. A number of new destinations have been developed in the Mexican Riviera, and some U.S. ports have made major improvements to their facilities as a point of embarkation.

Here's the reason behind my visit to Kiribati: For the past few years, Norwegian Cruise Line has operated cruises among the Hawaiian Islands in the spring and fall in between winter assignments in the Caribbean and summers in Alaska. To sail from Hawaii and meet the requirements of the Jones Act, the vessels sail a 1,200-mile side trip to an island in the Republic of Kiribati near the equator.

THE BATTLE FOR REPEAL

In recent years several attempts have been made to repeal or modify the Jones Act, led in one way or another by cruise lines or their American representatives and supporters. Opposition to change has come from what remains of the U.S. shipping industry and from American unions. It is unclear whether the U.S. Congress will change the law.

One bill would have removed most restrictions, allowing foreign-flagged ships to cruise between U.S. ports. A more modest version would create waivers to permit ships that are repositioned from the Caribbean to Alaska and the Mediterranean to make multiple U.S. port stops along the West and East Coasts and grant a limited number of thirty-day permits for foreign-flagged ships to sail between U.S. ports. It would also permit U.S. companies to reflag foreign ships.

According to its supporters, the removal of the Jones Act could virtually destroy the U.S. domestic shipping industry and its 124,000 jobs. According to an industry association, owners and builders of U.S.-flagged vessels pay approximately $300 million annually in federal taxes and $55 million annually in state taxes. The foreign-ship cruise industry operating out of U.S. ports earns hundreds of millions of dollars a year from American consumers, yet pays no taxes on that income.

American employees pay some $1.1 billion in federal income taxes and $272 million in state taxes; again, foreign workers on foreign-flagged ships do not pay taxes. Foreign operators are also exempt from minimum wage laws, the provisions of the National Labor Relations Act, the Occupational Safety and Health Act, and some safety regulations applied to U.S. ships and industries.

It is important to note, though, that foreign-owned cruise lines do contribute to employment of port personnel, purchasing supplies from domestic sources and supporting American travel agencies, airlines, hotels, and other elements of vacation travel.

■ PROJECT AMERICA

In 2003 there was not a single major cruise ship flying the American flag. In recent years there had been two U.S.-flagged ships: the elderly *Independence* of American Hawaii Cruises and the reflagged *Patriot*, the former *Nieuw Amsterdam* of Holland America Lines. Both of these ships were laid up with the bankruptcy of the reborn United States Line.

But in 2004 some fancy political footwork by Norwegian Cruise Line will enable the first two of a small fleet of new or reflagged ships to sail in Hawaii under the brand NCL America. On July 4, 2004, *Pride of Aloha* began year-round service from Honolulu; that ship sailed under a Bahamian flag as *Norwegian Sky* for four years. Sometime in 2005, *Pride of America* is due to arrive; she will become the first new ship expressly built to sail under the American flag in decades.

The NCL America ships will be able to sail in and among the Hawaiian islands without the need for a mad dash of several days to touch the Republic of Kiribati, or to make one-way trips from Hawaii to Mexico or Canada.

How complex a deal was NCL America? Consider this: *Pride of America* was originally begun as an American ship under special federal concessions at a shipyard in Mississippi. When the would-be owner of the vessel went bankrupt, the uncompleted hull was purchased by Norwegian Cruise Line and towed to a German shipyard for completion. NCL long ago lost its tenuous links to Scandinavia, and is now a subsidiary of Star Cruises, a Malaysian company which has its headquarters in Hong Kong. (I discuss the tangled history of NCL America in Chapter 13.)

A few smaller ships fly the American standard: The historic *Delta Queen* and her modern cousin the *Mississippi Queen* sail the rivers of the heartland. There are also a number of small American cruise ships on the East Coast and several boats in Alaskan waters.

PORTS OF EMBARKATION AND PORTS OF CALL

Three-quarters of the earth is covered by the oceans, forming the highway to thousands of wondrous ports on the continents and islands of the world. The busiest ports for cruise ships are in the Caribbean, the Mediterranean and northern Europe, and Alaska. In this section I'll discuss some of the most interesting places where cruise ships call.

■ THE CARIBBEAN

The Caribbean basin is the most popular cruising area in the world, and for good reason. There are dozens of attractive and interesting small island nations, lovely beaches, and easygoing and friendly cultures that have their roots in Africa and Europe.

The Caribbean islands are made up of the Greater Antilles and the Lesser Antilles. The first group is closest to the United States and includes the large islands of Cuba, Jamaica, Hispaniola (which includes Haiti and the Dominican Republic), the U.S. territory of Puerto Rico, and the Cayman Islands.

The Lesser Antilles occupy the southern portion of the Caribbean, comprising the Virgin, Windward, and Leeward Islands. Included here are the U.S. Virgin Islands of Saint John, Saint Thomas, and Saint Croix, as well as Dutch/French Saint Martin, Saint Eustatius, Tortola, Virgin Gorda, Anguilla, Saint-Barthélemy, Saba, Saint Kitts, Nevis, Montserrat, Antigua, Guadeloupe, Dominica, Martinique, Saint Lucia, Saint Vincent, Barbados, the Grenadines, Grenada, and Trinidad and Tobago. Just off the coast of Venezuela are the ABCs: Aruba, Bonaire, and Curaçao.

(By the way, the generally preferred pronunciation is *kar-ih-BEE-en,* as opposed to *kah-RIB-ee-en.* The name is derived from Caribs, the indigenous people of the area who were mostly killed by imperial explorers or died as the result of diseases brought to the islands by outsiders.)

Cruises to the Caribbean leave from Florida ports that include Tampa, Miami, and Port Canaveral and from Gulf of Mexico ports, including Galveston, Houston, and New Orleans. Other major ports of embarkation located in the islands themselves are San Juan, Puerto Rico; Santo Domingo, Dominican Republic; and Montego Bay, Jamaica.

Caribbean cruising is usually a series of short island hops. A typical schedule has a ship arriving in port (or offshore for transfer by ship's tender) in the early morning and departing in the evening. This is enough time to get a brief taste of the islands: a shopping expedition, a visit to a beach or historical site, or a jaunt to an island casino, but not much else. And there may be relatively little pure cruising—days when the ship is out to sea.

June through November is hurricane season; August is generally the most active month. That does not mean there are constant storms. In some seasons hurricanes miss the area; even when they do arrive, the storms can hit one port and miss another, and ships can alter course.

You can count on cruise operators to exercise due caution with their expensive ships and litigious passengers. They reserve the right to reroute ships, cancel port calls, and, in rare circumstances, cancel an entire trip. It's all spelled out in the fine print in cruise brochures and contracts, along with policies on refunds and credits that result from cruise changes.

Another feature of some Caribbean cruises is a visit to a private island, an extension of the sealed world of the ship. Just as the cruise ship is a city unto its own, a private island is a way to spend some time ashore without the hassles of tourist traps, or other tourists for that matter (other than the few thousand or so close friends traveling with you). To some, that's a real appeal; to others, it's an unreal way to travel.

Among the private islands:
- Disney Cruise Line's Castaway Cay in the Bahamas near Nassau.
- Costa Cruise Line's Catalina Island off the coast of the Dominican Republic.
- Royal Caribbean's Coco Cay in the Bahamas.
- Royal Caribbean and Celebrity's Labadee off Haiti.
- Norwegian Cruise Line's Great Stirrup Cay.
- Holland America Line's Half Moon Cay.
- Princess Cruises' Princess Cay in the Bahamas.

In most cases the cruise ships will anchor offshore and guests will have to transfer to the island by tender, which can result in delays and a shorter visit. (And in rough seas, the tenders might not run or could be uncomfortable for some guests.) Disney Cruise Line, which sails year-round to the Bahamas and the Caribbean, is the only line to construct a pier to tie up its ships at its private island.

If you are booked for a visit to a private island, be sure to inquire about what is included in your cruise package. Some of the private islands are clearly profit centers for the cruise lines, with extra charges levied for water sports and other services.

Selected Caribbean Ports of Call

- **Anguilla.** A relatively quiet British dependency, first settled in 1650, it was named by Columbus, who thought the wandering coastline looked like an eel.
- **Antigua.** Largest of the British Leeward Islands, it was headquarters to Admiral Horatio Nelson's fleet in the colonial era. The island is home to at least 365 beaches, one for each day of the year if you're on a very long shore leave. The main port town is Saint John's. Another port, for smaller vessels, is at English Harbor in Falmouth, where Admiral Nelson set up the base for the British Navy in 1785. Many of the naval facilities have been restored to their Georgian splendor at Nelson's Dockyard.
- **Aruba.** A mostly independent piece of the Netherlands, the "A" of the "ABC" Islands of Aruba, Bonaire, and Curaçao. The desertlike island of cactus, jungles, and shopping lies just off the coast of Venezuela. The cruise port is at Oranjestad.
- **Bahamas.** The capital city of the Bahamas and one of the busiest cruise ports anywhere is Nassau on New Providence Island. Cruise ships pull up to Prince George Wharf at the foot of town, a short walk to the shops and the famed straw market where native handicrafts and souvenirs are sold.

■ **Barbados.** The port at Bridgetown is still a bit of Britain, with its own Trafalgar Square complete with a statue of Lord Nelson; out of town, the island is a sea of green sugarcane that stretches to the white granulated beaches. Bridgetown is a lively commercial center that has a distinctly British flavor; out in the countryside are forests of flowers, caverns, and beaches. The island is the farthest east of any of the Caribbean islands, sitting on the line between the Atlantic and the Caribbean, approximately 100 miles east of the Lesser Antilles.

■ **Curaçao.** A mixture of Dutch, Spanish, English, and native cultures in the Netherlands Antilles, Curaçao is 35 miles off the coast of Venezuela. The famed Queen Emma Floating Bridge will move to the side to permit your cruise ship to enter the harbor at Willemstad. Beaches are more rock and coral than sand, and there is a busy refining industry. Willemstad was established by Dutch settlers in the 1630s, about the same time as other Dutch settlers arrived on Manhattan Island. Curaçao has maintained much of its original color, including red-tiled gable roofs.

■ **Dominica.** One of the most naturally diverse and relatively unspoiled islands of the Caribbean, Dominica is an independent nation; it is not related to the Dominican Republic, which lies on the island of Hispaniola. The interior is mostly an inaccessible rain forest; something like 365 rivers cascade down three mountain ranges. A few ecotours enter the rain forest by boat. The island, whose name is pronounced *dom-in-EEK-ah,* is also home to one of the last surviving groups of Caribs and a thriving set of folklore and superstitions that have their roots in Africa. The main port is at Portsmouth; some ships also call at Roseau in the southwest and at Prince Rupert Bay.

The dock in Nassau is regularly a billion-dollar parking lot; from left to right are *Norwegian Wind, Carnival Ecstasy,* and *CostaAtlantica. Photo by Corey Sandler*

■ **Grand Cayman.** A former hideout for pirates, today George Town is legal home to offshore tax shelters and trendy shops. The island's beaches and coral reefs are among the best in the Caribbean. The conservative culture there has banned cruise ship visits on Sunday and has taken unfriendly positions against what it broadly defines as "undesirable" elements.

■ **Grenada.** The Spice Island of the Caribbean, Grenada is known for its nutmeg, cinnamon, and cocoa in particular. Formerly a British colony, it had a rocky beginning as an independent nation in the late 1970s and early 1980s, including a questionable U.S. intervention and "rescue" of some medical students. More recently, the island has concentrated on tourism and agriculture. The famed Grand Anse beach is about ten minutes away by bus or taxi from the cruise dock in Saint George's Harbour. Plans are under way for the construction of a new deepwater cruise ship port on the western side of the capital city of Saint George's, including a visitor reception area, duty-free shops, restaurants, and a bus terminal.

■ **Guadeloupe.** Two French islands in one: Basse-Terre has volcanic peaks and a mountainous coast; Grande-Terre has beaches and shopping. The port is at Pointe-à-Pitre. The two islands are separated by the River Salée. Basse-Terre is dominated by La Soufrière, an active volcano; hot water cascades down its sides in several streams. Cruise ships pull into a bay near Pointe-à-Pitre, billed as the "Paris of the Antilles." Guadeloupe is a region of France, along with Martinique, Saint Bart's, and half of Saint Martin.

■ **Îles des Saintes.** This very French set of islands off Guadeloupe was originally settled by Breton fishermen. More recent arrivals include some of the jet set of Europe who have built fancy vacation homes.

U.S. Virgin Islands

The islands of Saint Thomas, Saint Croix, and Saint John have been under Spanish, French, English, and Dutch control. Saint Croix was at the heart of the slave trade, a way station from Africa to the West Indies, America, and South America. All three islands were sold by the Dutch to the U.S. government in 1917 during World War I, amid American fears of the Germans establishing a U-boat base in the area.

■ **Jamaica.** The famed resort port of Montego Bay is on the north shore of Jamaica, home to modern high-rise hotels and all the tourist amenities that go with them. The showplace beach is Doctor's Cave, which stretches for nearly 5 miles. Cruise ships also land on the north shore of this large independent island at Ocho Rios. The rivers of Ocho Rios include the one that tumbles down famed Dunn's River Falls, a 600-foot-high waterfall that has a well-worn set of natural steps, allowing visitors to climb its wet face. The bustling capital of Kingston lies on the other side of the Blue Mountains that run down the spine of Jamaica. Kingston, with nearly a million residents, is the largest English-speaking city south of Miami.

■ **Jost Van Dyke.** A tiny island northwest of Tortola, renowned as the "party island" of the British Virgin Islands, it has a port for small vessels at Great Harbour. There are fewer than 200 permanent residents, a dozen restaurants and bars, and a stunning white sand beach at White Bay.

■ **Martinique.** Very French—still a region of France—and very pretty, Martinique is abloom with orchids, hibiscus, and other tropical flowers. The island is also blooming with expensive shops in Fort-de-France, and it offers a European-tinged nightlife.

■ **Puerto Rico.** The capital port city of San Juan is home to ancient forts and cobblestone streets in Old San Juan, as well as some of the liveliest modern nightspots, casinos, and restaurants in the Caribbean. San Juan is also the most active cruise port in the basin. The island itself, a semiautonomous territory of the United States, is 110 miles long and 35 miles wide and home to nearly four million residents.

■ **Saint-Barthélemy.** Just eight square miles, this is considered one of the most attractive of the islands. The town of Gustavia, still tinged with Swedish and French designs, is a world-class shopping district. By the way, everyone calls the place Saint Bart's.

■ **Saint Croix** is one of the largest and more developed of the U.S. Virgin Islands. Christiansted, its capital and principal port, offers superb golf courses, beaches, and shopping. Another cruise port is located at Frederiksted on the west side of the island, near the popular West End beaches and the island's rain forest. Parts of the island have experienced high crime rates, and some cruise lines have canceled or reduced the frequency of calls there.

■ **Saint Eustatius (Statia).** This Dutch island was historically the merchant center of the Caribbean, at least until the U.S. Revolutionary War, when a British fleet destroyed many of the island's structures because of minor support of the upstart Americans by the local governor. The port is at Oranjestad. The waters surrounding it are cluttered with shipwrecks, coral reefs, and rare fish. Hikers can climb to the rim of an extinct volcano and look into the cone. By the way, anyone with a clue calls it "Statia," pronounced *STAY-sha.*

■ **Saint John.** About 3 miles east of Saint Thomas, this island in the U.S. Virgin Islands is an unusual mix of luxury resorts and a wondrous protected natural park preserve that occupies two-thirds of the island. The main port anchorage for smaller vessels is at Cruz Bay.

■ **Saint Kitts.** This island was the first English settlement in the Leeward Islands. Most ships visit Basseterre. Today Saint Kitts has moved from a sleepy sugarcane economy to an increasingly upscale tourist industry, including quite a few restored plantation houses. Across the sound is the sister island of Nevis, a near-perfect volcano cone that still belches sulphur. Together the two islands are now an independent nation.

■ **Saint Lucia.** The lush port on the northwest coast of the island is at Castries, not far from the twin peaks of Les Pitons at Soufrière Bay and La Soufrière herself, sometimes referred to as the "drive-in volcano." Saint Lucia, an independent member of the British Commonwealth, had a small coal mining industry until early in the twentieth century; a sugarcane economy continued until later in the century, supplanted by bananas, and, relatively recently, by crops of tourists.

■ **Saint Martin/Sint Maarten.** On the French side of this binational island, Marigot has a pretty harbor, an old fort, and an attractive shopping district. The beaches on the French side are all lovely, and many of the sunbathers seem to have misplaced their suits. Philipsburg is the cosmopolitan port at the capital of

A billion or so dollars in cruise ships join more humble fishing vessels in Philipsburg Harbor on the island of Saint Martin. *Photo by Corey Sandler*

the Dutch half of this split-personality island. The Dutch area is more built up, with large hotels and resorts, a few casinos, and a shopping district. The best beaches are at Mullet Bay and Cupecoy and across the unpatrolled border on the French half.

■ **Saint Thomas.** The port city of Charlotte Amalie (*a-MAHL-ya*) is the capital of the U.S. Virgin Islands, but its roots as a Dutch port are very much evident in the architecture. One of the busiest cruise ports in the world, it is home to a staggering assortment of duty-free shops and other commercial ventures aimed at visitors who have dollars to spend. Outside of town is the famed Magen's Bay beach, a white swath of sand that follows the outline of a horseshoe bay.

■ **Tortola.** The largest and most populated of the British Virgin Islands, Tortola is home to the major airport of the area. The port is at Road Town. The best beaches lie on the north side of the island, more or less easily reached on a day trip by car on some rather primitive roads.

■ **Venezuela.** The coastal port of La Guaira offers access to the inland capital city of Caracas.

■ **Vieques.** A lovely, lightly developed island, Vieques is part of Puerto Rico, just off the east coast of the main island. The island's bays are home to microscopic bioluminescent organisms that put on a light show in the wake of your boat. The U.S. Navy ran a controversial bombing range for many years at one end of the island. Most of this land was transferred in 2001 to Puerto Rico and the U.S. Department of the Interior. More than 3,800 acres will be wildlife refuge; the Navy retains 100 acres.

■ **Virgin Gorda.** Supposedly named by Columbus because the island's rolling hills somehow reminded him of an overly ample young woman (the name translates to "fat virgin"), the island is best known for its interesting beach and rock formation at The Baths, where gigantic boulders form grottoes, caves, and pools. Its man-made jewels include the opulent Little Dix Bay, Biras Creek, and Bitter End Yacht Club resorts. The principal port is at Spanish Town. Roads are very limited; the best way around is by boat.

■ BERMUDA

Britain's oldest colony, dating back to the early seventeenth century, Bermuda is still very much a bit of Old England, from afternoon tea to cricket matches to a good-natured formality in business and social matters. The island was first settled in 1609 by the survivors of the shipwrecked *Sea Venture,* British colonists who had been heading for Jamestown, Virginia.

Bermuda, about 600 miles east of Cape Hatteras, North Carolina, actually includes some 150 islands, with the six main islands connected by bridges and causeways. The preferred method of transportation is moped or bicycle.

The climate is temperate, not as hot as the islands of the Caribbean, which lie much farther south. The season runs from May through September. The best bargains are often available at the beginning and end of the season, before Memorial Day and after Labor Day.

The port of King's Wharf is at the tip of Bermuda's West End, home to the Royal Naval Dockyard and the Bermuda Arts Centre and Crafts Market. Saint George is another port on Bermuda, known for its narrow cobblestone streets and the restored 300-year-old King's Square on the waterfront. Although discovered by Spanish explorer Juan de Bermúdez in 1515, Bermuda was first occupied by Sir George Somers and other British colonists who were shipwrecked there in 1609, an event noted by William Shakespeare in *The Tempest.* The island was a haven for pirates and privateers and later used as a base for Confederate blockade runners during the U.S. Civil War.

■ CUBA

Politics aside, one of the most appealing cruise destinations is the island nation of Cuba. It has beautiful beaches, a lively culture, and ports just 90 miles off the coast of Florida.

Cuba is, of course, off-limits to ships sailing from U.S. ports and to most U.S. passport holders. It is legal for journalists and educators with a particular reason to visit Cuba; consult the U.S. Department of State for details. But the political climate could change rapidly.

A number of cruise ships visit Havana from ports in the Dominican Republic, Mexico, or Jamaica without touching American ports. In 2002 European lines making port calls at Cuba included Festival (the *Mistral*); Fred Olsen Cruise Line (the *Black Watch*), and Sun Cruises (*Sundream*).

All the major cruise lines have plans to bring their ships to Cuba as soon as they are permitted.

■ ALASKA

The hottest waters for cruising in recent years have been in the Inside Passage to Alaska, with nearly a half million passengers visiting coastal towns each year.

Alaska has some magnificent appeals: the spectacular frozen rivers of Glacier Bay and other inlets; the fascinating native, Russian, and American cultures of trading and fishing towns such as Ketchikan and Sitka; and the Gold Rush history of Skagway. Just as appealing: a pod of whales shadowing your ship in a narrow passage between thickly forested slopes, and frolicking families of seals on bobbing ice floes.

Alaska is still one of the last great frontiers of the world, and it's certainly among the most remote places in North America. There are almost no roads between towns in the state; residents are served by a fleet of small floatplanes and ferries.

For the cruise passenger, one of the major appeals of an Alaskan visit is that your ship will be within sight of land in protected waters for most of the cruise. The Inside Passage is sandwiched between the mainland and a series of large and small islands. You can expect generally calm waters in the sheltered arms of the Pacific, with only an occasional jaunt into the open ocean to visit ports such as Sitka.

Many of the cruise ships depart from Vancouver in Canada's British Columbia; Vancouver is one of the most attractive ports I know, combining a thriving cosmopolitan city with mountains and the ocean. It's worth a few days as a

The *Regal Princess* under way in Alaska's Inside Passage. *Courtesy of Princess Cruises*

stopover at the start or end of a cruise. Another beautiful Canadian port is Victoria on Vancouver Island. You can also sail to Alaska from Seattle, and some repositioning cruises depart from elsewhere on the West Coast or from Hawaii.

Most of the cruises visit the southernmost reaches of Alaska, from Ketchikan to Juneau and Glacier Bay. The more adventurous ships venture farther north through the open waters of the Gulf of Alaska and Prince William Sound to Seward.

Many larger ships must anchor offshore because they are unable to enter shallow or narrow harbors.

Holland America Line and Princess Cruises are major players in Alaska, and both have extensive facilities on shore, including hotels and tours. In fact, Holland America is one of the state's largest private employers.

It's not quite accurate to say that the Alaskan towns visited by cruise ships are untouched. You'll find more than your share of T-shirt and gift shops, tacky tourist bars, and unimpressive bus tours. The appeal of Alaska instead lies off the beaten path in the pristine bays and fjords of places such as Glacier Bay, Tracy Arm, and the sprawling Misty Fjords National Park.

Don't go for the weather. It can be cold and rainy any day of the year, although you could be blessed with a spectacular, warm day when you least expect it.

Selected Ports of Call in Alaska

■ **College Fjord.** In Prince William Sound, College Fjord is home to twenty-six glaciers, each named for an Ivy League college by the Harriman Expedition in 1899; the trip was financed by the schools.

■ **Haines.** Gateway to a rich Gold Rush history, thousands of bald eagles, and the Tlingit and Chilkat Indian cultures, the tiny town at the dock is not geared to tourists.

■ **Juneau.** This is the nation's only state capital with a glacier in its backyard; the Mendenhall Glacier is just outside town, reachable by public bus, taxi, or guided tour. Juneau is also home to the Alaska State Museum and other cultural attractions.

■ **Ketchikan.** Ketchikan lays claim to the largest collection of totem poles in the world, at Totem Bight and elsewhere around town. It's also the gateway to float-plane and boat expeditions into the spectacular Misty Fjord National Park, which spreads over more than two million acres and includes sheer granite cliffs that rise thousands of feet out of the water. The area has countless lakes and ponds and sprawling forests that are home to bears, deer, mountain goats, and other wildlife.

■ **Prince William Sound.** A large saltwater bay northwest of Juneau, the sound is some 15,000 square miles in size and as much as 2,850 feet deep. It contains more glaciers than any other single area in Alaska.

■ **Seward.** This tiny fishing village is the gateway to some of America's natural jewels: Chugach National Forest, Kenai Fjords National Park and Wildlife Refuge, and the Alaska Maritime National Wildlife Refuge.

■ **Sitka.** The keeper of Alaska's Russian heritage, Sitka's attractions include an onion-domed cathedral, a restored fort site, and a cultural center. The harbor looks out on a dramatic volcano.

■ **Skagway.** The northernmost point in the Inside Passage, this was the jumping-off point for many Gold Rushers of the 1890s. Its history is saluted by many shops and restaurants. It is also the terminal for the White Pass & Yukon Railroad, which retraces some of the routes taken by the Gold Rushers.

■ **Tracy Arm.** Tracy Arm is a fjord that wends its way to the face of two dramatic glaciers, North and South Sawyer.

■ **Valdez.** Laying claim to the title of the "Switzerland of Alaska," with its perch beneath the snowcapped peaks along Prince William Sound, Valdez is the southern terminus of the 800-mile trans-Alaska oil pipeline.

■ **Yakutat Bay.** The bay is home to Hubbard Glacier, which let loose in 1986 to advance more than a hundred feet in a single day, blocking off Russell Fjord. At more than 6 miles in width and nearly 500 feet in height, Hubbard is the largest valley glacier in North America.

Selected Ports of Call in Western Canada

■ **Vancouver, British Columbia.** One of the most cosmopolitan cities in Canada, Vancouver shares British, Asian, native, and many other cultures. It's home to the spectacular Capilano footbridge that sways over a deep gorge; sprawling Stanley Park with its world-class aquarium; several significant museums of science, anthropology, and art; and a thriving commercial district and Chinatown.

■ **Victoria, British Columbia.** A very English outpost on the far western edge of Canada on Vancouver Island, Victoria is the capital of the province of British Columbia and home to the famed Royal British Columbia Museum and the Empress Hotel. Just outside town are the world-famous Butchart Gardens.

■ HAWAII

Hawaii's weather is fine year-round. Norwegian Cruise Line circles the islands, making a long detour to the Republic of Kiribati. Other major cruise lines visit Hawaii mostly as part of repositioning schedules. A typical schedule has ships coming to Hawaii in the fall as they move south from Alaska en route to the Panama Canal and the Caribbean Sea. The schedule is reversed in the spring.

The complication comes from the provisions of the Jones Act, which requires foreign-flagged cruise lines to visit at least one other country after embarkation from a U.S. port. Itineraries sometimes begin in Vancouver or Mexico for repositioning trips. A few lines, including Norwegian Cruise Line, have extended their Hawaiian seasons with long detours to obscure island nations such as the Republic of Kiribati.

In 2004 NCL America began sailing round-trips from Honolulu under the American flag.

Selected Ports of Call in Hawaii

■ **Hilo, Hawaii.** Hilo is a commercial center on the east coast of the Big Island of Hawaii. The island is nearly twice the size of all the other Hawaiian Islands combined, and it is still growing as lava slowly but steadily flows into the sea from several active volcanoes. A visit to Volcanoes National Park by vehicle, or overhead by helicopter or plane, is a tourist highlight.

- **Honolulu, Oahu.** The best-known city of Hawaii is located on the island of Oahu. Near the port is the famed beach at Waikiki, as well as the U.S. naval base at Pearl Harbor. The waterfront Aloha Tower has greeted ships since 1926.
- **Kona, Hawaii.** The second port on the Big Island, on the west side, is a quiet backwater. Expeditions leave to tourist destinations and several nearby golf courses and resorts.
- **Lahaina, Maui.** Lahaina has some touches of an old New England fishing port, a remembrance of its days as an important Pacific port for the whaling ships of Nantucket and eastern America. The whaling ships are gone, but the whales still swim by in winter. The island is also home to some of the best beaches in the Hawaiian chain. Another port on the island is Kahului, 24 miles from Lahaina.
- **Nawiliwili, Kauai.** The very lush and mountainous island of Kauai includes the colorful Waimea Canyon, a small-scale geological feature somewhat grandly billed as the "Grand Canyon of the Pacific," as well as some spectacular waterfalls that are like a scene from Shangri-la.

◼ EAST COAST

New York and Boston were once among the great transatlantic ports; today they are busy in season with cruise ships to Atlantic Canada, Bermuda, and the occasional crossing of the pond to Europe.

A typical cruise heads north from New York along the coast, sometimes through the Cape Cod Canal, to Boston and on to Nova Scotia and sometimes Montreal. Some ships leave from Boston and head north to Canada.

The season for cruises runs from May to October, with the best bargains available before Memorial Day. Weather in New England and Atlantic Canada can be very capricious, especially in the spring and fall. There can be some spectacular October days and ferocious nor'easter storms.

Selected Ports in New England, Atlantic Coast, and Eastern Canada

- **Baltimore.** The port of Baltimore, founded in 1706 on the banks of the Patapsco River, is just minutes from Interstate 95, the main north-south highway of the East Coast.
- **Boston.** A modern metropolis, Boston also has a great colonial and Revolutionary War history. The port lies directly across the water from Logan Airport and just a few miles by taxi from South Station for Amtrak and bus connections.
- **Halifax, Nova Scotia.** Halifax is a historic fishing town of maritime Canada. Many victims of the sinking of the *Titanic* were buried in Fairview Cemetery, where rows of headstones form the shape of a ship's hull. Nearby is picturesque Peggy's Cove, a tourist magnet that has engulfed a little fishing village.
- **Martha's Vineyard, Massachusetts.** The tony resort island off the coast of Cape Cod, Massachusetts, is home to artists, musicians, and fine Atlantic Ocean beaches.
- **Montreal, Quebec.** The largest French-speaking city outside France, Montreal is one of the most cosmopolitan cities anywhere.

■ **Nantucket, Massachusetts.** A onetime whaling island 30 miles south of Cape Cod, Nantucket is now primarily a tourist community of galleries, shops, museums, and beaches—and home to the author of this book. The narrow and shallow harbor does not permit large ships to enter; they set anchor well outside the harbor and send guests ashore by tender.

■ **New York.** The Big Apple was once one of the most important ports for transatlantic ocean liners. Today the port is home to seasonal service to Bermuda and to maritime Canada, as well as transatlantic crossings. Sailing into or out of New York is one of the most dramatic transits anywhere in the world.

■ **Norfolk, Virginia.** A newly renovated pier, capable of handling Megaships, adjoins Nauticus, the National Maritime Center, home to the USS *Wisconsin.* In the heart of the Mid-Atlantic coastal region, Norfolk was founded in 1862.

■ **Quebec City, Quebec.** Cruise ships dock on the river below the famed Château Frontenac Hotel.

■ **Saint-Pierre and Miquelon.** This pair of tiny fishing outposts of France lies just south of Newfoundland, Canada.

■ FLORIDA AND THE GULF OF MEXICO

From Florida to Texas, the Atlantic and Gulf of Mexico ports are the busiest cruise ports in the United States. Ships travel deep into the Caribbean and west to Central America, South America, and through the Panama Canal to the Pacific Ocean.

The historic sailing bark *Elissa* frames Carnival's *Celebration* in Galveston. *Photo by Corey Sandler*

Selected Ports in Florida and the Gulf of Mexico

■ **Fort Lauderdale.** The third busiest domestic cruise port, Port Everglades has eleven terminals that are used by more than fifty ships each year, with more than 2,000 departures annually. Fort Lauderdale Airport is a few miles away; the larger Miami International Airport is 25 miles to the south.

■ **Galveston.** The historic port of Galveston was the second busiest port of immigration, after New York's Ellis Island, in the early part of the twentieth century. Today's terminal is a block away from the historic Strand shopping and entertainment district. Air service is through Houston, about ninety minutes away. Pirate Jean Laffite arrived on the island in 1817, making it his base of operations and naming it Campeche. The little village contained huts for the pirates, a large slave market, boardinghouses for visiting buyers, a shipyard, saloons, pool halls, and gambling houses. It is believed that Laffite buried treasure on the island, but it has never been found. The town prospered as a trading port until September 8, 1900, when the deadliest natural disaster in United States history hit Galveston Island. A storm with winds exceeding 120 miles per hour and the subsequent tidal surge devastated the island and killed more than 6,000 people.

- **Houston.** The Port of Houston is part of the 25-mile-long Houston Ship Channel that leads to the Gulf of Mexico at Galveston. The port is the busiest in the United States in terms of foreign commerce. Cruise ships tie up at Barbour's Cut Terminal near La Porte, less than an hour from Houston.
- **Miami.** The port sits at the feet of the shorefront skyscrapers of Miami, along the causeway to Miami Beach; it's one of the most attractive cruise terminal locations anywhere. In 2003 nearly twenty-four cruise ships had their home port at Miami; one out of every three North American cruise passengers sailed from there.
- **New Orleans.** More than 125 ships make calls or depart from the Julia Street terminal at the foot of downtown on the Mississippi River. The *Delta Queen* docks nearby at Robin Street Wharf.
- **Port Canaveral.** The protected harbor is about an hour east of Orlando, within sight of the launch pads of the Kennedy Space Center at Cape Canaveral. Disney built its own impressive terminal for the three weekly departures of its ships; other lines have their own structures.
- **Tampa.** The busy port of Tampa is about twenty minutes from the international airport there. The thriving downtown, including the Cuban-flavored Ybor City, is nearby.

■ MEXICAN RIVIERA AND CENTRAL AMERICA

The sunny ports of upper Mexico are becoming more popular each year, with ships making calls at port cities on the Pacific side, including Ensenada near the U.S. border with California and farther south at Cabo San Lucas at the tip of Baja California. Pacific mainland ports include Mazatlán, Puerto Vallarta, and Acapulco. On the Caribbean side are Calica, Cancun, and Cozumel.

Some cruise ships heading through the Panama Canal make port calls in Caldera, Costa Rica, and points off the eastern coast of Panama, including San Andrés Island, a northern outpost of Colombia.

The Mexican Riviera has generally fine weather year-round, with high season in the winter.

Selected Ports in the Mexican Riviera

- **Acapulco.** The most famous and most developed port in the Mexican Riviera, Acapulco has grown from a sleepy fishing village to a world-class resort during the past few decades. Among the best-known sights of the area are the cliff divers of La Quebrada, who plunge more than 100 feet into the waters below.

- **Cabo San Lucas.** Cabo San Lucas lies at the extreme southern tip of Baja California, between the Pacific Ocean and the Sea of Cortez. The bay once sheltered treasure ships from the Orient—and pirate ships waiting to prey on them. The pounding surf has carved some spectacular sea arches and rock formations.
- **Calica.** A recently developed port on Mexico's Quintana Roo coast on the Yucatan Peninsula on the Caribbean Sea, Calica provides access to the Mayan ruins at Tulum and the lagoons of Xel-Há.
- **Cozumel.** Just off the coast of the Yucatan Peninsula in Mexico, Cozumel is near the Mayan ruins at Chichén Itzá and San Gervasio. Palancar Reef, discovered by Jacques Cousteau about thirty years ago, is the second largest known reef in the world.
- **Huatulco.** On Mexico's Oaxaca coast, set against the dramatic backdrop of the Sierra Madres, the area's resorts lie along Tangolunda Bay.
- **Manzanillo.** This small but very stylish port of call was built around the Las Hadas resort and its dreamscape of a beach.
- **Mazatlán.** This is Mexico's largest Pacific port.
- **Playa del Carmen.** The gateway port to the resort center of Cancun, which is almost entirely made up of fancy tourist hotels and pricey shops, Playa del Carmen, referred to as Playa by residents, has the nicer beach and is a bit less developed. You can also catch a ferry (about an hour) from Playa to Cozumel.
- **Progreso.** The port city for Mérida, the capital of Yucatán, Progreso is the gateway to numerous Mayan ruins, including Chichén Itzá and Uxmal. Chichén Itzá was founded about A.D. 432, spreading over 6 square miles. At its heart is the Pyramid of Kukulcan, also known as El Castillo. Visitors can hike 180 feet up the ninety-one steep steps on one side of the pyramid (four sides times ninety-one steps plus the platform at the top equal 365 days, a calendar year). At the top is a fabulous view of the surrounding structures and the flat jungle; between the abandonment of the city about 1194 and its rediscovery in the mid-nineteenth century, the jungle took over, completely obscuring the buildings.
- **Puerto Vallarta.** A small fishing village on the Bay of Banderas, it has embraced visitors and has become a world-class resort.

Selected Ports in Central America

- **Belize.** The principal port and city of Belize, formerly British Honduras, is Belize City. North of the port is Altun-Ha, a significant Mayan ruin accidentally discovered in 1957 by a road construction crew. An extraordinary shore excursion from Belize City travels toward San Ignacio and into the jungle to the Jaguar Paw Resort, which includes the mouths of three large caves that extend more than 7 miles, carrying the slow-moving Caves Branch River. Guests are given miners' headlamps and inflated inner tubes and guided on a mile-long drift through the mostly dark caves.
- **Colombia.** At the top of South America on the Caribbean Sea, the port of Cartagena was one of the principal ports from which the riches of the New World were sent back to the Old in the days of colonial control. The walled city on Colombia's northern coast was built centuries ago to protect against pirate raids. Today the port is famed as a shopping mecca, especially for emeralds. San

Andrés Island is a small piece of land off the eastern coast of Panama that is home to a Colombian naval base and not much else. The island is a reminder that Panama was once part of Colombia, before a U.S.-backed revolution, which helped pave the way to American development of the Panama Canal.

■ **Costa Rica.** On the Pacific coast of Central America, the commercial port of Puerto Caldera is the gateway to a tropical paradise, home to exotic birds, butterflies, and tourists enjoying its white- and black-sand beaches. The port lies below San José, Costa Rica's capital.

■ **Honduras.** The port city of Puerto Cortes is an industrial center for San Pedro Sula, the commercial center of Honduras. Many visitors head for the Mayan ruins at Copán. Lago de Yojoa, the largest natural lake in Honduras, is at the base of interior mountains about 60 miles from the port of Puerto Cortes. The lake, at an elevation of 2,063 feet, is home to nearly 400 species of birds and teems with large-mouth bass and tilapia. The lake is drained to the north by the Río Blanco, which leads to the 140-foot-high Pullhapanzak Falls. Visitors can hire a guide to show the way along a steep and narrow path by walls of the canyon to a cave behind the waterfall.

The fabulous Copán ruins are about three and a half hours by bus from Puerto Cortes; Copán is considered the most artistically embellished Mayan site; its central acropolis includes pyramids, a ball court, temples, and decorative stelae.

■ **Panama.** Cruise ships rarely make calls at Cristobal or Balboa, the ports at either end of the Panama Canal, although some ships send shore excursions to plantations on Gatun Lake in the middle. More popular ports for ships are the San Blas Islands, a group of 360 lush, low-lying isles off the east coast. They are little changed from the way they were when Columbus visited more than 500 years ago and are home to the Cuna Indians.

▓ PANAMA CANAL

The Panama Canal was built to speed transit of ships from the East Coast of the United States to the West Coast, allowing vessels to avoid the lengthy and sometimes dangerous 8,000-mile passage around Cape Horn at the bottom of South America. The canal still serves that purpose, but its extraordinary man-made and natural wonders are today a tourist draw of their own.

From the Caribbean to the Pacific, ships are lifted 85 feet in three steps at Gatun Locks to Gatun Lake. They cross Gatun Lake to Gaillard Cut, where the canal passes the Continental Divide. From there ships are lowered 31 feet to Miraflores Lake and then proceed through two more locks at Miraflores Lock before entering the Pacific Ocean. The 50-mile transit takes approximately nine hours.

Until recent years, cruise ships passed through the canal only on repositioning itineraries, usually on journeys from Alaska or Hawaii to the Caribbean and returning. Now you'll find some cruise ships that pass back and forth from the Pacific to the Caribbean for much of the year. Other ships make a partial transit, entering from the Caribbean side and going as far as Gatun Lake midway across; there they turn around and exit.

■ EUROPE AND THE MEDITERRANEAN

Europe is one of the fastest-growing cruise markets and will continue to expand as a number of cruise companies position their ships there for the summer.

Many of the finest cities of Europe are ocean harbors, including Amsterdam, Barcelona, Copenhagen, Genoa, Helsinki, Lisbon, Monte Carlo, Nice, Oslo, Saint Petersburg, Stockholm, and Venice. London is up the Thames River from the sea.

Selected Ports in Europe and the Mediterranean

■ **Crete.** The fabled birthplace of Zeus and home of the ancient Minoans is Iráklion; you can visit the 4,000-year-old Knossos Palace.

■ **Croatia.** The ancient city of Dubrovnik, repaired from war damage, is one of the world's treasures.

■ **Germany.** The port for the bustling city of Berlin is Rostock.

■ **Greece.** The cruise port for Athens is Piraeus. Newcomers visit the Acropolis; veteran travelers head for the wineries, nightclubs, and shops. Among many Greek islands visited by cruise ships is Corfu in the Adriatic.

■ **France.** The queen of the French Riviera is Cannes, home to some of the most ostentatious displays of wealth in Europe. Ships dock a few miles away from La Croisette, the seafront promenade. Le Havre has served as the port for Paris since the sixteenth century. Marseille is the gateway to Provence, about an hour from the ancient hilltop town of Aix-en-Provence. Corsica, birthplace of Napoleon, is a French island with an Italian temperament. The principal port is Ajaccio. Located south of Marseilles, Corsica offers spectacular mountains and seashore and a culture just a bit different from elsewhere in the Mediterranean.

■ **Italy.** The ancient port of Civitavecchia is about an hour's bus, taxi, or train ride from Rome, the Eternal City that is home to the Vatican, the Colosseum, and hundreds of thousands of awestruck tourists. Livorno, also known as Leghorn, is the port for Florence, about an hour away. Among the treasures of Florence are Michelangelo's *David,* the Pitti Palace, and Santa Croce, the burial place of Galileo and Machiavelli. Also near Livorno is Pisa. Bella Napoli, the port city of Naples, is worth a visit of its own; Mount Vesuvius and the Isle of Capri are nearby. Cruise ships can also pull into a port complex just outside the heart of Venice. A vaporetto or water bus takes visitors to Saint Mark's Square, the Doge's Palace, the Bridge of Sighs, and the canals, which are every bit as thrilling as you've imagined. Messina is one of the most handsome cities in Sicily, within sight and visit of Mount Etna and the ancient Greek theater at Taormina.

■ **Malta.** The capital city and principal port of the ancient island nation of Malta is Valletta. The vibrant city has churches, mosques, museums, and stores. Worth a visit by public bus, taxi, or tour is the nearby old city of Mdina, a spectacular living museum.

■ **Netherlands.** Amsterdam is a lively center of culture in Western Europe.

■ **Russia.** Saint Petersburg is home to the fabulous Hermitage art museum.

■ **Spain.** Cruise ships bound for Barcelona dock a few minutes away from Las Ramblas, the famed downtown promenade. You can hop on the subway for a visit to Gaudi's quirky Sagrada Familia. Alicante is a jewel of the Spanish Riviera, with a Carthaginian fortress above the harbor dating from about 3 B.C.

■ The **Balearic Islands** of Majorca, Minorca, and Ibiza lie south of Spain, of which they are part. Palma de Mallorca on Majorca is the most cosmopolitan city of the Balearics, home to a medieval cathedral that took more than 400 years to complete. Downtown shopping is among the best in the Mediterranean.

■ **Turkey.** The famed Blue Mosque of Istanbul holds the culture, the Grand Bazaar holds the pursestrings. Some cruise lines canceled calls here in 2002 and 2003 because of security concerns.

■ REPOSITIONING CRUISES

The cruise companies have to move their ships from place to place to accommodate changing itineraries; the trips between ports of embarkation are known as "repositioning" cruises. Many cruise veterans seek out these trips because they often offer unusual ports of call, extra days at sea, and generally lower prices.

Many cruise ships follow a seasonal schedule, matching the changing interests of travelers. Here are a few typical cycles:

■ **Alaska/Caribbean.** Ships may spend the summer in Alaska, then move south through Hawaii or the Mexican Riviera in the fall, passing through the Panama Canal before winter, and finishing out the season in the Caribbean. In spring the migration is reversed.

■ **New England/Bermuda/Caribbean.** Some ships finish up their winters in the Caribbean and head north to New York or Boston for cruises to Bermuda in the spring. They then cruise New England and Atlantic Canada in summer and early fall.

■ **Caribbean/Europe.** After finishing Caribbean winter runs, some cruise ships then sail across the Atlantic to the Mediterranean for the summer. A typical itinerary runs from Florida or the Caribbean to Italy or Spain, or in the other direction.

CHAPTER FOUR

HOW TO BUY A CRUISE

THE MAJORITY OF CRUISE BOOKINGS are made through travel agents, although some cruise lines sell a portion of their available space directly.

In theory, it shouldn't matter to you as a buyer. Most travel agents do not charge customers a fee for cruise bookings. Instead they make their income from commissions received from the cruise lines and most other elements of a travel package they put together, including airlines, hotels, and car rental agencies.

Sometimes the best prices can be found by buying directly from a cruise line, especially when it comes to last-minute bookings. On the other hand, cruise lines recognize that the major portion of their sales still come from travel agencies, and they don't want to damage that relationship. A travel agent who sells a large volume of cruises often receives special offers at deeper discounts than are available elsewhere.

Airlines have been cutting back or eliminating commissions to travel agents, and some agencies have instituted a charge to book airline tickets. Because agents continue to receive significant payments from cruise lines, though, I don't think a fee to the consumer is appropriate. In any case, be sure to compare the bottom line—the cost, convenience, and special features—put forth by a travel agent with a booking you can put together yourself.

Most larger travel agencies are members of or associated with a national association, such as ASTA (American Society of Travel Agents), the CLIA (Cruise Line Industry Association), or NACOA (National Association of Cruise-Oriented Agencies). If you see one of these logos on the door of an agency, on a brochure, or on a Web site, you have some assurance the agency meets some level of industry standard. Among other things, the company may have posted a bond to protect deposits and advance payments made by clients; you may be able to enlist the association in any dispute you have with the agency.

Some industry groups offer training for members, awarding "master" and other titles to agents with particular expertise on cruises or other specialties. However, no matter what the string of letters after a travel agency's or agent's name, you should closely judge the quality of service you receive from any travel agency. Be willing to take your business elsewhere if you do not feel you are receiving proper treatment and the best available deal.

My recommendation is that you begin with research of your own, starting with this book, before you speak with a travel agent. Understand the industry, learn about the cruise lines and their ships, and find out about destinations. Check prices in newspaper and magazine ads, then make a phone call to the cruise line or check its Web page on the Internet, or both. Some cruise lines have begun accepting direct bookings from their Web sites, and it is reasonable to expect special deals, especially on unsold cabins close to the sailing date.

HOW TO CHOOSE A TRAVEL AGENT

Good travel agents remember whom they work for: you. There is, though, a built-in conflict of interest here because the agent is in most cases paid by someone other than you. Agents receive a commission from the sellers of the products they recommend. The more they sell (or the higher the price), the more they earn.

I recommend that you start planning for any trip by calling the cruise lines and airlines, and even a few hotels if you'll need to stay over at a port. Find the best package you can put together for yourself; then call a travel agency and ask them to do better.

If your agent contributes knowledge or experience, comes up with money-saving alternatives to your own package, or offers some other kind of convenience, then go ahead and book through the agency. If, as I often find, you know a lot more about your destination and are willing to spend a lot more time to save money than will the agent, you can do some or all of the booking yourself.

You'll have to judge whether an agent is looking out for your best interests by determining the best cruise line, vessel, and itinerary for you, or whether the promise of a higher commission is clouding your agent's judgment.

My best advice: Interview a travel agent carefully, and don't be afraid to ask questions about commissions and special promotions the agent receives from the cruise lines. If the agent refuses to discuss the matter or does so in a rude manner, take your business elsewhere. Remember that this is a business transaction, and it is your money and your vacation that are at stake.

Bids and Rebates

If you are booking an expensive cruise, don't be afraid to devote a little time and effort to saving some money:

▶ **Put your business out to bid.** There is nothing that says you cannot call two or three agencies and ask for a price on a particular cruise. Some agencies might have better pricing than others or could be receiving a bonus from the cruise line, and they may be willing to share some of that money with you to get your business.

▶ **Ask for a rebate from your agent.** If you're booking a $10,000 two-week luxury cruise, the agency stands to earn as much as $1,500 in commission for perhaps an hour's work. Ask for a reduction in price, a free cabin or hotel upgrade, first-class airline tickets, or something else back from the travel agency. It's not an unreasonable thing to do, and it's common practice in dealings between agencies and business clients.

Inside Info

The ordinary commission payment from cruise lines to travel agents is 10 to 15 percent, with some companies paying bonuses above that level for promotions. Most airlines have reduced their commissions significantly or have completely ended payments to agencies.

If you go to a travel agency with one cruise line in mind and are steered toward a different line, make sure the switch makes sense to you. Ask yourself: *Who gets a better deal because of the switch, me or the travel agent?*

UNBUNDLING THE PACKAGE

You might want to consider "unbundling" a vacation by giving your cruise business to a travel agency or consolidator, your airline reservations directly to the air carrier or a consolidator of tickets, and so on. Your goal, of course, is to compare the bottom line of a mixed purchase with the all-inclusive package put together by a travel agent.

In some cases, a cruise line may have negotiated special prices for airline tickets from many major gateway airports. Some cruise packages include airfare from these cities. Either way, you should compare the airfare price you could obtain by directly booking a flight to the cost in the package. Find out from the cruise line the credit you would receive if you were to make your own arrangements.

All this said, keep in mind that if you provide your own transportation to the ship, the cruise line is not likely to be very accommodating if your flight is late or canceled. If you purchase a package that includes airfare, the cruise line usually will take responsibility for getting you and your baggage to the ship, from the moment your journey begins. You'll read more about embarkation in Chapter 10.

INTERNET AND DISCOUNT TRAVEL AGENTS

Some large agencies offer travelers rebates on part of their commissions. Some of these companies cater only to frequent fliers who will bring in a lot of business; other rebate agencies offer only limited services to clients.

You can find discount travel agencies through many major credit card companies (Citibank and American Express among them) or through associations and clubs. Some warehouse shopping clubs have rebate or discount travel agencies. If you establish a regular relationship with your local travel agency and bring in enough business to make the agent glad to see you walk through the door, don't be afraid to ask for a discount equal to a few percentage points.

One other important new tool for travelers is the Internet. Here you'll find computerized travel agencies that offer airline, hotel, car, cruise, and package reservations. You won't receive personalized assistance, but you will be able to make as many price checks and itinerary routings as you'd like without apology. Several of the services feature special deals, including companion fares and rebates you won't find elsewhere.

Some of the best Internet agencies include:

- **Microsoft Expedia,** www.expedia.com.
- **Orbitz.com,** www.orbitz.com.
- **Travelocity,** www.travelocity.com.
- **Trip.com,** www.trip.com.

You can link directly to Travelocity from the *Econoguide* Web site: www .econoguide.com.

You can also book directly with a number of major airlines, sometimes taking advantage of special Internet prices or bonus frequent flyer mileage. Among the airlines that offer on-line booking are:

- **American Airlines,** www.aa.com.
- **Continental Airlines,** www.continental.com.
- **Delta Airlines,** www.delta.com.
- **Jet Blue,** www.jetblue.com.
- **Northwest Airlines,** www.nwa.com.
- **Southwest Airlines,** www.southwest.com.
- **United Airlines,** www.united.com.
- **US Airways,** www.usairways.com.

Don't be afraid to do your business over the phone or on the Internet. You should expect the same sort of personalized attention and service over the phone. In many instances I have received better service than I would have received had I walked into a travel agency.

You can also check Internet portals such as AOL or links from major newspaper or magazine Web sites.

UNDERSTANDING CANCELLATION POLICIES

One of the problems with booking a cruise is that you are paying in advance for a product not yet delivered. If you take advantage of some discount programs, you could be laying out thousands of dollars as much as a year before your cruise date.

In theory, that's OK. You're reaping the benefits of a discount for advance payment or securing a reservation for a commodity that's in very limited supply. There is a value that can be assigned to either situation, and if it makes sense to you, making an advance deposit and payment is acceptable behavior.

But what happens if your vacation schedule changes? What if there is an illness in your family? What if the cruise line changes the itinerary or substitutes a different ship? And, alas, what if the threat—or reality—of terrorism changes your dream into a nightmare?

I'll start with the last question first: In light of recent terrorist activities and the war in Iraq, most cruise lines and airlines have relaxed their cancellation policies. Most companies will permit travelers to cancel or postpone their trips on short notice because of military action; the value of any prepayment can usually be applied to a future trip without penalty or for a small charge. Keep in close contact with the cruise line if you have travel plans during such periods.

Other than terrorism and acts of war, if you are unable to show up at the appointed time, cruise lines generally claim the right to keep some or all of your

A Sample Cancellation Policy

Here's an example of a basic, inflexible policy from a major cruise line:

All cancellations and requests for refunds must be submitted in writing to the cruise company. All documents (deposit receipt or tickets) must be returned before the refund can be processed.

The cruise company will assess cancellation charges as follows:

- *76 or more days prior to sailing: Full refund*
- *75–46 days prior to sailing: Loss of deposit of $100 per person*
- *45–15 days prior to sailing: 50 percent of cruise/package price per person*
- *14–3 days prior to sailing: 75 percent of cruise/package price per person*
- *Less than 3 days prior to sailing: No refund, 100 percent cancellation charge per person*

These charges are just for the cruise portion of the trip and do not include cancellation or change fees that may be applied by air carriers, hotels, shore excursion suppliers, and others.

To add insult to injury, some cruise lines will add an "administrative fee" for changes to bookings after cruise documents have been issued.

deposit or advance payment. Some lines are more accommodating than others. The careful buyer spends the time to closely read the small print at the back of the cruise brochure.

On the other hand, if the cruise line makes a substantial change—such as changing the port of departure, changing the dates, or substituting a different ship—you don't have to accept the new deal; you can ask for all of your money back.

Enlist the assistance of your travel agency, the cruise line, and experienced travelers. But remember this: Put no trust in anything you are told verbally. The only thing that really matters is the written contract. If the cruise line or a travel agent tells you something different from what you see in the brochure or on the booking papers, ask that it be put in writing, signed, and made part of the contract.

TRIP CANCELLATION INSURANCE

So what is there to do about the not insignificant risk to your wallet from cancellations?

You might want to consider buying trip cancellation insurance. These policies pay the penalties assessed for any cancellation or interruption due to unforeseen, nonpreexisting medical conditions of travelers, their immediate family members, or traveling companions. Cancellation insurance will also often add coverage for illness or injury while on the cruise, including emergency evacuation, as well as damage, loss, delay, or theft of baggage.

As with other forms of insurance, the higher the potential payout, or the more likely it is that the insurance company will have to pay it, the higher the premium. Spend the time to read the insurance offering carefully. Pay special attention to the medical sections that cover preexisting conditions, generally excluded from coverage.

Unforeseen circumstances might include a traffic accident while en route to the port of departure, jury duty or subpoena, quarantine, a hijacking, or a home rendered uninhabitable by natural disaster. In all of these cases, you'll have to provide legal proof.

If your trip is interrupted midway because of illness, the refund will most likely be for the unused, nonrefundable portion of your cruise payment, plus the cost of returning home. For example, if you must leave the ship eight days into a ten-day trip, the insurance policy might pay only 20 percent of the cruise cost.

Take care not to purchase more coverage than you need. If you have a $5,000 prepayment on a cruise but the cruise line's cancellation policy says you will lose 50 percent of your advance payment in the case of a late cancellation, you need $2,500 in coverage, not $5,000. Be sure to include in your calculations all the elements of the package, such as airfare, noncancelable hotel reservations, and other bills explicitly covered by the insurance policy.

ACCIDENT AND SICKNESS INSURANCE

The idea of falling ill or suffering an injury while hundreds or thousands of miles away from home and your family doctor can be a terrifying thought. Although nearly all cruise ships have a medical doctor and small infirmary aboard ship, in the event of serious illness or injury, you'll almost certainly have to be taken to a hospital onshore or even airlifted home.

On one cruise I took, the captain told me that on the previous sailing the ship had to reverse course and sail several hours out of the way to meet up with a Coast Guard helicopter for an at-sea transfer of an ill passenger. On another cruise, an elderly passenger suffered a serious cardiac problem and was treated in the ship's hospital overnight until he could be transferred to a shoreside facility the next morning.

On a transatlantic repositioning cruise from Europe to New York on Silversea's *Silver Shadow,* a passenger with chest pains was left in a hospital in the remote Faroe Islands in the North Atlantic between Scotland and Iceland. He remained there for a week before being released to fly home.

As we'll discuss in greater detail in Chapter 7, most standard medical insurance policies do not cover expenses incurred onboard a cruise ship or in foreign countries. Consult your own insurance agent or your company's personnel office to see how far your personal medical insurance policy will reach. Does the policy cover vacation trips but exclude business travel? Are all international locations excluded? Can you purchase a "rider" or extension to your personal policy to cover travel?

If you are not covered under your own policy, you can choose to buy coverage that is part of the trip cancellation insurance packages sold by cruise com-

Travel Insurance Providers

Here is a listing of some of the companies that sell travel insurance directly to travelers or through travel agents. If you purchase insurance, be sure not to buy more than you need; check with your own insurance agent to determine the coverage provided by your own medical policy. If you plan to make more than one trip in a year, it is usually less expensive to purchase a policy that covers the entire year rather than individual policies for each trip.

▶ **CSA Travel Protection.** www.csatravelprotection .com; (800) 873–9855

▶ **Global Travel Insurance.** www.globaltravelinsurance .com; (800) 232–9415

▶ **Travelex.** www.travelex insurance.com

▶ **Travel Guard.** www .travelguard.com; (800) 826–4919

▶ **Travel Insurance Services.** www.travelinsure .com; (800) 937–1387, (925) 932–1387

panies; many include some level of accident and sickness coverage.

The only reason to purchase an accident and sickness policy is to fill in any gaps in the coverage you already have. If you don't have health insurance of any kind, a travel policy is certainly valuable, but you might want to consider whether you should spend the money on a year-round policy instead of taking a vacation in the first place.

Also be aware that nearly every kind of health insurance has an exclusionary period for preexisting conditions. If you are sick before you set out on a trip, you might find that the policy will not pay for treating the problem.

CRUISE LINE BANKRUPTCIES

Every year or so, the cruise industry adds—and loses—a few lines. Competition is very fierce among cruise lines, and some, especially those in the second tier of companies, operate on very tight margins. It doesn't take much to push some smaller cruise lines into treacherous waters.

If you purchase your cruise through a travel agency, the agent should be able to inform you about the financial viability of a line. In some cases, a cruise line will bolster its image by promising to place all advance payments in an escrow account that cannot be tapped until after completion of a voyage.

All ships embarking from American ports must post a performance bond administered by the Federal Maritime Commission that is intended to cover refunds to passengers if the line is unable to provide promised transportation. If you are departing from a foreign port, you might not be covered for financial failure.

You can also protect yourself by purchasing a traveler's insurance policy that specifically provides coverage for trip cancellation for any reason, including financial problems by the cruise line. If the insurance company refuses to cover a specific cruise company, that's a pretty good indication of potential problems.

Note that the cancellation coverage sold directly by cruise lines might not offer protection against financial difficulties; insurance companies don't want to encourage cruise lines to be fiscally irresponsible.

HOW TO PAY FOR YOUR CRUISE VACATION

In general, the best way to pay the fare for your cruise vacation is with a major credit card. This also applies to all the other elements involved, including airfare to the port and any necessary hotel and car rental expenses.

I am not endorsing paying high credit card interest rates. Rather, my advice is to pay for vacations from savings: Charge the expenses to your credit card, and pay the bill when it arrives. This allows you to take advantage of a credit card's built-in protection against fraud and other problems.

Here are some reasons to use your credit card:

■ You can enlist the bank or card issuer in any dispute with the seller. Although you have authorized a charge to be put on your account, you hold on to your money for the moment. If the seller does not deliver the goods, or if whatever you bought is not what you contracted for, you can withhold payment and enlist the assistance of the company that issued the credit card.

■ You'll have the federal Fair Credit Billing Act on your side, which allows you to refuse to pay for a purchase and any finance charges while you make good-faith efforts to resolve a dispute. Your credit card company can put pressure on the merchant on your behalf, too.

Be sure to follow the rules for disputing a credit card charge; they're generally listed on the back of your monthly statement. You can also discuss these rules with the customer service department of the credit card company.

■ It's fun to go "native" when you travel in a foreign land, paying for your meals and souvenirs with euros in Europe, pounds in England, and pesos in Mexico. But you could end up losing 10 to 20 percent or more of your purchasing power by cashing in your dollars at a money-changing counter at the airport or a hotel, where you may have to pay a service charge and almost certainly will receive less than the best rate. You'll get a better exchange rate at a major bank and an even squarer deal by using your credit card.

When you are traveling abroad and are paying local currency, your credit card company will convert the bill to dollars at the bank rate, almost always lower than the rate charged by local merchants or money-changing outlets. (Call the customer service department for each of your credit cards and find out how they calculate foreign transactions, then use the card that has the lowest markup fee.)

■ Use your credit card's automobile insurance coverage when you rent a car. Many credit cards, especially "gold" and "platinum" cards, offer special automobile insurance coverage for rentals made using the card. Be sure to read the fine print from the credit card company, and don't hesitate to call customer service for clarification before you use the card to rent a car. The insurance coverage usually has exceptions that exclude luxury cars, and payment can be withheld if it is deemed that an accident was due to negligence by the driver. Finally, some credit card companies do not extend coverage to international rentals.

■ You can obtain free airline accident insurance on tickets purchased with your credit card. Special insurance coverage for airline flights, purchased from an airport kiosk or directly from an insurance company, is generally not a good deal;

you're better off buying and maintaining a good life insurance policy. But if your credit card company offers free coverage for tickets purchased with its card, take advantage of the offer.

■ You want an interest-free loan from your credit card company from the time you make your purchase until the due date on your statement. Here's one of the best uses of a credit card, but it's only for the financially well disciplined: Make as many purchases as you can on your credit card—and then be sure to pay off the entire bill when it is due. The finest art here involves making major purchases just after the closing day of one billing period, which can give you thirty days until the next statement and up to thirty more days until the bill must be paid.

■ PAYING FOR A VACATION ON THE INSTALLMENT PLAN

Do you really want to be paying for your vacation memories for years after you're back home? That's what you'll be doing if you put your cruise on an installment plan, credit card, or other loan arrangement. What's even worse is taking out a home equity loan or a second mortgage for a vacation. In this case, you could be putting the roof over your head at risk.

All that said, if you do use a loan or credit card, be sure to pay close attention to the APR (annual percentage rate) for the interest charged. Don't be shy about changing credit cards to get a lower rate or asking your current card issuer to reduce the APR to match another offer you have received.

One plan I cautiously endorse is a pay-in-advance installment plan—sort of a layaway plan for a cruise. Here you put away money before you travel. The sponsor of the plan should pay you interest on your money or offer some other enticement to you, such as a discount or upgrade. Be sure to understand your rights to receive a full or partial refund if you must cancel your plans before you travel.

Carnival, the world's largest cruise company, tries to make it as easy as possible for passengers to scrape up the cash to travel. Among recent options is an arrangement that allows guests to have money taken directly out of their paychecks and deposited into a layaway account for a future cruise. Another option is a vacation club that includes the up-front purchase of points toward future cruises.

CHAPTER FIVE

YOUR HOME ON THE WATER

HERE'S MY IDEA of the perfect ship's cabin (and hotel room): a comfortable, clean, and quiet home away from home with a fabulous and regularly changing view out the window or off the private balcony.

What's your idea of the perfect cabin? As you thumb through cruise line brochures you'll see glorious color photos of spectacular suites and glimpses of the better-looking portions of the smaller outside cabins. If there is a picture of one of the lowest-priced inside cabins at all, it is usually with a wide-angle view that rarely hints at just how minimal the accommodation is.

My wife and I like to watch the sunrise and sunset in privacy and to retire to our cabin on a sunny afternoon to read and write. When our children travel with us, they love the guilty pleasure of room service between lunch and late-seating dinner. But some travelers use their rooms only as a place to sleep and hang their clothes. If you spend all your waking time outside on the pool deck or down in the bar or casino, you might not want to spend money on a veranda or panoramic window; if you don't expect to make it down to your room until way after dark, you might be perfectly happy with a windowless inside stateroom.

Think, too, about the nature of the cruise itself. If you're on a Caribbean island-hopper, the ship will travel by night and tie up or set anchor in a new port each morning. On this sort of cruise, you might be willing to accept a lesser cabin than you would prefer on an itinerary with several days between ports.

We've also been on cruises where we've had a fabulous veranda but the outside temperature was too cold or the seas too rough for us to take advantage of the million-dollar views.

Once you're out of your room, there's no class distinction on most modern ships: All guests eat in the same restaurants, swim in the same pools, traverse the same promenades and lobbies, and participate in the same onboard and shore excursions. (The exception: On some very luxurious cruise ships, a few suites have their own pool or deck area and a concierge area.)

CHOOSING A CABIN

Are you the sort of person who wants to spend time lounging around your luxurious cabin, or would you rather spend time (and the money you've saved) in luxurious public spaces and onshore shopping expeditions?

This is not to say you should seek out (or accept) substandard accommodations, but there have been many times when I've checked into a first-class hotel room at midnight and left at six o'clock the next morning for a business appointment. The sitting room was unsat in, the luxurious bathrobe unlounged in, and the spectacular view unviewed.

The same goes for cabins on a ship. Ask yourself how important it is to have a window. Are you willing to accept an obstructed view or an inside cabin with no view at all? You can save big bucks if you choose to spend most of your time up on deck or in one of the public rooms of the ship.

One step deeper into the budget section are especially small inside cabins, or staterooms in a particularly unappealing location such as the very bottom of the ship or next door to the disco or the laundry room. If you can put up with living in the low-rent district, you can expect to pay a lower rent.

Going in the other direction, there is little to match the luxury of a private veranda at sea, especially when there are spectacular sights to see—in Europe, in Alaska, entering a big city port, and sometimes merely watching the sunset over an empty sea.

Study the cabin diagrams and ship layouts carefully before booking passage, and have all your questions answered before you commit to a cruise. Although it is sometimes possible to upgrade to a better class of cabin once onboard the ship, you cannot rely on that on all cruises, especially those taken during peak seasons when ships may be completely booked.

Cabin size can vary from a tiny closet to a penthouselike suite. Although some modern ships have small cabins, to allow for more passengers, the trend has reversed somewhat with the arrival of the largest Megaships. Consult the brochures and online Web sites to compare the square footage of available cabins.

Today most basic staterooms are in the range of about 150 to 200 square feet. Think of a rectangular space about 8 feet wide and 20 to 25 feet in length; part of that space is taken up with a bathroom and closet. If that sounds small, it is, but a lot depends on the skills of the designer. The smallest cabins are usually inside, without windows or veranda.

Luxury staterooms are usually larger, and some suites are the size of small apartments or houses. Be sure to determine whether a cruise line's stated cabin size includes the square footage of a veranda (typically about 50 to 75 square feet) or just the cabin itself.

Here are a few examples of stateroom sizes from several cruise lines:

Royal Caribbean. An outside cabin can be as small as 108 square feet on *Empress of the Seas;* more standard are ocean-view staterooms, which range from about 154 to 211 square feet in size.

Princess Cruises. A basic outside double cabin on *Dawn Princess* ranges in size from about 147 to 155 square feet. Adding a veranda brings the size to 183 square feet.

Disney Cruise Line. The basic outside cabin is a relatively expansive 214 square feet in size, including a bathroom and a separate sink and shower/tub room.

Radisson Seven Seas Cruises. The basic stateroom, available in various levels of luxury, is 306 square feet in size plus a veranda of 50 feet.

Silversea Cruises. This luxury cruise line's smallest stateroom is 287 square feet in size. A basic veranda cabin totals 345 square feet, and the extraordinary collection of suites run from 701 to 1,435 square feet.

Suites offer superior accommodations; some of the most expensive come equipped with concierge or butler service, and a few may have access to a private swimming pool or lounge. Among the most spectacular: NCL's Garden Villas on the *Norwegian Dawn,* which are like a yacht to themselves. The two suites on the top, fourteenth deck, include three bedrooms, a forward facing glass-walled living room, and a dining room, as well as a private outdoor garden.

■ A ROOM WITH A VIEW

A balcony or veranda is a lovely extra, especially on a warm-water cruise. It's a great place to salute the sunset or the sunrise or to conduct a romantic interlude. Be aware, though, that not all balconies are that private; there could be a view from above, or there might not be full partitions on the sides. And the open veranda may be a concern to families with young children.

A handful of ships include forward-facing balconies at the bow. This affords a great view, but in most conditions, you'll also have something like a 20-knot wind in your face when the ship is moving.

Some newer vessels, including *Carnival Pride* and sister ships, have decks full of balconies on the stern. You'll have a great view of where you've been, with less breeze than at the bow unless you've got a following wind. (The downside: the absence of the traditional multideck lido restaurant and bar at the ship's stern.)

Study the ship's diagrams and check with the cruise line or a trusted travel agent to learn if your chosen cabin has an obstructed or partial view. What does that mean? On many ships, the lifeboats and other necessary equipment are mounted on the side of the ship or on an exterior deck. Try to get as much information as you can from the cruise line: A small winch in a corner of your view is very different from the broad side of a lifeboat completely filling your window.

Is there a promenade deck outside your cabin window or porthole? If so, you can't count on much privacy when the curtain is open.

By the way, on most ships the windows or portholes can't be opened. The exceptions: suites on upper decks and cabins that have verandas.

■ MAKING YOUR BED

Many cabins are equipped with twin beds, even on the "Love Boats." It may be possible to have the beds moved together to create a double bed, albeit one with a small gap between the mattresses.

In some especially small cabins, the beds are arranged in an L-shape. Some older boats use upper and lower berths with twin mattresses on each level. A few cabins have pulldown beds that fold up against the wall when they are not being used.

If you have any particular requirements or desires, study the ship diagrams before you book a cabin; you may also want to call the cruise line and discuss specific staterooms.

By the way, don't move furniture in your cabin. Ask the stateroom attendant whether beds can be rearranged, and allow the ship's staff to make changes and add appropriate bed linens.

WHERE ON THE SHIP?

The better and higher priced cabins are generally on the upper decks because these afford better views and larger windows or even verandas. As you move lower in the ship, the windows or portholes become smaller, and the chance you will feel vibrations or hear engine or machinery noise increases. (But lower decks experience less side-to-side roll than upper levels.) On some older vessels, elevators do not go all the way to the lower levels, requiring the use of stairs for the final approach.

Cabins at the front of the ship may have an angular outer wall because of the shape of the bow. More important, these cabins can be noisier during the time the ship is departing or arriving in a port because of the location of the anchor chain or docking ropes. Cabins at the stern, especially those on low decks, may be more susceptible to engine noises and heat.

An outside cabin offers views, light, and sometimes air. Watch out for obstructed views, usually lifeboats or docking winches on the outside decks.

The middle of the ship is usually less likely to carry engine noise and vibration. Cabins amidships (the middle of the ship in nautical terms) are affected less by the up-and-down pitching of the ship.

Avoid rooms that are located near nightclubs, lobbies, elevators, and other locations likely to have late-night noise.

■ INSIDE AND OUT

The most important distinction between cabins is that of "inside" and "outside" locations.

Posh Digs

According to some maritime historians, the preference for location on the ship is the source of the term "posh." British travelers heading out on grand expeditions on P&O ships to India and Asia would specify "port outbound, starboard home" to seek shelter from the sun.

Cabin Locations to Avoid

Here are locations on the ship to avoid:

▶ **Near the disco** or near the gathering place for a public area, such as the theater or dining room.

▶ **Below the jogging track** or the exercise room.

▶ **Staterooms near the ship's machinery.** All things being equal, the quietest rooms are amidships (the middle of the vessel), away from the propeller at the stern and the anchor and winch mechanisms at the bow and stern. The mid-ship area may also be less susceptible to roll and pitch.

▶ **Obstructed views.** Read the plan carefully to understand whether an available room has a veranda, a full window, or a large or small porthole. (Inside cabins, of course, have no windows or portholes.) Then check to see if the view out the window is obstructed by a lifeboat. Note that some "outside" cabins may lie across from an open promenade instead of being directly over the water. It's still a view, but you might have less privacy than you'd like.

An outside cabin, as the name suggests, includes at least one wall that is part of the exterior of the ship, usually one of the sides but sometimes overlooking the bow or stern. You can expect at least one porthole or window; on new ships many outside cabins include a veranda with a glass door.

An inside cabin is one that has no windows or portholes; on many ships these are also the smallest accommodations onboard. Some passengers will find them unbearably claustrophobic, while others will see them as a comfortable den to sleep in when they are not moving about the ship's public places.

There's one other class of inside cabins on some of the newest and grandest of ships: those with an inside balcony and a view of the ship's interior atrium. The first major ships with this sort of accommodation were Royal Caribbean's Voyager-class vessels, which offer a set of "Atrium Staterooms." (This strikes me as wholly unappealing, like a veranda in a shopping mall. Then again, it might match some travelers' concept of nirvana.)

▪ LEFT OR RIGHT?

You might also want to pay attention to whether your room is on the port (left) or starboard (right) side of the vessel. Only one side of the ship may be facing the sunrise or sunset or receive direct sunlight during the course of the day. Just as on land, the southern exposure receives more sun than east, west, and, especially, northern exposures. If your vessel is heading west, the port side faces south; heading east, the starboard side will receive more sun.

Some travelers also pay attention to the orientation of their beds in relation to the ship. If the berths are parallel with the sides of the vessel, your head and

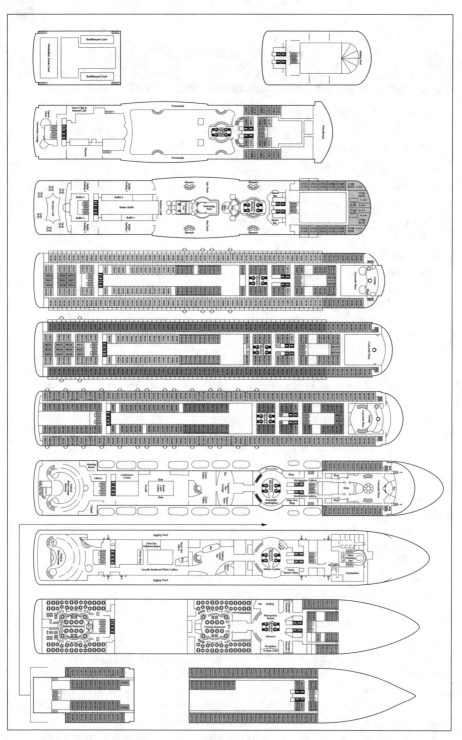

The deck plan for the *CostaVictoria,* a modern 76,000-ton Megaship that has 964 cabins and nine decks. *Courtesy of Costa Cruises*

feet will rise and fall with the pitch of the ship; if the berths lie across the beam, your head and feet will rise and fall with the ship's roll.

Which is better? Beats me. I sleep like a bobbing log either way.

■ YOUR FLOOR, PLEASE?

The "floors" of the ship, known as decks in marine parlance, run down the length of the ship and are stacked from the keel to the topmost sundeck.

The lowest level decks are used for the ship's mechanical rooms, including the engines, fuel tanks, saltwater desalination machinery and freshwater storage, and some of the refrigerators, freezers, and larders for the galley. The lowest decks are below the water level and there are no windows. It's a dark, sometimes noisy underworld.

On a ship of any significant size, the next few decks are given over to the galley or food preparation areas as well as cabins for most of the crew. On many ships, the lower decks may also house a movie theater or show room, where the absence of windows is not a problem.

The restaurant deck or a combined stateroom and restaurant level is typically three or four passenger decks up the ship or about six decks from the keel. On many modern ships, the dining room is at the stern, allowing a wall of windows.

The main deck is the central deck of the ship, usually the home of the purser's office and the reception desk. On many ships, this is the level where you will board the ship at the port of embarkation.

One level is often denoted as the boat deck, because that is the location of the boarding areas for most or all the lifeboats. Most modern ships hang their lifeboats way up high to avoid blocking the views from staterooms. The lifeboats would be lowered to a boarding platform if needed.

The promenade deck offers an open or enclosed walkway down one or both sides of the ship. An open walkway is pleasant for strolls or power walks in good weather, although high winds or rain can make the promenade disagreeable. On older vessels the promenade deck was often up high, between the main and boat decks; on more modern ships the promenade deck may be the same as the boat deck. On some ships the promenade has been shortened at the bow or stern or both by placement of luxury suites; walkers will have to reverse course for longer walks.

CHAPTER SIX

EXPENSES ONBOARD THE SHIP

YOUR CRUISE FARE is an all-in-one ticket for transportation, meals, a hotel room, and entertainment. Does that mean you can leave your wallet behind? No way.

There are many, many ways to spend money aboard ship and in ports of call. There are bars, health spas, art auctions, gift shops, and much more. There are shore excursions, bingo games, and casinos.

The truth is, most cruise lines realize a great deal of their profit from shipboard activities. You can run from their entreaties, but I'm afraid you can't completely hide.

ALCOHOLIC DRINKS AND SODA

On most cruise ships, you'll have to pay for drinks from the bar as well as wine at the table or drinks in your room. You can expect to find waiters hovering over you any time you sit down by the pool, in one of the lounges, and at your dining table. You may also find waiters standing by with a tray of welcome-aboard concoctions as your ship prepares to depart the terminal.

On all but the topmost ranks of cruise ships, the drinks are on you. It's perfectly fine to just say no. You don't have to order a drink to visit any part of the ship, including lounges and show rooms.

The waiters quickly learn to distinguish their best customers from those who don't indulge. By the end of a weeklong cruise you may have to wave very insistently to nab a farewell drink if waiters are not used to taking your order.

As with most other expenses onboard ship, if you do order a drink, you'll likely be asked to sign a receipt or hand over your onboard credit card, and the charge will appear on your final bill for the trip.

Drink prices onboard ship are usually comparably priced with what you'll find in an upscale bar on land, approximately $3.00 to $5.00 for most selections. Many cruise lines feature a drink of the day at a reduced price; you'll often find the specialty listed in the daily onboard newsletter.

Watch out for bottles of water, soda, or wine on the dresser in your room or in a minibar in some cabins. Find out from your cabin attendant whether there is a charge for opening one of the bottles (there usually is).

Here are some ways to save: First of all, juice, iced tea, and ice water are free, usually available in cafes and lounges onboard.

Most ships have rules against guests bringing their own alcohol aboard. Just between you and me: I have been known to pack my bags with a few bottles of wine from home or from a shoreside liquor store, keeping the bottle discreetly out of sight in a drawer or a closet. I can't imagine that a room steward is going to risk losing his or her end-of-the-cruise gratuity by turning me in to the purser.

You may also choose to purchase some wine in ports of call; on one cruise I took in the Mediterranean, we engaged in a floating wine tasting, sampling local offerings from Croatia, Greece, Italy, Corsica, and Spain. (Some cruise lines will insist on collecting any liquor purchased ashore to store it for you until the end of the cruise; there's no good reason for this except to protect their onboard liquor sales.)

Speaking for myself, I can accept the exclusion of alcohol from freebies—I don't want to subsidize someone else's binges—but I do think that paying for soda is a bit of an imposition, especially when I travel with my kids. They are, alas, used to traveling by airplane, where the soda flows free and freely. On a weeklong cruise, it's easy to run up a bill of $50 per kid for a few $2.50 Cokes a day. (A few lines, including Disney, Holland America, and others, offer all-you-can-drink soda cards at a discount for kids.)

If you want to be really tight—and I'm willing to include myself in that category when appropriate—bring a few six-packs of soda in your luggage or buy them from a store in port and keep them cool with a free bucket of ice or the refrigerator found in some cabins.

ALTERNATIVE RESTAURANTS

Eating is at the heart of the daily routine on most cruise ships. Your basic vessel includes a dining room, a lido or poolside buffet, and a pizza and ice-cream counter. They're all included in your cruise fare, and the food is usually good and always plentiful.

As ships grew in size and passengers increased in number, cruise lines began to add more options for dining. Today, nearly all Megaships and larger ships offer main restaurants as well as "alternative" dining places: Italian, Asian, seafood, and other specialties. Then there are the "gourmet" restaurants (which makes me wonder whether cruise lines are admitting that their standard dining rooms are subgourmet).

Although some lines offer the alternative restaurants as just another option in the basic package, an increasing number of cruise lines levy an extra charge for the special service and food. Fees range from as little as $5.00 to as much as $25.00 per person.

Is that a good deal? Perhaps. The alternative restaurants deliver an unusually high level of service, even by cruise ship standards. You can expect tableside preparation of salads, entrees, and desserts. The dining "experience" is more leisurely, and in most cases you can expect a small table matched to the size of your party.

You can also expect a bit more persistent sales pitch from wine stewards and cocktail waitresses for added-cost beverages during the meal, and you should take into account the fact that you have already paid for your meal in the main dining room, whether you eat there or not.

See the cruise diary about the *Norwegian Dawn* in Chapter 11 for the description of one ship that offers an unusual variety of specialty restaurants.

SHORE EXCURSIONS

Within hours of departure at the start of a cruise, you can expect to hear the persistent drumbeats of the shore excursion staff. You'll be invited to a meeting where you will hear about the wondrous excitement of a guided tour to Mayan ruins or the Alaskan bush or a Hawaiian volcano. The shore excursion host or hostess might tell you, in a hushed, conspiratorial tone, about the fabulous bargains available at a particular shop in an upcoming port. The deals get even better, you're told, if you flash your cabin key or wear a cruise line sticker.

In a phrase: Caveat emptor . . . let the buyer beware. Although the shore excursions offered by most cruise ships may well be worthy of your time, they are almost always marked up in price from a tour you might arrange for yourself. The stores touted by the staff are often advertised for a reason: They might pay the cruise line to be included in the excursion spiel or in some way make the ship or the cruise director's staff happy for delivering a boatload of tourists.

One advantage of booking a tour through the shore excursion desk is that the cruise line will then know where a group of its passengers is for the day, and will generally promise to hold the ship if an excursion is delayed.

Here are some important questions to ask before you purchase a shore excursion onboard a ship:

- What kind of transportation will be provided? How large is the vehicle? Is it air-conditioned? Is there a restroom onboard?
- Will an accredited guide accompany the group?
- How long is the drive? Are there any intermediate stops for comfort, shopping, or sightseeing?
- Will you have free time in cities or tourist destinations to explore on your own?
- Will you return in the same vehicle? Will it remain locked and attended while you are away, allowing you to leave personal possessions at your seat?
- Are there any extra charges for admission to attractions? If a meal is offered, are drinks included?
- How much walking or climbing is involved? Is the trip appropriate for your physical condition?
- What time is the group due back at the ship?

Be aware that in many ports, excursion operators have booths on shore offering tours. These might be the same companies and tours sold by the cruise line, or they could be similar trips offered by independent operators. If you haven't made arrangements in advance, be one of the first passengers off your ship when it docks and look for the booths; ask for a discount.

You can also hire a taxi or van and ask the driver to take you to the same places that the cruise line's bus will visit.

My recommendation for shore expeditions: Research the ports of call before you set out on your cruise. Buy a good travel book specific to your destinations and learn about the best sights to see and the recommended shops as laid out by a writer who has no vested interest in anyone but you. Make a few phone calls to the visitor bureaus for the ports before you travel, and ask about places to go on your own. The Internet is a wonderful source of information; many visitor bureaus maintain Web pages with links to individual tour operators.

Some cruise lines will send you a brochure of shore excursions a few weeks before you leave for your trip, to whet your appetite for their offerings. I use that brochure as the basis for my own research.

One word of warning: In some cases, a major cruise line may have locked up a particular excursion for its passengers, booking the only floatplane, for example, or arranging for the best seats at a particular show or event. Before you pay top dollar in the face of that sort of argument, make a phone call and see what you can arrange. In my experience, there's almost always something you can do for yourself.

I consulted some Web pages and made a few phone calls before I embarked on an Alaskan cruise; I found that I could save $50 per person on a seaplane tour of the bush by booking it myself instead of paying the price asked by the shore excursion desk onboard the cruise.

In the Caribbean, I regularly rent a car from a dockside agency and drive to the same beaches others take taxis or buses to reach. Some of the best islands for drives include Saint Martin and Saint Thomas.

In Europe, many ports are served by high-speed rail links to major cities, making it easy to make your own tour and save money.

Here are further savings opportunities:

■ A submarine voyage to the floor of the harbor in several Hawaiian ports is $20 to $30 cheaper when you buy a ticket onshore instead of from the shipboard excursion desk.

Too Good to Be True

In some ports you'll see booths touting "free" or deeply discounted tours with deals that seem too good to be true. In many cases, that's exactly what they are. These are come-ons for time-share vacation offers, and the price for the free helicopter tour or luau or submarine trip is that you'll have to sit through several hours of a high-pressure sales presentation.

First, a real estate or time-share presentation is not a very good use of your precious shore time; you might not have enough time for both the sales pitch and the "free" excursion anyway. Second, in my opinion, time-shares are not a good investment nor a rational way to plan future vacations.

Just say no.

■ You should be able to negotiate a better price for a private guided tour by taxi, Jeep, or limousine by contacting ahead of time tourist agencies in the ports you will visit. Split the fare with someone else you meet onboard the ship to save even more.

■ Floatplanes for visits to the Alaskan bush, an experience I recommend very highly, can be reserved ahead of time by calling tour operators directly or by calling tourism agencies in the ports. The same goes for helicopter trips to the volcanoes of Hawaii.

■ If you are planning to make a shopping expedition to a specific store and are reasonably certain you will be making a purchase there, why not call ahead to the store and make an appointment to come in? You can hope for more personalized attention, and the shop may even arrange to pick you up at the dock.

■ You can often catch a water taxi to a Caribbean beach at a much lower price than you'd pay to take a party boat.

■ When it comes to bus tours to tourist attractions and natural wonders, I figure that if the bus can drive there, so can I. It is almost always much more satisfying to rent a car in port and drive wherever you want, whenever, and with whomever; sometimes it's even considerably less expensive. You can set your own itinerary and stop at any shop or attraction. Best of all, at least in my view, you're not a sardine on a bus.

■ RENTING A CAR

Start out by calling major car rental agencies. You'll generally find rental companies at airports of most any size and in many important towns and cities. Bear in mind that the port where your ship docks or drops anchor could be some distance away from an airport. Call directly to a rental counter to arrange for shuttle service. If the car company wants to charge for a pickup and delivery, try another agency.

You should be able to save $20 or more per day on a car rental in port if you make a few phone calls to rental agencies ahead of time instead of relying on the excursion desk to make arrangements for you.

Car rental rates in obscure locations may be slightly higher than you would find at home, and gasoline prices are almost certainly more expensive on distant islands and ports. But I have yet to see a case in which renting a car is not less expensive or comparable in price to a prepackaged tour for two to four travelers.

Check with your insurance agent about your liability and collision coverage, and make sure you make the agent aware of your itinerary if it includes a stop in a foreign country. Some insurance companies will not extend coverage for rental of four-wheel-drive off-road vehicles. In any case, you probably should not use your vacation as the place to learn to drive off-road.

Be aware, too, that on islands with a British heritage, including a number of ports in the Caribbean, cars travel on the left side of the road. For some drivers, the changeover to the "wrong" side of the road is a simple adjustment; for others, it is an exercise in terror.

■ A WORD OF WARNING

When you go it alone onshore, you assume the responsibility for getting back to your ship before it leaves port at the end of the day. If you drive too far away from port, if your car suffers a flat tire, if your fishing expedition makes a wrong turn, or if you simply make a mistake in your planning, you could end up with the extra expense of catching up with your ship at its next stop.

If you're driving, discuss local road conditions and travel times with the rental company, and carry a good map. Ask about how breakdowns are handled, and bring with you the phone number for the local office, not the toll-free number for reservations. Plan your trip to give yourself at least an hour's cushion at the end of the day.

If you're taking a tour, make sure the operator knows when you need to be back onboard the ship. Again, leave yourself an extra cushion of time.

Finally, any time you leave the ship, be sure to carry with you the ship's identification number and the name and telephone number of the cruise line's local agent in the port; it is usually listed on the day's newsletter. In case you run into trouble or miss the departure of the ship, the local agent should be able to help you communicate with the line and help you catch up with the ship in a later port—at your expense.

TELEPHONE SERVICE

One of the reasons to travel by cruise ship is to cut the cord to the "real world." But, alas, there is always the tug to stay in touch with the family and the office. In today's world of cellular and digital communication, it is relatively easy to make phone calls as you travel. You will, however, have to pay a premium rate to use the ship's long-distance services.

Until fairly recently, communications from a ship were exclusively by radio. The ship's radio officer could patch a cabin telephone or a phone on the bridge into a radio signal to shore, where it could be tied into a land-based telephone system. You may still find radio-based telephone service on some older vessels; typical radio charges range from $10 to $15 per minute.

The latest in shipboard telecommunications, however, is the satellite phone. On most ships, passengers can place calls from their cabins directly to a phone located anywhere on the planet. Typical charges range from about $6.00 to $10.00 per minute; billing sometimes starts as soon as the call is initiated, and a session of two minutes and one second is billed at three minutes.

Either telephone system will work quite well in the most popular cruising areas, including the Caribbean, but there are still places that even satellites don't cover.

On one cruise I found myself at Fanning Island, which lies just above the equator, nearly 2,000 miles west of South America and a thousand miles south of Hawaii. The standard satellite links for the ship, including telephone and television, were useless in the vast emptiness of that part of the South Pacific. I was able, though, to visit the radio officer on the bridge and place a call that bounced off a satellite somewhere over Japan and then back to my home in Massachusetts; I've got the bill to prove it.

■ BETTER WAYS TO KEEP IN TOUCH

Before you travel, think about your telephone and Internet needs and strategies. In this modern age, you will rarely be out of reach of an electronic connection, but some arrangements are much better than others.

The most expensive way to call is to use the phones onboard the ship. Make your phone calls as short as possible. Prearrange with family or the office to set a particular time for your call—you don't want to be put on hold at $10 per minute—and keep the calls businesslike. You can always discuss the weather when you return.

You'll do much better by calling from shore. Use a telephone credit card with a reasonable per-minute charge. If you are going to be calling to or from a foreign country, check with your long-distance credit card provider before you set out on your cruise and inquire about the most economical way to place the call.

The lowest calling card rates are found in countries that have deregulated their phone companies. Rates from Europe are generally about 30 to 50 cents per minute plus a service charge of about $1.00 for the first minute. At the other end of the spectrum are Mexico and Central America and parts of the Caribbean, where you can expect to be charged about $3.00 to $4.00 per minute plus a service charge of about $4.00.

Apply for several telephone calling cards before you leave. AT&T will usually work in ports both familiar and strange, but the company's prices are generally the highest. Slightly better deals are available from Sprint and other carriers. Before you leave for your voyage, check with the issuers of each of your cards to obtain the latest local access phone numbers.

Another way to keep in touch is to purchase phone cards in port; visit the shops that cater to members of the crew. Ask your dining room waiter or stateroom attendant where he or she goes to call home. In Mexico, for example, phone cards cost about 100 pesos for 12 minutes, a bit less than $1.00 per minute for calls to the United States. In Europe, phone cards cost about 30 to 50 cents per minute.

■ CELL PHONES

One way to keep in touch is to use a cell phone, but don't expect to receive a signal when your ship is way offshore or in an obscure port. Be sure you understand your cell phone company's policy on roaming out of your home area.

You should be able to use a U.S.-based cell phone in major ports in Alaska and Hawaii; some companies have local connections in American territories in the Caribbean, including Saint Thomas and Puerto Rico, and a few companies extend their coverage into major cities in Canada.

Most domestic cell phones will not work in Europe, Asia, South America, and elsewhere, but a new class of "world phones" can extend your digital phone to roam in many other countries; check with your cellular company. My "triband" phone works throughout most of Europe and Asia, at a rate of about $1.00 to $2.00 per minute; it does not work in Mexico and Central America, and coverage in the Caribbean is spotty.

Another solution is to rent a cell phone with a foreign account, either before you travel or on arrival. Expect to pay a few dollars per day for rental of the phone plus about $1.00 to $3.00 per minute for calls. I took one such cell phone with me on a cruise around the Mediterranean. The phone, from Roadpost (formerly RentExpress), came equipped with a telephone number in England; it worked in that country as well as in most of my ports of call in Italy, Greece, France, Spain, and even in parts of Croatia.

One nice feature of some world phones is the ability to receive text messages sent over the Internet. Messages cost less than a dollar to send or receive, a reasonable way to keep in touch between voice calls. For information call (888) 290–1616 or visit www.roadpost.com.

INTERNET CAFES

Communicating by e-mail offers many advantages, including cost (if you're careful) and a way to get around time zone differences. The beauty of using the Internet is that messages can be sent on an asynchronous basis, meaning that both parties do not need to be on-line at the same time.

I'd suggest that you set up an account with one of several free-mail Web sites. You don't even need to have a regular Internet account to use one; you can sign up on a free terminal at a library or school or borrow a friend's system. Among mail Web sites are www.hotmail.com and www.juno.com. You should also be able to set up an account that can retrieve messages from your regular e-mail provider, using services including www.hotmail.com and www.mail2web.com.

Some computer users make arrangements for an AOL Instant Messenger account and try to coordinate being on-line at the same time as friends or family members; be sure to take into account time zone differences. AIM permits near-instantaneous messaging among users.

Many cruise lines now have Internet cafes onboard their ships, allowing guests to sign on to mail Web sites or Internet providers, including America Online. The cafes at sea typically charge 50¢ cents to $1.00 per minute, which is rather pricey, and connection speeds can be slow in some parts of the world. Expect to spend at least five minutes on-line to retrieve messages and dash off a reply.

Some cafes offer unlimited service for a onetime fee, usually about $100 for a week's pass. A number of cruise lines have begun to extend Internet access to staterooms using plug-in Ethernet connections for guests who bring their own laptop computers. And companies, including Holland America, have begun to create wireless "hot spots" in libraries, cafes, and elsewhere onboard; users will need to have wireless receivers in their laptops to attach in this way.

A better deal is to visit an Internet cafe on land. You'll find one in nearly every port; check in the terminal for advertisements, or ask a crew member for advice. Typical rates are about 10 cents per minute; I've found charges as low as a few pennies per minute in Europe. Check to see if the cafe is part of a chain with locations in other stops on your itinerary. If so, it probably makes sense to purchase a block of time that can be used at several ports.

SHIP'S PHOTOGRAPHER

On some cruise lines the ship's photographers will be on you like flies on jam, happy to document your every moment for posterity. They'll be there as you come onboard for the first time, they'll be there at the captain's welcome-aboard dinner, and they'll be there at most every onboard activity.

If you'd like to come home from your trip with pictures to prove you've really been on a cruise, or to show yourself stuffed into a tuxedo and cummerbund or a cocktail dress at the captain's dinner, the photographers will be happy to oblige.

On some of the most spectacular of the modern ships, you'll even find a state-of-the-art "blue screen" studio, where a bit of electronic magic can place you against most any backdrop. Didn't quite make it to the lip of the volcano? Who's to know? Even stranger: How about a picture of you in front of an Alaskan glacier, taken onboard your Caribbean cruise?

Photographs are not cheap; on most ships a 5×7 picture costs $5.00 to $10.00. Multiple copies of the same picture should be priced at a lower rate; ask for a discount if one is not offered. Formal studio portraits cost more.

You are under no obligation to make a purchase. If you don't like the picture, don't buy it. There is nothing wrong with waving off the photographers if you're not interested in posing; tell them to save their film or digits for someone else. As with waiters in the bars, by a few days into the cruise, the ship's photographers will have a pretty good idea of which passengers are going to be their customers and which ones don't want to be spotted.

On many cruises you can also sit for a formal family portrait in a studio setting; in this instance there may be an obligation to make a purchase. Be sure you understand the terms before saying cheese.

One deal you might want to consider: On the most modern of ships you can arrange to have your own film developed, printed, and delivered to you within a day or so. Compare the prices with what you would pay onshore and add in the convenience and amazement factor: You can show off your pictures on the plane ride home.

The latest wrinkle: A switch to digital cameras and the installation of video kiosks on some ships allow guests to search for pictures on a screen and then order prints. The highest-tech version of this system includes a computer program that can search for your face from among the thousands of images stored on disk.

GIFT SHOPS

On most modern ships, a small shopping arcade offers a reasonable selection of gifts and necessities. Many of the items are duty-free; that makes a difference on certain items such as some liquor, jewelry, and perfume. You'll also find cruise clothing, pharmaceuticals, cosmetics, cameras, binoculars, and all manner of souvenirs. The shops seem to be constantly offering some sort of a "once in a lifetime" sale.

My opinion, since you asked, is that you should consider these shops as emergency resources, kind of a floating 7-Eleven for things you need in a hurry and can't wait to purchase in the next port of call. The only exception: On most ships the prices for liquor are about the same or a bit less than you'll find onshore; it's a lot more convenient to buy on the ship. Note that the selection is usually limited to major brands. If you're looking for unusual local wines or liquors, you're still going to have to shop onshore.

The shops may be of value if you are unexpectedly invited to sit at the captain's table and your most formal outfit is a T-shirt that proclaims, I'M WITH STU-PID. Many shops sell or rent formal wear, albeit at premium prices.

Another reason to visit the ship's gift shop is if you absolutely must own a T-shirt or a jacket emblazoned with the name of the ship or cruise line.

Remember that on most ships, you can obtain free aspirin or Tylenol, Band-Aids, shampoo, and other sundries from your cabin attendant or from the purser's office. You should also be able to obtain seasickness pills and Tylenol from the office of the ship's doctor.

ART AUCTIONS AND GALLERIES

We all know the official slogan of the amateur art collector: "I don't know much about art, but I know what I like."

That's all very well and good, but do you also know how much the art you like is worth? On many cruise lines, especially those in the mid- to upper price range, you'll find an onboard art gallery or auction.

On one cruise I took, an earnest young man was passing himself off as an expert in "fine art" and conducting several auctions of paintings and sculptures that he declared at various times to be priced at either "80 percent off retail" or "80 percent of retail." There's a huge difference between those two discounts; even more scary is the fact that I have absolutely no idea what the true "retail" price for a piece of art should be.

The auctions he conducted were also not pure exercises in capitalism. The seller had a reserve price—a minimum price—for each piece, and although the bidding might start low, the painting or sculpture was not going anywhere until someone offered at least that minimum amount.

So is an onboard art auction a fraud? I couldn't tell you because, as I said, I have no idea of the true value of the items. My advice: If you know the value of art, go forth and drink the free champagne and hunt for a bargain. If you don't know the

Disney Magic and *Golden Princess* tied up in Saint Maarten. *Photo by Corey Sandler*

value of art, but you find something you really like, decide for yourself what the item is worth to you and see if you can buy it for that price. Don't, however, try to make an "investment" in art unless you do know the value of the items for sale.

Oh, and be sure you understand any shipping costs, duties, and other charges that might be assessed on your purchase before you make a bid. For example, "fine" art is generally exempt from U.S. Customs duty, but you may be assessed tax on the frame that surrounds it.

HEALTH SPA AND BEAUTY SALON

If the rockabye motion of the ocean, lying by the pool, and the overall cruise experience are not quite relaxing enough—or if you feel the urge to beautify yourself or undertake a new course of exercise—most ships offer an onboard health spa that is fully prepared to coddle you in luxury. The spa is also ready to give your credit card a serious workout.

Basic facilities include everything from beauty parlors and barbers to manicures, massage rooms, saunas, and steam rooms. But on many ships, that's just the starting point. On a typical voyage you might find such offerings as a full body massage with aromatic oils and therapeutic heat for about $90, a reflexology consultation and analysis for about $70, and something called an Ionithermie superdetoxification treatment for about $120.

(That last is described as a regime in which lotions rich in kelp, ivy, and seaweed are placed on the body and covered with a blue clay, then excited with electrodes. The treatment is supposed to reduce cellulite and remove toxins in the body that contribute to cellulite and reduce energy. Or so they say.)

SPORTS AFLOAT

Swimming in the pool, working out in the gym, playing basketball on the sundeck or shuffleboard alongside the pool, hiking around the promenade deck, and repeated trips to and from the buffet line are all included in your fare. You'll also find some additional sports facilities that are generally offered at an extra cost. These include:

- **Golf.** The offerings here include driving ranges and golf simulators that allow you to step up to the tee with a real club and drive a ball into a screen that carries the image of a famous fairway. On some cruises you'll also find a PGA-certified instructor who can help you with your game. Some of the golf programs are tied into shore excursions to courses in ports of call.
- **Specialty sports.** The biggest of the new ships include some unusual sports options, including rock climbing on an artifical wall attached to one of the ship's funnels or ice-skating on a small rink. You can expect to be charged for the right to tell your friends and family, "You won't believe what I did on my cruise."
- **Water sports.** In warm waters you may be able to rent snorkeling or scuba diving equipment or sailboats or arrange for waterskiing and other activities in port. (You'll need to be certified to use scuba devices; some cruises can arrange for the training onboard the ship.)
- **Skeet shooting.** This holdover from the glory days of the transatlantic liner is available on a few ships. The modernized version uses biodegradeable targets and quieter guns.

Some of the smaller luxury ships make their advanced sports part of the basic package. For example, the Radisson *Diamond* and the Windstar sailing vessels include a marina at the stern used to launch watercraft available to all guests in certain ports.

BABYSITTING AND KIDS' ACTIVITIES

Many cruise lines offer free activities for children. Among the best programs are those offered by Disney Cruise Line. Other companies that promote kiddie-friendliness include Holland America, Carnival, Royal Caribbean, and Princess.

You'll likely have to pay for private babysitting in your room or for special group babysitting activities. You'll also have to pay for video arcades. Some companies, including Disney Cruise Line, make it very easy to run up a bill. Kids (if you give the cruise line permission) have their own credit cards they can use to purchase arcade time, as well as soda and gifts from the stores.

GRATUITIES

Like it or not, nearly all the service staff onboard most cruise ships receive very little in the way of salary, sometimes the equivalent of only a few dollars a day. They make their incomes from gratuities offered by guests.

There is no requirement that you give a tip, but the fact is, tipping is considered part of today's cruise environment. Most cruise lines will helpfully provide passengers with a "suggested" schedule of tips. On most ships the amount ranges from $7.50 to $12.00 per person per day.

Here's a typical breakdown:

Cabin attendant	$3.50 per person per day
Waiter	$3.50 per person per day
Busboy	$1.50 per person per day

The cruise line may also recommend that you tip the headwaiter and/or maître d' another $1.50 per person per day. Those tips are truly voluntary. If the managers of the restaurant have performed some especially notable service for you, go ahead and remember them with a gratuity. If not, take solace in the fact that the managers are paid a reasonable salary, while the cabin attendants and waiters are not. (Want some scary math? Multiply 2,000 passengers times $1.50 per day for the headwaiter and maître d' and ask yourself if you're in the wrong business.)

Drinks from the bar and many other special services, such as the health spa and special-order room service deliveries, will typically have a 15 percent service charge added to the bill.

As I have noted earlier, on many ships you can charge the gratuities to your shipboard account and hand your servers a card indicating that. You can also give cash.

The traditional time to extend gratuities is at the final dinner before disembarkation, known among the staff as "the last supper." You can expect all the service staff to be especially attentive to your needs that evening.

If you do expect to give a tip, some veterans recommend giving your room steward and dining room staff $20 or more at the start of the cruise; you can expect just a bit more attention and special service if they envision you as a big tipper. It'll be up to you whether to stay with the standard amount of gratuity when you make a second gift at the end of the trip.

A handful of cruise lines charge their passengers enough of a premium to allow a "no tipping permitted" or a "no tipping required" policy. The lines that completely prohibit tipping include Seabourn and Silversea. Among lines that say tipping is not required are Cunard, Holland America Line, Radisson, and Windstar.

Note that it is also customary to extend a small gratuity to the escort on a shore excursion.

PORT CHARGES

Many cruise lines advertise their rates without including port charges and fees levied by the various places the ship departs from and visits. These can easily add $150 or more to each ticket on a seven-day cruise, and much more on a longer voyage. Be sure you know whether these fees are included in the price of your cruise.

FLOATING CRAPS GAMES AND SLOT MACHINES

If you want to gamble, many cruise ship companies are perfectly happy to take your money. Onboard casinos range from a few slot machines in a bar to glitzy miniatures of Las Vegas.

You won't find casinos on many smaller ships and adventure cruises and the Disney Cruise Line decided to forgo gambling on its family-oriented vessels.

In most cases, the casinos do not operate when the ship is in port.

Let's get a few things straight right away: First of all, the fancy casino onboard your ship, just like those of Las Vegas, Reno, Lake Tahoe, Laughlin, southeastern Connecticut, Atlantic City, and everywhere in between, was not built as entertainment but as a place of business. That business is the extraction of cash from your wallet or purse.

Second, the success of that business is based on the fact that nearly every visitor can be counted on to lose money at gambling tables and slot machines. Some will lose more than others, and a few will even come away with an occasional small or large or huge win; but always remember that the pockets of the casino operators are lined with the money left behind by the losers.

Third, if you are a serious gambler, shipboard casinos may not be the best place to invest your capital. Passengers on a ship are a captive audience, and slot and video poker machines might not be as liberal in their payouts as their land-based equivalents.

I'm not going to offer lessons on gambling here. If you're going to bet serious money, I'd suggest you buy a book or two about gambling. I will, though, offer my **Three *Econoguide* Rules of Gambling**.

- **Rule Number One for Gamblers:** Don't bet more than you can afford to lose.
- **Corollary to Rule Number One:** Don't bring with you to the table (or with you onboard the ship) more money than you can afford to lose.
- **Second Corollary to Rule Number One:** Don't beg, borrow, or steal more money than you can afford to lose. The casinos will make it very easy for you to tap into credit cards or savings accounts, and they may even offer unsecured loans. Whatever the source, it will still be a debt, and it probably will include an unpleasant interest rate.

The casino onboard *Celebrity Millennium. Photo by Corey Sandler*

■ SLOT MACHINES

At one time, the conventional wisdom may have been that table games, from roulette to 21 to baccarat, were where the real action was at a casino. Slot machines were looked down upon as the province of the low roller.

The average bet in a casino is still considerably higher at the tables, but don't believe for a moment that casinos look down on slot machines. At most casinos, slots deliver about half the revenue. That percentage is even higher on most cruise ships.

Here's the rap on slots: They are dumb, require no skill, and provide no human interaction. They are pure exercises in luck, and, like other casino bets, they ask the player to put aside the knowledge that the casino is almost sure to win over time. They aren't called "one-armed bandits" for nothing.

The odds against winning are based on the number of reels (rolling sets of symbols), the number of symbols on each reel, and the computer settings made by the casino operator. A "liberal" machine is one that returns about 98 percent of the money put into it. What that means is that over an extended period of time, the machine pays out about $98 for every $100 bet. In practice, this could mean that unlucky players might lose nearly everything they bet, while a lucky bettor could walk away with a nice payoff. The highest-payoff five-reel machines may work out to a chance of something like 1 in 3.2 million pulls for the jackpot.

Most slot machines pay better jackpots to bettors who play the maximum number of coins on a pull. If you are willing to bet about $1.00 per pull, you generally would be better off at a quarter machine putting in five coins at a time ($1.25 per pull) than putting in a single dollar token at a dollar machine.

■ VIDEO POKER

Video poker machines are very popular, offering the chance for a bit of reward to players who have a bit of skill. There are dozens of different formats, but most of them come down to versions of stud poker. The machine will deal you five cards; you can choose to hold any or all of them or draw up to five new cards. After the second round of cards, the hand is evaluated and winning hands are paid off.

Most machines pay off only on a pair of jacks or better. In addition, the relative payoffs are much higher for the best hands. Therefore, professional video poker players generally recommend throwing away any low hands and always making a play for the high-payoff hands. For example, in standard poker you would almost never draw to an inside straight (seeking to fill out a straight with a gap in the middle, as in 9-10-Q-K), but in video poker it might be worth a chance.

■ THE ROULETTE WHEEL

Round and round she goes; where she stops, nobody knows. Some historians track the roulette wheel back to the ancient Chinese or Tibetans of 1,000 years ago. Famous French scientist and mathematician Blaise Pascal is credited with adapting the wheel to a casino game in 1655.

Of the four major table games (roulette, craps, blackjack, and baccarat), roulette offers the poorest odds to the player. It is, though, one of the simplest of games to play. In the standard game as played in Nevada and onboard most ships, the wheel is divided into alternating red and black compartments that are numbered from 1 to 36; in addition, one compartment is numbered 0 and another 00. A player can bet on any of the 38 numbers directly and is paid off at 35:1. (Here is the house advantage presented about as clearly as possible: There is a 1 in 38 chance of a particular number coming up, and the winning payoff is 35:1.)

The 0 and 00 are excluded from the payoffs on red/black, odd/even, columns, or rows. In other words, the casino wins all bets on color, odd/even, or groups of numbers if 0 or 00 comes up.

The American game with the 0 and 00 numbers added to the layout gives the house a 5.26 percent advantage on most bets; the worst gamble for the player is the five-number bet, which gives the house an advantage of more than 7 percent.

■ BLACKJACK (21)

Blackjack, also known as 21, is one of the more popular casino games and, on one level, one of the easiest to play. All you have to do is request cards from the dealer, one at a time, until you get as close to a card value of 21 as you can. If you get closer to 21 than the dealer, you win; if you go over 21 or if the dealer is closer to that magic number, you lose. If you and the dealer tie, your bet is returned to you.

Betting is relatively simple too. You are always betting against the dealer that your card value will be better than the dealer's. But although blackjack is easy to play, it is not easy to win. It is, however, one of the few games at the casino that can be consistently beaten, or at least fought to a draw, by a well-educated and careful player.

A player who understands the basic strategy and bets conservatively can expect to win about 1 percent of total action over the course of time, which doesn't sound like much, but it can quickly mount up to serious money. Players who can count cards and adjust the levels of betting and strategies based on the current condition of the deck can expect to win much more.

The line between winning and losing is always slim, and the casino always stands to benefit from a player's mistake.

Watch the players at the table or ask the dealer about the protocol for indicating whether you want to hit or stand. Some casinos are more picky than others about hand signs used at the table. In most casinos, you indicate you want another card by scratching your current cards toward you on the felt or by waving at the dealer with a "come to me" gesture. (Looser dealers will permit you to nod your head "yes" or perform some other positive signal.) To indicate that you want to stand, you can slip your cards, face down, under your bet or give some sort of a "wave off" signal. The reason casinos are sometimes picky about the signals used is they don't want a bettor to ask for his money back on a losing bet because of any ambiguity about betting intentions.

Other casino protocol: Handle the cards with one hand only; don't take the cards off the table, and don't touch your bet once cards have been dealt. If you are busted, turn over all your cards and watch the dealer take away your bet.

■ CRAPS: A FLURRY OF ACTION

Craps is one of the more exciting games at the casino, one in which the players and even various casino employees are encouraged to yell, shout, and otherwise encourage the little cubes of plastic to come up properly.

The thrower (called the shooter) makes a money bet, covered by one or more opponents. The shooter throws the two dice against the far wall of the craps table. (This is an important rule of the casino; the boxman or pit boss may halt the game if they don't feel you are throwing the dice with enough force to ensure an honest tumble.) If the first throw totals 7 or 11, the player wins; but if 2, 3, or 12 is thrown, the player loses. In any of these cases, betting and throwing are repeated.

If the throw totals 4, 5, 6, 8, 9, or 10, that number becomes the player's point, and throwing is continued until the same point is made again or a 7 is thrown. If the point is made, the player wins, but if a 7 is thrown, the player loses both the bet and the right to throw again.

Even more complex is the betting protocol for craps. If you're going to be risking your capital at the craps table, pick up a specialized book on gaming or ask the casino management for a lesson.

■ THE BINGO PARLOR

Your grandma might not refer to bingo as gambling, but that's what it is, and on many ships this is where you'll find the big action.

Every ship has its own prices and special promotions, but in general, bingo is bingo. You'll find traditional games, the goal of which is to fill in a straight or diagonal line, as well as "coverall" versions, in which the winner must fill in all the numbers to win.

There are basic prizes of $25 to $100 per game, and there are jackpot and progressive rounds, with the prize rising after each unsuccessful game until one player takes home a large payment.

And then there are lotteries intended to keep you coming back for more bingo games. A number of cruise lines, including Holland America and Norwegian Cruise Line, routinely award a grand prize of a free cruise to the winner of a lottery or a special high-priced round of bingo.

Bingo cards typically cost between $5.00 and $10.00 per game. Less expensive cards and twofer promotions are offered on most cruises, too, although the prize payout for lower-priced cards is usually concomitantly lower.

Don't look to finance your kids' college education or even your next cruise vacation on the basis of your bingo winnings. The careful player performs a rough calculation of the odds of winning based on the number of players, and then looks at the price to play and the possible prize. If you go to all of that trouble, you'll probably decide the game is a pretty poor bet. Instead, if you think of an hour of bingo as fun, pay the price as entertainment.

A CASHLESS SOCIETY

On most cruise ships, cash is either not expected or not accepted. Instead, you'll be asked to establish a credit account with the purser's office when you board. From that point on, you'll be able to sign for all expenses onboard the ship. If you do not have a credit card or choose not to use one, you will likely be asked to make a cash deposit to open an account.

Some ships issue a magnetically encoded charge card for use aboard. Others give you a printed card with your name and cabin number on it, while on some cruises all you need to do is announce your stateroom number. On the most modern of ships, your cabin key is also your personal credit card as well as your embarkation and disembarkation pass.

On many ships you can also charge gratuities to your charge account. You should receive a receipt for the tips and a card to give to your room attendant, waiter, and busboy to inform them you have paid for a tip that should be credited to their accounts.

Some ships provide a preliminary accounting of your bill a few days before the end of the trip; take the time then to check over the statement and bring any errors to the attention of the purser's office. You'll receive a final itemized bill early on the morning of disembarkation. If the bill is correct, you're usually set to leave; on some ships you'll have to visit the purser's office to check out.

If there are errors on the bill, head for the purser early. It is not unheard of for someone else's charges to be applied to your account, or for accidental double billing. Stand your ground and politely demand that the purser show you the signed receipts for all charges posted to your account.

On most ships, the one place where the onboard charge card is not valid is at the casino. Here they expect visitors to use (and lose) cash or traveler's checks. You can, though, arrange for a separate line of credit with the casino manager. Some shipboard casinos also have credit card cash-advance ATMs, a convenience I find fiscally appalling.

CHAPTER SEVEN

SAFETY AT SEA

BEFORE THE TERRORIST ATTACKS in 2001, the most common fear among cruisegoers was an errant iceberg: Precious few travelers could resist making nervous jokes about the famous marine disaster when they put on their life vests for lifeboat drills. And some nervous cruisers kept a lookout for icebergs in waters, like the Caribbean, almost warm enough to make tea.

Today the travel industry has been forced to be on the lookout for threats from terrorists as well. A cruise ship on the open sea is a rather remote target, although experts do express concern about threats from within, either from passengers or from crew members with ill intent. More worrisome is the huge target presented by a cruise ship in a harbor or tied up at a dock.

In our changed world, cruise lines have stepped up their inspection of checked and hand-carried luggage. You can also expect to have your passport or other identification closely examined at embarkation. The cruise lines promise more close screening of the crew as well.

In ports, the U.S. Coast Guard and foreign equivalents are keeping a close eye on ships in the harbor. It's definitely in the government's interest to do so; a cruise ship with 2,000 guests brings with it hundreds of thousands or even millions of dollars in spending.

Cruise lines also realize that an incident on one of their ships could deeply injure the industry. The cruise lines' immediate reaction to the attacks was to reposition most of their fleets from Europe and Asia, sailing from American ports and nearby ports in the Caribbean and Canada for the winter of 2002. In 2003 most lines offered reduced service in distant waters, moving more ships to the Caribbean, the Northeast, and the Gulf of Mexico. The move to closer waters continued in 2004 and in plans for 2005, with a record number of ships and passengers heading to the Caribbean, Atlantic Canada, and Alaska. Cruise lines still operating in Europe and Asia adjusted their itineraries to avoid or reduce exposure in hot spots including Turkey, parts of the Middle East, and Indonesia.

No one I know is able to predict world events very well. We may have peace, or we may have to endure a long period during which whole sections of the world—the Middle East, Asia, and parts of the Mediterranean among them—present real or perceived threats to cruisegoers. I intend to keep traveling, but with a new attention to security in the ports I choose to visit.

In the aftermath of the terrorist attacks, cruise lines went to "Level 3" security in cooperation with the U.S. Coast Guard. Here's part of what that means:

■ Advanced screening of passengers and crew based on passport and visa information before departure; commercial vessels must give ninety-six hours advance notice before entering a U.S. port.

■ Screening of passenger baggage and carry-ons as well as supplies and cargo loaded on ships at various ports. Cruise lines are expected to check in guests with photo ID or ship's identification. Some lines have added metal detectors at entry points.

■ Cruise lines have beefed up their onboard security staff with former military personnel or police officers; Princess Cruises has employed Gurkhas, former members of the specialized Nepalese brigade of the British Army.

■ There is greatly tightened access to sensitive areas of the ship, including the bridge and engine room. Many cruise lines have ended tours of the bridge.

■ In U.S. ports, the Coast Guard maintains a security zone around cruise ships in the harbor and escorts them into open water.

Safety at sea is not a joking matter. In a real disaster, passengers and crew can find themselves with nowhere to go but into the water, hundreds or even thousands of miles away from the security of dry land and shelter.

In the past few years, there were about a dozen significant accidents involving cruise ships: One liner sank off Malaysia, a classic eighty-three-year-old Tall Ship was blown from her moorage and lost at sea in a hurricane in the Caribbean, another lost power in the Gulf of Mexico as a tropical storm bore down on her. Three small vessels ran aground in Alaska, one Megaship on her maiden voyage washed up on the rocks in the Saint Lawrence River, and another large cruise ship had a middle-of-the-night collision with a freighter in the English Channel. That sounds scary, but consider this: In all of these accidents, not a single person was killed, and only a handful of injuries were sustained.

Today the biggest fear doesn't have to do with striking an iceberg in the North Atlantic. Radar, satellite navigation systems, and improved construction have pretty much solved that problem. Instead, the real threats to travelers are fire at sea, contagious diseases, or contaminated food.

In May 2003, the classic steamship *Norway* suffered a boiler explosion as the vessel was preparing to disembark passengers in Miami at the conclusion of a cruise. Seven crew members were killed and more than a dozen others injured; no passengers were hurt. Most recently there have been a series of shipyard accidents involving vessels under construction, including the collapse of a temporary walkway in France at the *Queen Mary 2*, a fire onboard an uncompleted Princess ship in Japan, and the swamping of NCL's *Pride of America* in Germany.

MODERN SAFETY: AFTER THE *TITANIC*

For the record: The "unsinkable" RMS *Titanic* struck a glancing blow against a large iceberg some 400 miles from Newfoundland in the cold North Atlantic on April 14, 1912, at 11:40 P.M. The ship sank two hours and forty minutes later.

Although the ship went down quickly, that would still seem to be more than enough time to evacuate the 2,200 passengers and crew. However, the designers of the *Titanic* trusted too much in the promises of technology; the supposedly unsinkable ship did not have enough lifeboats to carry all aboard, and the lifeboats were not designed well enough to overcome the severe list of the sinking ship. Only about 700 people survived.

▪ SOLAS: THE LEGACY OF THE TITANIC

From the *Titanic* disaster came one positive development: the convening in 1914 of the first international convention for the Safety of Life at Sea, which became known by its comforting acronym, SOLAS. This agreement among shipping nations has been updated and expanded numerous times since.

Today most of the world's nearly 140 seagoing nations are parties to the agreement. The countries that subscribe promise to apply the regulations of SOLAS to any ships that fly their flag. (Panama, the Bahamas, and Liberia, common "flags of convenience" for cruise lines, are signatories.)

In North American waters, the cruise industry cooperates with the U.S. Coast Guard, which inspects all foreign-flagged vessels operating from American ports and issues certification that is required before U.S. passengers can embark. Coast Guard certification also includes quarterly lifeboat and firefighting inspections.

The original SOLAS convention set rules that ships have enough lifeboat seats for every person aboard and mandated a lifeboat drill on each voyage. Ships were required to staff their radio rooms at all times.

The SOLAS regulations have been improved over the years. Modern ships now must have partially or totally enclosed lifeboats as well as other equipment, such as self-righting rafts.

In recent years, much attention has been shifted to fire safety at sea. Nearly all older vessels are now under orders to be refitted to add fire sprinklers and automatic controls of fire doors.

SAVE OUR SHIP!

With the advent of satellite navigation, improved radar and radio systems, and computers, the chances of collisions between ships or accidents involving obstacles in the water have become more and more remote. This is especially true for modern cruise ships. The owners of your basic $300 million Megaship that has a few thousand vacationers aboard have what lawyers would call a huge liability exposure; most cruise lines are extremely conservative in their operations. That doesn't mean, though, that accidents don't happen.

Royal Caribbean's *Monarch of the Seas* struck a rock off the coast of Saint Martin just after midnight on December 15, 1998; three of her eighteen water-tight compartments began taking on water. The captain was able to steer the ship back to port, where it was intentionally beached on a bed of sand. Meanwhile, all 2,557 passengers were called from their cabins and sent to their muster stations. By 4:15 A.M., all had been evacuated from the ship in tender boats, without injury.

In May 1999, the 30,000-ton *Sun Vista* suffered a fire in its engine room; all 1,104 passengers and crew were forced to take to lifeboats off the coast of Malaysia in the middle of the night, where they watched the ship go down.

In September of the same year, a fire on board Carnival's *Tropicale* disabled its engines, leaving it to drift in the Gulf of Mexico as Tropical Storm Harvey approached. The ship, with 1,700 passengers and crew aboard, drifted for nearly a day in rough seas before the crew was able to restart one of the engines and move slowly out of the way of the storm, eventually heading back to port in Tampa. Passengers complained of lack of air-conditioning, faulty toilets, and other issues of comfort, but there were no injuries.

In summer 1999, three small ships had problems in Alaska's Inside Passage. The *Spirit of '98* struck a shoal in Tracy Arm, a narrow fjord that leads to a pair of glaciers, about 40 miles southeast of Juneau. All ninety-three passengers were transferred by raft to another ship. Earlier, the *Wilderness Adventurer* ran aground in Glacier Bay National Park, and a sister ship, the *Wilderness Explorer*, ran aground in an inlet 70 miles west of Juneau.

In August and September 1999, Norwegian Cruise Line suffered a pair of costly mishaps. First, the *Norwegian Dream* inexplicably collided with a large freighter in the English Channel; passengers were able to stay onboard as the ship continued to port in England, but the ship was disabled for more than a month for repairs. And then the line's brand-new *Norwegian Sky*, on its first official cruise after arriving from the shipyard in Europe, ran aground in the upper Saint Lawrence River at the mouth of the Saguenay River in Quebec. Ferries, whale-watching vessels, and private boats were mobilized to help evacuate passengers, but the ship eventually floated free and was brought into Quebec City for repairs to its hull, rudder, and one of its propellers. NCL was forced to cancel the next six weeks of sailings for the much anticipated ship.

HURRICANES AND BAD WEATHER

Cruises are rarely canceled because of storms, but the weather can result in a choppy ride, a rerouting that may include cancellation of a port visit, or substitution of a destination out of the way of the storm. In some extreme cases the ship may be unable to return to its planned port of disembarkation, and passengers may have to travel by bus or other conveyance to their intended destination.

All that said, it would take one heck of a storm to threaten a large cruise ship. But cruise companies don't want to risk their customers' falling or have a ship full of vacationers too green to come out of their cabins. Modern weather equipment, including satellite receivers aboard ship, permit captains to outrun a hurricane or steer around massive storms.

In Chapter 11 you can read the cruise diary about a trip on *Radisson Seven Seas Navigator* in 2003 where we packed for a cruise to Bermuda but ended up with a trip north to Canada to avoid a severe storm.

In late October 1998, disaster struck the venerable *Fantome*, flagship of the Windjammer fleet, a 282-foot-long, four-masted schooner built in 1927.

As Hurricane Mitch approached Central America, the *Fantome* was ordered to stop at Belize City to drop off its passengers so that they could be flown back to Miami. The ship then headed out to sea with its crew of thirty-one to avoid the storm, but the hurricane kept changing its path and eventually overtook the ship. The *Fantome*'s last radio message said it was experiencing 100-knot winds and the ship was rolling 40 degrees. After more than a week, the search for the ship and its crew was abandoned.

In late November 1999, the cruise world lost another classic when the eighty-three-year-old *Sir Francis Drake* apparently broke free of her mooring in a hurricane and was swept out to sea and lost. Hurricane Lenny, one of the most severe storms of the twentieth century, parked off the Caribbean island of Saint Martin for several days.

The 165-foot-long ship had been built in Germany in 1917 and in recent years had sailed throughout the British Virgin Islands. She was in port at Marigot for repairs on her auxiliary engine. As the storm approached, all passengers and crew were disembarked to shore. The ship was secured with fifteen lines and both anchors at a huge commercial-ship mooring buoy in Marigot Harbor. When visibility returned after three days, the *Drake* and another Tall Ship were gone. An intensive search with private aircraft and ships, aided by U.S. Coast Guard satellite data, was unsuccessful. No trace was found of either vessel, except for a floating life raft, later identified as being from the *Sir Francis Drake*.

DOCTORS ONBOARD

Cruise ships carrying more than fifty passengers will have a doctor onboard; some smaller luxury ships, especially those that venture to remote corners of the world, also carry a doctor. Most ships also have an infirmary or hospital and nursing staff. Few on-ship facilities are suitable for surgery, though.

That said, there is no guarantee that a ship's doctor will be well qualified or that the ship's hospital is well equipped for such critical emergencies as heart attacks. The goals of most medical facilities are to treat any minor illnesses or injuries and stabilize seriously injured patients until they can be transferred to a full-service hospital. If you have any particular medical concerns, be sure to discuss your travel plans with your own physician and with the cruise line.

Medical services aboard most ships are not free; passengers must pay consultation fees (typically about $50) plus charges for medication and tests. Most private health plans and Medicare do not cover the costs of medical care at sea and in foreign ports; consult your insurance agent or corporate benefits department. You might want to consider purchasing supplemental health and emergency evacuation insurance; this coverage may be included as part of a cancellation policy offered by many cruise lines or available separately from the cruise line, through your own insurance agent, or from independent agencies.

In recent years, some cruise lines have upgraded their medical facilities as ships have grown into small floating cities. As an example, most modern ships have an infirmary equipped with much of the equipment used in hospital emergency rooms, including an X-ray machine, defibrillator, electrocardiogram machine, and an intensive care unit.

Princess is among the major lines offering a telemedicine program that links the ship's medical staff with the emergency department physicians and specialists at a major American hospital onshore. This "virtual ER" allows X rays, electrocardiograms, and other monitoring signals to be transmitted from the ship to the hospital by satellite.

Just for the record: Most cruise ships have a small refrigerated morgue below decks. I've inspected a few . . . from the outside.

TRAVELERS WITH MEDICAL CONDITIONS

Most cruise lines will not book passage to a woman in the third trimester of pregnancy. Beyond that, most companies require that passengers notify them at the time of booking of any physical or mental illness or disability for which special services or the use of a wheelchair may be necessary.

Cruise lines reserve the right to refuse passage or terminate a vacation if the ship's doctor determines travel may pose a risk to the passenger or others.

■ A PRECRUISE MEDICAL CHECKLIST

There are few of us who don't have a health or diet concern of some sort. Consider the fact that soon after you embark on a cruise you will find yourself hundreds or even thousands of miles away from the nearest full-service pharmacy and potentially in the hands of a doctor and clinic that have no record of your medical history.

Here are some ways to protect yourself; these suggestions are adapted from Holland America's excellent precruise brochure.

■ Gather a supply of all prescription drugs and medications sufficient to cover your trip from home to the port of embarkation, the entire cruise, your return home, plus a few extra days in case of delay. Most major cruise ships have a supply of common medications onboard, but they might not have your precise prescription.

■ Place all medications in a carry-on bag that is not checked on your airplane flight and not given to the stevedores at the cruise port. In other words, carry your medications with you from home to your stateroom.

■ Carry a written list of all medications with the brand names and generic equivalents and the dosage you take. Put the list in a separate place from the carry-on bag with the medications.

■ Bring with you the names and phone numbers of your doctors at home.

■ If you have a medical condition, consult with your doctor about your cruise plans, including flights from home to the port of embarkation. If you have a significant medical condition, bring a copy of your medical records. If you have a heart condition, bring a copy of your most recent EKG.

■ Make sure you or your travel agent conveys all special needs to the cruise company before you travel. Inform the company about the need for a wheelchair, oxygen, or other equipment.

■ Consider the purchase of travel insurance to cover cancellations due to medical conditions. If you have a medical condition that is of concern, look for a policy (more expensive, but more valuable) that does not exclude preexisting conditions from coverage.

■ Consider purchase of supplemental insurance to cover medical expenses at shipboard infirmaries or in foreign ports. This sort of coverage may be included with trip cancellation policies. Again, pay attention to exclusions of preexisting conditions.

■ If you require a special meal, such as low-sodium, low-cholesterol, low-fat, or other arrangements, be sure to inform the cruise line several weeks in advance of your trip.

■ TRAVELERS WHO HAVE DISABILITIES

Although most cruise lines can be counted on to be accommodating to persons with disabilities, the fact of the matter is that not all ships are appropriate for persons in wheelchairs or those who have significant medical problems.

To begin with, many older ships were designed before consideration was given to persons with special needs. It's possible that only a handful of rooms and few, if any, public restrooms are accessible to guests in wheelchairs. Antique ships, such as Tall Ships and windjammers, do not have elevators and so present difficulties for persons with disabilities.

If you do book passage on a ship that claims wheelchair accessibility, be aware that not all areas of the vessel may be served by elevators. You may also find that some ports of call are not equipped to handle all visitors. In some ports the cruise ship might not tie up at a dock, instead transferring guests to shore by tender boats, which might not be easily navigated by all guests. This is an area where you may be able to ask your travel agent to do some detailed research for you.

SEASICKNESS

Could there be anything worse than spending thousands of dollars, traveling thousands of miles to a port, setting sail on a fabulous cruise ship, and then finding yourself so seasick you cannot leave your bed?

That scary thought keeps many travelers away from cruises and causes more than a bit of concern among those who do go down to the sea in ships.

The good news is that modern ships are pretty stable, and there are a number of things you can do, from common sense to common medication, that can help you ignore the rolling and pitching of a cruise ship. (Rolling is the side-to-side motion caused by seas that move across the beam of the ship; pitching is the up-and-down movement of the ship as the bow rides waves coming at the ship or a following sea that attacks from the stern.)

Modern ships use one or more forms of stabilizers to reduce roll. These devices are like underwater wings that work against the motion of the ship in rough water. The size and length of larger ships goes a long way toward reducing pitch, and sailing ships are relatively less likely to roll because they are held to an angle of heel by the pressure of the wind on the sails.

Here are some things you can do to reduce your chances of seasickness:

■ Give some thought to the waters your ship will travel. The Caribbean and the Inside Passage of Alaska are usually calmer than the waters of the Pacific and the North Atlantic. The Gulf of Mexico can vary weekly, from dead calm to moderately or severely rough. The Mediterranean is usually calm in summer.

■ Choose the time of year you cruise. June through late fall is hurricane season along the East Coast and sometimes the Gulf of Mexico. That doesn't mean the seas are always stormy at that time of the year, but, on average, one or two hurricanes a year disrupt the cruise calendar.

■ Pay attention to the cruise itinerary. Some ships spend one or more days out to sea without making a port call. Most cruisegoers relish the calming effects of nothing but ocean, but if you do suffer from occasional seasickness, you might want to seek out an itinerary that allows you to set foot on land every eight or twelve hours.

■ Select a more stable cabin. Most cruisegoers find that a cabin amidships (in the middle of the ship) and on a lower deck will roll and pitch less than a cabin that is up high and at the stern or bow.

■ Reduce your alcohol intake. Alcohol can make you dizzy and disoriented and upset your stomach. Need I say more?

■ Consider taking a seasickness medication such as Dramamine or Bonine before the ship gets under way. In my experience, both work quite well, although they may make you drowsy. (Be sure to consult with your physician if you have any other medical conditions that might complicate use of such medication.) Many cruise ships have stocks of seasickness pills available for guests; check with the purser's office or the medical office. Some travelers find relief with the use of accupressure wristbands and other devices.

EPIDEMICS ONBOARD

Cruise ships are a near-perfect environment for the transmission and spread of disease. You have passengers gathering from all over the world, then mingling in enclosed dining rooms, theaters, and show rooms. Add to the equation the large central kitchens and the tons of food that must be stored onboard the ship and prepared for the almost continuous round of meals, snacks, and buffets. Finally, consider the fact that passengers are visiting remote ports where the sanitation may not be as advanced as onboard ship or at home.

In recent years, hundreds of cruise vacationers suffered from a series of nasty viruses at sea. Television crews met cruise ships as they docked, interviewing passengers about their ordeal.

The primary culprit: the Norwalk virus or something just like it. As a cause of illness, the Norwalk virus—your basic stomach bug—is second only to the common cold. According to the Centers for Disease Control and Prevention (CDC) in Atlanta, each year more than twenty-three million persons in the United States are infected by that virus—and only a few thousand are on cruise ships. That compares with 1.4 million illnesses caused by salmonella, 79,000 cases from E. coli contamination, and 2,500 instances of listeriosis.

The CDC typically requires a cruise line to immediately file a report when more than 3 percent of passengers are ill. In a typical year, you can expect to see fewer than a dozen outbreaks on cruise ships.

Another recent problem has been SARS (Severe Acute Respiratory Syndrome). During winter months guests may be asked if they have experienced any symptoms of the disease or have traveled to areas in Asia where the disease has been reported; cruise lines can deny boarding to guests who are ill or who may represent a health threat to others.

The key to stopping epidemics onboard a cruise ship is to step up the already-continual cleaning process and to break the cycle of transmission. Cruise ships pay special attention to sanitizing handrails and doorknobs touched by guests and to request regular handwashing by all onboard (it's required for employees after restroom use). If an epidemic does occur, the ultimate solution is to take a ship out of service for a week or two to prevent passing the disease to and from the crew and passengers.

During the removal from service of several ships in recent years, virtually everything on the ship was cleaned—from TV remotes to ice buckets and Gideon bibles—and pillows and bedding were replaced.

Most cruise ships visiting American ports do a good job of maintaining proper hygiene under the watchful eye of the CDC. Every vessel that has thirteen or more passengers is subject to inspections at least twice a year by the CDC. The resulting scores are published every two weeks in the Summary of Sanitation Inspections of International Cruise Ships, known in the industry as the Green Sheet.

A ship must receive a score of 86 percent or higher to be acceptable; ships that fail are subject to reinspections and could eventually be prevented from sailing from a U.S. port if problems are not fixed. The CDC also distributes the list of inspections to travel agents and the press.

You can view a list of recent cruise ships inspections on the Internet at www2 .cdc.gov/nceh/vsp/vspmain.asp. You can also contact the CDC by phone at (888) 232–6789 and request a copy of the most recent Green Sheet, although I was warned that the agency is understaffed and may not be able to respond quickly over the phone.

And you should use good judgment. Don't eat foods onboard you wouldn't have at home. Make sure hamburgers and seafood are fully cooked, for example. And take special care with anything you eat or drink in foreign ports.

In many parts of the world, it's a good idea to avoid drinking the local water and any products prepared with unsterilized water. That means limiting yourself to commercially bottled water or bottles filled with the water prepared on your cruise ship, sodas, and beer and avoiding unpeeled and uncooked fruits and vegetables. (This is not to say that water in other countries is necessarily "bad," but it may contain organisms that your body is not prepared to deal with without a few weeks of acclimation.)

CRIME ONBOARD

In recent years, several newspapers and television shows have made a big deal about a supposed "crime wave" aboard cruise ships. Here are the facts: Cruise ships are a relatively safe environment, less dangerous than most small towns. But like a small town, they are not without an occasional problem.

Onboard, there are two sources of threat to your possessions and personal safety: the crew and the passengers. A third danger lies in some ports of call.

The fact is that cruise ships draw their crews from all over the world, often from areas of relative poverty. The crew is often out to sea for six months or longer, without return visits to their homes. Add to all this the fact that some travelers, including single women, may be overly relaxed on their sea vacations.

Most cruise lines are very specific in their instructions to crew members regarding prohibitions on fraternization with passengers outside their official duties in the dining room, bar, or elsewhere. But that does not mean you should totally abandon any concern for safety: Lock your door when you are in your cabin, keep valuables in the safe (or at home), and take the same sort of care with strangers you meet on ship that you would with someone you met in a bar in your town.

Finally, there is this: When you are in international waters in a vessel that (like nearly all cruise ships) flies a foreign flag, you are outside the reach of U.S. laws and enforcement agencies. Theoretically, the laws of the nation of registry apply while on the seas. How much do you know about the legal code of Liberia, Panama, or the Bahamas? For most intents and purposes, a cruise ship is like an independent floating nation.

If a crime or incident does occur while you are at sea, be sure to document every detail for the ship's officers, as well as for yourself. Then do the same when the ship reaches its next port of call, and again with the U.S. Coast Guard if the ship touches an American port.

Most cruise lines do not permit visitors onboard ship without prearrangements through the purser or other officer. Hand-carried luggage is X-rayed, and passengers go through a metal detector prior to boarding.

The most modern of ships include a passenger cruise card ID with a magnetic strip. The card is used as an identity instrument to disembark or reboard the ship at port calls (allowing the purser to know if all of the guests have returned at the end of the visit), as a shipboard charge card, and as an electronic key to the stateroom.

SHORE EXCURSIONS

When you leave the ship, you are out of the cruise line's protective cocoon of security and safety. In a foreign country, you could find that American definitions of safety—shaped by lawyers, lawsuits, and legislation—do not apply.

Rental cars might not have seat belts, and they often are closer to "rent-a-wreck" condition than the near-new condition we expect at home. Buses can be overcrowded and rickety. (In some countries, including parts of Central America, you'll discover where all the old American school buses and city buses go after they have been "retired" from our streets and highways.)

Part of the charm of many attractions in strange places may also bring some serious safety hazards. I've climbed trails hacked into the sides of mountain canyons with nothing between me and the edge but the tread on my sneakers. I've crossed bridges in the jungle that Indiana Jones would have turned away from; I fell through the planking of a pontoon bridge on a lake in Honduras, coming within millimeters of snapping my leg on the support below. And my wife and I have strolled through areas of some ports where even the police demand escorts.

Does this mean you shouldn't leave the ship? Of course not, but you do need to be on guard for your own safety. Here are some suggestions:

■ A cruise ship's excursion desk should vouch for the quality of any bus or car provided for an excursion. If you're on your own, take a look at the tires and general condition of a taxi before you enter for a long trip. If you don't feel comfortable with the safety of the transport, reconsider your trip.

■ Carefully follow any safety instructions given by tour providers. Wear life preservers if asked. Don't undertake an activity you know to be beyond your physical abilities.

■ Never carry nonessential valuables. Leave your jewelry in the safe in your cabin, and bring only enough spending money for minor purchases. Credit cards are accepted almost everywhere and, in any case, are generally the best way to pay for items in a foreign currency.

■ If you are accosted, give over what little you have with you without a fight. Objects are not worth endangering your life for.

■ Carry the name and phone number of the ship's agent with you. If you are stranded or injured, the agent should be able to help you make contact with the ship.

■ In subtropical and tropical climates, bring with you a high-SPF sunscreen— and use it regularly. Drink plenty of liquids and wear a hat. Consult with your family doctor for advice on innoculations and preventive medications recommended for the destinations you will visit.

■ If you're in a country where you are concerned about the water or food, bring your own. You can purchase bottled water onboard ships, or fill your own bottle from the water in your cabin. It is generally considered safe to drink bottled beer or soda; avoid ice cubes and fruits and vegetables washed in local water.

CHAPTER EIGHT

DINING ON THE HIGH SEAS

SOMETIMES IT SEEMS as though the logic of many cruise vacationers is this: I paid $250 a night for this cruise, and by God, I'm going to eat $250 worth of food every day.

It doesn't help your waistline one bit when you realize that most cruise lines go out of their way to encourage you to eat. In fact, there's a bit of a war of the restaurants and buffets among most of the major cruise lines: Call it the Floating Battle of the Bulge.

The staff is going to be pushing food at you at most every turn, and in most cases the food ranges from good to excellent. When you sit down to dinner, your waiter is going to encourage you to sample anything and everything on the menu: Look twice at the dessert offerings, and he is likely to bring you both the cheesecake *and* the double dark chocolate dream cake.

EAT UNTIL YOU DROP

There's a lot of eating onboard a cruise ship. In fact, on some ships you could just about go from meal to snack to meal, from dawn until after midnight. And then you could probably order room service to get you past the munchies at 3:00 A.M.

Here's a typical day onboard a major cruise ship, in this case NCL's *Norwegian Dawn* on an itinerary from New York to Florida and the Bahamas and back:

Breakfast	
6:00–7:00 A.M.	Early Risers. Blue Lagoon, Deck 7 aft
7:00–11:00 A.M.	Morning coffee, Dawn Club Casino, Deck 6 fwd
7:30–9:30 A.M.	Breakfast, Venetian Restaurant, Deck 6 aft
7:30–10:30 A.M.	Breakfast buffet, Garden Cafe, Deck 12 mid

Lunch and afternoon snacks

11:30 A.M.–2:30 P.M.	Luncheon buffet, Garden Cafe, Deck 12 mid
11:30 A.M.–2:30 P.M.	Vegetarian buffet, Garden Cafe, Deck 12, mid portside
11:30 A.M.–2:30 P.M.	New York Deli, Garden Cafe, Deck 12, aft portside
Noon–1:30 P.M.	Barbecue, Oasis Poolside, Deck 12, mid
Noon–2:00 P.M.	Luncheon, Venetian Restaurant, Deck 6, aft
Noon–2:00 P.M.	Teppanyaki/Sushi Lunch, Bamboo Restaurant, Deck 7 mid
2:00–3:00 P.M.	Chocoholic Buffet, Impressions Restaurant, Deck 6 mid
3:30–4:30 P.M.	Afternoon snacks, Garden Cafe, Deck 12 mid
4:30–5:30 P.M.	Mini-Chocoholic Buffet, Dawn Club Casino, Deck 6 fwd

Dinner and late-night snacks

5:30–9:00 P.M.	International Night Buffet, Garden Cafe, Deck 12 mid
5:30–10:00 P.M.	Welcome Dinner, Venetian Restaurant, Deck 6 aft
5:30–10:00 P.M.	Welcome Dinner, Aqua Restaurant, Deck 6 mid
5:30–10:00 P.M.	Welcome Dinner, Impressions Restaurant, Deck 6 mid
Midnight–1:00 A.M.	Casino Late-Night Snacks, Dawn Club Casino, Deck 6 fwd

Specialty restaurants (*with cover charge)

5:30 P.M.–close	La Trattoria, Italian, Deck 12 mid
5:30 P.M.–close	*Le Bistro, French, Deck 6 mid
5:30 P.M.–close	Salsa's, Tex-Mex, Deck 8 mid
5:30 P.M.–close	*Bamboo, Asian-Fusion, Deck 7 mid
5:30 P.M.–close	*Cagney's, Steakhouse, Deck 13 mid

But wait: If you're in one of the suites, your cabin attendant will deliver a small tray of hors d'oeuvres in late afternoon to stave off sudden pangs of hunger. And, oh yes, there is also twenty-four-hour room service if you have a desperate need for a turkey sandwich between dining room seatings. And the *Dawn's* Blue Lagoon is a twenty-four-hour snack bar specializing in hot dogs, hamburgers, and a touch of Asian fare if you can't hold on for the waiter to arrive at your door.

To me, that late-night buffet, sometimes known as the midnight buffet, is the ultimate in wretched excess—and an occasional wicked delight. Typical offerings range from crab legs to steamship round of beef to gourmet pizza. On all Norwegian Cruise Line ships, one night of each cruise is given over to the aptly named Chocoholic Buffet, an absolutely sybaritic exercise in late-night gluttony. Oh, yes, we gave in to our baser instincts, too.

DINNER SEATINGS

For some travelers, the most exciting news in recent years is the arrival of "freestyle" or open seating at restaurants. Today you can choose when, where, and with whom you dine on many ships. Cruise lines have added alternative restaurants and more staffs to accommodate freedom of choice.

Still, on most ships, the dining rooms have two seatings: a main or first seating and a second or late seating. On many ships, breakfast is open to all from about 7:00 to 9:00 A.M.; lunch may have a first seating at noon and a second seating at 1:30 P.M., or it may be open seating. Dinner is usually served at 6:00 or 6:30 P.M. and again at about 8:00 or 8:15 P.M.

For most Americans, an 8:00 P.M. dining time is a bit later than we're used to. You'll waddle out of the dining room close to ten o'clock, perhaps to catch a show, and then be well situated for the midnight buffet. Still, it can be gotten used to.

If you are flying from the East to the West Coast, however, factor in the time change. When we flew from Massachusetts to Honolulu to pick up a cruise there, we lost six hours. Our internal clocks were set at 2:00 A.M. for the 8:00 P.M. seating for the first few days of the cruise; we quickly changed to the 6:00 P.M. main seating, which was ever so slightly better. The same would apply for Europeans flying to Florida or the Caribbean to pick up a cruise. Coming from the West Coast to Florida, the late seating will be more comfortable, at least for the start of the trip.

Great masterpieces line the wall of Le Bistro on *Norwegian Dawn*. *Photo by Corey Sandler*

Room Service

Most cruise ships offer room service food without extra charge. On some lines, you can order from that day's restaurant menu; other ships offer a more limited menu for meals taken in the cabin.

You can also pay for drinks and wine from the bar and order canapés—a bucket of shrimp, for example—if you have an appetite for something special.

Know thyself. If you're the sort of person who expects to enjoy every possible moment in port, taking shore excursions or going native, choose the late seating for dinner. You don't want to cut short your time ashore to rush back for a 6:00 P.M. assignment. On the other hand, if you value your time on the ship above all else, you'll probably want to eat early and then enjoy the shows and other activities aboard. This is another reason many travelers prefer cruises without assigned times for meals. You can adjust your onboard schedule to your plans for each day at sea or in port.

If you have a strong preference for a particular seating, make your wishes known early and often; enlist your travel agent if necessary. In some cases, you may find that your preference is not available; some cruisers don't accept no for an answer and take up the issue with the maître d' on arrival. Remember: Most cruise crew members depend on tips for much of their income, and a subtle reminder of this may grease the way to the dining time or table you want.

On many ships, you can expect to find yourself assigned to a table with others. A typical dining room has tables for four, six, eight, and occasionally even more. You should also be able to find a two-seat hideaway, although the "deuces" are often tucked away in corners. My wife and I are quiet and private by nature, and we always push for a table for two; one way or another, we always get one.

You can expect that the occupants of your cabin will be seated together; you may have to work to bring together friends or family members in other cabins.

Can you change your table assignment once you are onboard? Perhaps. A lot depends on how full the vessel is and the reasonableness of your request. If you cannot stand your tablemates, take the subject up quietly and in private with the maître d' or the cruise director.

For many cruisers, the freestyle or open dining is a welcome change. Depending on the size of the ship and the number of dining rooms, you might be free to show up whenever and wherever you want, or you may need to make a reservation for a table. You could still end up at a large table with whoever arrives at the same time you do, or the cruise line may be flexible enough—like a shoreside restaurant—to rearrange tables to suit the sizes of the parties. Cruisers who look forward to making friends onboard can still do so, gathering their own tables.

The downside, for some, of freestyle dining is that you won't have the same servers and tableside staff throughout the cruise. (For that reason, most cruise lines that have gone away from assigned seating have also instituted an automatic gratuity program that pools tips and distributes them among the dining room staff.)

A cook carves a decorative vegetable display in the galley of Holland America's *Veendam.*
Photo by Corey Sandler

CRUISE CUISINE

Start with this: Imagine the challenge of every day preparing 2,000 sit-down breakfasts, 2,000 lunches, and 2,000 dinners, plus buffets for breakfast, brunch, lunch, afternoon, and midnight. Then prepare to carry nearly all your food supplies with you, reprovisioning once every seven to ten days.

And, oh yes: Your cramped kitchen is in a pitching, rolling ship. You cannot use an open flame because of safety concerns, and your staff is a mini–United Nations.

Then there are the passengers, many of whom look at their all-inclusive cruise fare as a license to make demands of waiters and the chef—demands they would never attempt at home or at a restaurant where they were paying a la carte.

All that said, it is nevertheless true that most cruise cuisine is pretty good. In general, the budget end of the cruise market delivers decent institutional-quality food. The top-of-the-line ships offer quality approaching that of a first-class restaurant on land. The ultraluxury ships add caviar, champagne, and an extra level of personal attention.

The most luxurious ships will sometimes offer to prepare any special request the galley can possibly accommodate. Don't assume they'll be able to rustle up some fresh venison in the middle of a transatlantic crossing, but if you give the chef enough advance notice, he may be able to find some at an upcoming port of call.

Most cruise lines offer vegetarian and low-calorie alternatives on every menu. If you require a special diet beyond that, such as kosher, low-sodium, or gluten-free, be sure to advise the cruise line several weeks before sailing. In some cases, the special meals will be prepared and frozen off the ship and then warmed as needed.

A SENSIBLE DINING STRATEGY

Face it: You're going to go off your diet on a cruise vacation; that's one of the appeals of cruising. But you don't have to overdo it. Here are a few tips:

■ **Choose your meals.** You don't really need to visit every food offering every day. Pick the ones that most appeal to you.

■ **Eat in moderation.** Take smaller portions or avoid cleaning every morsel off your plate. You might be able to get your waiter to deliver half portions.

■ **Consider the "spa" dishes**—low-calorie or heart-healthy offerings found on most menus. Eat an extra portion of salad, with a fat-free dressing, instead of a cream-based chowder.

■ **Increase your level of exercise,** especially on days at sea when you won't be walking onshore. Use the health spa or take a half dozen laps around the promenade deck. It's romantic, fun, and helps work off the calories.

■ **Don't be afraid to skip a meal.** Missing an occasional breakfast or lunch won't kill you.

CHAPTER NINE

GET ME TO THE PORT ON TIME

FOR MOST OF US, before we get onboard our cruise ship, we have to travel to the port, which could involve a lengthy flight or a long drive. Among your first decisions as a savvy consumer is whether to book your own transportation from home to the port or to take advantage of travel packages offered by the cruise companies.

In some cases, the cruise line may be able to offer you a discounted airline ticket because of arrangements with major carriers. You might, though, find you can do better by yourself. In any case, making your own arrangements offers you the greatest flexibility with your schedule, including the ability to stay over en route or before or after your cruise.

One of the effects of the terrorist attacks of 2001 was a new emphasis on "homeland" ports. If you choose to drive, you'll find more ships sailing from U.S. ports than ever before. There are four major ports in Florida (Miami, Fort Lauderdale, Tampa, and Port Canaveral), a burgeoning resurgence from New York, a new port complex in New Jersey, and regular service departing from other East Coast ports including Montreal, Boston, Baltimore, Philadelphia, Norfolk, and Charleston. On the Gulf, there's a growing presence in Galveston and New Orleans. And on the West Coast, cruise lines have added facilities and ships to Los Angeles, Seattle, and Vancouver, plus occasional sailings from San Diego.

THE ADVANTAGES OF BOOKING A PACKAGE

One advantage of booking your travel package through the cruise company is that the line may take responsibility for you from your home airport to the ship. Many cruise lines dispatch employees to arrival airports to help with transfers to the ship. If your flight is delayed, canceled, or diverted, they'll know about the situation and may help you get to the ship.

Be sure you understand the commitment of the cruise line to tracking its incoming passengers. In some instances, the cruise line might hold the departure of the ship by a few hours to accommodate late arrivals. In other situations, the line will make arrangements to fly passengers to the next port call.

During a "sickout" by one airline's pilots in 1999, several major cruise lines chartered planes and made other special arrangements to get their guests to the waiting ships. On a cruise I took in 2004, I found that the cruise line was well aware of the problems one particular airline was having in keeping to its schedule; the ship at that port was regularly held several hours beyond its published departure time because the captain and hotel director knew there were dozens of anxious passengers on the late flight.

The cruise line should also take responsibility for matching you up with misdirected luggage. On an Alaskan cruise I took, a group of passengers made it to the ship while their baggage took a vacation somewhere else. The cruise line delivered the guests to their cabins, offered a basic kit of personal supplies, and arranged to have their bags catch up with them two days later at the first port call.

A few weeks later, I was cruising in the South Pacific and met a couple whose clothing was a week behind them. They had to do without their luggage for six days out of a ten-day voyage because the ship was heading out to sea for a stop at a remote island that had no airport. The cruise line chose to offer them a few sets of T-shirts and shorts from the gift shop, outfits that did not work very well on formal nights in the dining room.

Note that I say the cruise line "may" be able to help. Be sure to check with the company and discuss their policies before you book tickets. Then make certain everything you are told verbally is also presented in writing in the cruise line's brochures, contracts, or other confirmations you receive.

WHY YOU MIGHT MAKE YOUR OWN ARRANGEMENTS

If, on the other hand, you make your own arrangements to get to the port, you could end up waving at the stern of your cruise ship as it leaves the pier. The cost of overnight accommodations and transportation to the ship's next port of call will probably be your responsibility.

That said, making your own arrangements is usually less expensive than the flights and transfers offered by the cruise line. I'd suggest that you do the research yourself before you accept the cruise company's travel arrangements. For domestic departures you may well be able to obtain a lower price or make a better set of connections. If your ship is departing from an unusual location, the cruise company might be able to offer better prices, sometimes using a charter airline.

Here are a few tips to lessen the chances of missing your ship:

- Consider traveling to the port the night before your departure.
- Notify the cruise line of the flight arrangements you have made. The line might have other passengers on the same plane and may be making special arrangements for them.
- If you encounter problems with the airline, be sure to inform them you are flying to catch a cruise departure. They may be able to rebook you on another flight or another airline if necessary.

If you do end up missing the ship, immediately call the cruise line's port representative. Most companies have an office at ports of embarkation; if not, call the phone number listed in your cruise confirmation papers.

If you arrive at the port but your bags are off on a trip of their own, you should be able to engage the assistance of the cruise line in notifying the airline of your ship's schedule and providing the names and phone numbers of the ship's agents in upcoming ports. Be sure to keep copies of the missing baggage form you file with the airline, and record the names of any airline personnel you speak with and the details of conversations you have with them.

If you've planned ahead properly, you should have your passports, cruise tickets, medications, and a change of clothing in your carry-on bag.

ARRIVING EARLY

There is one other situation in which you might have to make your own arrangements: if you choose to fly to the port the day before your cruise (my preference) or stay afterward in the final port.

Why do I prefer to fly to the port a day ahead of departure? First of all, I don't want the stress of worrying about missing a departure because of a delay while flying to the port. This is especially true in the wintertime, when bad weather can wreak havoc on airports and schedules everywhere in the country.

Second, I prefer to spend a day of rest in a port city before getting onboard the ship. Many cruise travelers pass too quickly through some of the most interesting cities in the world, rushing from the airport directly to the ship and missing exciting places such as Vancouver, Miami, Boston, New Orleans, and other points of departure.

This also allows me a day or so to become acclimated to time zone changes in distant ports before I get on the ship. On the day of the cruise, I take a quick taxi to the port instead of suffering through a day of high-stress airline travel. In that way, while the passengers who have been traveling all day to get to the port head for bed, I'm immediately ready to enjoy the cruise.

GETTING FROM THE AIRPORT TO THE SHIP

Your cruise company is likely to offer a service to transport guests from the airport to the ship. This could be included in your cruise if you have booked airfare through the cruise line, or you might be able to purchase the transfer service separately.

I can see the advantages of having a prearranged service with a direct connection to the cruise company, but I also know that in general, transfer service is overpriced and can be less convenient than arrangements you make on your own.

Do a little research and compare the cruise line's transportation with the cost and convenience of a taxi, a rental car, or a limousine service from the airport to the pier.

Just how overpriced are transfers? On one trip in the Hawaiian Islands, the cruise line charged $20 per person for a bus trip from the pier to the Honolulu airport, a distance of just a few miles. Guests had to wait while their bags were collected and loaded onto a huge bus and then wait again at the airport while the bus was unloaded and bags distributed. Meanwhile, my wife and I got off the ship a half hour later and grabbed a taxi. The fare was $17 for the two of us, including a tip, and we got to the airline counter ahead of the bus-borne horde.

The same applied in Vancouver on the return from a voyage north to Alaska. The cruise company's bus was not only overpriced, but it would have delivered us to the airport four hours before we needed to be there. Instead, we arranged for a rental car that was delivered right to the dock; we spent the morning at a museum, had lunch in Chinatown, and drove to the airport on our own schedule.

Among ports that are very close to major airports are Boston and Fort Lauderdale. North American ports that are distant from airports include Houston (about seventy-five minutes) and Galveston (about ninety minutes). Port Canaveral is about an hour from Orlando and just a bit farther from Daytona Beach. Long Beach is about a half hour from Los Angeles International Airport.

If you're concerned about making a tight connection, contact a taxi company or a limousine service before you embark, and arrange for a pickup at the dock when your ship returns.

AIRLINE TRAVEL

Why is there a section about airline travel in a book about cruising? Simply because the vast majority of cruise passengers begin their vacations by boarding an airplane and flying to a port in Florida, San Juan, Vancouver, New Orleans, or other major locations.

Let's start with a real-life scenario: It's May 2004, and I'm flying south from Providence to Fort Lauderdale to pick up a cruise from the bustling port there. My ticket, a special deep-discount Web fare, cost a mere $188 round-trip. The businessman seated a few rows ahead of me in business class will eat a slightly better meal, watch the same crummy movie, and arrive in Florida at the same millisecond I do. The only difference: He paid $813.90 for the same flight. And in first class, someone who (in my humble opinion) has more money than sense has paid an astounding $892 for a slightly wider, slightly plusher seat, and a relatively better meal. (I'd rather spend just some of that money on a better place to sleep and a meal at a restaurant where half the food doesn't end up in your lap.)

All of those prices are real. Now consider a few more positive examples.

Somewhere else on this same plane is a couple who were bumped off a previous flight because of overbooking. They are happily discussing where to use the two free round-trip tickets they received in compensation.

And up front in first class, where you arrive at your destination a millisecond earlier, a family of four is traveling on free tickets earned through Mom's frequent flier plan.

Me, I'm perfectly happy with that cut-rate ticket. I use some of the money I saved to buy a bag lunch to eat on the plane, and I'm daydreaming about where to use the frequent flier miles I'm earning on the airfare, hotel, and car rental.

ALICE IN AIRLINELAND

In today's strange world of air travel, there is a lot of room for the dollarwise and clever traveler to wiggle. You can pay an inflated full price, you can take advantage of the lowest fares, or you can play the ultimate game and parlay tickets into free travel.

There are three golden rules when it comes to saving hundreds of dollars on travel: Be flexible, be flexible, and be flexible. Here's how to translate that flexibility into extra dollars in your pocket:

■ Be flexible about when you choose to travel. Go during the off-season or low season when airfares, hotel rooms, cruises, and attractions are offered at substantial discounts. Try to avoid school vacations, Spring Break, and the prime summer travel months of July and August, unless you enjoy a lot of company.

■ Be flexible about the day of the week you travel. In many cases you can save hundreds of dollars by bumping your departure date one or two days in either direction. Ask your travel agent or airline ticket agent for current fare rules and restrictions. If this puts you into port a day or two ahead of the departure of the ship, use the time to become acclimated to a new time zone and to explore.

The lightest air travel generally occurs midweek, Saturday afternoon, and Sunday morning. The busiest times are Sunday evening, Monday morning, and Friday afternoon and evening. In many cases, you will receive the lowest possible fare if your stay includes all day Saturday; this class of ticket is sold as an excursion fare. Airlines use this as a way to exclude business travelers from the cheapest fares, assuming that businesspeople will want to be home by Friday night. Many airlines have been forced by economic conditions to end this discrimination against business travelers, but you may still run into price differentials.

■ Be flexible about your hours of departure. There is generally lower demand, and therefore lower prices, for flights that leave in the middle of the day or very late at night. The highest rates are usually assigned to breakfast time (7:00–11:00 A.M.) and cocktail hour (4:00–7:00 P.M.) departures.

■ Be flexible on the route you will take, and be willing to put up with a change of plane or a stopover. Once again, you are using the law of supply and demand to your advantage. For example, a nonstop flight from Boston to Tampa for a family of four may cost hundreds more than a flight from Boston that includes a change of planes in Atlanta (a Delta hub) or Charlotte (a US Airways hub) before proceeding to Florida.

Consider flying on one of the newer, deep-discount airlines, but don't let economy cloud your judgment. Some carriers are simply better run than others. Read the newspapers, check with a trusted travel agent, and use common sense. Two of the best new airlines also generally deliver very good service: JetBlue and Southwest. (One way they keep prices down is to operate their own online and telephone booking services; you won't find them listed on multi-airline Web

Airline Speak

In airline terminology, a "direct" flight does not mean a "nonstop" flight. Nonstop means the plane goes from Point A to Point B without stopping anywhere else. A direct flight may go from Point A to Point B, but it might include a stopover at Point C or at more than one airport along the way. A connecting flight means you must get off the plane at an airport en route and change to another plane. And to add one more level of confusion, some airlines have "direct" flights that involve a change of plane along the way: The flight number stays the same, but passengers have to get off at an intermediate stop, dragging all their carry-on luggage to another gate and aircraft. Go figure.

sites and travel agents may not offer them to you as alternatives.)

Delta has been experimenting with a discount offshoot, Song, and United has similar plans for Ted. Even if you don't fly one of the professed cheapo airlines there is always the pressure they put on the established carriers to lower prices, or even to match fares on certain flights. Look for the cheapest fare you can find, and then call your favorite big airline and see if it will sell you a ticket at the same price—it just might work.

■ Don't overlook the possibility of flying out of a different airport. For example, metropolitan New Yorkers can find domestic flights from LaGuardia, Newark, White Plains, and a developing discount mecca at Islip. Suburbanites of Boston might want to consider flights from Providence as possibly cheaper alternatives to Logan Airport. Chicago has O'Hare and Midway. From Southern California there are major airports at Los Angeles, Orange County, Burbank, Long Beach, and San Diego.

■ Plan way ahead of time and purchase the most deeply discounted advance tickets, which usually are nonrefundable. Most carriers limit the number of discount tickets on any particular flight. Although there may be plenty of seats left on the day you want to travel, they might be offered at higher rates.

■ Understand the difference between nonrefundable and noncancelable. Most airlines interpret *nonrefundable* to mean that they can keep all your money if you cancel a reservation or fail to show up for a flight. You can, though, apply the value of the ticket (minus a fee of as much as $150) to the purchase of another ticket.

A *noncancelable* fare means that you have bought a specific seat on a specific flight, and if your plans change or you are forced to cancel your trip, you lose the value of the tickets. (Think of missing a concert performance; you can't use your ticket another day.) Of course, if the airline cancels your flight or makes a schedule or routing change you find does not meet your needs, you are entitled to a refund of your fare.

■ If you're feeling adventurous, you can take a big chance and wait for the last possible moment, keeping in contact with charter tour operators and accepting a bargain price on a leftover seat and hotel reservation. You may also find that some airlines will reduce the prices on leftover seats within a few weeks of your departure date; don't be afraid to check with the airline regularly or ask your travel agent to do it for you. In fact, some travel agencies have automated computer programs that keep a constant electronic eye on available seats and fares.

■ Take advantage of special discount programs such as senior citizens' clubs, military discounts, or offerings from other organizations to which you belong. If you are in the broadly defined "senior" category, you might not even have to belong to a group such as AARP; simply ask the airline ticket agent if there is a discount available. You might have to prove your age or show a membership card when you pick up your ticket or boarding pass.

■ Consider doing business with discounters, known in the industry as consolidators or, less flatteringly, as bucket shops. These companies buy airlines' slow-to-sell tickets in volume and resell them to consumers at rock-bottom prices. Look for their ads in the classified listings of many Sunday newspaper travel sections. Be sure to study and understand the restrictions; if they fit your needs and wants, this is a good way to fly. In general, bucket shops offer the best deals on long domestic and international flights, like trips to and from Asia and Europe. Only occasionally will you find prices below the already deeply cut tickets in the east coast corridor from New York or Boston to Florida.

■ Shop online through one of the Internet travel sites or the Web sites of individual airlines. You can expect to receive the lowest possible airfares—usually a few percent below the best prices offered if you call the airline directly—but little assistance in choosing among the offerings. Be sure to pay close attention to details such as the number of connections required between origin and destination. Note too that tickets sold in this way may have severe restrictions on changes and cancellations.

I list some of the best Internet agencies and airline Web sites in Chapter 4.

■ Consider, very carefully, buying tickets from an on-line travel auction site such as www.priceline.com or www.hotwire.com. These sites promise to match your travel plans with available seats on major airlines at deep-discount prices, but you will not be able to choose departure or arrival times or a particular airline. The way to use these sites is to do your research beforehand on one of the regular Web sites to find the best price you can; compare that with the "blind" offerings from the auction sites. Although the auction sites can often deliver the best prices, the tickets come with some detractions: You cannot time your arrival to meet cruise ships and may have to build in an extra hotel stay at each end of the trip; it may be impossible to make changes or obtain a refund if your plans change; and you might not be permitted to stand by for another flight with your limited ticket. Read the fine print carefully: Prices might not include taxes and fees, and the sites could tack on a service charge. Be sure to compare the true bottom line with the price quoted on other Web sites or from a travel agent.

These auction sites have also begun offering a more traditional form of ticket booking, where the airline and flight times are displayed before you make your purchase. Be sure to check the prices against another Web travel site to make sure you are receiving a real discount from the regular fare.

■ The day of the week on which you buy your tickets may also make a price difference. Airlines often test out higher fares over the relatively quiet weekends. They're looking to see if their competitors will match their higher rates; if the other carriers don't bite, the fares often float back down by Monday morning. Shop during the week.

■ Use an electronic ticket when necessary. Most major airlines have dispensed with their former practice of producing an individualized ticket for your travel and mailing it to you; instead, you'll be given a confirmation number (sometimes called a record locator) and asked to show up at the airport with proper identification and receive your ticket and boarding pass there. If you absolutely insist on receiving an actual ticket in advance of your flight, some airlines charge as much as $50 per ticket for their trouble.

In general, electronic ticketing works well. At many major airports, airlines have begun installing automated check-in machines, similar in operation to a bank's ATM. You'll be asked to insert a credit card or a frequent flyer ID card just for the purposes of identification, and the device will print out your ticket and boarding pass there. A nearby attendant will take your bags and attach luggage tags.

■ STANDING UP FOR STANDING BY

Until our world was turned upside-down by terrorists in 2001, one of the little-known secrets of air travel on most airlines and for most types of tickets was the fact that travelers with valid tickets were allowed to stand by for flights other than the ones for which they have reservations; if there were empty seats on the flight, standby ticket holders were permitted to board at no additional charge.

Today, though, be sure to check airlines' current policies. Some companies will allow holders of full-fare tickets to stand by for other flights without charge. Others apply a reticketing charge, and some airlines have banned the practice completely.

If I have a changeable ticket, here's my strategy: If I can't get the exact flight I want, I make the closest acceptable reservation available after that flight, then I show up early at the airport and head for the check-in counter for the flight I really want to take. Unless I am traveling during an impossibly overbooked holiday period or arrive on a bad-weather day when flights have been canceled, my chances of successfully standing by for a flight are usually pretty good.

One trick is to call the airline the day before the flight and check on the availability of seats for the flight you want to try for. Some reservation clerks are very forthcoming with information; many times I have been told something like, "There are seventy seats open on that flight."

Be careful with standby maneuvers if your itinerary requires a change of plane en route; you'll need to check the availability of seats on all legs of your journey.

The fly in the ointment in today's strict security environment is this: Airlines are required to match bags to passengers before a flight takes off. It is difficult, if not impossible, to stand by for a flight other than the one you hold a ticket for if you have checked a bag. Your chances are much better if you limit yourself to carry-on bags. Security screeners might not let you into the concourse for flights more than two hours before scheduled departure. Consult with the ticket agents at check-in counters *outside* the security barriers for advice.

A final note: Be especially careful about standing by for the very last flight of the day. If you are unable to get on that flight, you're stuck for the night.

■ YOUR RIGHTS AS A CONSUMER

The era of airline deregulation has been a mixed blessing for the industry and for the consumer. After an era of wild competition based mostly on price, we now are left with fewer but larger airlines and a dizzying array of confusing rules.

The U.S. Department of Transportation and its Federal Aviation Administration (FAA) still regulate safety issues. Almost everything else is between you and the airline. Policies on fares, cancellations, reconfirmation, check-in requirements, and compensation for lost or damaged baggage or for delays all vary by airline. Your rights are limited and defined by the terms of the contract you make with an airline when you buy your ticket. The contract might be included with the ticket you purchase, or the airlines may "incorporate terms by reference" to a separate document that you will have to request to see.

Whether you are buying your ticket through a travel agent or dealing directly with the airline, here are some important questions to ask:

■ Is the price guaranteed, or can it change from the time the reservation is made until you actually purchase the ticket?

■ Can the price change between the time you buy the ticket and the date of departure?

■ Is there a penalty for canceling the ticket?

■ Can the reservation be changed without penalty or for a reasonable fee? Be sure you understand the sort of service you are buying.

■ Is this a nonstop flight, a direct flight (your plane will make one or more stops en route to its destination), or a flight that requires you to change planes one or more times?

■ What seat has been issued? Do you really want the center seat in a three-seat row, between two strangers?

You might also want to ask your travel agent:

■ Is there anything I should know about the financial health of this airline?

■ Are you aware of any threats of work stoppages or legal actions that could ruin my trip?

How to Get Bumped

Why in the world would you want to be bumped? Well, perhaps you'd like to look at missing your plane not as an annoyance but as an opportunity to earn a little money for your time. Is a two-hour delay worth $100 an hour to you? For the inconvenience of waiting a few hours on the way home, a family of four might receive a voucher for $800; that could pay for a week's hotel plus a heck of a meal at the airport.

If you're not in a rush to get to your destination or to get back home, you might want to volunteer to be bumped. We wouldn't recommend doing this on the busiest travel days of the year or if you are booked on the last flight of the day, unless you are also looking forward to a free night in an airport motel.

■ OVERBOOKING

Overbooking is a polite industry term for the legal business practice of selling more than an airline can deliver. It all stems from the rudeness of many travelers who neglect to cancel flight reservations that will not be used. Airlines study the patterns on various flights and city pairs and apply a formula that allows them to sell more tickets than there are seats on the plane in the expectation that a certain percentage of ticket holders will not show up.

But what happens if all passengers holding a reservation do show up? Obviously, the result will be more passengers than seats, and some will have to be left behind. The involuntary bump list will begin with passengers who check in late. Airlines must ask for volunteers before bumping any passengers who have followed the rules on check-in.

Now, assuming that no one is willing to give up a seat just for the fun of it, the airline will offer some sort of compensation, either a free ticket or cash, or sometimes both. It is up to the passenger and the airline to negotiate a deal.

Some air travelers, including this author, look forward to an overbooked flight when their schedules are flexible. My most profitable score: $4,000 in vouchers on a set of four $450 international tickets. The airline was desperate to clear a large block of seats, and it didn't matter to us if we arrived home a few hours late. We received the equivalent of three tickets for the price of one, and to add to the package, we went on to earn some more free frequent-flier mileage on the tickets we later purchased with those vouchers.

The U.S. Department of Transportation's consumer protection regulations set some minimum levels of compensation for passengers who are bumped from a flight due to overbooking. If you are bumped involuntarily, the airline must provide a ticket on its next available flight. Unfortunately, there is no guarantee that there will be a seat on that plane or that it will arrive at your destination at a convenient time. If you are traveling to the port on the day your ship is scheduled to depart, you probably don't want to even consider the possibility of being bumped. Let the airline staff know you are flying to a cruise, and stand your ground if you feel your vacation is threatened.

If the airline can get you on another flight that will get you to your destination within one hour of the original arrival time, no compensation need be paid. If you are scheduled to get to your destination more than one hour but less than two hours late, you're entitled to receive an amount equal to the one-way fare of the oversold flight, up to $200. If the delay is more than two hours, the bumpee will receive an amount equal to twice the one-way fare of the original flight, up to $400.

It is not considered bumping if a flight is canceled because of weather, equipment problems, or lack of a flight crew. You are also not eligible for compensation if the airline substitutes a smaller aircraft for operational or safety reasons, or if the flight involves an aircraft with sixty seats or less.

■ THE NEW WORLD OF AIRPORT SECURITY

Travel has become all the more complicated and less convenient in the wake of the terrorist attacks of 2001. The bottom line for well-meaning business and pleasure travelers is this: You'll need to add an hour or more to the check-in process, and your options to stand by for a different flight or make other changes to your itinerary are severely limited.

Here are some things you can do to lessen the pain:

■ Consult with the airline or your travel agent about current policies regarding check-in times.

■ Consider your departure time. Lines for check-in and security clearance are longest during peak travel times: early morning and late afternoon.

■ An alternate airport might have shorter lines. Some major hubs are, by necessity, more efficient at processing huge crowds, but smaller airports with fewer crowds can be easier to navigate.

■ Try to avoid carrying unnecessary metallic items on your person. Choose a belt with a small buckle rather than the one with the three-pound championship steer-wrestling medallion. Put your cell phone, keys, coins, and wristwatch in a plastic bag and place it in your carry-on bag as you approach the magnetometer; this will speed your passage and reduce the chances of losing items.

■ Travel in a pair of simple sneakers instead of heavy boots or high heels; you are less likely to have to remove your shoes.

■ Be cooperative, remember that the screening is intended to keep you safe, and hope that the guards do their job well.

SHOULD YOU DRIVE?

Everyone's conception of the perfect vacation is different, but for me, I draw a distinction between getting there and being there. I want the getting there part to be as quick and simple as possible and the being there part to be as long as I can manage and afford. Therefore, I fly to just about any destination that is more than a few hundred miles from my home. The cost of driving, hotels, meals en route, and general physical and mental wear and tear rarely equals a deeply discounted excursion fare.

If you do drive to the port, you can save a few dollars by using the services of AAA or another major automobile club. Before you head out, spend a bit of time and money to make certain your vehicle is in traveling shape: A tune-up and fully inflated, fully inspected tires will certainly save gas, money, and headaches. If you are taking your own car to the port, be sure to inquire ahead of time about parking facilities. Find out the charges, and determine what level of security is provided. You might want to look into leaving your car at a secured garage away from the port.

■ RENTING A CAR

Your travel agent can be of assistance in finding the best rates on rental cars; make a few phone calls on your own, too. Sometimes you'll find significant variations in prices from one agency to another. Be sure to check Web sites as well; sites such as www.expedia.com and www.travelocity.com allow you to compare rates from several rental agencies for the dates and locations you specify.

You might also find lower rental rates at the Web sites of the rental car companies themselves. Join the agencies' priority clubs, which usually are free, to receive special offers.

Although prices for rental cars have gone up in some markets, they still represent a great bargain. Think of the deal as borrowing $15,000 for a $35 fee, to put things in perspective.

Car rental companies will try, with varying levels of pressure, to convince you to purchase special insurance coverage. They'll tell you it's "only" $7.00 or $9.00 per day. What a deal! That works out to about $2,500 or $3,330 per year for a set of rental wheels. Of course the coverage is intended primarily to protect the rental company, not you.

Before you travel, check with your insurance agent to determine how well your personal automobile policy will cover a rental car and its contents. I strongly recommend using a credit card that offers rental car insurance; such insurance usually will reimburse you for the deductible and other out-of-pocket expenses under your personal auto insurance policy. The extra auto insurance by itself is usually worth an upgrade to a gold card or other extra-service credit card. The only sticky area comes for those visitors who have a driver's license but no car, and therefore no insurance. Again, consult your credit card company and your insurance agent to see what kind of coverage you have or what kind you need.

Pay attention, too, when the rental agent explains the gas policy. Under the most common plan, you must return the car with a full tank; if the agency must refill the tank, you will usually be billed a very high per-gallon rate and sometimes a service charge as well.

Although it is theoretically possible to rent a car without a credit card, you will find it to be an inconvenient process. If the rental agency can't hold your credit card account hostage, it will most often require a large cash deposit, perhaps as much as several thousand dollars, before it will give you the keys.

CHAPTER TEN

BEFORE YOU SET SAIL

WHAT KIND OF WEATHER can you expect at your destination and your ports of call? If you're sailing from Vancouver to Alaska, you can expect a wide range of conditions, from warm and sunny to cold and drizzly. If you head to the mountains on a shore excursion, you could find a bit of winter in July on a glacier. In eastern Canada, it can be damp and cool in spring and fall; the inland port of Montreal can be surprisingly cold in spring and immoderately hot in summer and fall.

In Hawaii, the Caribbean, and Mexico, temperatures are generally moderate to hot all the time; of more import is the difference between the dry and wet seasons. In Central America and Mexico, it's hot all the time, with a rainy season that begins in early May and continues through October and November, when hurricanes sometimes arrive in the Gulf of Mexico. European coastal ports can reach extremes of cold and heat.

Wherever you go, pack some light sweaters or jackets to wear on deck in the evening when temperatures drop. Your ship will be moving, too, usually adding a 15- to 20-mile-per-hour breeze to whatever wind there is at sea.

The Internet offers a great way to check average weather and specific forecasts around the world. Among the sites you should visit are:

- www.accuweather.com
- www.cnn.com/weather
- www.intellicast.com/Travel
- www.mytravelweather.com
- www.travelforecast.com
- www.usatoday.com/weather
- www.weather.com

Smart travelers also give some thought to changes in time zones as they head to the port of departure. The clock gets set back as you travel east to west, and forward moving west to east. (And if you travel far enough east or west, you will run into the International Date Line, where today becomes tomorrow or yesterday.)

When you're onboard ship, the cruise director and captain will keep passengers up-to-the-moment on local time but things can become more complex when you're dealing with airline schedules. And you may also want to keep in touch with friends and family back home; a midnight call may not be welcome.

Here are a few Internet sites that help you determine the local time almost anywhere in the world:

- www.timeanddate.com/worldclock
- www.timezoneconverter.com
- www.worldtimeserver.com/

FASHION TIPS

Find out from the cruise line about the dress suggestions for dinner; details are usually included in the packet of information that arrives with your cruise tickets. Most ships have one or more "formal" nights. Many add optional theme nights: Western, the '50s, Island, Mexican, Greek, and so on.

Like it or not, the definition of "formal" has loosened up greatly on most ships. Only a few lines require men to wear tuxedos; a conservative suit or a blue blazer and gray slacks will not raise any eyebrows. On nearly every cruise I've taken, at least one man has chosen to arrive at the formal dinner in a kilt. Women have a range of options, from cocktail gowns to pantsuits. Put another way, on most ships "formal" means the night when you don't wear a T-shirt and jeans.

What happens if you show up at dinner on a formal night inappropriately dressed? On some ships, the maître d' may discreetly suggest that you return to your cabin and seek new attire. On other ships, he might suggest that you visit an alternative casual dining room that night. Or he might look away, preferring to keep his relations with you—and his potential gratuity—undamaged. You might have to endure some sideways glances from cruisers in fancy duds though.

On some ships you can arrange to rent a tuxedo and other formal wear; check before you depart to see if such services are available.

Ask if the ship has an onboard Laundromat or a reasonably priced laundry or dry cleaning service. On a longer cruise this can allow you to pack less clothing.

Find out about health club and sports facilities onboard the ship, and think about whether you will be visiting any beaches onshore. Pack a bathing suit, sandals, sun hat, sneakers, and any other appropriate articles, including sunblock. The cruise line will provide beach towels and might offer other amenities such as bathrobes and slippers for some or all of its passengers, sometimes discriminating on the basis of your class of cabin.

One other thing: Think twice and even three times about whether you want to bring any valuable jewelry with you. You'll have to worry about its security while getting to the ship, onboard the ship, in port, and getting home.

Another worthwhile fashion accessory: a pair of neat rubber-sole shoes for strolls on the promenade deck or other outside parts of the ship. Plastic or leather soles might be too slippery for comfort.

PAPERWORK AND PASSPORTS

Almost every cruise visits a foreign port. That's part of the romance of it all, as well as a legal requirement for any vessel that does not fly a U.S. flag.

Many tourist ports in the Caribbean and Canada do not require visitors to have a passport to enter and will accept a birth certificate or a driver's license. The same generally applies for U.S. citizens returning to this country from those destinations. Immigration laws and regulations can change, however, and you might find some immigration inspectors are more picky than others. In today's heightened security atmosphere, you should be prepared for a more stringent examination at border points.

I strongly recommend that you bring a passport. If you don't have one, it's not a huge bother to obtain one. Your travel agent, U.S. post office, or county clerk can usually help you with the paperwork. The standard process can take a few months, but for an extra fee, there are ways to speed it up considerably.

Regulations now require all cruise lines to provide government agencies with the names of each cruise passenger as well as his or her passport number, nationality, date of birth, and permanent address. Non-U.S. guests must provide additional information including visa details and destination address once the cruise is completed. Most cruise lines ask passengers to fill out an embarkation registration form at the time of booking; some companies, including Carnival, have streamlined the process by allowing passengers to fill out the forms online through Web sites.

On most cruise lines, U.S. immigration officials board the ship on the last morning of the trip; all guests are required to come before them with their passports and immigration forms before any passengers are permitted off the ship. Customs officials either board the ship or wait to meet guests as they pick up their bags in the terminal.

Some cruise lines will send passengers a personal questionnaire to be used in producing a shipboard newsletter or a registry that will allow people to locate guests with similar interests or backgrounds or those from particular locations. You do not have to participate or fill out this sort of form. The forms ask for your date of birth and sometimes for your wedding anniversary. Don't be surprised if this information is conveyed to the serving staff in the dining room.

The cruise line will likely send you a set of luggage tags. If you have purchased an airport transfer service from the cruise line, these will be used to identify your bags when you arrive at the airport. If you make your own way to the ship, these luggage tags will be used by cabin attendants who deliver bags to staterooms. Fill out the tags, including your cabin number, which you should find on your cruise contract.

MEDICAL NEEDS AND PERSONAL SUPPLIES

If you are taking any medications or have any significant medical conditions, speak with your doctor before heading out on your trip. Consider bringing a copy of your current medical records in case you need to visit the shipboard clinic or an onshore facility. If you have a heart condition, for example, your doctor might want you to bring a copy of a recent electrocardiogram.

If you are on medication or have a medical condition, ask your doctor whether you can safely take one of several commonly used seasickness preventives or remedies. (Most are considered quite safe and effective, but the question is worth asking.)

Be sure to pack a full supply of required medicines; bring along a few additional days' worth to deal with possible delays on your return. You might want to ask your doctor for a backup set of prescriptions in case you need to replace bottles during your trip. Pack your medication in a carry-on bag that does not get checked at the airport or at the dock.

Although most cruise ships can supply you with seasickness pills, aspirin, and most personal toiletries, you're better off bringing your own supply. Again, pack these in your carry-on bags.

I also recommend bringing a sunscreen that has an SPF rating of at least 30, especially on Caribbean, Mexican, Central American, and Hawaiian voyages but also for Alaska and other destinations. It is quite easy to ruin your vacation with a bad sunburn, and overexposure to the sun's rays is a long-term health risk.

In some areas, including Central America and Mexico, it can be worthwhile to take a prescription antimalarial drug; most require that you begin the course of medication a week before arrival in the region and continue for several weeks after your return. Seek the guidance of your physician.

Finally, consult with your insurance agent or personnel office about the limits of your health insurance. Most policies don't cover emergency medical treatment onboard a ship, and many exclude coverage for treatment in foreign countries. Policies also might not pay for expensive emergency medical evacuation from a ship or from a foreign port.

You can, however, purchase special medical insurance for your trip. Policies are offered by most cruise lines and some travel agencies or insurance agencies. Be aware that most policies exclude coverage for preexisting conditions. Be sure you understand all the terms of a policy before you buy one.

CAMERAS

Most travelers document their vacations on film, but not everyone is happy with the results.

If you're strictly an amateur, consider buying an autofocus, autoexposure, pocket camera with a zoom lens. These cameras do just about everything but take the picture for you, and the quality is generally quite good. Expect a decent model to cost approximately $100 to $200.

A standard lens for 35mm film is about 50mm, a typical wide-angle lens is 35mm, and a moderate telephoto focal length is 100mm. Therefore, a zoom lens that runs from 35mm to 100mm covers most situations; even better is a zoom that is slightly wider and longer, say 28mm to 135mm.

When you buy film, pay attention to the speed, also called ASA or ISO rating. The higher the number, the "faster" the film. A fast film allows you to shoot in lower-light conditions, at a higher shutter speed to stop the action, or at a smaller lens aperture, which generally gives you a sharper image with a better depth of field. Professional photographers will tell you that faster film doesn't deliver perfect color or

> ## Centers for Disease Control
>
> The Centers for Disease Control and Prevention maintains an excellent Web site with advisories for travelers: www.cdc.gov/travel. You can also call a toll-free hot line at (877) 394–8747 or request information by fax at (888) 232–3299.

that your photos may be more grainy in appearance when larger prints are made. That is true, but you are taking vacation snapshots, not studio portraits. And today's "fast" films have nearly as fine a grain and as much color saturation as the slower films of just a few years ago.

I recommend using film that has a rating of at least 400, which allows picture-taking at the midnight buffet as well as on deck and in port. If you know you're going to be shooting mostly low-light images in museums and onboard, look for film with an 800 rating.

It's a good idea to buy your film at a reputable dealer before you leave for your trip. You'll pay less than at a tourist port, and you can expect that the film is fresh and has been stored properly.

A word of caution: Film can be damaged by exposure to heat. Don't leave your film out in the sun. You'll also get the best results if you have your film processed sooner rather than later. Try to avoid leaving a roll of film in your camera for months just because there are a few unexposed frames.

In theory, airport X-ray machines will not harm film in carry-on bags. However, faster film, such as ASA 800 stock, is more susceptible than slower film, and there can be a cumulative effect from passing through six or eight machines over the course of a trip. In today's security-conscious airports, you might have no choice but to pass your film through the screening machines. Don't put film—exposed or unexposed—in checked luggage. The X-ray equipment used for checked luggage is much stronger and can "fog" or damage film in just one pass.

You can do without film entirely by using a digital camera that records images in magnetic memory. You can transfer the data from the camera to your personal computer and send the images to a laboratory for prints, or stay electronic and transmit the pictures to friends and family by e-mail. A basic point-and-shoot digital camera, acceptable for e-mail and small prints, starts at about

$200. More sophisticated digital cameras are capable of storing higher-resolution images that can be enlarged to wall-size frames. The key to look for is the "pixel" (picture element) rating for the camera. A camera that records 640 kilobyte images is appropriate for Web and e-mail use. In order to make large prints, look for a camera that records at least two megabytes per image; more is even better. (Nearly all of the photos in this book were produced using a five-megabyte digital camera.)

It's also a good idea to pack one or more sets of replacement batteries for your camera; even better are rechargeable batteries. You don't want to discover that you've run out of juice just at the moment a humpback whale breaches alongside your ship.

If you are traveling with a digital or video camera, be sure to bring the battery charger with you. Most modern cruise ships offer standard 110-volt electrical outlets in the cabins. You might need a voltage adapter on some older ships and certain European cruise ships that supply 220 volts. And if (like me) you travel with a suitcase full of electronic and electrical devices—a digital camera, a personal computer, a cell phone, a shaver, and a CD player—you might want to also carry a multiple-outlet plug with you. Most cruise ships offer only one or two outlets. Even better is a multiple-outlet device with a surge protector.

ARRIVING AT THE PIER

Most ships have a window of several hours for arriving passengers to check in and get onboard. Cruise ships generally depart in the early evening, and may be open for check-in as early as 1:00 P.M. You'll probably find that lunch will be served to arriving passengers, sometimes in the dining room but more often as a casual buffet.

When you arrive at the pier, you might find a curbside check-in for your bags. Be sure to determine that the persons reaching for your bags are legitimate employees of the cruise line or stevedores from the port; look for an ID badge or card. Cruise line staff might have a list of arriving passengers. Be sure, too, that they are checking in your ship and not another one at the same port.

At some ports, you might have to drag your bags into the terminal for check-in. Again, be sure that you deposit your bags with the right cruise line. Your luggage tags should have your name and cabin number clearly marked on them. Double-check to see that the tags have not come off en route to the pier.

Hold on to your overnight bag with a change of clothes, medications, cameras, jewelry, and other valuables. Be sure you also hold on to your cruise documents, including your passport.

On nearly every ship, your bags will be delivered to your cabin. Sometimes they will arrive before you get to your cabin, but they might not make it to your stateroom until after the ship has sailed from the port. (On most ships, the first night's dinner has a casual dress code.)

It is not necessary to tip a cabin attendant who brings your bags to your room onboard the ship; protocol calls for a tip to be delivered at the end of the voyage.

If your bags are taken at the curb by a stevedore or employee of the port, a tip may be in order; check with the cruise line in advance or ask a representative of the cruise company at the dock whether the service is included in your fare.

BOARDING THE SHIP

When you get onboard, you will likely be escorted to your room by a cabin attendant. (The fancier cruise lines make this into a bit of an event, outfitting the attendants in starched jackets and white gloves.) Check out your room. Be sure the attendant shows you how to operate the heating and cooling system. Find out if there is a safe in the room. If you're lucky enough to have a veranda, learn how to open and close the door. Locate the life vests. If you want extra pillows or blankets, ask for them. If the cabin has two single beds that can be brought together to serve as a queen-size bed, ask the attendant to rearrange them.

Of course, if you find that the cabin is not what you thought you had purchased—it has a porthole instead of a window, there are upper-and-lower berths instead of a double bed, it's a broom closet rather than the Owner's Suite—now is the time to make a beeline to the reception desk or purser's office onboard the ship. It may be possible to switch to another cabin if the ship is not full.

If no mistake has been made, you may still be able to upgrade your cabin if better accommodations are available. On many ships, this is one way to obtain an upgraded room at a decreased price: The purser or onboard hotel manager might offer deep discounts on any available upgraded cabins once it is absolutely impossible to sell them to someone not already onboard the ship.

Your first few hours on the ship may also be the time to visit the dining room to meet with the maître d' to attempt to change your dining room assignment if it is not to your liking.

IMMIGRATION AND CUSTOMS INFORMATION

There are two official steps in the process of entering a foreign country and returning to your home nation: immigration and customs.

Put simply, *immigration* is the process of clearing you into a country, and *customs* is the process of allowing your possessions the same privilege.

In this section, I'll concentrate on customs and immigration processes for American citizens leaving and returning to the United States. Similar requirements apply to citizens of other countries; ask the cruise line or your travel agent any specific questions about your situation.

■ IMMIGRATION

The Immigration and Naturalization Service (INS), part of the Department of Justice, is responsible for the movement of people in and out of the United States.

The cruise line will ask to see your passport or identification papers before you embark on the ship. This allows the company to certify to foreign destinations that all passengers are legally able to enter; in most cases you will not have to produce your passport to actually enter the country at the port. The next time you will have to produce your passport is likely to be upon your return to the United States. Under tightened security controls, cruise lines may supply information to the INS and the U.S. Coast Guard ahead of time to speed up the processing of passengers when they return to the United States.

Depending on the itinerary and the cruise line's policy, your passport may be held by the purser's office and returned at the end of the trip when immigration officials are onboard to clear the reentry of passengers. Be sure you understand the official policy before you leave your passport in someone else's hands.

For information on obtaining a passport or other immigration questions, contact the nearest passport agency in person or by mail or phone, or through a Web site at http://travel.state.gov/passport_services.html. For information on renewing a passport, you can also consult a Web site at http://travel.state.gov/passport/get_renew.html. You may be able to obtain assistance from some U.S. post offices and some town or city clerks of court. Your travel agency should also be able to direct you to the nearest and most convenient office.

You can write for information by addressing a letter to the passport agency at the nearest of the following zip codes: Boston 02222-0123; Chicago 60604-1564; Honolulu 96850; Houston 77002-4874; Los Angeles 90024-3614; Miami 33130-1680; New Orleans 70113-1931; New York 10111-0031; Philadelphia 19106-1684; San Francisco 94105-2773; Seattle 98174-1091; Stamford, Connecticut 06901-2767; Washington, D.C. 20524-0002.

Be aware that if a single parent is traveling with a minor child, the cruise line or immigration authorities may refuse boarding or entry without a legally binding letter from both parents, even if they are divorced, granting permission for the minor to leave the country. Consult an attorney and the cruise line for advice if you fall into this category.

CUSTOMS

On the customs side, administered by U.S. Customs & Border Protection, there are two principal concerns: security and duties.

Obviously, it is not a smart idea to go through an inspection point with illegal drugs or weapons. Also prohibited are foreign lottery tickets, obscene articles and publications, seditious and treasonable materials, and hazardous articles such as fireworks, dangerous toys, and toxic or poisonous substances.

In most ports, visitors are on the honor system; customs agents do not inspect every incoming bag. Some travelers may be honored with a random search of their person and possessions. Many ports are adding X-ray machines and devices that screen for explosives.

It's a good idea to carry prescription drugs in a pharmacist's bottle or with a copy of the prescription from your doctor. In a pinch, your hometown pharmacy should be able to give you a letter certifying that the pills you carry have been ordered by an accredited physician. Be especially careful to obtain this sort of proof if you are carrying any painkillers or sedatives.

Duties are a special form of taxes levied on certain types or amounts of imported goods. As this book goes to press, each returning U.S. resident is permitted to bring home up to $800 in goods without having to pay duty. Included in that $800 exemption is up to one hundred cigars and two hundred cigarettes; residents over age twenty-one can also bring back one liter (33.8 ounces) of alcohol duty-free. The next $1,000 worth of items is taxed at a flat duty rate of 10 percent.

Note that certain items, including Cuban cigars and other products, are generally not allowed into the United States, even though they are readily available in nearby countries. Although you can purchase Cuban cigars in Canada, Jamaica, Mexico, and elsewhere, you cannot bring them back to the United States; the only exception is if you are returning from Cuba itself, and that requires a special license that is generally limited to American journalists and academics. In 1998, restrictions on travel to Cuba were relaxed slightly, and U.S. residents who are allowed to visit are now permitted to bring back up to $100 in Cuban goods purchased in Cuba.

Other acquisitions may qualify for duty-free treatment under other exemptions, such as the generalized system of preferences, which awards duty-free treatment to many goods from developing countries. Fine art (not handicrafts) and antiques older than one hundred years are commonly acquired items that also do not require the payment of duty. There are all sorts of interesting side trips in the regulations. For example, although fine art is exempted from duty, you may be liable for tax on the picture frame that surrounds it.

The "Duty-Free" Confusion

In most seaports and airports, the streets and corridors are chock-a-block with "duty-free" stores. You'll also find some duty-free items available onboard cruise ships. If you didn't know better, you could reasonably assume this meant that items for sale there are free from duty when travelers return home. That's not the case.

Articles sold in duty-free shops are free of duty and taxes for the country in which the shop is located, and items sold there are intended for export. When you arrive in the United States, these items are subject to duty after you exceed your personal exemption.

If your cruise includes a visit to one of the U.S. Virgin Islands, the personal exemption is $1,200, although no more than $800 worth of items within that $1,200 exemption can come from foreign nations outside the U.S. Virgin Islands ($600 for Caribbean Basin countries).

If you are returning directly from any of the following countries, your customs exemption is $600: Antigua and Barbuda, Aruba, Bahamas, Barbados, Belize, British Virgin Islands, Costa Rica, Dominica, Dominican Republic, El Salvador, Grenada, Guatemala, Guyana, Honduras, Jamaica, Montserrat, Netherlands Antilles, Nicaragua, Panama, Saint Kitts and Nevis, Saint Lucia, Saint Vincent and the Grenadines, and Trinidad and Tobago. If you make an intermediate stop at another country, say, Venezuela, the $800 exemption applies, although only $600 may come from the noted Caribbean countries.

Finally, to qualify for an exemption, you must be returning from a stay abroad of at least forty-eight hours and you cannot use more than one exemption within a thirty-day period. If you have been out of the country more than once in a thirty-day period, or if your trip out of the United States lasted less than forty-eight hours, you will be limited to bringing back $200 free of duty and tax.

Be sure to check with the cruise line or U.S. Customs & Border Protection for the latest regulations. The Customs Service lists some valuable information on their Web site at www.customs.ustreas.gov.

Regulations for returning Canadian citizens are similar, with an exemption of up to $750 (Canadian) for travelers who have been out of the country for at least seven days, including up to forty ounces of alcohol, two hundred cigarettes, and fifty cigars. The Canada Border Services Agency maintains a Web site at www .cbsa-asfc.gc.ca/menu-e.html.

■ REGISTERING FOREIGN-MADE VALUABLES

If you cross through customs with an expensive Japanese camera on your shoulder, an Italian scarf on your neck, and a fancy watch or piece of jewelry on your arm, the inspector can assume that all these items were purchased abroad and not in your neighborhood mall.

To establish that you brought these items from your home, bring proof of purchase, an insurance policy, or jeweler's appraisal. You can also register the serial numbers or other marks with customs before you leave home.

Customs pays particular attention to expensive cameras (including special lenses and video equipment), binoculars, radios, foreign-made watches, and other similar items. To register items, take them to the customs office and obtain a validated Certificate of Registration (CF 4457) form; bring the form with you on your travels.

■ PROHIBITED FOOD PRODUCTS

In general, you can bring home packaged foods in sealed cans, bottles, and boxes. Baked goods and cured cheeses are also permitted.

Most fruits and vegetables are either prohibited from entering the country or require an import permit. Every fruit or vegetable must be declared to the customs officer and must be presented for inspection, no matter how free of pests it appears to be. Note that Hawaii and California also have very strict prohibitions against the import of fruits and vegetables; the regulations are in place to protect against the introduction of pests and diseases that could be damaging to the native crops. Plants, cuttings, seeds, unprocessed plant products, and certain endangered species either require an import permit or are prohibited from entering the United States.

Unpasteurized cheeses, meat, poultry, and processed food products including ham, frankfurters, sausage, and pâté are either prohibited or restricted, depending on the animal diseases prevalent in the country of origin. Canned meat is permitted if the inspector can determine it is commercially canned and can be kept without refrigeration.

■ TRANSPORTATION OF CURRENCY

You may take on your trip as much currency or monetary equivalents as you wish. However, if you take out or bring into the United States more than $10,000 in cash, you are required to file a report with the U.S. Customs Service.

LIFEBOAT DRILLS

One of the first scheduled events on a cruise is the lifeboat drill, often conducted in port before departure. It's something that could save your life in the extremely unlikely event of an emergency at sea, and it's a requirement of vessels operating throughout most of the world.

Listen for the instructions that will be announced over the ship's public address system; you'll likely be asked to return to your cabin, pick up your life vest, and proceed to the assembly station. When you arrive, a member of the crew will check your name off the list of passengers assigned to that lifeboat; in theory, a crew member will come looking for you if you don't show up.

Finally, you'll be instructed on how to put on the vest properly, shown the location of the emergency whistle and beacon on each vest, and given an explanation of how the lifeboats are lowered into position for boarding.

A lifeboat drill aboard Royal Caribbean's *Rhapsody of the Seas* while in port in Vancouver.
Photo by Corey Sandler

CHAPTER ELEVEN

CRUISE DIARIES

EVERY CRUISE HAS A STORY: an amazing sight, a particular luxury, an exciting encounter. Here are cruise diaries from a few of my favorite recent trips to New Zealand and Australia, from New York to Nova Scotia, and all over the Caribbean. It's a tough job, but someone has to do it.

A VOYAGE OF DISCOVERY ON *SILVER SHADOW*

Captain James Cook cruised the waters of the South Seas in 1770 on one of his three great voyages to survey uncharted waters, collect unexamined plants, and classifiy some of the strangest of animals. Along the way Cook and his crew survived assaults from high seas, island natives, and a near-fatal encounter with the Great Barrier Reef that fringes much of the east coast of Australia.

Cook's ship, the *Endeavour,* was a box-like 97-foot-long vessel with three masts and a nearly flat bottom that was appropriate for its previous use as a collier. Its design made it extremely ungainly when its cargo was sailors, botanists, and artists—rather than coal.

In 2004 my wife and I cruised from Auckland, New Zealand, to Sydney, Australia, and up the coast of the great southern continent aboard Silversea's *Silver Shadow,* which is in nearly every way the antithesis of Cook's collier.

Even in the lap of luxury, though, a trip from North America to Australia is a strange experience, a voyage down under in so many ways. We were in the antipodes—a marvelous word that literally means the opposite side of the globe. The word is sometimes used to mean something that is the exact opposite or contrary. In common usage, appropriately, it simply means Australia and New Zealand.

In the antipodes, the night sky is confusingly unrecognizable. The cars drive on the left side of the road. You head north to hot weather. And, to adapt George Bernard Shaw's famed quip, America and Australia are two countries divided by a common language.

But the most outrageous antipode for us was our luxurious accommodations on *Silver Shadow.* Nothing about a Silversea cruise is cheap: not the handsome

Silversea's *Silver Shadow.* Photo by Corey Sandler

appointments in the suites, not the food and wine and other drinks (all included), and certainly not the level of service. And though the fare for a cruise on this line is not cheap, either, when it comes to value for your money, Silversea is a great deal.

Cook traveled completely out of touch with his sponsors and beyond reach of rescuers, with a sextant, a compass, and some very sketchy—often incorrect—charts. The captain of *Silver Shadow* had a bridge with satellite positioning, radio, television, and e-mail. We were so much in touch that we were able to handle an urgent request for college money from one of our children, transferring money from the onboard Internet cafe while sailing in the Tasman Sea.

■ EXOTIC PORTS

At the core of the modern cruise industry are voyages in the warm and familiar waters south of Florida. Sooner or later, though, the prospect of yet another cruise to the Caribbean becomes a dispensable been-there, done-that excursion. Experienced travelers begin to look for new horizons.

The cruise lines, of course, want to hold on to their customers as they expand their fleets with more—and much larger—ships every year.

And so there comes the search for "new" ports of call. There are, of course, no new oceans being added to the planet and relatively few new harbors being opened for the first time. But there are many places on earth that are very anxious to entice cruise ships and their sometimes free-spending passengers to town; in a small port, when even a midsize vessel like the *Silver Shadow* ties up at the quay, it becomes the largest building in town.

Our voyage began in Auckland, New Zealand, and included two days in the handsome port of Sydney, Australia; as well-known as those ports are, they are not often visited by cruise ships. And along the way, we also visited less-known places like Russell in New Zealand; and Newcastle, Hayman Island, Townsville, and Cairns in Australia.

■ AN ENCOUNTER WITH A MODERN ADVENTURER

We arrived in New Zealand after a long day in the air; six hours from Boston to Los Angeles and thirteen more on to Auckland. It is an attractive city, a mix of British colonial architecture and modern mirrored glass skyscrapers with Asian and Pacific Rim flourishes. In Viaduct Harbour on Waitemata Harbour is a bustling village and museum dedicated to one of New Zealand's recent victories on the world scene: the capture of the America's Cup, the sailing championship that Team New Zealand took from Young America in 1995, and successfully defended against Italian Prada in 2000. Alas, Kiwi pride took a dent in 2003 when the cup was taken away by the Swiss Alinghi team. But then they did walk away with all of those Oscars for *Lord of the Rings* in 2004.

We walked up Queen Street to Auckland Town Hall and stumbled into an encounter with one of the world's greatest living adventurers: Sir Edmund Hillary, who in 1953 (with his Sherpa guide Tenzing Norgay) was the first to climb Mount Everest in the Himalayas of Nepal. Born in Auckland in 1919, Sir Edmund was being honored by the Lord Mayor on the anniversary of one of his many accomplishments as an explorer.

Queen Elizabeth had sent over a platoon of her personal Lifeguards, one of the most famous marching bands in the world, and they strutted through downtown in the noonday sun. The Queen of England and Hillary are both quite familiar to New Zealanders: Sir Edmund graces the country's five-dollar bill and her royal highness is on the twenty. It was an auspicious send-off for our voyage of discovery.

■ A BAY OF ISLANDS AND MUFFLED HISTORY

We sailed 150 miles north to Russell, anchoring in the green and peaceful Bay of Islands. The pebble beach was lined with palm trees, graceful yachts bobbed at anchor, and the town's neat houses were gathered around a small but handsome church.

It was a lovely setting for a place once known around the world as the Hellhole of the Pacific.

The town began as the native Maori village of Kororareka. In the early 1800s, the first Europeans and Americans arrived, mostly aboard whaling ships that put into port for provisions. Very quickly the port became a lawless mix of grogshops, crooked merchants, prostitutes, and missionaries.

Add to the blend government functionaries from England who decided in 1840 for some reason to make the place the first capital of New Zealand, a position it held for just nine months; it was renamed after Lord John Russell, secretary of state for the colonies and later Prime Minister of Great Britain. Christ Church, built in 1836, is the oldest surviving church in New Zealand.

While many of the guests on *Silver Shadow* luxuriated in the calm splendor of modern Russell, we explored the churchyard and found the graves of British seamen and American whalers, including Henri Turner of the *Mohawk*, from our home town of Nantucket, Massachusetts, on the other side of the world.

ACROSS THE TASMAN SEA TO SYDNEY

I was accompanied on my voyage of discovery by a box of wondrous books about the region, including a transcript of Captain Cook's journal, and *Blue Latitudes*, Tony Horwitz's modern-day retracing of some of Cook's voyages. I was thus well-prepared for the often-wild weather of the Tasman Sea that lies between New Zealand and Australia.

We sailed out of Russell and north to the end of the island nation and at midnight turned due west into the oncoming heavy weather of the Tasman Sea. By daybreak we were plowing through squalls with winds of 50 to 60 knots in seas with 12- to 18-foot swells.

Silver Shadow, like most modern cruise ships, handles rough seas pretty well; coming from our island home, my wife and I are generally comfortable at sea in any weather. That said, some of the guests and crew were not to be seen for about twenty-four hours as the ship plowed westward.

Two days later we sighted Australia. The port of Sydney is one of the best-known places in the world, even though relatively few North Americans can claim to have visited. The *Silver Shadow* sailed into the wide, sheltered harbor and all eyes turned to the city's two very familiar icons: the Sydney Opera House and the massive Harbour Bridge nearby.

Sydney's handsome downtown—dominated by mirror-glass skyscrapers intermixed with Victorian colonial structures—is a great walking city. *Silver Shadow* docked in bustling Darling Harbour on the west side of town; the main cruise ship slip at Circular Quay near the opera house was occupied by the *QE2* making her final world circumnavigation enroute to refitting for cruises from Southampton in England.

That night we were picked up by limousine and taken to the opera for a performance of "The Merry Widow." We waltzed our way back to the ship for late-night cocktails.

BRINGING OENOPHILES TO NEWCASTLE

Silver Shadow was one of the first cruise ships in many years to make a call at Newcastle, a once-bustling coal and steel port north of Sydney. Our arrival was big news: We were met by the Newcastle Regional High School marching band, the Marching Koalas.

The sleepy beachside city, with some of the quirky charm of Brighton in England and one of the most active commercial ports in Australia, is not much of a tourist lure. But less than an hour inland is a surprising world of European sophistication and California chic; the Hunter Valley region is eastern Australia's wine country. The lush valley is home to dozens of small and midsize wineries and some of the trappings that inevitably come with them: luxury resorts, horse farms, gourmet restaurants, art galleries, and antique shops.

The Hunter Valley Gardens in the town of Pokolbin is an ambitious project to create a set of formal and fanciful gardens: Protected from the broiling February summer sun by umbrellas, we explored an exquisite *feng shui* arch, a desert rose planting, and a children's garden of nursery tales. We retired for a gourmet lunch to rival Paris, California . . . or the *Silver Shadow*, at Robert's at Pepper Tree nearby. The restaurant, set in a restored 1850 farmhouse, is on the grounds of the Pepper Tree winery.

■ THE GREAT BARRIER REEF, IN STYLE

Our next great discovery is near the top of the natural wonders of the world, the Great Barrier Reef. Here are just a few of the statistics: It is the biggest structure on earth constructed by living organisms, stretching about 1,250 miles along the east coast of Australia; there are actually more than 2,900 reefs and cays, plus 618 islands that were once part of the mainland.

Today's modern mariners have charts and global satellite positioning equipment; early explorers came to grief when their ships hit the hard, sharp coral of the reef. Captain Cook went aground in 1770 and was forced to put in to shore

Silver Shadow near Hayman Island. *Photo by Corey Sandler*

for six weeks to make repairs; once he set out to sea again, the winds nearly blew him back into the reef. Twenty years later, the HMS *Pandora*—dispatched to Tahiti to capture the *Bounty* mutineers—hit the reef and sank.

The fortunate guests on *Silver Shadow* were transported in comfort to an anchorage in the Whitsunday Islands and met by a catamaran. The fast ferry took us to Hardy Reef, where one of several carefully regulated eco-tourism companies maintains a platform.

While we happily snorkeled with the clown fish (and 1,499 other species) and gaped at some 400 species of coral and 4,000 different types of mollusks, *Silver Shadow* sailed on without us to Hayman Island; the catamaran delivered us to the ship in the afternoon. Hayman is a six-star luxury resort that is among the most exclusive anchorages in the world. Silversea passengers were allowed to tender ashore to use the beach, pools, and bars at Hayman and gawk at the lucky guests staying there; the guests gawked at the lucky passengers visiting for the afternoon and at the handsome ship in the harbor.

TOWNSVILLE AND CAIRNS

Townsville, two days sailing further north into tropical Queensland, was another surprise on our voyage of discovery. We found a sparkling seaside town with a handsome palm-lined oceanfront strand and a jumping shopping and entertainment district.

We began our day with a quick 5-mile ferry trip across the harbor to Magnetic Island, a lightly developed tropical paradise with secluded bays, dramatic lookouts, and abundant wildlife, including koalas and rock wallabies. We rented a "moke" (an open mini-jeep) to visit several settlements on the eastern half of the island; most of the western side is devoted to a national park.

Back in Townsville, the Reef HQ is almost as thrilling as a visit to the Great Barrier Reef itself. Within you'll find the world's largest living coral reef aquarium. You'll also come closer than you'd ordinarily want to predators including reef sharks, moray eels, sea snakes, and box jellyfish.

Next door is the Museum of Tropical Queensland. The fine collection is based around a partial reconstruction of HMS *Pandora* and many artifacts brought up from the wreck on the Great Barrier Reef, including china, cutlery, cannons, and coins. Another section displays the skeleton of a huge deep-sea reptile.

And then it was time to meet some of the current residents of Australia. Billabong Sanctuary, 10 miles south of Townsville, is a hands-on nature preserve that celebrates the local flora and fauna. There are not all that many places in the world where you can hand-feed a kangaroo, hold a koala to your breast, cuddle a sixty-pound wombat in your lap, and handle (carefully) an infant crocodile. We could hardly tear ourselves away.

The next morning we sailed into steamy Cairns (pronounced Cans), the largest city in the north of Australia, closer to New Guinea than Sydney. The streets are fronted by well-kept colonial buildings; it was like stepping into a scene from a Graham Greene novel.

■ GIVING UP THE SHIP

Thrilled with our voyage of discovery, we grudgingly disembarked *Silver Shadow* in Cairns; the ship was due to continue around the top of Australia to Thursday Island and Darwin and on to Singapore.

Although I've noted that Silversea is by no means the least expensive cruise line, it is also gratifying to see the value for dollars it delivers. There's not a spot on the ship that is crowded. You cannot walk from the luncheon buffet to your seat without a waiter taking your plate. And at dinner, the staff quickly gets to know your every want . . . and delivers it without an outstretched palm. And then there are the dozens of little luxuries, like wine and drinks without additional charge, and free laundry service for certain classes of suites.

On many lines you get the feeling that everything is designed from the bottom line up. From the moment you step onboard, you'll be accosted by staff selling tropical drinks with paper umbrellas; at dinner you get the feeling that your wait staff is calculating the gratuity they expect you to pay at the end of the cruise. In the restaurant the beef is good but you've had better, the lobster tail is recently defrosted, and the chocolate in the cake looks great but tastes quite ordinary.

Not so on Silversea. When it comes time to make a decision between good and excellent, ordinary and extraordinary, budget or expensive, this cruise line always seems to choose excellence.

■ OUR MODEST PIED-À-MER

The basic accommodation on *Silver Shadow* and her sister ship *Silver Whisper* is the Vista Suite; 287 square feet in size (about 50 percent larger than the lowest category cabin on most other ships), the room includes a panoramic window, a refrigerator and cocktail cabinet, walk-in closet, sitting area and writing desk, and a marble bathroom with bathtub and separate shower. The most common suite is the Veranda Suite, at 345 square feet, which adds a teak veranda.

Our accommodations were in a Silver Suite, an especially elegant and spacious home at sea. Spread across 701 square feet was a bedroom, a dining room, a living room, a double-size veranda, a walk-in closet, two televisions with VCRs, a CD player, a whirlpool bathtub, and many other lovely little touches. There are thirteen such Silver Suites on Deck 7 of the two sister ships, and they are very popular.

(There are even more spectacular digs: the Owner's, Royal, and Grand Suites—as big as 1,435 square feet, larger than many landlocked apartments.)

Accommodations on the slightly smaller *Silver Cloud* and *Silver Wind* sisters are similar, although a bit downsized.

Everything is up a notch or two—or three—from most other cruise lines. The furniture is more like an upscale home than a budget motel. The beds are appointed with luxurious Frette bed linens from Italy, and the marble bathrooms are stocked with Bulgari amenities.

Philipponat champagne flows like water throughout the ship and in the suites; guests can also order complimentary wine, beer, and spirits from an extensive selection for delivery to their rooms or at any of the bars, lounges, and restaurants.

The Restaurant is large and bright, more like a traditional dining room on a cruise ship. Meals are served on an open seating, and the quality of food is like that of a gourmet restaurant on shore. Silversea attempts to shop for fresh fish and vegetables in ports of call, and menus usually include local specialties.

Once each cruise, the Restaurant opens the doors at the back of the dining room for an unusual luncheon buffet: a fabulous spread of dishes on steam tables, countertops, and machinery in the sparkling galley. Of course, on Silversea there are also liveried waiters standing by to carry your treasures to the table and music by the ship's classical trio.

Le Champagne, an intimate wine room, offers an haute cuisine French menu accompanied by special vintages; it is one of the few places onboard ship where it is possible to spend extra money.

The Terrace is a small, lovely hideaway up top, offering a preset gourmet menu that changes each day; the sous-chef visits every table to discuss the night's delights.

As we sailed out of Newcastle, the Terrace presented a meal of Australian specialties, which proved to be my favorite. We began with steamed Balmain Bugs . . . which sounds just a bit more frightening than what they were: The locals call them "squagga," but they are also known as flapjacks or shovelnose lobsters. Other appetizers included citrus-smoked salmon with a wattle seed beurre blanc; the seeds come from an acacia tree and are roasted and ground to yield a nutty, coffee-like taste. The main course, prepared on an outdoor "barbie" or barbecue, was peppered sirloin steak marinated with local Castlemaine XXXX Bitter beer as it cooked. Dessert was an almost indescribable Australian specialty called Pavlova cake; a baked meringue and whipped cream creation named after Russian ballerina Anna Pavlova who visited the nation in the 1920s. (New Zealand also lays claim to a similar dessert.)

The wine steward quickly learned that I prefer an interesting beer at dinner. I sampled a variety of Australian brews each night; my wife enjoyed wines from around the world including a few from the Hunter Valley wine district near Newcastle.

Many Silversea guests avail themselves of yet another unique luxury from time to time: ordering from the menu and having it served course by course in the privacy of their suites. Room service will also bring up your choices of wine. That is, without a doubt, the way I would enjoy dinner on my private yacht.

GOLDEN PRINCESS: WHEN MORE IS LESS

The amazing thing about the *Golden Princess* is not how large she is, but rather how small she seems.

Yes, this handsome ship is a city afloat, 951 feet long and 118 feet across, with beds for 3,300 passengers and 1,150 crew. There are eighteen decks from her keel to the spectacular cantilevered lounge high above the stern.

But the designers of the *Golden Princess* have done a marvelous job of dividing the city into smaller and more comfortable neighborhoods. (A very similar design is used in the other ships in the Grand Class: *Grand Princess, Star Princess, Diamond Princess, Crown Princess,* and *Sapphire Princess.*)

We spent a crisp fall week on a cruise from New York, north to Nova Scotia and New Brunswick, Canada, returning to the Big Apple by way of the handsome New England ports of Bar Harbor, Boston, and Newport. After seven nights, at least twenty-one meals, and dozens of adventures, we disembarked without having completed a full tour of the ship; there are still a few more clubs and lounges waiting for a future visit.

We have sailed on much smaller ships that had a single gigantic dining room, filled with tables for eight and twelve and lorded over by a maitre d' who kept time like a symphony conductor; diners at the early assigned seating had to move along so that the room could be cleared for the next hungry horde.

But on *Golden Princess,* instead of one large dining room with multiple seatings there are three midsize rooms with a variety of schedule options. While other ships may add a single reservations-only specialty restaurant, the Grand Class ships offer at least two different choices, as well as separate pizzeria and barbecue counters. And even the lido buffet presents several choices for seating.

Rather than construct a gigantic theater to hold at least half the ship's complement at one seating, the elegant Princess Theater is of a more manageable size; popular production shows are offered at least three times per sailing, allowing guests to attend on their own schedule.

There's a traditional outdoor swimming pool with chaise longues, as well as a second pool under a retractable roof. All the way forward on the sun deck, there's a third "current" pool that allows swimmers to exercise against an oncoming stream of water.

There are sufficient saloons to permit a full week's worth of unduplicated bar-hopping, ranging from intimate hideaways to a raucous sports tavern to a show lounge. And way up high, on Deck 17, is Skywalkers Night Club, which is suspended 200 feet above the stern. There's a dramatic moving walkway that delivers you to Skywalkers; visitors are warned that the return trip is under their own power.

After dinner, you're likely to find a Broadway-style revue in the Princess Theater, a light jazz or Big Band show in one of the lounges, a rock group in another, and a comedian or singer holding sway elsewhere.

At 10:00 P.M. one night, as *Golden Princess* sailed down the coast of Maine toward Boston, the following was going on at various locations on the ship:

- A magician performed the first of two shows in the Princess Theater
- The Golden Princess Orchestra and the Golden Princess Dancers presented "Shake, Rattle & Roll" in the Vista Lounge
- A trio played dance music in the Wheelhouse Lounge
- A lounge singer played requests and musical games in the Promenade Lounge
- A country music band performed in the Desert Rose restaurant

Golden Princess. Photo by Corey Sandler

■ The Major League Baseball playoffs and World Series were offered in the rowdy Players Bar as well as on a huge projection screen in the spacious Explorers Lounge

■ A '50s Sock Hop, displaced from the Explorers Lounge by the baseball game, moved into another club

■ Way up top in Skywalkers Nightclub, a disc jockey produced Disco Inferno

Of course, the restaurants were still open, the Atlantis Casino was humming, the library and Internet Cafe were well attended, and in the cabins the ship's television was showing a current movie. The swimming pools, hot tubs, athletic club, and the small-but-worth-bragging-about miniature golf course on the sports deck were also open.

■ EXPLORERS AT SEA

For us, the best thing about going on a cruise is the chance for new discoveries onboard the ship and in the ports we visit.

Princess has gone beyond the traditional shipboard entertainment of shuffleboard, ice carving, and trivia quizzes (all still offered) to the ScholarShip@Sea program that offers classes and learning experiences.

On our cruise *Golden Princess* was introducing a ceramics class that allowed guests to decorate and glaze pre-formed pieces of pottery including small vases, boxes, and picture frames; the objects are then fired in an electric kiln, a most unusual appliance onboard a cruise ship. Future ships may expand the program to allow guests to work with wet clay and potter's wheels.

Other classes included introductory and advanced computer programs, ballroom dancing . . . and fruit and vegetable carving.

The guest speaker on our cruise turned out to be a most distinguished member of the family: Commodore Mike Moulin, the recently retired senior captain of the Princess Cruises fleet. Moulin had spent his entire career of forty-three years at sea with P&O, the parent company for Princess; he began as a fifteen-year-old indentured cadet on a small freighter out of Singapore. He went on to a succession of freighters and tankers; in 1962 a ship he was on was escorted through the middle of the blockade around Cuba for the missile crisis.

Moulin moved on to cruise ships in 1974, as an officer and eventually master of vessels including *Sea Princess,* the original *Island Princess* and *Pacific Princess, Sky Princess, Royal Princess,* and *Grand Princess.*

Moulin gave a lecture about the *Titanic* as our ship sailed within a few hundred miles of her burial place in a cold stretch of the North Atlantic. Later he was joined by his wife Maggie to speak about a career at sea.

We joined Moulin at dinner one night and asked him what were the most significant changes he had seen in moving from a modest 1,500-ton coastal steamer to a 109,000-ton state-of-the-art behemoth like the *Golden Princess.*

The biggest changes, he said, were in the crew culture. "When I started, junior officers never questioned orders. It was very autocratic," he said. "Now, everything involves teamwork.

"On the bridge now, you have a group of people who are all interacting. A junior officer can and must hold his head up and say something when he is not happy with what is going on."

"On the technical side, everything I was taught to do, from using a sextant to reading charts has been taken over by small electronic boxes," Moulin said.

I asked him which of the ships in the fleet was his favorite. "The traditional answer is always the one you are on. But to be honest, the Grand Class of ships is the epitome of ship handling. These ships are a total joy to handle because of modern power systems including bow and stern thrusters, independently controlled rudders," said Moulin. "You have all this power at your command. The ship can spin on a dime, or move sideways at 2.5 knots."

For all of their advanced technology, the Grand Class ships use traditional fixed pitch propellers. Princess chose not to adopt the new Azipod propulsion units, rotatable units that are like huge outboard motors mounted beneath the keel. "That was one of the best decisions we made," Moulin said. "We can wait until they get all the bugs out before we get into that design."

■ A LIFE ASHORE

A fall cruise to Atlantic Canada and New England is a thrill for the leaf-peepers and lobster-lovers, and we certainly saw more than our share of both. But we also managed to break away on shore to make some of our own discoveries.

We wandered far from the guided tour in Lunenberg, Nova Scotia, to a section of town frozen in time. There we met Greg Ernst, at work in the Thomas Walter blacksmith shop. Little has changed since the shop was opened in 1876.

Today Ernst works on custom fittings and ironwork for fishing boats and sailing vessels. The shop also produced nine tons of iron work for the replica of HMS *Bounty* created in 1960 for a Hollywood film and rebuilt in 2001, and nearly as much iron for Canada's sailing icon *Bluenose II*.

In Saint John, New Brunswick, I went for a little cruise that was a bit different than our pampered cabin on the "Love Boat." My transportation was in an aluminum-hull jet boat driven by a self-declared and demonstrably insane driver; we headed directly into the oncoming waves and wicked whirlpools of the changing tides in the Bay of Fundy.

The Reversing Falls just outside downtown Saint John are an unusual natural phenomenon caused by the tremendous rise and fall of the tides in the Bay of Fundy, the highest in the world. The south-facing opening of the bay receives the on-rushing ocean tides like a funnel; as it travels further up the bay it is squeezed by the narrowing sides and the increasingly shallower bottom. Twice a day, the incoming high tide collides with the receding low tide from further up the bay. The result is wild water.

At Fallsview Park, an underwater ledge 36 feet below the surface causes the full flow of the water to tumble downward into a 175-to-200 foot deep pool. The Reversing Falls Jet Boats take ten or twelve volunteers out into the onslaught; our driver—between theatrical cackles and well-honed jokes—described the ride as going through river rapids uphill. His favorite maneuver, the "pile driver," drove the bow of the boat into a hole in the water and delivered a solid wave of water into the cabin. Though we were dressed top-to-bottom in rain gear, we could not have gotten more wet if we had dived into the water for a swim. And we loved every minute.

Another stop on the *Golden Princess* itinerary was Bar Harbor, gateway to Acadia National Park, the third-most-visited national park after Yosemite and Yellowstone. Each summer 3.5 million visitors descend on a town of 10,000, which is one good reason why a fall visit on a cruise ship is a great way to visit.

The final port call was Newport, home to a fabulous collection of American castles built during the Gilded Age of the 1890s; the enormously wealthy railroad, silver, and merchant-built "cottages" by the sea including the Breakers, the Elms, and Marble House. In recent years Doris Duke's Rough Point was opened to the public for the first time.

Growing up with almost unimaginable wealth given her by her tobacco-baron father, Duke lived an unconventional and by most accounts unhappy life. Rough Point, designed like an English manor house, was commissioned by Frederick Vanderbilt in 1887.

Doris Duke filled the home with magnificent tapestries, Ming dynasty ceramics, and European antiques. She also kept a pair of ill-behaved camels on the back lawn and a few personal pieces of kitsch. In the Billiard Room we came across a pair of embroidered pillows on a couch: one bore the message MY DECISION IS MAYBE AND THAT'S FINAL. And the other, with credit to her friend Malcolm Forbes, read FAMILIARITY BREEDS.

Our final stop before returning to the ship was Rosecliff, designed in 1898 by famed architect Stanford White for Comstock Lode silver heiress Theresa "Tessie" Fair and her husband Oelrichs. The modest cottage includes a huge formal ballroom that was used as the stage set for many of the dinners, balls, and costume parties of the time. The house and gardens were used in several major films, including *The Great Gatsby* and for the spectacular party scene that opens *True Lies*.

■ TRAFFIC JAMS

Across seven days at sea, we hung out in our favorite neighborhoods and all but forgot about the other 2,498 or so temporary residents of our floating city. We met baseball fans in one corner, early morning exercisers in another, and thin-crust pizza aficionados up top when we needed emergency rations between lunch and the pre-dinner cocktail party.

It is only at certain times, like embarkation and debarkation, and customs and immigration that you're likely to catch a glimpse of the teeming masses. Getting on or off a ship in New York is always a challenge, especially when there are four or five ships at berth. You'll also encounter delays in other ports of call.

The traffic jams in the terminals are not particularly the fault of Princess Cruises; yes, they built a really big ship, but when the cruise is underway, there's so much to do that the crowds are spread out very nicely. Push comes to shove only when a couple of thousand people all want to do the same thing at the same time, like all going for the same solitary taxi. My advice: plan on an extra hour or so at each end of the cruise and take pleasure in everything there is to enjoy in between.

RESTAURANT ROW: FREESTYLING ON THE *NORWEGIAN DAWN*

Manhattan's famed Restaurant Row is home to two dozen fine dining spots on one block, 46th Street from Eighth Avenue to Ninth Avenue. For a lucky few thousand locals and visitors, fine dining continues just a few blocks west at New York's passenger cruise terminal, home to weekly visits by NCL's *Norwegian Dawn*.

On board the handsome ship are ten first-class restaurants and another dozen bars and nightspots. The food is fine, and the views are fantastic.

We sailed from New York on a seven-day trip to Port Canaveral and Miami in Florida, and Nassau and NCL's private island Great Stirrup Cay in the Bahamas. The ship departed New York just after Thanksgiving with a bit of a nip in the air, returning a week later in the teeth of an historic early blizzard that dropped more than a foot of snow on Manhattan.

NCL bills itself as the home of "freestyle" cruising. In theory, here's what that means: Guests can choose to eat at any of the ten onboard restaurants at any time they are open, at a private table or one shared with other guests. Most of the restaurants are open for dinner from 5:30 P.M. until midnight, and the Garden Cafe is open twenty-four hours a day for buffet service.

In practice, guests should act as if they were on shore: Make a reservation ahead of time, and take advantage of early or late dining to avoid the busiest times. If you show up with no advance notice at 7:00 P.M. and ask for a table for two, or a table for twelve, you may have to wait to be seated. But no one goes hungry.

Dress codes, too, are freestyle: On our week of cruising there was only one "suggested" formal night and the handful of guests in tuxedos and gowns were way outnumbered by decidedly less formal garb. At Cagney's and Le Bistro, guests are asked to wear at least resort casual garb; jeans, t-shirts, or shorts are discouraged.

▓ IN THE NEIGHBORHOOD

The *Norwegian Dawn* is a 965-foot-long, 91,000-ton Megaship that rivals the size of the nearby skyscrapers of Manhattan. But like the very best of the newest and largest cruise ships, it is very nicely divided into smaller neighborhoods. Instead of one or two gigantic main restaurants, there is one midsize traditional room and two more intimate rooms. Add to that an informal Tex-Mex eatery and tapas bar, a family-style Italian trattoria, an all-day all-night buffet, and a fast-food burger and stir-fry joint.

And then there is a trio of premium restaurants, intimate settings for a leisurely and elegant steakhouse, French-Continental, or Asian meal that would be fit for service on Restaurant Row in Manhattan.

All but the premium restaurants are included as part of the cruise fare. If you choose to visit a specialty restaurant, your room account will be billed an additional service charge.

Norwegian Dawn's sushi bar, Bamboo. *Photo by Corey Sandler*

The onboard entertainment, by the Jean Ann Ryan company, was a notch or two above the standard on other cruise lines. Perhaps the weekly proximity to Broadway had an effect on the talented cast.

Here's a cruise diary through our seven days on the *Norwegian Dawn:* seven dinners, seven breakfasts, seven lunches, a cocktail party, and a few snacks here and there including a sybaritic mid-afternoon Chocoholic Buffet.

Day One: Asian Delicacies. Sitting on our private veranda, we watched a brilliant red sunset over the shoulder of the Statue of Liberty as our ship sailed out of New York harbor, one of the world's most spectacular ports. And then we began our week-long visit to NCL's floating Restaurant Row.

On the upper level of an open alcove of a midship mini-atrium is Bamboo, a teppanyaki room, and a sushi bar; the deck below is home to Le Bistro, the Wine Cellar, the Impressions Restaurant, and Gatsby's Champagne Bar.

Bamboo combines Chinese, Japanese, and Thai cuisines with an elegance well above the level of your neighborhood Golden Palace. Teams of servers, dressed in formal kimonos, wait attentively.

Our meal began with an *amuse bouche,* a tasty tidbit of seaweed with sesame dressing. We enjoyed bowls of Tom Yum Koong, a Thai soup of Black Tiger Shrimp and rice noodles in a spicy lemon grass fish broth. For entrees, we shared seared Ahi tuna with a wasabi, ginger, and brown sugar dressing. The second entree was beef tenderloin with black bean sauce. And we each savored a plate of sliced Mandarin Peking Duck with sour plum sauce and savory pancakes. I topped off the meal with green tea ice cream; my wife made it through an order of Thai banana pancakes with coconut ice cream.

The current cover charge for Bamboo is $12.50 per person; guests who arrive for dinner before 6:30 P.M. are charged just $5.00. The standard meal includes a choice of two items (soups or entrees) and a dessert; that may be less than cruise guests expect, but additional entrees or sushi selections are priced at only a few dollars apiece.

Bamboo also includes a handsome sushi bar, offering a wide selection of fresh sushi, sashimi, and maki dishes. Individual items were very inexpensive, and there was an all-you-can-eat special for $10.00. At the other end of the restaurant was a small teppanyaki room with a la carte chicken, shrimp, scallop, calamari, and steak dishes.

Day Two: American morning, Italian noon, chocolate afternoon, Chicago night. At breakfast we watched the North Atlantic from a window seat in the Garden Cafe, up high on Deck 12. The six buffet lines are augmented by omelet and fresh fruit stations.

For lunch we made our first visit to the Venetian Restaurant, the largest traditional dining room on the ship. Under the Freestyle program, there are no assigned seats and a two-hour window for lunch; you can ask to be seated by yourselves or join others at larger tables.

As befits its name, the Venetian salutes Italy's city of canals with attractive murals and decor. The restaurant spreads across the entire stern, with many tables along the windows.

The menu also spread across a few cultures: Appetizers and entrees included Balinese beef and chicken satay skewers, spaghetti Bolognese, yellow fin tuna steak with mango salsa, Indian beef curry, and Greek moussaka.

Although prudence would have dictated a siesta in preparation for the evening's meal, we could not resist a visit to NCL's famed Chocoholic Buffet, which was laid out in the Impressions Restaurant, a smaller alternative to the main traditional restaurant decorated with reproductions of Impressionist artwork evoking Paris of the 1900s. A long line snaked its way into a twin buffet line stacked with chocolate cakes, cookies, pies . . . ending with an ice cream bar for those who wanted their calories a la mode.

Somehow, on this leisurely day at sea, we found room for dinner, and it was a well-catered affair: Cagney's Steak House is a small and elegant hideaway on Deck 13. Decorated in rich wood, leather, and brass, Cagney's evokes Chicago of the 1930s with framed newspaper clippings and other artifacts of the time.

We feasted on crab cakes with aioli mayonnaise; a recreation of Cardini's original Caesar Salad born in Tijuana, Mexico, in 1924; a gigantic T-Bone steak with steamed asparagus, and a dessert that was appropriately named Sinful Chocolate Obsession.

Cagney's is one of the specialty restaurants on the ship, and guests are charged a $20 service charge for the basic menu, or $25 for either a whole Nova Scotia lobster or a plate-filling 24-ounce Angus Beef porterhouse steak.

Day Three: Mexican sunset. We arrived early in the morning at Port Canaveral, Florida. We had made prior arrangements to rent a car and we drove an hour west to Orlando to spend the day at SeaWorld. Many other guests took advantage of charter buses to Walt Disney World or Universal Studios arranged by NCL's excursion desk.

We worked up an appropriate appetite visiting Shamu and friends, and arrived back at the ship in time to make our next visit to *Norwegian Dawn's* Restaurant Row. We had reservations for a table for two at Salsa, a Tex-Mex and tapas bar and restaurant that sits on a balcony of the main atrium. Tables are arranged along the port and starboard windows of the balcony. There is no service charge for meals at Salsa.

They wish you *buen provecho* as you are seated, and a good appetite is something to wish for here: The assorted hot and cold tapas plate is almost a meal in itself with a small quiche, chicken wing, grilled vegetables, and olives. Other appetizers include a crispy onion blossom and fiery jalapeño poppers. We savored a rich black bean soup with chorizo.

Entrees included quesadillas, carnitas burrito, and fajitas, with fillings including chicken, skirt steak, or pork. Also on the menu was Momma's Meatloaf and blackened mahi-mahi. We waddled off to bed after sampling cranberry-pecan pie and Mexican chocolate and mascarpone cheesecake.

Day Four: Miami Vices and French Masters. We spent the day in Miami Beach, exploring the art deco wonders of South Beach and the quirky fashions of Lincoln Road, returning to the ship for a late lunch at the Garden Cafe.

That evening we dined with the masters at Le Bistro. I have visited some of the greatest museums in the world, and eaten in some of the most exclusive restaurants. But I have never before broken bread in the presence of Renoir, Matisse, Monet, and Van Gogh.

Each of the tables in the intimate dining room is in sight of four works of art, part of the personal collection of the chairman of Star Cruises, the Malaysian parent company of NCL.

We studied Pierre August Renoir's *The Bather* while enjoying an appetizer of warm asparagus with Hollandaise sauce and French escargots in garlic butter.

We turned to appreciate Henri Matisse's *Nude in a Turban* to accompany French onion soup and cream of forest mushroom in a sourdough loaf.

Our main course of filet mignon with foie gras and truffled veal jus was served in the reflected light of Claude Monet's *Vetheuil in the Sun*.

And for dessert, I savored a lemon sorbet while Janice dipped fresh fruit into a chocolate fondue; as we sipped tea and cappuccino, we admired Vincent Van Gogh's *A Park in Spring*.

Guests at Le Bistro are assessed a service charge of $15.00; visitors can come to tour the art gallery during the day.

Day Five: A Change in the Weather. As the sun rose, the *Norwegian Dawn* arrived at NCL's private island, Great Stirrup Cay, to find high seas and wind. Though the ship handled the waves well, there is no dock on the island and guests have to be shuttled to and from the beach on tenders. The decision was made to proceed instead to nearby Nassau and attempt to return to Great Stirrup Cay the next day.

We discussed the weather and the handling of the ship that night; we were the guests of Captain Idar Hoydal and Hotel Director Tony Becker on a return visit to Cagney's Steak House. This time we sampled the seafood side of the menu, enjoying an Oyster Rockefeller casserole and a broiled salmon steak.

Day Six: Back to the Beach. Captain Hoydal's reading of the weather charts proved correct, and the next morning dawned calm and clear. *Norwegian Dawn* arrived at Great Stirrup Cay at 7:00 A.M., and guests began tendering to shore after breakfast.

NCL's private island, just 2.5 miles in length and 1.5 miles across, is at the northern end of the Berry Island chain of the Bahamas, about 140 miles due east of Fort Lauderdale.

The first settlers were believed to be Lucayan Indians around 600 A.D. Christopher Columbus brought the Spanish to the area beginning in 1492, followed by British explorers and settlers in the early 1600s. The cove at Great Stirrup Cay was a favorite safe anchorage for pirates lying in wait for Spanish ships returning home with gold from South America.

During the U.S. Civil War, the island was held by Union troops and used to provision warships, a role that returned in World War II when American troops were stationed there to help guard the east coast of the United States.

NCL became the first cruise line to buy its own private island when it purchased Great Stirrup Cay in 1977. Just to the north is Little Stirrup Cay, used by Royal Caribbean Cruise Line for visits to a beach it calls Coco Cay.

The island includes two beaches along a cove protected by a coral reef. One section of the reef is intended for snorkelers, and cruise line staff conduct tours of aquatic life. We were accompanied on our swim by stingrays, barracuda, and millions of bright tropical fish.

Along with a few thousand guests, the tenders also brought a barbecue lunch ashore: ribs, burgers, and hot dogs. We chose instead to take an early tender back to the ship and have our own private picnic on our veranda: We ordered a room service lunch of Japanese ramen soup, a roast beef sandwich, and a chicken Caesar salad. The view, and the room service menu, were priceless.

That afternoon we enjoyed the irony of watching the film *Pirates of the Caribbean* in the cinema as we sailed through the Berry Islands, once home to Blackbeard, Henry Morgan, and Anne Bonney, among other celebrated brigands.

That evening we visited Aqua, the third of *Norwegian Dawn*'s traditional dining rooms. This midsize room is decorated in its namesake color, beneath a starlight ceiling; think of under-the-sea with bread baskets. We found the room a bit crowded and noisy, the least attractive of the restaurants onboard ship.

Aqua shares most of its menus with the Venetian and Impressions restaurant, adding a few seafood items on some evenings. We sampled Oysters Rockefeller, salmon bisque, grilled fresh tuna with tangy onions, and roast Long Island duck with green peppercorn-cognac sauce. Other diners chose a roasted lobster tail, part of the Captain's Farewell Menu offered throughout the ship.

Day Seven: From the beach to the blizzard. Cruising north toward New York, *Norwegian Dawn* faced 48 knot winds (55 miles per hour) and seas as high as 12 feet, but the ship was more stable than a crosstown bus. The modern ship's advanced stabilizers and broad and squat hull smoothed out almost all rolling motion, and the ship's navigators sought a course that minimized front-to-back pitch.

We made a return visit to Bamboo that evening to sample some of the other gourmet Asian specialties served there. In addition to a repeat order of Peking Duck, we tried Tempura Soba, black tiger shrimp tempura-style with buckwheat noodles in Japanese broth. Our final dessert course included a frozen pineapple soufflé.

Believe it or not, at the end of our seven-day cruise we had not managed to eat in every room of the floating Restaurant Row. We never made it to the Blue Lagoon, a twenty-four-hour food court that serves burgers, fries, and Asian stir-fries. And we were unable to squeeze in a visit to La Trattoria, a section of the Garden Cafe that is converted each evening to an informal Italian restaurant serving salads, pizzas, and pasta. We strolled through the Pearly Kings Pub without stopping to eat there; it's a sports bar that offers fish and chips and other finger food. In the main lobby, Java Cafe serves frozen coffees, espresso, cappuccino, and tea, accompanied by specialty a la carte pastries and cookies.

New York looked a bit like a frozen soufflé itself when we arrived the next morning. Embarkation and debarkation can be a real New-Yawk hassle. In NCL's defense, most of the problems are not of their making; the terminal is in the control of Customs and Immigration officials and the powerful longshore unions.

More so than in any other port, you should leave a large cushion of time for arrival and departure.

NCL does show the best of intentions over the things it can control: A full breakfast is served on the final morning and guests are allowed to stay in their cabins until they are called for debarkation. And the line arranged for clearing a foot of snow off cars parked on the rooftop lot alongside the terminal.

We passed by Manhattan's Restaurant Row once again as we headed out of town; there was no need to stop for a pick-me-up.

NIGHT MOVES: *RADISSON SEVEN SEAS NAVIGATOR*

The elegant *Seven Seas Navigator* sailed out of Boston at midnight, carrying about 400 pampered guests. While they were sleeping, the pilot came aboard at 3:58 A.M. north of the East Breakwater of the Cape Cod Canal.

This is what it means for a pilot to come aboard when a ship is underway at sea: The *Seven Seas Navigator* plowed through slightly choppy seas, a few miles offshore and unaccompanied in the shipping channel by any other vessels. Though a nearly full moon crossed the sky early in the evening, it had set beneath the horizon in the waning hours of the night, and the heavens were lit only by the stars and by the red glow of Mars on one of its closest visits.

The ship slowed from cruising speed of 20 knots to 12 knots (nearly 14 miles per hour) and held a steady course. From the bridge, the officer on duty turned on the bright lights along the starboard side of ship, and watched as the small pilot boat approached. On one of the lower decks, crewmen opened a small door and extended a ladder to just above the wave tops.

The little pilot boat edged alongside, almost—but not quite—touching the 560-foot-long cruise ship. From the cabin of the boat, a lone figure walked out onto the heaving gunwales and grabbed hold of a rail. And then, in a move that would give an acrobat pause and an insurance agent the jitters, the pilot stepped across the gap and grabbed hold of the ladder.

Once inside, the pilot rode an elevator through the quiet ship to the eleventh deck and entered the navigational bridge.

The bridge was in its nighttime darkness, lit only by the sweep of radar screens and the reports of computer monitors; a few red lights marked the length and depth of the wheelhouse. The lights also showed the way to a silver tray of coffee, cappuccino, and juices laid out for the pilot and the ship's officers.

Our ascent to the bridge was a good deal easier than the route taken by the pilot. The phone in our suite rang as the pilot approached. Captain Alfredo Romeo, making good his promise, called to tell us we were about to enter the mouth of the canal and invited us to join him.

■ THE CAPE COD CANAL

We've been in navigational bridges many times, all around the world, but this visit was special for us: Although we had crossed the high bridges over the Cape Cod Canal hundreds of times to and from the ferry docks that connect our home on Nantucket island to the mainland, we had never sailed through the waterway.

The canal is a manmade sea-level shortcut that separates Cape Cod from the mainland of southeastern Massachusetts. A trip through the 17-mile-long channel saves about 135 miles of travel through open and sometimes rough seas around the tip of Cape Cod.

The idea for the canal dates all the way back to the Pilgrims; William Bradford and Myles Standish, among the leaders of the *Mayflower* expedition, explored the area around Plymouth settlement in 1626. According to historical documents, they discovered that two rivers, the Manomet on Buzzards Bay at the west end of the Cape, and the Scusset on Cape Cod Bay to the east, were separated by a short distance of land.

In 1776 General George Washington sent an engineer to Cape Cod to study the possibility of a canal to help get around the British blockade.

It wasn't until early in the twentieth century that work actually began, with backing from New York financier Augustus Belmont. Work began in 1907 and was completed seven years later; the opening of the Cape Cod Canal on July 29, 1914, beat the inauguration of the Panama Canal by seventeen days.

Operated by the military during World War I and later purchased by the federal government, the canal was widened and deepened during the depression and three bridges were constructed. The Bourne and Sagamore bridges, each with a span of 616 feet, are among the longest continuous truss bridges in North America. The 544-foot-long railroad bridge near Buzzards Bay is today the third-longest vertical lift drawbridge in the country. The bridges clear the water by 135 feet.

Today the canal is nearly 500 feet wide, with a depth of about 32 feet. The shortcut runs at sea level, which means there are no locks to go through. However the waters of Cape Cod Bay to the east are about five feet higher than those at Buzzards Bay and so there is a strong current through the waterway. At high tide, waters move through the canal at an average of 4 to 5 miles per hour. Under a full moon or in adverse weather, the current can move at more than 7 miles per hour.

■ THE PILOT TAKES CHARGE

The pilot took control of the ship, standing at the front window of the bridge and at first commanding adjustments to the ship's rudder and speed in the tiniest of increments—a degree to starboard or a knot faster or slower.

Before we entered the canal, he radioed the Coast Guard controller; for the nearly one-hour duration of our passage, the waterway was ours alone, a one-way route from northeast to southwest. We sailed down the center of the canal, keeping our ship's masts and superstructure in line with the highest points of the Sagamore and Bourne bridges.

It was at the Sagamore where the pilot earned his keep. A combination of the full moon, a change in tide, and the remnants of Hurricane Fabian put a stiff current through the canal, a flow of 7 or 8 knots—nearly 9 miles per hour—against our forward progress.

Seven Seas Navigator in Bar Harbor. *Photo by Corey Sandler*

At the point where the bridge crosses the canal—a roadway that carries tens of thousands of Bostonians and visitors to the Cape on summer weekends, the canal bends like the crook of an elbow.

The oncoming current pushed *Seven Seas Navigator* first to port and then to starboard. Under the pilot's command, the ship's rudder was moved at first slightly, then a bit more, and then finally hard over.

In the narrow canal, the captain had retracted the wing-like stabilizers that extend out from the sides of the vessel; while nearly everyone but the ship's senior officers and the engine room crew slept the ship heeled 9 degrees over to port. In the predawn stillness, we heard the tinkle of a hundred bedside water glasses and watches tumble to the floor.

Around the bend, the canal straightened and the rudder was set midship for the remainder of the way. Passing beneath the Bourne Bridge and finally the rarely used railroad overpass, we reached the end of the canal and entered Buzzards Bay between the mainland and the Elizabeth Islands and just beyond, Martha's Vineyard. Two hours later, as we approached Newport and Narragansett, Rhode Island, a small boat came alongside once again and the pilot took a step across the sea and into a small boat that would take him home.

A few hours later, Captain Romeo apologized to the passengers for the unexpected tilt in the night.

■ THE BERMUDA TRIANGLE

This wasn't the first, or the last, impact that the sometimes fickle weather of late summer and early fall had on our trip.

We had happily planned a September journey, saluting the end of a cool summer with a visit to the warm and proper isle of Bermuda. As experienced cruisers, we knew that September is the heart of hurricane season, but we also knew that these hugely powerful storms are also relatively small. What would be the chances that a hurricane could interfere with our simple plans?

The itinerary for Radisson's *Seven Seas Navigator* was an appealing one for a luxury liner: a spectacular departure from New York harbor, a three-day stay in Bermuda, and a visit to Norfolk, Virginia, on the way back to the Big Apple. We packed our summery clothes, bathing suits, and suntan lotion.

But in the days leading up to our departure, we began tracking a tropical depression off the Cape Verde Islands that became a tropical storm and eventually a full-blown Category 4 tempest. Given the name Fabian, at first the storm appeared to be heading for the Florida coast; then projections took it a bit offshore, moving north on a track between the Carolinas and Bermuda. By the day before our departure, the forecasters had moved the storm eastward: There was a chance that Fabian would head directly to Bermuda, arriving half a day after our ship was due to dock in the port of Hamilton.

Here is where cruise lines are very different from landlocked resorts. A ship is a moveable feast, a hotel that can sail to more promising—or less threatening—waters. Relatively few cruises are canceled outright because of adverse weather.

We drove to New York with no certainty of the ship's plans: Would we hug the coast and come in behind the hurricane after it passed? Would we visit nearby East Coast ports like Baltimore and even Florida before looping back through the Bahamas or Bermuda?

It wasn't until we got on board the ship and settled into our handsome suite that we received the first update from the friendly and very accessible Captain Romeo. The latest projection, he told us, called for Fabian to make a direct hit on Bermuda with winds of 120 miles per hour. Not that we particularly wanted to test the forecast, but the deal was sealed by authorities on the island who were sending away any cruise ships already there and closing the harbor to new arrivals.

And so, we learned, we were the latest victims of the Bermuda Triangle: We were going to head north before we went south. The new itinerary took us from New York to Halifax, then back down the coast to Bar Harbor, Maine, and then Boston before making our previously scheduled visit to Norfolk, Virginia.

It was a bit like packing for a week at the beach and ending up at a ski resort.

There was a bit of grousing—and cancellations by about fifty guests. The not-quite-so-good news is that large cruise ships cannot go just anywhere. They need ports large enough to accommodate them, and not already occupied by other ships. And in most cases ships departing from a domestic port must make a port call at a foreign destination.

It was for that reason that instead of sailing 769 miles southeast to Bermuda, the *Seven Seas Navigator* headed 595 miles northeast to Halifax, Nova Scotia.

Our revised itinerary took us out to sea for a day, then to Halifax, Nova Scotia; Bar Harbor, Maine; Boston; Norfolk, Virginia, and then back to New York. (You can read about some of the port calls in Chapter 3.)

Radisson offered guests an onboard credit of $100 per person and a larger discount on any future cruise booked onboard the ship. Although the line was not obligated to make refunds to passengers who canceled, most were able to apply their fare to another itinerary.

■ ABOUT THE *NAVIGATOR*

Radisson's fleet delivers a first class hotel at sea, with superb service, food, and a high degree of luxury and refinement. It's hard to quantify luxury: One woman's necessities are another's dreams; one man's basic comfort is another's extravagance.

That said, Radisson is just half a notch below the most *luxe* of the deluxe cruise lines. If Silversea, Crystal, and Seabourn are Rolls Royces, then Radisson is a Lexus: a bit less flashy, a bit less well-known, and for some buyers, an excellent deal.

As we unloaded our bags at the cruise terminal in New York, we were met by a white-gloved ship's stewardess who escorted us to the check-in desk. Our bags followed us to our suite in record time, one of the advantages of a relatively small ship with a low passenger-to-crew ratio.

Our accommodations were a penthouse balcony suite, an upgraded version of the basic cabin. Classes A through H on the ship are each a comfortable 301 square feet in size—as much as 50 to 70 percent larger than the basic cabin on most modern cruise ships. All but the lowest two classes also include a 55-square-foot private veranda.

Our Class B suite came with the services of John, a butler who stood ready to handle any request—special or ordinary—during our cruise. Among our modest needs: reservations for dinner, personal delivery and attention to our daily room service breakfast, and arrangements for the ship's tailor to make a visit to the cabin to take measurements for an adjustment to one of my wife's cocktail dresses. Butler service is offered to Class A and B cabins, plus the larger and fancier Navigator, Grand, and Master suites.

Even without a butler, guests on Radisson ships receive a very high level of service. Gratuities are included in the fare, as is wine, beer, and aperitifs at dinner; it is always a pleasure to deal with crew who do not seem to be measuring you for a tip.

The food and service at the Compass Rose Restaurant, the main dining room, was very good. At Portofino, the alternative restaurant, the quality and attentiveness of the staff was even better. Portofino serves a buffet breakfast and lunch, and then converts to an elegant and small bistro with mostly Northern Italian specialties for dinner. You'll need a reservation for Portofino; we managed to find a table for two there nearly every night.

This is not the Fun Ship, which seemed to suit the generally quiet and refined passengers on our cruise. There was a harpist and a classical pianist who each made concert and informal appearances; the nightly entertainment also included a song and dance troupe of average off-off-Broadway caliber. Our cruise also included a cameo appearance by the executive chef of the Four Seasons in New York; he presented two cooking lessons and supervised a special gourmet meal at Portofino.

After a full day in Beantown that included a poolside late-night dessert spectacular, we sailed at midnight for the Cape Cod Canal and then out to sea for a final day in Norfolk, Virginia.

Our final night from Norfolk to New York turned out to be a bumpy ride through the remnants of hurricane Fabian. The ship pitched from one roller to another, a bit like a bus with a flat tire.

But we were rewarded the next morning with a stunning late summer morning and a triumphant sail into New York harbor, the classy way to arrive in the Big Apple. As we debarked, we were thankful for the fact that our five-star hotel had wheels . . . err, propellers . . . and had safely transported us away from a hurricane in high style.

WINDSTAR *WIND SURF*: SAILING INTO HISTORY

Wind Surf is lying at anchor in the aqua seas of the Caribbean in Philipsburg, Saint Maarten. A few hundred yards away, tied up to the dock, are Royal Caribbean's *Adventure of the Seas* and Radisson's *Seven Seas Navigator.*

■ *Adventure of the Seas* is a modern megaship, a 138,000-ton behemoth that stretches 1,021 feet along the quay—three-and-a-half football fields. She holds 1,557 cabins and suites and typically carries more than 3,114 passengers and another 1,181 in crew. The Royal Caribbean ship is too wide and too long to fit through the Panama Canal, which suits her primary assignment of sailing loops among the islands of the Caribbean Sea. *Adventure of the Seas* needs all that space, of course, in order to make room for an ice-skating rink, a rock-climbing wall, a nine-hole miniature golf course, a full-size basketball court, a song and dance troupe with a well-equipped theater, and a twenty-four-hour shopping mall.

■ The second ship tied up at the dock, *Seven Seas Navigator,* is about half the length and width of *Adventure of the Seas.* She is an elegant, upscale, midsize cruise ship with 245 suites—almost all of them with private verandas. A typical sailing on the 560-foot-long Radisson ship carries about 490 guests and a high ratio of crew, about 340. The emphasis is on fine dining, wine with dinner, bridge in the card room, and a guest lecturer from a university, museum, or government. It's a five-star hotel with a changing view out the windows.

And then there is our vessel, the *Wind Surf,* which includes a bit of each of her neighbors in the harbor. *Wind Surf* is about the same length and width as *Seven Seas Navigator,* and in some ways she is as modern as any new ship like *Adventure of the Seas.* Dining was fine, served in an open-seating restaurant or a reservations-only bistro. But in some other ways, *Wind Surf* is unlike almost any other ship afloat today.

To begin with, *Wind Surf* is a sailing vessel. Depending on your measuring tool, *Wind Surf* may be the largest sailing vessel on the seven seas and perhaps the biggest ever built. She is 535 feet long, 617 feet if you include the bowsprit spar that hangs out over the bow; her five aluminum masts can hang five mainsails, a jib, and a mizzenmast. She has 156 cabins for about 312 passengers.

A sailing vessel, *Wind Surf* is unlike almost any other ship afloat today. *Photo by Corey Sandler*

And, unlike most other cruise vessels, *Wind Surf* is first and foremost a ship. She is not a floating amusement park, a moveable five-star hotel, or a shopping mall at sea. The ship, large as she is, can pretty much go anywhere there is water, without need of a dock or the services required for a behemoth carrying 5,000 people.

On this sailing vessel, the cabins are shipshape and attractive with portholes instead of condo-like balconies. There are several levels of outdoor promenades. The doors to the navigational bridge are open, and passengers are welcome to visit when the ship is at sea and in most foreign ports.

This is a cruise line for people who don't need ice shows, twenty-four-hour bingo, and off-off-Broadway dance reviews. The guests on the *Wind Surf*— including an unusually high number of repeat guests—come aboard for the romanticism of a sailing vessel and pampered but unstructured relaxation. The excitement comes from the ports of call—many of which are less-visited anchorages where the big cruise ships don't venture.

▉ SAILING AWAY

It is the five 164-foot-tall masts and the 26,881 square feet of white sails that define this ship. When guests on a cruise liner cross paths with *Wind Surf* when she is under sail, they see a massive windjammer—something that was common a century ago and very rare today.

That said, *Wind Surf* is a decidedly modern ship. When the officer on watch wants to unfurl the sails he doesn't have to dispatch dozens of able-bodied seamen to climb the masts and walk out on the yardarms to maneuver tons of canvas—the way sailors have worked for hundreds of years on the great exploration and trading ships. Instead he walks to a panels of dials and switches tied into a computer program. With the click of a mouse, hydraulic winches unwind the triangular Dacron sails that are reefed around each mast like window shades.

There are five mainsails, a smaller jib at the bow, and a mizzenmast near the stern. For all of her high-tech design elements, *Wind Surf* is essentially a staysail schooner, using triangular sails supported by wires and heavy ropes.

Depending on the season and location, *Wind Surf* may spend hours or days under sail; as a cruise ship she has to make her regular schedule of port calls even if the wind is not strong enough to move the ship quickly or if the winds are from the wrong direction. Below decks, *Wind Surf* has four diesel engines for use when there is insufficient wind and for maneuvering in harbor. In addition to the two propellers, the ship includes bow and stern thrusters and a segmented rudder that serves as an extra stern thruster, deflecting the propeller's wash as much as 80 degrees.

On our cruise from Saint Thomas into the Leeward Islands of the Caribbean, we spent a full day at sea and parts of two others with most of the sails hoisted. When the ship repositions from Europe to the Caribbean each fall, much of the nearly two-week crossing is made under sail; going the other way in the spring, the winds often fail to cooperate and the engines are used to keep on schedule.

With all seven sails fully extended and a forceful wind, *Wind Surf* can easily reach 12.9 knots with her propellers turned off and feathered so that they create the least drag on forward motion; the presence of the props actually limits the top speed under sail. With both sails and propellers working, she can reach about 14 knots.

Wind Surf was built in France in 1990 and first sailed as the *Club Med 1*; she was extensively renovated and additional cabins and facilities were added in 1998 and 2000, making her a bit larger in gross tonnage than her sister ship, *Club Med 2*, which is still in service.

Most sailing ships make use of a deep V-shaped keel to provide a counter-weight to the heel produced by a sail under the load of wind, and to resist the sideways force that results when the wind is pushing on the sails from a direction other than directly over the stern. *Wind Surf,* though, has a nearly flat bottom like most cruise ships; its designers use the sides of the ship like a keel and a sophisticated ballast system that can pump 150 tons of sea water from one side of the ship to the other to adjust the heel to keep it within 3 or 4 degrees of upright. Even with her nontraditional lines, *Wind Surf* is capable of sailing close to 60 degrees off the wind.

■ SHIPSHAPE AMENITIES

The small, attractive cabins are as shipshape as any I've traveled in; we found plenty of closet and desk space, a refrigerator, and a high-tech flat screen LCD television and a DVD player. (The ship's library had a good selection of current and classic movies for guests.)

The cruise line keeps its promise not to annoy guests with announcements of art auctions, spa treatments, and other sales events. On the downside, cabins include a drawer full of minibottles of liquor, a quart of Scotch in the closet, and a basket of other goodies—charges will appear on your account if you use any.

Don't look for dance troupes, comedians, bingo, and toga nights on a Windstar cruise. You will find low-key lounge singers and a dance band if you prowl by night; the most spirited entertainment was delivered by many of the enthusiastic Philippine and Indonesian amateurs in a crew show.

For many of us, a favorite place to visit was the marina. In most ports, *Wind Surf* opens a large door at the stern and extends a floating platform into the sea. Guests can take out small sailboats and kayaks, join with four or five others in hanging on to an air-filled float called a banana boat that is towed at high speed by a skiff, or go water skiing. Certified divers can sign up for organized scuba expeditions for an extra charge, or borrow snorkel masks and fins to take ashore to beaches.

The only activity not allowed off the marina is swimming, because the platform on the *Wind Surf* sits directly in the water, creating a bit of suction under the stern. The similar but much smaller platforms on the two other ships in the Windstar fleet have a different design without that problem.

THE MODEL OF A MODERN SAILING CAPTAIN

Mark Boylin, master of the ship, brings with him the necessary unusual resume to run this unusual hybrid. His background includes extensive service on sail training ships in Europe.

"*Wind Surf* was designed from scratch to be a sailing vessel with a minimum of manpower," he told me. "It's crossover technology between sailing and cruise ships."

A bit of a naval historian, he pointed out that up until the start of the twentieth century most commercial sailing vessels had flat bottoms, to allow carriage of more cargo and the ability to sit on beaches for loading and unloading.

Boylin started his career as a seaman on banana boats, but moved over to the more romantic world of sailing vessels. His first such service was on the *Sir Winston Churchill*, a three-masted topsail schooner sail training vessel, built in 1966 for Britain's Sail Training Association as an educational program for young people. The 135-foot-long schooner was replaced in 2001 by the newly built *Prince William*.

His first command came on the *Golden Hind*, a replica of the ship captained by Sir Francis Drake on a circumnavigation of the world between 1577 and 1580. Boylin captained a crew of twenty-four who sailed from England to San Diego. He later was master of *Malaysia*, the sailing trainer for the Malaysian Navy. Boylin joined Windstar in 1994, and is now the senior captain for the flagship *Wind Surf*.

Hotel manager Frank Ulbricht, who came up through the ranks as a sous-chef and later executive chef on various cruise ships, says guests on *Wind Surf* are of a slightly different breed than those found on other vessels. As many as 50 percent of passengers are repeat customers, he said. "They don't want to be on bigger ships. They don't want everything organized, with bingo games and constant announcements. And they don't want to have to dress up for dinner," Ulbricht said.

PORTS OF ANCHORAGE

Our cruise on *Wind Surf* departed from Saint Thomas in the U.S. Virgin Islands and made calls at some of the less-visited islands of the Leewards: Îles des Saintes, Nevis, Saint Bart's, and the smallest and least-developed of the U.S. Virgin Islands, Saint John; nearly three-quarters of the land is part of the Virgin Islands National Park. We also visited the popular island of Saint Martin, best known for its shopping.

Îles des Saintes is one of the more obscure and most charming far-flung outposts of the once-great French empire. There are eight little islands in Les Saintes, only two of them occupied, and thus far the place has almost completely escaped the trendy development that has changed forever places like Saint Bart's and Nevis.

The principal island is Terre-de-Haut, with a village at the harbor in Bourg des Saintes. The island is just 3 miles long by 2 miles wide, a walkable tropical paradise through bougainvilleas and past a cemetery where conch shells line the graves.

There are about 3,000 *saintoises* living on Terre-de-Haut and nearby Terre-de-Bas. There's a tiny tourism industry with a few small hotels and guest houses; many of the locals still earn their living as fishermen. A handful of the old-timers still wear a *salako* on their head, a flat dish of straw or bamboo covered with cloth; the unusual design may have been brought to Les Saintes centuries ago by Chinese or Indonesian sailors. The other local specialty is sold by some of the women of the island at little stands: *tourments d'amour,* small round and soft cakes filled with coconut or other nuts. These memorials to the "torments of love" were once baked by the fishermen's wives to carry out to sea for sustenance.

Les Saintes are dependencies of the nearby, more developed island of Guadeloupe, which is itself an overseas *departement* of France. Guadeloupe also oversees Marie-Galante, Saint Martin, and Saint Barthélemy.

There's a bit of history in Les Saintes. They were spotted by Columbus in 1493 soon after the Feast of All Saints, and he named them Los Santos. (If you're on the island on November 1, the predominately Roman Catholic *santoises* decorate the cemetery stones with candles in celebration of the holiday.)

The first European permanent settlers arrived from France in the mid-seventeenth century, and the seas around Les Saintes and Guadeloupe were the site of numerous skirmishes between the French and British fleets, culminating in the decisive Battle of the Saintes on April 17, 1782, when English Admiral Lord George Rodney all but destroyed the French West Indies fleet of Admiral François de Grasse with some fancy maneuvering. (Rodney had been the most successful British naval commander in the American War of Independence, while in 1781 de Grasse had played an important role in blockading the mouth of Chesapeake Bay, helping the Americans defeat the British at the end of the Revolutionary War.)

High above the town of Bourg is Fort Napoleon, built by the French in 1867 after the island was returned to their rule and never used in military action. It was restored by volunteers a few decades ago and includes fabulous views of the island and across the water to Guadeloupe.

The volcanic island of Nevis has some stronger claims for listing in the history books of the Caribbean, Europe, and the United States. Its European history starts in 1493 when Columbus—either because of bad eyesight, poor logic, or artistic license—named it Las Nievas, which means "the snows," because of the ring of fluffy white clouds that usually surrounds the still-active volcano.

The island had been settled by Awaraks and Caribs, and there is ample evidence of prehistoric peoples. British and other European settlers arrived in large numbers about 1624, and by 1626 nearly all of the Caribs on Nevis and nearby Saint Kitts had been massacred or taken into slavery in Venezuela. To replace them, Nevis imported thousands of slaves from Africa to work on sugar plantations there. In 1774 the island was populated by about 1,000 whites and 10,000 slaves.

Wind Surf at Nevis. *Photo by Corey Sandler*

On March 24, 1667, a ship carrying 144 English made a six-day stop at Nevis. Two months later the same group landed at what is now Jamestown, Virginia, to found the first permanent English settlement in the new world.

Alexander Hamilton, one of America's founding fathers, was born on Nevis in 1757. He left the island at the age of fifteen to pursue formal education and became a leader in the Revolutionary movement while still in his teens; before the age of twenty he commanded artillery troops in several battles and when he was twenty-five became a member of the Continental Congress. A signer of the U.S. Constitution in 1787, he became George Washington's first Secretary of the Treasury in 1789. If you look carefully, you'll find a small bronze monument at his place of birth just north of downtown Charlestown; if you seek his picture, consult a $10 bill from your wallet.

In 1784 famed British Admiral Horatio Nelson was given command of the gunship *Boreas* and sent to Nevis to enforce the Navigation Act, a form of economic reprisal against the American colonies. Nelson was tasked to prevent non-English and certain European-owned ships from trading with England or her colonies. From his base in Nevis, Nelson seized four American vessels; he was in turn sued by the captains of those ships with the support of the merchants of Nevis. To avoid imprisonment, Nelson was forced to remain on board *Boreas* for eight months. Somehow during that period Nelson met wealthy Nevisian widow Fanny Nisbet, whom he would later marry.

Nevis remained a British colony until 1967 when it received commonwealth status; in 1983 Nevis became partners with Saint Kitt's as an independent nation.

Today Charlestown has many remaining eighteenth- and nineteenth- century Georgian buildings. Small museums celebrate Nelson and Hamilton. Around the circumference of the nearly circular island are former plantations including several that have been reincarnated as high-end spas and hotels.

Saint Barthélemy (more commonly known as Saint Barth or Saint Bart's) is one of the toniest of the French islands in the West Indies, vacation home to multimillion-dollar yachts and vacationing movie stars. The hilly island, composed of just 8 square miles, has some of the best beaches in the Caribbean.

Columbus named the place for his brother Bartolomeo in 1493. It was first settled about 1648 by French colonists; that community did not succeed, and in 1651 the island was sold to the Knights of Malta, the island state in the Mediterranean Sea. Five years later, the island was raided by Carib Indians and it was abandoned until 1673 when French settlers from Normandy and Brittany returned.

One reason the renewed French settlement succeeded was a wink-and-nod accommodation with French pirates who made their base there and brought with them some of their plunder taken mostly from Spanish galleons that were themselves bringing swag from the new world back to Europe. One of the most famous of the buccaneers was Monbars the Exterminator, whose treasure trove is supposedly still hidden somewhere on the island between Anse du Gouverneur and Grande Saline.

The British resurgence in the West Indies resulted in a brief takeover in 1758, but the island returned to French hands until 1784. In that year, the island once again went to unusual hands when the faraway government of Louis XVI sold

Saint Bart's to Sweden in exchange for a European trade agreement. The Swedes renamed the harbor Gustavia in honor of their king, and it became a highly profitable neutral free port, with a still mostly French population. When France repurchased the island in 1878, trade had almost completely fallen off and the place went into sleepy decline.

Today the principal city retains the name Gustavia and some of the street signs are still in Swedish, but otherwise Saint Bart's is very French with very chic boutiques and restaurants. The villages of Colombier and Corossol are more French than Normandy, with some of the women shaded from the sun beneath shoulder-length *quichenottes*.

Many of the women are much less modest at the fabulous beaches, including Baie Saint Jean and Lorient. We rented a four-wheel-drive car in Gustavia and toured the island's narrow and precipitous roads, stopping at three beaches. We visited a boulangerie in Saint Jean to spend a few euros on a fresh baguette, a wedge of Reblochon de Savoie cheese, and a bottle of vin de pays imported from mother France.

It was a cruise that will live on in our personal history.

DISNEY MAGIC: THE KIDS ARE ALL RIGHT

Dear Mom and Dad:

While you were sleeping, I was hanging out under the stars in the Caribbean, dancing with my new friends and visiting the late-night all-dessert buffet extravaganza. We partied in the atrium, went to teens-only shows, and strolled around the promenade in the dark. One night we watched a cool lightning storm way out to sea.

When you were upstairs at that fancy adults-only restaurant, nibbling eggs Benedict and sipping champagne for Sunday brunch, we were ordering pizza, fabulous french fries, and ice cream from the restaurants around the pool deck: all the basic food groups for the healthy teenager.

We were doing the hokey-pokey while you were watching Roxie Hart and Velma Kelly put on their moves in the movie *Chicago,* part of the nightly double feature of first-run movies in the gorgeous Buena Vista Theatre. Then we all went to see *Holes,* which debuted on the ship the same week it opened on land.

I don't know about you, but this was pretty close to my perfect vacation: Mom and Dad took care of all the details. They got me down to Florida and on the ship, and then we had our own separate holidays. You were up early to sit out on the veranda or go to a cooking lesson. I was out all night, coming back to the cabin about 2:00 A.M. and sleeping late in the morning. We met to attend the stage shows and go to dinner every night, and then you headed off to bed while the teens took over the ship.

They call this *Disney Magic* a cruise ship, but I think of it more as a floating city that traveled to some great places and a fantastic beach. We partied hearty every day, and I felt safe everywhere I went. And I didn't have to pack up and unpack every day.

I really enjoyed the three days at sea and the shopping and sightseeing in Saint Martin and Saint Thomas, and then there was Castaway Cay, where I soared like a bird. More about that later.

This was my sixth cruise; it's pretty nice having a dad who travels for a living. I've liked all the ships I've been on, but Disney is definitely the best when it comes to things for kids of all ages.

■ NO ADULTS ALLOWED

Our headquarters was in a private club where no parent is allowed—called The Stack on *Disney Magic* and Common Grounds on *Disney Wonder.* About fifty kids, age thirteen to seventeen, hung out there. It was our home base from noon to 2:00 A.M., with couches, a huge television set with a library of tapes and video games, Internet terminals, board games, and a coffee and soft drink bar.

We had three crazy Canadian counselors. On the first night we were told the rules: no swearing, no fighting, and no forgetting that there were counselors— and video cameras—watching us in the club and nearly 1,000 members of the crew in one place or another on the ship. No problem: We had way too much fun to get into trouble.

Those Canadians were obsessed with the movie *Coyote Ugly*; they danced on top of the bar when they showed the movie one night.

I mentioned that there were about fifty older teens; there had to be three or four hundred younger kids on board. Many of them spent a lot of time at the Oceaneer Club, for kids from three to twelve years old; the little babies were parked at Flounder's Reef Nursery while their moms and dads chilled. And there was a lot going on at Mickey's Kids' Pool, with the big water slide, or at Goofy's Family Pool. Several nights they pulled the cover over Goofy's and made the whole middle of the ship into a dance floor facing the stage; we had a great sail-away party the night we left Saint Martin.

After the young kids went to bed most nights, we took over the Studio Sea club for midnight dances and karaoke sessions. Other times we made our own animation cels; I brought "Stitch" home in my suitcase.

One day at sea we played "Gotcha." Everyone was given a secret assignment to track down another kid somewhere on the ship and kill them off in the game: You got points for stabbing with a paper spoon, delivering the kiss of death on their hand, giving a water torture on the pool deck, or poisoning them by slipping a piece of paper marked POISON under their drink without being noticed. You never knew who had your name—until they got you. Let me tell you, this is a big ship with ten decks, four restaurants, three pools, a whole bunch of elevators, and lots of stairs. I put up a good fight.

One of the best things about this cruise is the way they treat kids; we felt like full citizens in this city. Of course I also really liked the way our Filipino servers Andrew and Rowena fussed over us at dinner. Disney does this cool thing: They have three restaurants, and our servers travel with us to a different one each night.

They did a great job of figuring out what I liked to eat, and they had my soda and steak sauce and my favorite green tea at the table before I even thought to order. Andrew had a new puzzle for me to solve each night. Rowena, who was so sweet, insisted on calling my dad "Sir Corey."

On the last night of the cruise, Andrew gave me a stainless-steel plate cover to bang during the servers' parade; maybe it was because he heard me running around on the deck with a cow bell given to me by one of those crazy Canadians.

Back in the room, our stewardess Lijljana made a different animal out of towels each night. Dad found out that she was a former journalist with a degree in political science who was earning some money before heading back to Croatia, where she hoped to work as a diplomat. That was cool, too.

■ BROADWAY AT SEA

I loved the shows, even if they kept bringing out Mickey and Minnie at the end of each performance. I mean, please, I'm almost eighteen years old. (I prefer Pluto and Belle.)

They did this comedy and magic show called "Morty the Magnificent" about a pretty bad magician. His girlfriend, Daphne, made a wish on her birthday candles, and the Sorceror's Apprentice (Mickey) made Morty magnificent. The magic tricks were cool, and the singing and dancing was really good.

Dad, you told me the little inside joke about the name Morty; it's short for Mortimer, Walt Disney's intended name for his cartoon mouse before his wife convinced him to go with Mickey. It had nothing to do with the show, but, as always, you see things differently than most other people do.

The best magic trick was when Morty sawed the stage manager in half. He said he needed a single woman for the trick because she had to remain unattached. Anyhow, after sawing, the stage manager's legs danced away all by themselves.

There were two other shows. "Hercules—A Muse-ical" was really funny, full of wisecracks and references to pop songs and singers. Hades, lord of the underworld, and his goofy imps sang a few lines of "It's a Small Underworld After All." The big production number was "Zero to Hero."

"Disney Dreams" is like a review of all the Disney favorites, with Peter Pan helping a wishful little girl, Anne-Marie, to find her own magic. We meet Cinderella, Belle, the Beast, Ariel, the Lion King, and all the usual suspects . . . and Mickey.

The Walt Disney Theatre is just fabulous. There are three stage elevators, a fly loft for sets, indoor fireworks, fog machines, laser lights, video screens, and a starfield in the ceiling. And how many theaters on a ship have flying rigs so that Peter Pan can help a little girl soar out the window?

"Who wants to be a Mouseketeer?" was a game show named after guess-what, with prizes from $20 to $400 in shipboard credit and a top prize of a free seven-day cruise. Contestants are randomly selected from the audience, and I had it all worked out. I was going to go up there with dad; I could answer all the questions about *Lion King* and *The Little Mermaid* and dad could answer questions about Mortimer Mouse and all those other little details he knows about ships, theme parks, and other stuff.

They also had this really funny ventriloquist onboard; he had this hilarious routine where he took a five-year-old kid from the audience and made him into his dummy. And this juggler guy did some amazing tricks on stage. Both of them also appeared later in the smaller Off-beat and Rockin' Bar D clubs for some close-up tricks.

And then there was Castaway Cay, on the last full day of the cruise. I remember how you told me that when Disney was planning its cruise ships, the designers thought about how kids would imagine a fabulous ocean liner. That's why they gave it a pointy prow, a black hull, and two big funnels—even though only one of them is real.

I think they did the same thing when they worked on their private island: It's just the way I would want it. The beach is beautiful, there's a big barbecue, and there's snorkeling and floating and a fort with ropes to swing on. Inland, there are bike paths and hiking trails. The little kids have their own beach.

I know you both visited the adults-only beach at the other end of the island. I know that sounds pretty risqué, but this is a Disney place, right? It's a nice, quiet beach with no kids, its own restaurant, and private cabanas for massages.

I hung out with my friends at the teen beach, until the afternoon, when I met up with Dad at Marge's Barges at the end of the breakwater that protects the beach. We climbed into a speedboat and headed out into the open ocean beyond the *Disney Magic* at her dock. A guy strapped me into a harness, attached me to a parachute, and gunned the engine.

For the next ten minutes or so, I parasailed high above Castaway Cay, making a turn around the stern of the cruise ship. We had a nice wind, and once I was about 200 feet in the air, the speedboat stopped and I just hung there—a human kite.

I soared higher than Wendy ever did with Peter Pan; it was my Disney Dream. Dad, you did pretty well, too—for an old man.

I know I'm headed off to college in the fall, and I expect I'll find a few things to do there for the next four years. But if you need me to go with you on a cruise as a reporter, I'm there.

—Tessa

CARRYING CULTURE TO SEA: *VEENDAM* IN THE CARIBBEAN

Every modern cruise ship is globalization in action, a mini United Nations of guests, crew, cuisine, and culture. But few cruise lines are as conscious of their history and cultures as is Holland America Line.

We sailed on the *Veendam* from Fort Lauderdale on a basic weeklong eastern Caribbean cruise: Saint Thomas, San Juan, and Nassau. But we were surrounded by an often elegant, sometimes wondrously confusing, and always fascinating global stew of cultures on an exceptionally handsome ship. (*Veendam* is one of four nearly identical sisters in the fleet, along with *Maasdam*, *Ryndam*, and *Statendam*.)

We were aboard an Italian-built ship, registered in the Netherlands by the

Holland America Line division of the American company Carnival Corporation. The ship's captain and principal officers were British, while the dining room staff and cabin attendants were mostly Indonesian. We were sailing in the Caribbean, which is itself a mix of native, American, British, Dutch, French, and Spanish cultures, and we were carrying with us a floating art museum with pieces from as far away as Egypt and China.

Holland America Line (HAL) helped bring the huddled masses to the New World, carrying nearly a million European emigrants in the late nineteenth and early twentieth centuries. The company was founded in 1873 as the Netherlands-America Steamship Company.

Holland America ships, such as the *Veendam,* have a rolling roof over the swimming pool that allows for year-round and all-weather use. *Photo by Corey Sandler*

HAL celebrates some of its own history in the forward staircase with a set of paintings of the four company ships that have carried the *Veendam* name. The first was built as the *Baltic* for White Star Line. It entered service in 1871, was purchased by Holland America Line in 1888, and served until 1898. The 426-foot-long vessel, just 3,707 tons in capacity, carried 166 passengers in first class and 1,000 more in third class or steerage. The painting shows *Veendam* in New York's Upper Bay, off today's Liberty Island, at the start of a voyage to Rotterdam in summer 1891.

The second *Veendam* sailed from 1922 to 1953. *Veendam III* joined the fleet in 1972 and served until 1984; the ship was the reflagged liner *Argentina,* launched in 1958, which was the last major passenger liner built in the United States. *Argentina*'s sister ship *Brasil* sailed until 2002 as the *Universe Explorer.*

On today's modern *Veendam,* the entire ship is a floating art gallery, with hundreds of items small and large on walls and in display cases. Many of the pieces celebrate the connection of Holland to its former colonies and trading partners around the world.

Indonesian carvings, paintings, and fabrics adorn the walls of the piano bar. Within the Explorers Lounge on the upper promenade is a collection of feather masks and headdresses from the Tapirape, Kayabi, and Txukaramac tribes of Brazil. Nearby is an elegant mantel clock from mid-nineteenth-century France and a set of pewter plates from late-eighteenth-century England.

In a showcase outside the handsome library are some ancient artifacts from Mexico and Central America. Among the oldest items on the ship is a statue of a sower, holding a planting stick and a seedbag, from the Jama-Coaque culture of Ecuador and dated from 500 B.C. Nearby is an earthenware dog from the Colima culture of western Mexico, about 100 B.C.; the dog, which has a hollow space within to hold corn wine, was meant as a companion for the dead in the afterlife.

Near the puzzle room is an interesting mix of Chinese and Dutch porcelain and delft items. A Chinese dinner service and serving bowls dating from the seventeenth and eighteenth centuries sits alongside earthenware and delft pottery from Holland of about the same time. Some of the Chinese items were commissioned by Dutch traders and imported into Europe.

A corner of the Half-Moon Room holds a display of *ushabiti,* small mummy-like statues from about 1085 to 935 B.C. The 3,000-year-old icons were supposed to perform farm work in the afterworld for the deceased.

The attractive two-level Rubens Lounge was used for nightly entertainment, including a magician, an "edgy" juggler, and an above-average corps of singers and dancers. Special events included a "Rockin' Rolldies Show" that engaged some of the guests in some very funny (intentional and otherwise) send-ups of golden oldies; the highlight was a rendition of Bobby Darin's "Splish Splash," featuring a septuagenarian man in a towel and snorkel mask and a dancing chorus of good-natured women who had made more than a few extra trips through the buffet line in their lives.

But for many of us, the entertainment highlight was the Indonesian Crew Show, presented by a group of waiters from the dining room as we sailed toward San Juan, Puerto Rico. Dressed in spectacular native costumes, they performed a version of the classical Balinese *Kecak Ramayana* dance that tells the sad story of King Dasaratha and the unhappy succession of his less favored son to the throne. The finale of the show was a presentation by the Angklung West Java Bamboo Orchestra.

Captain James Russell-Dunford, master of the vessel on our cruise, was born in southern England and went to sea as a cadet on cargo ships at age eighteen. In 1978 he joined Cunard as a second officer and worked his way through the ranks to become the youngest chief officer on the transatlantic liner *QE2.* In 1982 he was aboard ship when the liner was taken over by the Ministry of Defence to transport troops during the Falklands War between Great Britain and Argentina. When not aboard ship, the captain, who joined HAL in 1998, lives in a small fishing village in Cornwall, England. On our cruise he was joined by his wife, Lynne, who served as social hostess for special events.

Holland America offers most of the amenities of the Megaships, although it does so with a nicely cultured restraint. You can play bingo or go to the casino or bid on art at an auction, but the ship's loudspeakers don't assault your senses with announcements.

The small movie theater is in regular use; we stocked up on fresh popcorn from the stand outside, augmented by cappuccino, espresso, and dessert—the sort of free snack bar every landside cinema ought to offer. The ice-cream bar and pizzeria on the lido deck were open most of the day as well.

We made good use of the attractive Internet cafe onboard the ship; on our cruise, the operator was offering a package deal of unlimited service for seven days for $99, which is a relatively good deal for those of us who need to or want to remain in near-constant touch with the office, friends, family, and the rest of the world. I joined a group of Canadians in listening to the Olympic gold medal hockey game over the Internet as we sailed near the Bahamas, yet another wondrous dish of global stew.

Another interesting package deal on our sailing was unlimited laundry service for $45 per cabin, or unlimited clothes pressing for $30.

As on any other cruise ship, much of the focus of the day revolves around three—or four or five—meals. We were not disappointed; the quality and presentation of food were excellent, several notches above the middle of the road. Each night's menu included an unusually expansive choice, typically offering five appetizers, several soups, and five entrees. Some sample entrees: sesame potato-crusted coho fillet; seared tuna steak with charmoula vinaigrette; grilled venison rack chop; pan-seared five-spiced duck breast; and sautéed garlic prawns. One dinner featured Dutch specialties, including *Zeevruchten Zeeland* (bay shrimp, scallops, mussels, and mushrooms in lobster sauce), and *Hutspot met klapstuk* (boiled brisket of beef over mashed potatoes).

There was also a separate vegetarian menu chosen by one of our tablemates; it included some dishes that deserved a spot on the menu alongside the thick steaks, fresh fish, and other specialties.

After I made a special request that our waiter visit the crew's galley below deck, my meals were accompanied by a bowl of Indonesian *sambal,* a fiery-hot chili sauce.

The exceptional pastry chef prepared a changing rotation of desserts and baked goods. Two of our tablemates, friends of the executive chef, reached an anniversary on our cruise: They were feted with a huge marzipan dessert that celebrated a few notable personal events.

In between stage shows, meals, dessert, and more dessert, we sailed happily through the Caribbean—although our visit to Holland America's private beach resort, Half Moon Cay, was canceled because of high winds and waves. We strolled the streets of San Juan and visited El Morro Castle. In Saint Thomas we rented a car and circled the mountainous island on our own, stopping for a swim at famed Magens Bay. We've explored Nassau enough times to know by heart its limited charm, but our daughter enjoyed bargaining for trinkets at the Straw Market.

On this cruise, the excitement and entertainment came from the ship and not the destinations. Happily, the *Veendam* held up her part of the bargain as a comfortable and cultured place to hang our sandals.

CELEBRITY *MILLENNIUM*: HIGH-TECH ON THE HIGH SEAS

Celebrity Cruises' *Millennium,* a technologically advanced beauty, was the first passenger ship to be powered by gas turbine engines. She also is equipped with state-of-the-art propulsion pods, advanced Internet connections aboard, Pay-

The high-tech Celebrity *Millennium* in the harbor at Saint Thomas. *Photo by Corey Sandler*

Per-View movies in the cabins, and a show stage with a control panel that would be at home on the space shuttle.

All of this would mean nothing were it not for the fact that *Millennium* is a stunner inside and out. The 965-foot-long, 105-foot-wide, 91,000-ton cruise ship is the first of at least four vessels in Celebrity's Millennium class. *Infinity* joined the fleet in 2001; *Summit* and *Constellation* were added in 2002.

The dark blue hull of the ship is topped with a white superstructure and a large blue funnel about two-thirds of the way to the ship's stern. Two smaller funnels, one near the stern and another near the bow, are for decoration only. The main funnel carries the large *X* of Celebrity's fleet, with a horizontal bar like the scarf of Hermes, messenger of the gods. (The *X* is a Greek chi, as in Chandris, founders of the line.)

Millennium boasts the first glass-enclosed panoramic elevators on a cruise ship; the lifts near the midships atrium offer unusual views of the sea as they traverse the decks. Eighty percent of the 975 staterooms have ocean views, and there are 578 cabins with private verandas. An interactive television network aboard the ship allows passengers to order room service, shore excursions, and Pay-Per-View movies.

The ship features a pair of handsome two-story libraries. "Words" offers one level of English-language books and a second in other languages. "Notes" is a music library offering 1,500 selections of music accessible from listening stations.

Online@CelebrityCruises, one of the first Internet cafes designed with the ship, has eighteen LCD screen stations and an ocean view. The Emporium, the largest retail shopping area on any current ships, includes name-brand shops such as DKNY, Versace, H. Stern, La Perla, Swarovski, and Fossil.

On our cruise we were entertained in the Celebrity Theater by high-energy stage shows, including *Spectacle of Broadway* with singer and actor Joel Grey as video host, and an interactive game show, *Dream Ticket*, in which members of the audience entered their answers by remote control from their seats to win the right to come up on stage and compete for prizes.

AquaSpa is among the largest and most luxurious floating spas. You'll find your basic thermal suite with a tropical shower, laconium grotto steam room, and fog shower. If that's not exotic enough, you can lose yourself in the ancient oriental ceremony of rasul, which demands the application of purifying muds followed by an herbal steam bath. There's also a thalassotherapy pool under a glass dome in a garden setting.

One of Celebrity's claims to fame is the quality of dining, and *Millennium* does not disappoint its many frequent eaters. Renowned chef Michel Roux oversees the fleet's dining rooms and specialty restaurants.

The Metropolitan Restaurant is lit from above by a blue faux skylight. At the back of the room a full-window wall looks out at the sea to the stern of the ship; by night, projectors can paint maritime scenes on a curtain at the stern. The upper level of the two-story dining room is a horseshoe-shaped balcony that overlooks the main floor. Galleys for the restaurant are one deck below; hidden escalators are used by servers.

The culinary star of the ship is the Olympic Restaurant, an elegant and oh-so-fancy eatery that includes some of the design elements and actual paneling from the famed SS *Olympic,* sister ship of the *Titanic.*

Cova Cafe Milano, an outpost of the famed cafe near the La Scala Opera House in Milan, offers coffees and pastries from an a la carte menu. Michael's Club, an English Georgian-style cigar lounge, is another premium room.

At the forward end of the Sunrise Deck is Cosmos, an observation lounge with a glass wall that replicates the sweeping view from the navigational bridge below. By night Cosmos becomes a cocktail lounge and later a disco. At the top of one of the stairwells on this deck

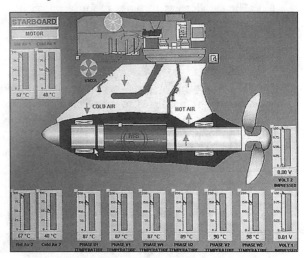

An engine room video display monitors the starboard engine pod on the Celebrity *Millennium. Photo by Corey Sandler*

is the Conservatory, a small greenhouse at sea that's filled with arranged plants, trees, and flowers.

We sailed from Fort Lauderdale to San Juan, Saint Thomas, Nassau, and Catalina Island, which is a private beach resort off the coast of the Dominican Republic. In winter, *Millennium* sails eastern Caribbean itineraries like ours, alternating with western Caribbean journeys to Key West, Calica and Cozumel in Mexico, and George Town, Grand Cayman.

■ THE GEE-WHIZ FACTOR

At her christening in Southampton, England, *Millennium*'s name was preceded by a new prefix, GTS, for gas turbine ship. Nearly every other modern cruise ship uses diesel engines as the source of power, carrying the label MS for motor ship. The diesels spin generators that produce electrical power for motors to turn the propellers. A few older ships directly drive the propeller shafts from diesel engines, and a handful of venerable antiques use steam turbines, classified as SS (steamship) vessels.

The state-of-the-art *Millennium* ship produces much less pollution from the combustion of its engines and its associated lubrication system. Gas turbines are adaptations of jet engines. Although they may be slightly less efficient than equivalent diesel engines, they produce only a small fraction of the noxious emissions of a diesel, and they are also much simpler to maintain. Diesels use oil for lubrication, and the material breaks down into sludge and waste over time. The gas turbines do without the bulky and environmentally hazardous oil storage and oil separation systems. And because the turbines are much smaller than diesels and do not require oil storage tanks, the space devoted to mechanical systems is reduced. What that means to a cruise line is more space for staterooms or public rooms.

The smaller gas turbines produce power by rotation rather than up-and-down reciprocation, which means they produce less vibration. Diesel engines emit low-frequency noise that is difficult to muffle, while the jet engine/gas turbines produce noise in a much higher frequency range that is easier for engineers to quiet.

The two turbines spin generators rated at fifty megawatts; an additional nine megawatts are produced by a low-pressure steam turbine spun by the exhaust gases from the turbines. *Millennium* uses a pair of General Electric LM2500+ gas turbine engines, manufactured in Cincinnati. They were sent by freighter to the Chantiers de l'Atlantique shipyard in Saint-Nazaire, France, to be installed in the hull under construction; this marked the first time in more than forty years that engines for a new cruise ship have been built in the United States.

When the shipyard completed *Millennium* in 2000, it was the largest vessel ever built there, surpassing the legendary *Normandie,* which launched in 1935 and weighed in at 82,799 tons.

The next design improvement for *Millennium* addressed the propulsion mechanism. The standard design for ships built in the past few decades placed large electric motors in chambers toward the back end of the ship; they spun propellers attached to shafts at the stern. Also at the stern were one or two huge movable rudders that could change the angle of the bow as it moved through the water. Rudders have been used on ships for thousands of years; among their drawbacks are mechanical complexity and the fact that ships have greatly reduced steering when they are moving at low speed.

Millennium is among the first cruise ships to use propulsion pods, which are like huge outboard motors. Forward-facing propellers, 19 feet in diameter, are mounted in units that can swivel in any direction. The ship's generators feed power to the electric motors in the pods by cable; the motors are directly connected to the propellers.

In ordinary operation the propulsion pods pull the ship through the water like airplane propellers; to turn, the angle of the pods is changed. Because the pods can swivel and produce thrust in any direction, the massive ship has no need for rudders and can quickly change from forward to reverse without the need for the propellers to come to a complete stop and change direction. And because the pods can generate thrust to either side, there is no need for separate stern thrusters like those used on nearly every major ship. (*Millennium* still has electric bow thrusters to swing the front of the ship in port and in emergency situations.)

I visited the engine control room of the *Millennium* as we sailed between Saint Thomas and the Bahamas. The video display panel used by the engineers to control the machinery showed that one pod was facing straight ahead while the other was angled slightly; the ship's computer had directed the unusual configuration to deal with a crosscurrent.

All of this high-tech equipment practically guaranteed some teething pain for the new class of ships. *Millennium* had to be pulled from service twice in her first six months, once to slightly modify the shape of the hull underwater to deal with an unexpected vibration detected during her initial cruises in Europe, and once in February 2001 to repair a problem with one of the electric motors within the propulsion pod. Neither problem was a threat to the safety of the passengers.

▥ THE OLYMPIC RESTAURANT

This most modern of cruise ships reaches back almost a century for some of its design. In 1909 the famed White Star Lines announced construction of three 45,000-ton ocean liners. The first was *Olympic,* huge for its time (about half the tonnage of today's *Millennium*). The ship was capable of carrying more than 2,400 passengers in three classes, including more than a thousand in cramped third class. The second ship in the series was the ill-fated *Titanic.*

One reason the huge ships of the time had relatively small public spaces and cabins was the need for huge mechanical spaces. *Olympic,* as originally built, had immense coal-fired boilers served by hundreds of stokers with shovels. She was later converted to oil burners.

Nevertheless, *Olympic* included the first indoor swimming pool at sea and a squash court, both located deep within the hull. The jewel of the ship was an alternative restaurant, an a la carte dining room for first-class passengers. The restaurant was paneled with elaborate hand-carved wood that was accented with gilded moldings and ornaments.

After *Titanic* sank in 1912, *Olympic* was withdrawn from service and renovated to improve its safety, with features including additional lifeboats and improvements to the ship's watertight compartments. The alternative dining room was expanded at that time as well.

The fabled *Olympic* came to the end of the line during the Depression, when she was cut up for scrap, but not before some of her finest appointments were set aside. In 1935 the paneling from the restaurant was sold at a pierside auction to a family who used the wood to decorate their own home in England. Celebrity purchased the paneling at a second auction in 1998.

Just as with the high-tech machinery on *Millennium,* the design of the Olympic Restaurant is merely a stage setting. The room seats just 134 guests, with a serving staff of ten chefs, ten servers, five sommeliers, and five maître d's. Reservations are necessary, and guests are charged a stiff $25 per person fee for gratuities.

The emphasis of the restaurant is placed on tableside finishing, with servers showing off their skills on appetizers, entrees, and desserts, including an elaborate Caesar salad, steak Diane, flambéed shrimp scampi, and crepes Suzette. Other attractively presented dishes included monkfish with sauce Nantua, saltimbocca alla Romana, and rack of lamb en croute.

On sister ship *Infinity,* the specialty restaurant is patterned after the decor of the famed liner *United States; Summit* salutes the French liner *Normandie.*

ON THE ROUTE OF THE GOLD RUSHERS

Here's the way to prepare for a cruise from Seattle into the Inside Passage of Alaska: Before you embark, make a stop at the Klondike Gold Rush Historic Park in downtown Seattle. Spend the time to absorb a bit of history about the years 1897 and 1898, when a hundred thousand prospectors set out on an almost impossibly difficult and unpleasant trek in search of gold.

The gold rushers were headed north, mostly to the new tent-and-shack towns of Skagway and Dyea in Alaska. From there they faced a 600-mile passage to the goldfields near Dawson in Canada's Yukon.

Alaska and the Yukon were almost completely wilderness made worse by severe winter weather and extremely difficult mountain passes. And then there was the "one ton" rule, enforced by Canada's Northwest Mounted Police: Every prospector had to carry with him a full year's provisions, which amounted to about a ton in weight.

At Dyea, the trail led to the shorter but extremely steep Chilkoot Trail, where prospectors had to carry their ton of supplies up the "Golden Stairs" carved in the ice; they had to make as many as thirty-five round-trips to the summit with their supplies. The longer, less steep White Pass Trail left from Skagway and allowed packhorses. Both trails led about 40 miles into the interior; from there the gold rushers had to build their own rafts and boats for a 550-mile trip on lakes and rivers.

Consider this: Of about 100,000 who sailed out of ports in the Pacific Northwest, only about 30,000 actually reached the goldfields in the Yukon. Of those, only about half actually did some prospecting, and only 4,000 or so found some gold. A few hundred became rich, and just a handful managed to hold on to their wealth and bring it back to the United States.

Now you've got a bit of perspective before you are shown to your luxurious stateroom, where you'll effortlessly float your way into Alaska.

■ FLOATING NORTH IN LUXURY

We thought about the Chilkoot Trail and the White Pass as we sat on our private veranda, eating a room service breakfast and watching the green hills and the sky blue glaciers as we cruised north.

On our cruise, we sailed on the *Norwegian Sky,* a modern "freestyle" ship that was renamed by NCL as *Pride of Aloha* in 2004 and reassigned to sail, under the American flag, from Hawaii. NCL, though, had its largest Alaska deployment ever in 2004 with four ships in service—three from Seattle (*Norwegian Star, Norwegian Spirit,* and *Norwegian Dream*) and one from Vancouver (*Norwegian Sun*).

Our cruise departed Seattle's new cruise terminal on a glorious late-summer Sunday. The first day was spent "at sea"—more properly, cruising the Inside Passage to the east of Canada's Vancouver Island and up toward the panhandle of lower Alaska.

Alaska has a longer coastline than the combined lower forty-eight states. Unlike cruises in the Caribbean and Europe, we could see land on one or both sides of the ship at all times. In some places, the channel between the islands and the mainland was only a few hundred feet wide; the 853-foot-long, 106-foot-wide *Norwegian Sky* eased its way through like a recumbent skyscraper with a propeller.

Except for a handful of small towns and cities, you won't see many signs of civilization. You'll see many more whales, eagles, and the occasional bear or mountain goat than you will humans. The huge state of Alaska (615,230 square miles) has the lowest population density of any state, just 1.1 residents per square mile. The cruise industry, however, has been a steadily growing influence in the state. Juneau, the state capital and a regular port of call, received about 718,633 cruise-borne visitors in 2002, a number about equal to the state's entire population.

On Tuesday we made a slow passage up Tracy Arm to the face of Sawyer Glacier, which is among the most spectacular sights on the planet, especially when you arrive in luxury on a cruise ship. (Some of the *Norwegian Sky*'s cruises visit Glacier Bay instead; cruise ships are allotted only a limited number of slots to enter the narrow and environmentally fragile glacial bays.)

The steep-walled watery canyon is approximately 50 miles south of Juneau, branching eastward off Stephens Passage. The *Norwegian Sky* steamed slowly through the fog at the entrance to the deep fjord, then followed the twists and turns of the canyon for nearly two hours, steering around some large ice floes along the way. Finally the ship came to the end of the passageway and we were face to face with an electric-blue wall of ice.

The color of a glacier is almost always a surprise to visitors. The ice at the face has been compressed, and most of the air has been pressed out. What remains is highly crystallized; as light strikes the surface, all colors of the spectrum are absorbed except blue, which is reflected back.

The next day we arrived in Skagway, the principal objective of the gold rushers. There we changed modes of transportation for a few hours, traveling back in time on the incredible White Pass & Yukon Railroad (WP&YR).

The White Pass route was discovered in the early 1890s—before the Gold Rush—by a survey team mapping the 141st meridian, the boundary between the United States and Canada. The extremely difficult Chilkoot Pass had already been found, but it was much too rugged for pack animals or vehicles. The longer White Pass route was a series of steep climbs and perilous switchbacks that finally leveled out at Lake Bennett near the headwaters of the Yukon. (The pass, by the way, was named not for the glaciers and snow, but instead for the Canadian Minister of the Interior at the time, Sir Thomas White.)

When the Gold Rush began in 1897, tens of thousands of prospectors came to the panhandle to cross over to the Yukon. Those who arrived in Dyea hand-carried their ton of supplies up the icy steps at the face of the Chilkoot Pass; eventually a primitive cable tramway was used to carry supplies to the top of the pass. At Skagway many gold rushers attempted to climb the White Pass using pack animals—horses, mules, and dogs. Thousands of the animals died along the way, and many of their skeletons can still be seen at Dead Horse Gulch partway along the trail.

A White Pass & Yukon Railroad train climbs White Pass along the route of the gold rushers. *Photo by Corey Sandler*

In 1897 a former construction engineer on the Northern Pacific Railroad attempted to construct an improved toll road up the canyon. George Brackett's road eventually extended 12 miles before he ran out of money. The next year, though, a group of British financiers and a Canadian railway contractor met in the bar of a Skagway hotel, and by May 1898 work was under way on a narrow-gauge railroad.

Work on the northernmost railroad in the Western Hemisphere was extremely difficult. The first stage of the track was a climb from sea level in Skagway to 2,865 feet at the summit, with grades as steep as 3.9 percent. Workers had to hang from ropes to blast and hack their way through granite walls. At mile 16, Tunnel Mountain, crews had to cut through the side of a 1,000-foot-high cliff.

Heavy snow and temperatures as low as 60 degrees below zero hampered the work. Many workers were killed or injured; others quit with each new rumor of a gold strike. On February 20, 1899, in the dead of winter, crews reached the summit of White Pass; by July 6 they reached Lake Bennett. At the same time, another crew worked south from Whitehorse in the Yukon. The two crews met, and the road was completed on July 29, 1900, at Carcross.

Alas, the completion of the railroad came at nearly the exact moment the Gold Rush went bust. Instead of carrying prospectors over the White Pass from Skagway, the railroad found business carrying copper, silver, and lead ore from large corporate mines in the Yukon. The WP&YR expanded to include stern-wheeler freighters that carried ore south to processing plants. During World War II the railroad helped supply the U.S. Army as it built the Alaska Highway as part of the defense of the West Coast. Steam engines were still in use until 1954.

In 1982 market prices for metals plummeted, and the major mines in the Yukon shut down. The WP&YR was forced to close. But in 1988 the historic railroad benefited from a new gold rush: tourism by cruise ship. Today the tracks of the railroad extend down onto the piers where the *Norwegian Sky* and other ships tie up for the day.

The three-hour trip from Skagway up to the summit is quite simply one of the most extraordinary journeys in the world. Diesel engines pull vintage passenger cars up the grade to the international border at the Canadian Yukon and then return. The views at every turn are spectacular, and guides explain the history of each mile.

Every cruise ship that visits Skagway sells shore excursions that include the WP&YR. You can also book your own tickets directly from the railroad; be sure to take a trip that returns you to the pier in time to reboard your ship. For information call (800) 343-7373 or visit www.whitepassrailroad.com.

From Skagway we progressed to Juneau. One of the highlights here is the small but rich Alaska State Museum. Among its treasures are the remains of a prehistoric mammoth found at Tolovana; the tusks are 11 feet long with a diameter of 7 inches at the base. You'll also find exhibits on the Tlingit and Athabascan Indians. One of the most poignant exhibits is a pom-pom dipped in oil that was used in the cleanup of the spill from the *Exxon Valdez* in March 1989.

The museum dates from 1900, when it was originally in Sitka, the capital of Alaska at the time. Some of the exhibits about Alaska include the returned show-cases from the Louisiana Purchase Centennial Exposition in Saint Louis in 1904 and the 1905 Lewis and Clark Centennial Exposition in Portland.

After a day cruising back south, we arrived in Vancouver, British Columbia, one of the prettiest and most vibrant big cities in the world. Vancouver is heav-ily influenced by its trade with the Pacific Rim, which is evident in its lively Chinatown and international shopping district.

SEA CLOUD: A CLASSIC AT SEA

I've always wanted my own sailing yacht. Until my ship comes in, I'll make do with the memories of a week of luxury aboard the *Sea Cloud* in the Caribbean.

The largest private sailing yacht ever built, *Sea Cloud* now carries passengers and crew on cruises around the world. On our round-trip from Antigua, we sailed in the company of thirty-seven guests (a full load is sixty-nine guests) and sixty crew.

The seventy-year-old ship is exquisite above and below decks; it is a place of marble and teak and gold-plated fixtures. Some of the original staterooms are beyond compare on land or sea, and several of the original owners' cabins in-clude fireplaces. The service is impeccable, and the food is superb. Oh, and the prices. . . .

Rates for a week onboard *Sea Cloud* can be as much as $17,000 for a cabin for two. How can they justify a fare equal to a year's college tuition? In a word, overhead.

You can rent a huge suite on a luxury cruise liner, but you won't be sleeping on a classic vessel with a storied history, almost certainly the last of her kind. You won't be able to watch the exquisite ballet of twenty able-bodied seamen (and a few women) climbing the twenty-story masts to let loose the sails by hand. You won't sail into port and find guests onshore and aboard cruise ships lining up to take pictures of your vessel.

If you're lucky (and you can pay the price), you might have the key to Cabin 1, a seagoing palace complete with a fireplace and bathroom of Carrara marble, mahogany furniture, Louis Philippe chairs, and an antique French bed. But even the lesser cabins are rather grand, outfitted with marble and fine furniture.

The restaurant, created from the ship's original salon, is like a fine private club. And the food: If there were any complaints on our voyage, I didn't hear them. In any case, if you don't like the menu posted each afternoon, all you need do is leave word with the chef, and he'll fix almost anything you can request. Beer and fine wine are included. Lunch is often served beneath a canopy on the fantail.

There's no television, no movie theater, no stage show, no casino, and no pool. There are also no kids, no ship's photographer intruding on your privacy, no art auctions, and no rah-rah cruise staff. Guests sail along in a semiprivate fraternity of privilege.

We were treated to a slide show of Tall Ships from the personal collection of the captain, a lecture about the history of the ship from the accommodating but most discreet cruise director, and a private performance by a twenty-piece steel band while we enjoyed a nighttime barbecue off Grenada. But our primary entertainment was the ship herself, a most elegant way to travel.

■ A CLASSIC SHIP

Sea Cloud stretches a bit more than a football field (360 feet) from stern to the end of the bowsprit, a little less than half the length of a typical cruise ship. About half the length of the ship is accessible to guests; the rest is given over to crew work areas. There are twelve of the original cabins on the main deck and fourteen more on the promenade deck. When the ship was refurbished for use as a passenger ship, eight simpler but still elegant cabins were added to the upper captain's deck.

Sea Cloud is classified as a bark or barkentine, and its sails are mostly near-square or rectangular. In the right conditions, the crew can hoist, by hand and winch, thirty sails from her four masts, about 32,000 square feet of canvas. The crew has to unravel a maze of ropes and operate a shipyard's worth of pulleys; guests can sit and watch, following along on a rigging chart.

At the very front of the ship is the bowsprit, extending nearly horizontally out over the water; here the captain can order an inner, outer, and flying jib. The first vertical mast is the foremast; the uppermost of five large sails here is the fore royal, followed by the fore topgallant. The main mast is the tallest of the uprights and holds six large sails, from the skysail (the origin of the term skyscraper) to the main royal and down to the mainsail. The third mast is the

The *Sea Cloud* at anchor off the little-visited Caribbean island of Carriacou. *Photo by Corey Sandler*

Cabin 1, an original stateroom on the *Sea Cloud*. Photo by Corey Sandler

mizzenmast, which holds aloft four nearly rectangular sails plus the triangular mizzen course or crossjack. Near the stern is the spanker topmast, with two sails that together form a triangle. By night the sails are lit from below, like a ghostly galleon.

Even with all her masts and canvas, *Sea Cloud* cannot sail very close into the wind like a modern sailboat; the wind has to be behind the sails or no more than 90 degrees across the direction of forward motion. When the wind does not cooperate, the ship's four diesel engines can move her through the water at a respectable 12 knots.

The ship is very stable in most conditions, and under sail the ship does not roll much because of the pressure of the sails against the ship. The sails do keep the ship at a near-constant heel of a few degrees; sometimes you might wonder if your downwind leg will become shorter over time. Sleeping under sail is also a bit unusual; rolling over against the direction of the heel can take a bit of extra effort.

Sea Cloud was built in 1931 for cereal food heiress Marjorie Merriweather Post by her husband, Wall Street broker Edward F. Hutton. Post, famous for her parties and social events, turned the ship into a gathering place for royalty, heads of state, and society hobnobbers. The ship was built during the Depression; the Post cereal empire was privately owned and not much affected by the stock market crash. *Sea Cloud* was constructed, at a cost of just over $1 million, by the Krupp shipyard in Germany, later to become the builder of much of the Nazi fleet. From the deck down, the steel-hulled *Sea Cloud* is designed almost as though she were a submarine, with ten hermetically sealed watertight compartments.

Marjorie Post and E. F. Hutton lived aboard for nearly four years, sailing in the Caribbean and Europe. When they divorced in 1935, Marjorie took the ship as part of the settlement, renaming her *Hussar V.* In the prewar years, the ship served as a floating diplomatic residence in the Soviet Union; during that time Marjorie Post bought millions of dollars worth of Russian art, including Fabergé eggs. Many of the eggs are now on display at the Hillwood Museum in Washington, one of her homes.

During World War II, the ship was leased to the U.S. Coast Guard for a nominal $1.00 per year. Her rigging was stripped down and she was equipped with guns, cannons, and depth charge launchers. Sailing as the *IX-99*, her primary assignment was as a weather observation ship (during the D-Day invasion in June

1944, she was stationed off the coast of Normandy to broadcast weather reports). She was, though, involved in several submarine spottings.

After the war the ship came into the hands of Dominican dictator Rafael Trujillo and was renamed *Angelita*. Son Rafael Trujillo Jr. took the ship to Los Angeles as a party boat while he was in school from 1954 to 1958; his crew of fifty-three included a nine-piece mambo band. During that time the original Krupp engines were replaced with motors from Dominican Republic gunboats.

In 1961 Trujillo Sr. was assassinated; his son took over for four months, just enough time to gather much of the national treasure and load it, along with the body of his father, aboard *Angelita* and attempt to flee to Cannes in France. The ship was seized and much of the treasure returned. Trujillo Jr. went into exile, a wealthy socialite. He died in 1969 from injuries suffered in an automobile accident.

The ship was taken to Panama, where she lay at anchor for eight years, rotting and filling with water while owners sought a new buyer. In 1975 Hugh Hefner was said to have offered the asking price of $5 million to buy the ship for use as a floating Playboy club, but the offer was refused. Two years later, Ross Perot reportedly tried to buy the ship and give it to the U.S. Navy while he retained tax advantages and visitation rights, but the Navy decided it didn't need the ship.

In 1978 a group of German businessmen and shipowners decided to resurrect *Sea Cloud*. They managed to bring the ship across the Atlantic to Germany, sailing her up the Elbe River; in 1979 she arrived in Kiel, where she had originally been built. Her steel hull was still in good condition, as were the original owners' cabins; much of the remainder of the ship had to be rebuilt. The original cabins have the same floor plan and are furnished with antiques, but not all are from the original ship. (Cabin 2 boasts a pair of Chippendale chairs valued at $15,000 each.)

In 1980 *Sea Cloud* returned to the seas but wasn't a success until she was used for an episode of the German equivalent of *The Love Boat* in 1988. The ship is often chartered for private groups or resold by various travel agencies and charter companies. At the busiest times of the year, you can expect to be asked to pay full rate. At other times, though, you could see discounts and special offers that reduce the fare by as much as 50 percent. Because of all of the wood paneling and furnishings aboard, *Sea Cloud* might have only a few more years at sea before she's no longer able to operate under exemptions from Safety of Life at Sea (SOLAS) regulations.

In 2001 the fleet doubled with the addition of *Sea Cloud II*, built in the style of her famous cousin. The new ship is slightly larger and includes some more modern features and amenities. She will follow a similar schedule, sailing in the Caribbean in winter and the Mediterranean in summer.

■ SAILING IN STYLE

In port in Antigua, we were tied up alongside the superluxury cruise ship *Crystal Harmony*. Many of the 900 passengers onboard lined the rails as she left port at sunset; most were admiring the *Sea Cloud* instead of the bright orange sun descending into the Caribbean Sea.

The dining room belowdecks of the *Sea Cloud*. *Photo by Corey Sandler*

Captain Richard Shannon, one of several masters of the vessel, was in charge; Shannon is among the world's most experienced Tall Ship skippers and is a former captain of the Coast Guard sailing vessel *Eagle*. On the *Sea Cloud* he commanded a United Nations of a crew: Swiss, Russian, and Ukrainian officers and mostly German and Filipino deckhands and stewards.

The passengers, too, were from around the world. They were mostly discreet, although there was a bit of subtle inquiry aimed at determining how the other guests could afford a voyage on this ship.

We left Antigua in a dead calm, and the second day was also an uncharacteristically gray and calm Caribbean morning. The crew hoisted the sails and we moved along slowly until the bridge received a distress call off the island of Dominica. The sails were dropped quickly, and we motored to the aid of a 30-foot motorboat taking on water. Arriving at the same time as a vessel from the local coast guard, we stood by ready to lend a hand. The owner was rescued, and then we watched as the motorboat dropped deeper and deeper into the water and then upended and sank.

Among the highlights of the cruise was a visit to the Îles des Saintes, a group of seven very French islands in a volcanic archipelago just south of Guadeloupe. The islands are a *Département d'Outre Mer* (an Overseas Department), and the inhabitants are French citizens.

We anchored off Terre de Haut and tendered into the small village of Bourg. From there we hiked to a hilltop to visit Fort Napoleon, which was built to protect French interests. At the fort, which offers views of Guadeloupe, Marie-

Galante, and Dominica, you can take in exhibits that document the single moment of military history in the area: the Battle of the Saintes, which was fought between thirty-six British and thirty-three French ships on April 12, 1782. The French ships were on their way to join Spanish troops in an invasion of Jamaica; the British victory that day prevented the invasion and essentially ended French expansion in the Caribbean.

Another port of call was Carriacou, a modest outpost of Grenada. Ship's tenders delivered us to Sandy Island National Park, a tiny coral isle that's home to many varieties of fish.

In Bequia and Grenada we anchored near the *Club Med II,* an ultramodern cruise ship whose five skyscraping aluminum masts have computer-controlled sails reefed around them. The entire sailing rig can be put into place with the push of a button. Unlike on the *Sea Cloud,* though, the masts seemed out of place, like a mistake in the shipyard. One of the *Sea Cloud* guests asked one of our crew about *Club Med II*'s sailing abilities. "The sails don't slow her down much," he responded dismissively.

CROSSING THE POND ON HOLLAND AMERICA'S *MAASDAM*

We decided to pop over to London to catch a musical in the West End. The trip east across the Atlantic began with a hectic trek through steamy Boston to a hellacious scene at Logan Airport: a blocklong line of passengers waiting to drag their bags to the check-in counter of Virgin Atlantic.

The 747 jumbo jet, crammed with more than 500 passengers, took off late, of course. We spent the night crammed into narrow seats in the economy section, sandwiched between a very large woman (with four bags of oddly configured stuff at her feet) and several caterwauling babies.

Tossing and turning in our seats, we desperately tried to snatch a few moments of sleep between interruptions: a meal served at 10:00 P.M. on tiny plastic dishes perched on the uncertain support of a tray table; a forgettable movie on a minuscule screen; and the sales pitches for useless trinkets from the onboard duty-free store.

The good news was that we were moving across the Atlantic at about 500 miles per hour. Mercifully, we landed at London's Gatwick Airport at the reasonable hour of 8:00 A.M., except that it was 3:00 A.M. to us and we had tossed and turned in our clothes all night.

After dragging our bags through customs, we squeezed onto a packed train from Gatwick to downtown London. It was two more hours before we were able to make it to our London hotel, where—miracle of miracles—we were able to check in and go to our room (although most of the others in line were told they would have to wait for the arrival of the cleaning staff). The room itself was typical for a European city: very small and relatively expensive, about $200 per night for a view of a back alley in Kensington.

We fortified ourselves with coffee, tea, chocolate, and other forms of caffeine to fight off the effects of the sleepless night and the sudden five-hour change in time zones. Exhausted and jittery, we managed to stay awake through *Miss Saigon* in the West End and stroll the streets of one of our favorite cities.

The bottom line: An overnight flight to Europe is a very efficient way to get from Point A to Point B. It is, in general, not all that pleasant in between.

■ COMING HOME

Two days later, we began our trip home. We floated westward, happily ensconced in an attractive stateroom—not huge, but larger than our room in London—with a picture window looking out on the ocean. We relaxed as we were waited on by a cabin attendant, room service, and the dining room staff.

As you may have guessed, we were not on a 747 this time. Instead, we crossed the Atlantic aboard the elegant *Maasdam* of the Holland America Line, on a weeklong trip at 20 knots that would deposit us back in Boston.

Our voyage was a repositioning cruise, a special trip to move a cruise ship from one part of the world to another. The *Maasdam* had traveled through Europe and the Baltic in the summer and was being dispatched to the East Coast of the United States for a series of trips through New England to the Maritime Provinces of Canada. Later in the fall, she would move south from Boston to Florida for winter cruises in the Caribbean.

Repositioning itineraries can offer some of the best bargains in cruising because of the extended periods at sea and unusual ports; however, they're not everyone's cup of tea. A transatlantic cruise is not one I would recommend for first-timers, and certainly not for someone who is apprehensive about the prospect of being cooped up on a ship for a week.

The ship departed from Harwich, about 70 miles east of London. Harwich (pronounced *HAR-itch*) is a busy commercial port on the English Channel and is home to cruise ships, freighters from around the world, and passenger and car ferries to the Hook of Holland and other destinations in Europe. The modern cruise terminal is about 50 yards from the train station, about an hour's ride from London's Liverpool Street Station.

For the middle five days of the trip we saw nothing but ocean—no ships, no planes, no shoreline. We carried our civilization with us, like moon explorers. However, no astronaut has ever lived in the lap of luxury as we did.

■ ELEGANCE AFLOAT

Holland America Line (HAL) is a notch above the middle of the market. It offers much of the refinement and a bit of the service of the luxury lines at a price closer to that of the economy brands. The company was purchased by Carnival Cruise Lines in 1989 but has maintained its own identity and class.

The *Maasdam* is an elegant ship, one of four nearly identical sister ships in the HAL fleet, including the *Veendam,* about which I wrote earlier in this chapter. It's a particularly workable design, with lots of attractive public space, including a stunning show room and handsome dining room. Although hardly a tiny ship, at 720 feet long and 55,451 tons, within it feels much larger.

As I've noted in the cruise diary about the *Veendam*, one of the hallmarks of Holland America is the onboard collection of art that's spread throughout the ships. At most every turn, you're greeted by paintings, sculptures, and antiques, most with a maritime link or a connection to great Dutch explorations. A large electronic map on the upper promenade charts the ship's progress and can be programmed to display famous maritime explorations, including those of Columbus, Captain Cook, and others.

One of the prettiest public rooms is Crows Nest, up high over the bow with views ahead, to port and starboard, and toward the stern over the Sports Deck.

On this cruise without any port calls, there was something going on almost everywhere at most times of the day. In fact, we found it hard to find a place that would remain private and quiet for more than a few hours before another activity or group began. Even the attractive library on the upper promenade deck, with a wall of windows behind the reading desks, was busy much of the day.

The *Maasdam* is among the few modern ships with a covered promenade that makes a complete circuit of the ship, four laps to the mile. Another nice touch, common to many of the Holland America ships, is a movable dome over the pool deck. In warm and dry weather, the dome is retracted to leave the pool area open to the sky but still protected from winds; in cool or wet weather, the dome remakes the deck into a large indoor pool and patio area. On our crossing of the Atlantic, we greatly appreciated both the covered promenade and the dome.

▓ CROSSING THE POND

We pulled out of Harwich on a Sunday, entering the English Channel in the company of large freighters and fishing vessels. Monday morning we continued through the channel with the south of England to starboard and France to port. We sailed past Penzance, the Scilly Islands, and the distant green shores of Ireland. And then we were out in the Atlantic.

It would be the following Friday before we saw another sign of human life, which came in the form of a huge oil rig anchored in the cold waters a few hundred miles off the coast of Labrador. And it would be Saturday before we saw distant land.

The summer of 1999 was a particularly active season for hurricanes. As we left port on Sunday we were aware of the progress of Hurricanes Cindy and Dennis, both of which were churning off the East Coast of the United States. But our course on the Great Circle Route, an arc to the northwest to above the 50th parallel, was well north of the storms—or so we thought.

In this modern age of satellites, weather radar, and in-room CNN, it's all but impossible for a ship to be caught unawares by a storm. Two days into our week-long journey, the captain—and most everyone else on the *Maasdam*—knew that Cindy had pulled away from the coast and was moving northward toward Iceland. In other words, it was due to cross our path.

On Wednesday, the master of the ship changed our course, heading due south off the Great Circle Route to drop below the storm. And so we did, but not without experiencing a few days of fierce weather in the North Atlantic: gale winds of up to 46 knots and seas to 27 feet. That said, we found the *Maasdam* to be extraordinarily stable in very rough seas; the modern stabilizers countered much of the rolling motion, leaving just a bit of end-to-end pitching. Up top, the water in the swimming pool was almost wild enough for a surfing competition; the crew finally had to drain the pool for safety. The mostly experienced passengers handled the weather pretty well, although we noted a few victims of seasickness, including our waiter in the dining room.

By Friday the storm was gone, and we proceeded down the coast of Labrador and Newfoundland, passing within 200 nautical miles of the location of the resting place of the *Titanic,* which is a particularly empty stretch of ocean, especially at night.

■ ENTERTAINMENT AFLOAT

The 800 or so guests (out of a possible capacity of about 1,200) represented a more sophisticated than usual group of travelers, aboard for the romance of it all and not for the ports of call.

The card rooms and libraries were packed for most of the trip. By night, the lounges were filled with an unusually diverse crew of entertainers, including a big band, two comedians, an instrumentalist, a pair of tap dancers forty years too late for the Borscht Belt, a troupe of dancers and singers, and the *Maasdam*'s capable house band.

A major attraction for some was the special presence of the Harry James Orchestra, a big-band troupe that carries on the name and arrangements of the famous bandleader; James died in 1983, but the band was continued by a former member of the group, Fred Radke. The orchestra performed a half dozen times on the trip.

Also onboard was comedian Marty Brill, a veteran performer and writer. He tailored his witty shows to the mellow crowd aboard the *Maasdam;* some will remember him for the sharper edge he displayed as a cohort of Lenny Bruce. In fact, Brill portrayed Bruce on Broadway in a one-man show.

The dance troupe put on enthusiastic and capable revues, right up the middle of the road. The dancing was pretty good, especially on the small (and sometimes pitching) stage. The singing was, well, enthusiastic; a Broadway medley was the best offering. Another night we saw an uninspired salute to great performers, most of whom were dead long before the young dancers first strapped on their shoes, plus soulless recountings of Frank Sinatra, the Supremes, Sammy Davis Jr., and Elvis Presley.

And then there was the food, which was somewhat mystifying: The presentation was very good, but the preparation was disappointing. In other words, the food looked great but tasted rather ordinary. It was a commentary we heard at most every turn at dinnertime.

We found the ship's photographers a bit too much in evidence at boarding, formal dinners, and many other shipboard activities. My wife and I are not at all keen on being interrupted at dinner by a member of the cruise director's staff made up as a pirate, or as a Dutch milkmaid, each accompanied by a cameraman. But they kept coming. If you're not comfortable shooing the photographer away, do remember that you don't have to buy any photos they take.

All in all, we greatly enjoyed the pure sailing experience of a transatlantic crossing on the *Maasdam*.

PACIFIC TO ATLANTIC IN HIGH STYLE: THE *RADISSON DIAMOND* THROUGH THE PANAMA CANAL

We made a slow and deliberate passage through the Panama Canal aboard the *Radisson Diamond*, a floating island of high-tech luxury passing through what was once one of the most inhospitable places on earth. We sat on the private veranda of our stateroom, sipping cool drinks and watching the sheer rock of the Gaillard Cut and the dense jungle go by. As we passed through the locks, the walls were just inches away from the railing of our balcony, and we were able to reach out and touch the concrete, bridging the old and new worlds with our fingers.

▓ A SHIP LIKE NO OTHER

The *Radisson Diamond* is one of a kind, the largest multihull cruise ship afloat; there are a handful of small catamaran ferries and cruise ships, but no others in her class of size or luxury. She has a capacity of 20,295 tons but carries no more than 320 passengers; other ships of her size carry as many as 800 guests.

You can think of the *Radisson Diamond* as a luxury hotel mounted atop a pair of submarines. Unlike high-speed catamarans that have more than one hull but

The unusual *Radisson Diamond* sits atop a pair of submarine-like hulls. *Courtesy Radisson Seven Seas Cruises*

very shallow drafts, the unusual *Radisson Diamond* floats on "tubes" that extend about 23 feet below the surface of the water; each contains a separate engine room.

The ship was intended as a great breakthrough in design, and on some counts it has been a success. The two hulls and their deep draft give the ship somewhat more stability than other cruise ships. The *Radisson Diamond* also presents an unusual profile and a startling head-on appearance: There's a huge open tunnel down the center of the ship. She attracts attention on the high seas and in every port. There are also some spectacular interior spaces, including a two-story lounge that has a wall of windows at the bow (the appropriately named Windows Lounge) and an open observation deck at the top that hangs over the bridge.

The ship is made up of three floors of cabins (all with outside views, and two levels with private verandas) plus an elegant dining room, an intimate lounge, and a pool deck. The design puts most of the public rooms and the sparkling atrium down the central spine of the ship, with cabins to the outside. All of this sits atop a tunnel approximately 60 feet wide and 30 feet tall that runs more than 400 feet down the full length of the ship.

The ship is relatively short, at 420 feet, but is a full 103 feet wide, a bargelike shape that just barely squeezes through the Panama Canal. Her deep draft means she must anchor offshore in many ports, sometimes a bit farther out than larger, more conventional craft.

The ship includes four stabilizers, one each at the bow and stern of each tube. Unlike every other cruise ship afloat, the stabilizers move inward from the tubes, into the tunnel between them. You can feel the ship start to roll and then correct itself in the other direction. The short swings can take a few hours to get used to, but after a while the voyage will likely be a bit more comfortable for travelers who are concerned about seasickness. The design works well at top speed but not so well at slower speeds.

The design, however, proved to be a not particularly efficient one, at least in terms of fuel usage and speed. The underwater body and decidedly nonaerodynamic shape of the front of the ship (it's hard to call it a "bow" since it is more like a ski slope than a classic narrow cake wedge) result in a top cruising speed of just 14 knots and a monumental fuel bill, as much as twice that of a more conventionally shaped vessel. The contour of the tubes results in a short, weak side wake, a wall of water the *Radisson Diamond* must plow through. And the squat design of the ship makes it somewhat susceptible to twisting in winds or seas that move across her amidships.

A single control room on Deck 6 oversees the operation of two separate engine rooms in the underwater pontoons of the ship. Down in the submarine tubes are four engines, two on each side; engineers must scurry down five flights of stairs to one or the other tube. Up and over is a trip of ten flights; there is no connection between the pontoons below the waterline.

One of the sustaining memories of our trip came when the tender boat returning us from a visit to shore made a transit down the length of the tunnel between the hulls. The white walls of the pontoons and the "roof" of the tunnel contrasted with a gorgeous iridescent Caribbean sea; at one end of the tunnel was the green jungle of San Andrés Island and at the other end the bright tropical sun.

TRAVELING IN STYLE

Like every other cruise ship, the *Radisson Diamond* has a dining room and lots of food; passenger cabins with a place to sleep and a bathroom; and show rooms, bars, and lounges. But at every turn, the *Radisson Diamond* delivers it all in great style.

The Grand Dining Room is one of the most elegant rooms at sea—or on land, for that matter. The two-floor-high glass wall at the stern of the ship offers spectacular views all through the day. There are also more than enough tables for two, a relative rarity on many cruise lines. Because of the stability of the ship, and also because this is a "customer is king" operation, the tables can be moved around the dining room and rearranged to create seating for groups large or small.

There is also an open seating policy in the dining room, with guests free to arrive at any time during serving hours. The dining room staff features female servers from Europe, not all that common on cruise ships.

That's the good news about the servers. The bad news, for some cruise veterans, is that you won't have the comfort of an assigned wait staff who will learn your favorites and become your short-term best friends aboard ship. But some other good news is that the ratio of guests to staff is low and the dedication to service so high that the entire crew seems devoted to your needs. We found a section of the dining room we liked and a pair of waitresses we enjoyed; by three days into the trip, the maître d' knew our preferences.

One other nice point: Tips are included in the cruise fare on Radisson ships. This means that members of the staff are paid a decent wage and are not reliant on gratuities from guests. Put another way, you do not feel that the waitresses, the maître d', the wine steward, and the cabin attendant are calculating the size of their tip each time they greet you or offer a service.

Of course, nothing is free; the cost of higher wages is reflected in stateroom charges. But for my money, I would just as soon see all cruise lines go this route. There certainly was no lack of effort, courtesy, or attention to detail on the tipless *Radisson Diamond*. In fact, the service was as good as or better than any we have received on a cruise ship.

ENTERTAINMENT ABOARD: LESS IS MORE

There are no lavish production shows, no parade of waiters with flaming baked Alaska (thank goodness), and no painful guest talent shows or costume balls onboard (even more thanks).

Instead, the *Radisson Diamond* presents a very laid-back atmosphere with a less-is-more philosophy. On our cruise there was a talented piano and violin duo who gave a few recitals and performed at dinner. The cruise director, an amiable Briton who had a respectable background in theater and cabaret, sang show tunes and pop songs. Each afternoon, the staff conducted an informal trivia quiz in the lounge during tea time.

There is a short jogging and walking track on the topmost deck, along with a golf driving net. At the stern, the *Radisson Diamond* has a small marina that can be lowered into the sea to allow guests to use personal watercraft and sailboats; the marina is mostly used in Europe and was not available on our particular cruise.

The real entertainment, however, was a lovely ship with superb service and luxurious accommodations and food. This is a cruise for the self-sufficient.

■ AND NOW FOR SOMETHING COMPLETELY DIFFERENT

Lest you fear that everything aboard the *Radisson Diamond* is prim and proper, there is also "An Evening at Don Vito's," an alternative dining experience that is not to be missed. Most evenings, the casual grill on the tenth deck is transformed into a small Italian bistro. Guests are offered an eclectic evening that's a cross between a fine Italian restaurant (the food would win raves anywhere on land) and a rollicking burlesque.

The evening starts out with a talented singer and musician performing Italian songs. Sometime around the second appetizer, the waiters begin to join in on the songs, and by the salad course there's a full chorus of wisecracking, singing, and dancing clowns bringing you your dinner. On our visit, a talented singer suddenly took the stage; a young Filipino waitress who had quietly been pouring wine took the microphone and contributed a lovely song in phonetic Italian.

By the end of the night, somewhat abetted by the free-flowing wine, one matron was in a near-swoon on the dance floor with the maître d', Guiseppe, and another took over from the singer for the final chorus.

There are only about fifty seats in the restaurant, enough room on a typical cruise for every passenger to visit once. After our first visit we immediately staked out a place on the waiting list for a second pass; we happily returned to Don Vito's for the final night of our cruise.

■ A SPARKLING ITINERARY

The *Radisson Diamond* makes a grand circuit each year from the Pacific to the Caribbean and on to Europe for the summer. The ship is also regularly chartered to major corporations for special events and "incentive" rewards.

We flew to San José, Costa Rica, to meet up with the *Radisson Diamond* for a trip through the Panama Canal that would end in Fort Lauderdale, Florida. Most of the guests on our cruise began their adventure with a day trip to a Costa Rican rain forest and animal preserve; we caught up with the group on the second day for a visit to the spectacular Poás volcano. From there we traveled the mountainous countryside to a private plantation for a peasant-style lunch. Late in the day we were delivered to Puntarenas, a port on an inlet of the Pacific Ocean.

Our first full day was spent cruising south down the untouched jungle coast of Costa Rica and northern Panama. We were accompanied in the morning by several schools of dolphins; they happily played in the ship's broad wake, launching themselves a few feet into the air.

On the second day, we arrived just before dawn at Panama City. As the sun came up we found ourselves threading our way through a few dozen freighters waiting their turn to enter the Panama Canal. At our appointed time, we passed beneath the Bridge of the Americas and entered the canal.

The construction of the Panama Canal stretched over more than thirty years, beginning in 1880 with the tragic French effort and finishing in 1914 under the sheer bravado of Teddy Roosevelt, the military prowess of George Goethals, and the not-insignificant solution to the deadly malaria and yellow fever plagues by Dr. William Gorgas.

The ten-hour passage through the six locks of the canal (three up and three down) was a fascinating voyage along the border where one of mankind's greatest feats of engineering meets nature's wildest challenges. We passed through the spectacular Gaillard Cut, where thousands of men labored for decades to cut a passage; from there we moved into Gatun Lake, a body of water created by a huge earthen dam in the jungle.

As night fell, we exited the canal and entered the Caribbean Ocean, passing through another floating waiting line of freighters heading for the Pacific.

Our first stop in the Caribbean was at San Andrés Island, a somewhat obscure possession of Colombia. From there we moved on to Grand Cayman Island and Cozumel, Mexico. On the last full day of the ten-day cruise, we moved along the mountainous northern coast of Cuba, en route to disembarkation in Fort Lauderdale, Florida.

Cuba is a Holy Grail for cruise lines. Nearly every company has plans already on the shelf for trips to the large, culturally rich, and exotic island that has been off-limits to most Americans for nearly forty years. Lying just 90 miles south of Miami, Cuba will likely one day be a popular destination for ships sailing out of Florida and the Gulf of Mexico.

■ *DIAMOND* ELEGANCE

Our cabin was decorated with an arrangement of exotic live flowers, an echo of the decorations throughout the ship. The bathroom was equipped with extra-plush towels and bathrobes. A refrigerator in the room was kept filled with soda, mixers, and bottled water.

When we boarded the ship, there was a bottle of French champagne on ice set up on our table. The cabin was also stocked with a personal bar set up with more liquor than I could personally consume over the course of a ten-day voyage; if you did manage to go through the bar, additional supplies were available for purchase.

Rooms are equipped with a video player, and the ship's library has a decent collection of classic and current movies for loan.

The cabin stewardess discreetly noted our schedule each day and made at least three visits to make the beds, remake them, and turn them down.

A small pleasure: Soda and juice flows freely and without charge at any of the bars and from wandering staff members. When you return from a shore excursion in a tropical port, a uniformed waitress stands just inside the reception area with a tray of chilled champagne or juice. At dinner, the steward pours from complimentary offerings of red or white wine selected to complement the evening's fare; there is also an extensive wine cellar for those who insist on paying extra.

And then there's the food. Nearly every cruise ship does a good job of feeding guests, but the offerings sometimes emphasize quantity over quality. On the *Radisson Diamond,* however, every meal was on the level of a four-star restaurant. The plates (Villeroy and Boch china, actually) were laid out like works of art. Each afternoon, the executive chef would appear on stateroom television to describe in luscious detail the menu for dinner and to demonstrate the creation of a sauce or stock.

Menus do not repeat over the course of a cruise. Guests are discreetly encouraged to make reasonable special requests; the chef will attempt to fulfill these requests for special dishes or preparation styles. I particularly enjoyed a gazpacho one evening; I put in a word of praise to the maître d', and the next night I was offered a second chance at the soup, freshly concocted just for me in the galley.

After dinner, if you somehow find the strength to resist dessert and order "nothing," your waitress may appear with a dinner plate decorated with "Nothing"—spelled out in chocolate icing and glaze. More than a few guests end up licking the plate in utter defeat.

Every cruise ship offers a lunchtime buffet on the upper deck, but on the *Radisson Diamond* it was more of a catered picnic than a casino smorgasbord. The silver serving dishes held rich goulash or lamb chops; an outside barbecue offered grilled fish, chicken, or beef; a cheese cart held hundreds of dollars worth of sinful international offerings. And waiters and waitresses stood by to carry your plate from station to station. Our favorite lunch included shrimp, crab legs, cold lobster, and an assortment of seafood salads. On a more ordinary cruise ship, a "gala" buffet might have featured just one of these premium dishes.

Although on most ships I spend little time in the cabin, preferring to watch the sea from the deck or from a library or lounge, when your cabin has its own balcony, everything is different. The *Radisson Diamond's* verandas are completely private, sheltered from one another and from the wind. When we were out to sea, the large sliding door to the outside stood open all day. We happily began every morning of our trip with breakfast on the veranda, delivered with clockwork precision and served on a linen tablecloth. Each night before retiring, we toasted a day of adventure or one of blissful indolence.

Although we preferred the elegance of the Grand Dining Room, guests can also ask room service to deliver a meal ordered from the evening menu; dishes are brought course by course to your veranda or sitting room.

We toured behind the scenes with Executive Chef Peter Spörndli, who met us in the galley with a chilled bottle of wine. The bright and open workspace is blessed with an unusual feature for cruise ships: a picture window. The dining room on the *Radisson Diamond* sits high on the eighth deck; most cruise ships set their dining rooms down low. Of course, on the *Radisson Diamond,* there is no space below the seventh deck for a wide open room.

The ship's larders were like an international gourmet shop: asparagus from Guatemala, tomatoes from Costa Rica, beef from the United States, and seafood from around the world. Shelves held fresh spices, including a case of horseradish roots. We watched as a sous-chef decorated the plates for one of the night's appetizers: exquisite cold mussels from New Zealand, served with a seasoned mayonnaise concocted fresh onboard.

Another nicety for experienced cruise travelers is the low-key shipboard commerce. On many cruises, there is a drumbeat of sales pitches for shore excursions, bingo games, "sales" at the boutique, come-ons from the ship's photographers, auctions of "fine art," and sprawling, beeping, and flashing casinos. For many cruise companies, a large portion of their profits come from onboard marketing and bar tabs.

Each day the ship's golf pro offered lessons in the net on the small sports deck above the bridge; husband-and-wife bridge experts delivered talks on arcane strategies and conducted tournaments, and a visiting professor offered several lectures on history and economics. We found it quite possible to enjoy our cruise in peaceful obliviousness to all the shipboard sideshows. They are still there, but we didn't have to go out of our way to avoid them.

In fact, that was the way we looked at our entire cruise: We let the *Radisson Diamond* transport us on the path between the seas while we laid back in the lap of luxury.

FROM HAWAII TO AN ALMOST UNTOUCHED SOUTH PACIFIC ISLAND

Norwegian Cruise Line has found a way to sail between ports in Hawaii and deal with the cabotage requirements of the Jones Act. In 1998 NCL began sailing round-trips from Honolulu with an extended five-day side trip to Fanning Island in the tiny Republic of Kiribati near the equator.

We sailed that itinerary on the *Norwegian Dynasty* in late fall 1998; that ship has since left the fleet. In 2005 NCL will send *Norwegian Wind* on ten- and eleven-day cruises from Honolulu for a similar itinerary.

■ CRUISING BACK IN TIME

On our cruise on the *Norwegian Dynasty*, we left Honolulu and sailed to Kailua on the Kona Coast on the Big Island of Hawaii. Kona, which means "leeward" or sheltered side, lives up to its name. This is the calm, sunny side of the island, home to some relatively isolated luxury resorts, golf courses, and tons of gift shops.

Then we headed south from Kona toward the Republic of Kiribati, a two-and-a-half-day, full-steam cruise toward the equator and a place back in time. We approached Fanning Island (Tabuaeran to the locals) just after breakfast and were greeted by a native in a wooden sailboat who paralleled us the last few miles to the entrance to the inner harbor.

Fanning is a broken Cheerio of an atoll, the land only a few hundred feet wide around an inner lagoon that is actually the collapsed cone of an ancient volcano. Beaches on the ocean are somewhere between tricky and dangerous. English Harbor, the interior of the atoll, is deep enough for a major ship but not wide

What's a Knot?

One knot is equal to one nautical mile per hour; a nautical mile is about 1.15 land-based miles. Here's a conversion chart:

15 knots	=	17.25 mph
16 knots	=	18.4 mph
17 knots	=	19.55 mph
18 knots	=	20.7 mph
19 knots	=	21.85 mph
20 knots	=	23 mph
21 knots	=	24.15 mph
22 knots	=	25.3 mph
23 knots	=	26.45 mph
24 knots	=	27.6 mph
25 knots	=	28.75 mph
30 knots	=	34.5 mph

enough for a cruise ship to enter and turn around comfortably, and the ocean currents and soft sand bottom make it impossible to set an anchor; there are believed to be wrecks of World War II ships and planes on the bottom. Our ship was forced to cruise slowly back and forth while passengers visited the island on tenders that surfed through the waves into the harbor.

Kiribati (pronounced *KUR-a-bass*) is made up of the Gilbert, Line, and Phoenix Islands. With a population of 75,000, the thirty-three islands comprise 268 square miles of land spread over 5 million square miles of ocean. Kiribati won its independence from Great Britain in 1979. The capital is Tarawa, site of some of the bloodiest battles of World War II.

Fanning Island is located 3 degrees, or 273 miles, north of the equator. A sister island, 50 miles away, is Christmas Island, which from 1954 to 1965 served as a base for American, British, and French atomic testing on more distant atolls.

Fanning Island was discovered in 1798 by Edmund Fanning, the American captain of the ship *Betsy*. A number of whaling ships visited the uninhabited island in succeeding years. Beginning in 1848, some 500 natives of other islands in the chain were moved to Fanning to operate a coconut oil plantation for a British company. A bit later in the century, the island was extensively mined for guano, and some 20,000 tons of the natural phosphate fertilizer were shipped to Honolulu.

In 1902 one of the first transoceanic telephone cables was brought ashore at Fanning. The cable stretched from near Vancouver, British Columbia, to New Zealand. During World War II, a small Japanese landing party damaged the cable station on Fanning. In another footnote to history, Fanning was one of Amelia Earhart's way points on her final voyage.

Modest plantation operations continued until midway through the twentieth century. Most of the approximately 1,600 residents of Fanning are descendants of the plantation workers who were abandoned when the company closed operations and pulled out.

■ FIRST CONTACT

NCL paid for the construction of a small pier built—like most everything else on Fanning Island—from coconut trees. Our arriving tenders were met by the town council and a band of about fifty dancers in grass skirts, along with musicians who performed continuously for the seven hours we were ashore.

We found a nearly untouched tropical paradise, where the I-Kiribati, as they call themselves, live a subsistence life of grabbing bonefish and the occasional lobster from the lagoon and harvesting taro, coconuts, and a few other crops. The local livestock includes foot-wide land crabs that make their homes in large holes in and among the coconut trees.

The island is almost untouched by modern influences, without electricity, plumbing, telephone service, and with little in the way of permanent changes to the coconut jungle. Most of the homes consist of open platforms a few feet above the ground, with thatched coconut-frond roofs. There are no doors, windows, or privacy except for the blackness of the night.

While most of the ship's passengers stayed near the pier and the pretty sand beach on the lagoon, my wife and I headed out on the packed-sand road that led from the pier. We passed some of the ruins of the old plantation and phosphate mining operations, including a few dozen feet of rusted narrow-gauge rails, and found a small overgrown cemetery that held the remains of some of the family members of the plantation people. Every few hundred feet we came to another little cluster of huts, each with its own name.

Children—and there were hundreds of them—peeked out at us from behind trees or came to the road to say hello. One group of little boys came forth to shake our hands. We walked past the atoll's primary school, listening for a while to the children reciting their numbers in math class. Once we were spotted, though, class came to a halt and dozens of heads crowded the doorway to catch a glimpse of the unusual visitors.

Alas, I expect that this island paradise will never be the same. The more visits by outsiders, the more likely the contamination of their culture. The kids will learn to stick out their hands for a dollar when they are photographed, and the native dancers will pass the hat instead of performing in welcome. And Fanning will become just another tourist island.

We were told a tragicomedy story of the ship's first visit to Fanning. It seems an intrepid American sailor had chosen Fanning as his destination for a solo journey from the West Coast of the United States. His research had told him he would be a modern-day Captain Cook, visiting a place that time had bypassed. After several weeks at sea, he arrived at the isolated speck of sand near the Equator . . . to find the *Norwegian Dynasty* pulling up with a load of 600 passengers.

■ BACK TO THE FUTURE

After our return from Fanning Island, we made port at Hilo on the other side of the Big Island. Hilo is the takeoff point for numerous helicopter tours of the Mauna Loa volcano. We chose instead to explore the island by car, renting a vehicle and driving to the extraordinary Volcano National Park. I have been to many strange places on this planet, but few exceed the peculiarity of a stroll across the miles of black lava left behind by dozens of recent flows. It's as close to a moonscape as most of us will ever experience and a scene that will stick with you forever. The lava is frozen in twisting ropes, undulating waves, and crunchy beaches of pumice.

The volcanoes of Hawaii are still very much alive, although eruptions are rarely violent explosions. Instead there are near-continuous slow flows of thick, superheated lava that bubbles out of cracks in the mountains and heads down the hillside and into the sea where it gives off clouds of steam that rise several miles into the sky.

Also in the park is the Thurston Lava Tube, a natural tunnel caused by a cooling lava flow; a walk in the long tunnel is like a journey to the center of the earth.

Lahaina, on the island of Maui, was once the royal capital of the Hawaiian kingdom and the seat of power for the Kamehameha Dynasty. In the early nineteenth century, Lahaina became the lusty port away from home for the American whaling fleet that had sailed all the way around the Horn of South America in search of "greasy luck" (whale oil). In a way, Lahaina became an extension of Nantucket, a whaling capital thousands of miles away in Massachusetts and the home of many of the ship owners and captains (and this author's home, too).

At the heyday of the whaling era, as many as 400 ships at a time were berthed in the harbor. Whalemen said there was no God west of the Horn, and they conducted themselves accordingly—at least until a band of puritanical missionaries arrived from New England to attempt to clean things up. Among the sailors was Herman Melville, who wrote about the whole scene in *Moby-Dick* and other works.

The weathered wooden buildings on Front Street now house boutiques, art galleries, and restaurants, but the sense of history in Lahaina is more intense than most anywhere else in the islands.

Lahaina also offered the most diverse collection of activities for visitors, from golf expeditions to helicopter and biplane routes to whale watching. We chose to make a visit to the floor of the harbor onboard one of the ships in the Atlantis submarine fleet; the 65-foot craft descended to a depth of 125 feet and allowed us to intrude on fish and other creatures of the sea and to view coral beds not often seen outside an aquarium. Atlantis operates similar subs at a number of ports in the Hawaiian Islands and in the Caribbean; it's a voyage worth the trip.

The last stop on our NCL tour around the fiftieth state was Nawiliwili on the lush island of Kauai, the most isolated of the major islands. Here we rented a car and drove west (there's really only one major road, and it does not quite circle the island because of the severe geography of the Na Pali Coast) and went for a visit to Waimea Canyon State Park. Waimea is called the Grand Canyon of Hawaii; just a little bit of exaggeration is involved. The steep, multicolored walls of the canyon are hidden from view until you complete a long, slow drive up the mountainside.

Kauai's scenery is unusual enough to have attracted a long line of Hollywood filmmakers who have used settings on the island for scenes in such films as *King Kong, South Pacific, Raiders of the Lost Ark,* and *Jurassic Park.*

CHAPTER TWELVE

ECONOGUIDE CRUISE SHIP RATINGS

SO MANY LOVELY cruise ships, so little time!

In the next chapters of the book, I'll give you a guided tour of 180 cruise ships from thirty cruise lines. This book concentrates on ships that regularly include calls at U.S. ports, the Caribbean, the Gulf of Mexico, the Mexican Riviera, and coastal Canada, as well as cruises in Europe and the Pacific marketed to Americans and Canadians.

Each section begins with information about the cruise line. You'll find telephone numbers and Web pages for information. Note that only a few companies accept direct reservations from travelers; in most cases you'll be referred to travel agencies or cruise specialists. If you do call directly, be sure to ask about special offers and last-minute booking.

The listings of each company's fleet are organized by the size of each ship. Sister ships are grouped together; sisters may have identical specifications, but in most cases there are slight differences in public rooms and facilities.

You'll also find a preview of new ships under construction for many major cruise lines. The names, sizes, and expected dates of maiden voyages are all subject to change.

Be aware that each year you can expect a few ships to be taken out of service or sold to another line. Most of the major lines tend to retire their ships somewhere around their early teenage years; this trend has accelerated because many of these older ships are smaller and have fewer special features, such as verandas and large show rooms, than their younger cousins. The older ships are usually sold to one of the second-tier cruise lines, which can happily operate a well-tended cruise ship for many decades.

ECONOGUIDE CRUISE CLASSIFICATIONS

Each of the cruise lines is given an overall rating, from one to six ribbons, indicating the overall quality of a cruising experience. The ratings for cruise lines are as follows:

Econoguide Cruise Line Rating

♀	Rusty tubs
♀♀	Oldies but goodies
♀♀♀	Middle of the fleet
♀♀♀♀	A cut above
♀♀♀♀♀	Luxury
♀♀♀♀♀♀	Ultraluxury

Each of the ships in this book is given an Econoguide rating that separates the superb from the merely wonderful and the very good from the good enough.

The scale runs from 0 to 100; our minimum acceptable rating is 50, and you won't find any ships here that fall below that level. The ratings get tighter (and the points harder to come by) near the top of the scale.

Here's an explanation of the cruise ship ratings:

Econoguide Cruise Ship Rating

★	Less than 50 Not acceptable
★★	50 to 64 Budget
★★★	65 to 79 Average
★★★★	80 to 89 Above Average
★★★★★	90 to 94 Excellent
★★★★★★	95 to 100 Ultraluxury

Ship Size

Gargantuan	130,000+ gross registered tons
Colossus	100,000–129,999 GRT
Megaship	70,000–99,999 GRT
Large	40,000–69,999 GRT
Medium	10,000–39,999 GRT
Small	Less than 10,000 GRT

Category

Ultraluxury	A semiprivate yacht
Top of the Line	Best of the large cruisers
Golden Oldie	A classic older ship
Vintage	A less-than-classic older ship
Adventure	Transport to far-flung places

Price Range

Budget $	$185 per night or less
Moderate $$	$186 to $250 per night
Premium $$$	$251 to $325 per night
Opulent $$$$	$326 to $400 per night
Beyond Opulent $$$$$	More than $400 per night

Prices are based on per-person, per-day brochure prices for midrange cabins in regular season. Nearly all cruise lines offer discounts for advance booking, off-season, and special promotions. Use the price range here for comparison purposes only.

WHO OWNS WHOM?

You're not a Carnival sort of cruiser, you say. Seabourn, or maybe Cunard, sounds more like your level of luxury. Or perhaps you like the cut of the jib of Princess Cruise Lines, with its promise of romance and elegance. That's just fine, although you might be interested to know that all four cruise lines are part of the same company.

One of the effects of the tremendous success of Carnival has been a consolidation among cruise lines into a family of brands that meet various price and luxury classes.

Here's a guide to who owns whom among the major cruise lines:

Carnival Corporation, parent company for Carnival Cruise Lines, has its headquarters in Miami and has mostly American executives. The publicly held corporation, however, is registered in Panama. Controlling interest in the company is held by the Arison family. Carnival Corporation owns Carnival Cruise Lines, Costa Cruise Line, Cunard Line, Holland America Line, Seabourn Cruise Line, and Windstar Cruises.

In 2003 Carnival completed its acquisition of Princess Cruises. Prior to the acquisition, Princess Cruises was the third-largest cruise company in the world. Its brands include Princess Cruises in the North American market, P&O Cruises for the United Kingdom and Australian market, Swan Hellenic in the United Kingdom and Europe, and Aida Cruises and A'ROSA for the German market.

Norwegian Cruise Line fought a hostile takeover bid by Carnival in 1999, only to find itself bought by Malaysia-based Star Cruises, the largest cruise line in Asia. Star, which also operates Orient Lines, has maintained its independence, although some observers speculate that it is a candidate for a merger or sale to a larger company.

Royal Caribbean Cruises Ltd., which also has its headquarters in Miami, is registered as a Liberian corporation. Controlling interests are held by a Bahamian partnership associated with the Pritzker family of Chicago and by a shipping company owned by the Wilhelmsen family in Norway. Royal Caribbean Cruises Ltd. owns Royal Caribbean International and Celebrity Cruises.

Radisson Seven Seas Cruises is part of Carlson Hospitality Worldwide. Its ships are owned by a variety of international companies and marketed by Radisson Hospitality Worldwide in joint ventures.

Silversea is owned by the Lefebvre family of Rome. Crystal Cruises is owned by the huge Japanese freighter company Nippon Yupen Kaiska (NYK).

ECONOGUIDE CRUISE RATINGS

ECONOGUIDE'S BEST CRUISE LINES

Celebrity Cruises. (800) 437–3111, (305) 262–6677; www.celebritycruises.com
Disney Cruise Line. (800) 326–0620; www.disneycruise.com
Holland America Line–Westours Inc. (800) 227–6482, (800) 426–0327; www .hollandamerica.com
Norwegian Cruise Line. (800) 327–7030; www.ncl.com
Princess Cruises. (800) 421–0522, (800) 774–6237; www.princess.com

ECONOGUIDE'S BEST LUXURY CRUISE LINES

Crystal Cruises. (800) 820–6663, (310) 785–9300; www.crystalcruises.com
Radisson Seven Seas Cruises. (800) 333–3333, (800) 285–1835; www.rssc.com
Sea Cloud Cruises. (888) 732–2568, (201) 227–9404; www.seacloud.com
Seabourn Cruise Line. (800) 929–9391; www.seabourn.com
Silversea Cruises. (800) 722–9955, (954) 522–4477; www.silversea.com

ECONOGUIDE'S BEST CRUISE VALUES

Celebrity Cruises. (800) 437–3111, (305) 262–6677; www.celebritycruises.com
Holland America Line. (800) 227–6482, (800) 426–0327; www.holland america.com
Norwegian Cruise Line. (800) 327–7030; www.ncl.com

ECONOGUIDE'S BEST CRUISE LINES FOR FAMILIES

Disney Cruise Line. (800) 326–0620; www.disneycruise.com
Royal Caribbean International. (800) 327–6700; www.royalcaribbean.com

ECONOGUIDE'S BEST DINING AT SEA

Celebrity Cruises. (800) 437–3111, (305) 262–6677; www.celebritycruises.com
Radisson Seven Seas Cruises. (800) 333–3333, (800) 285–1835; www.rssc.com
Sea Cloud Cruises. (888) 732–2568, (201) 227–9404; www.seacloud.com

ECONOGUIDE'S BEST ADVENTURE CRUISE LINES

Delta Queen Steamboat Company. (800) 543–7637; www.deltaqueen.com
Star Clippers. (800) 442–0551; www.star-clippers.com
Windstar Cruises. (800) 258–7245, (206) 281–3535; www.windstarcruises.com

ECONOGUIDE'S BEST PARTY SHIPS

Carnival Cruise Lines. (800) 227–6482, (305) 599–2600; www.carnival.com
Costa Cruise Lines. (800) 332–6782, (305) 358–7325; www.costacruises.com

CHAPTER THIRTEEN

ECONOGUIDE'S BEST CRUISE LINES

♔♔♔	Carnival Cruise Lines	♔♔♔♔	Holland America Line
♔♔♔♔	Celebrity Cruises	♔♔♔♔	Norwegian Cruise Line
♔♔♔	Costa Cruise Lines	♔♔♔♔	Princess Cruises
♔♔♔♔♔	Cunard Line	♔♔♔	Royal Caribbean
♔♔♔♔	Disney Cruise Line		

CARNIVAL CRUISE LINES   ◗Carnival.

Address: 3655 N.W. 87th Avenue
   Miami, FL 33178-2428   ♔ ♔ ♔
Information: (800) 227–6482, (305) 599–2600;
   www.carnival.com
Econoguide's Best Party Ships

The Carnival Fleet

Carnival Valor	2004	2,974 passengers	110,000 tons
Carnival Glory	2003	2,974 passengers	110,000 tons
Carnival Conquest	2002	2,974 passengers	110,000 tons
Carnival Victory	2000	2,758 passengers	102,000 tons
Carnival Triumph	1999	2,758 passengers	102,000 tons
Carnival Destiny	1999	2,642 passengers	101,353 tons
Carnival Miracle	2004	2,124 passengers	86,000 tons
Carnival Legend	2002	2,124 passengers	86,000 tons
Carnival Pride	2002	2,112 passengers	84,000 tons
Carnival Spirit	2001	2,112 passengers	84,000 tons
Elation	1998	2,040 passengers	70,367 tons
Paradise	1998	2,052 passengers	70,367 tons
Inspiration	1996	2,040 passengers	70,367 tons

Imagination	1995	2,040 passengers	70,367 tons
Fascination	1994	2,040 passengers	70,367 tons
Sensation	1993	2,040 passengers	70,367 tons
Ecstasy	1991	2,052 passengers	70,367 tons
Fantasy	1990	2,044 passengers	70,367 tons
Celebration	1987	1,486 passengers	47,262 tons
Holiday	1985	1,452 passengers	46,052 tons

FUTURE SHIPS

Carnival Liberty	Late 2005	2,974 passengers	110,000 tons

Carnival ships offer a Mardi Gras of glitz, pizzazz, and hoopla. These are theme parks on the water, with flashing lights, polished wood and chrome, and nearly nonstop parties, contests, and lavish Las Vegas style shows, magic, singers, and bands.

The Carnival crowd is more young, more single, more young family, and more party-seeking than the guests on most other lines; its nearest competitors are Royal Caribbean and Princess.

In other words, Carnival is not your father's Cunard . . . although Carnival now owns the separately operated Cunard Line. These are not superluxury ships like those of Seabourn (Carnival owns that line, too). And Carnival is not the Love Boat, although in 2003 the company completed a corporate merger with Princess Cruises.

On Carnival you're not likely to find an emphasis on hushed rosewood libraries and secluded deck chair hideaways; you're much more likely to hear about discos and beach blanket bingo on the pool deck.

▓ ITINERARIES

Carnival's "Fun Ships" sail to the Bahamas, the Caribbean, the Mexican Riviera, Alaska, Hawaii, the Panama Canal, and New England—on itineraries as short as three days and as long as sixteen.

In 2004 Carnival was due to operate from nineteen different North American home ports, the most in the cruise industry. Primary home ports were in Miami, San Juan, Long Beach, Tampa, New Orleans, Port Canaveral, Galveston, Vancouver, Anchorage, New York, Charleston, and Norfolk. Other ports of embarkation include San Diego, Jacksonville, Mobile, Alabama, Philadelphia, and Baltimore.

The new *Carnival Valor* began year-round seven-day Caribbean cruises from Miami in December 2004. The 2,974-passenger vessel, the largest member of Carnival's fleet to be based at the Port of Miami, joins five other 100,000-plus-ton Destiny- and Conquest-class vessels operating Caribbean departures from four North American home ports.

Carnival operated a record fifty-seven departures from New York in 2004, a 250 percent increase over the schedule in recent years. Trips from New York included seven-day round-trip Port Canaveral/Orlando and the Bahamas itineraries on the 2,124-passenger *Carnival Miracle;* four- and five-day Canada and seven-day "fall foliage" voyages on the 2,758-passenger *Carnival Victory;* and eight-day Caribbean sailings on the 2,124-passenger *Carnival Legend.*

In the fall of 2004, Carnival increased its capacity from Galveston by assigning the 2,052-passenger *Ecstasy* to replace the 1,486-passenger *Celebration* on year-round four- and five-day Mexico cruises. On this itinerary, four-day cruises depart the historic Port of Galveston to visit Cozumel; five-day cruises head to Cozumel and Calica/Playa del Carmen.

The 2,052-passenger *Paradise* took over *Ecstasy*'s three- and four-day Baja cruises from Long Beach, California. Three-day cruises call at Ensenada, Mexico, while four-day cruises add a visit to California's Catalina Island. Alas, in the process *Paradise* lost its distinction as a smoke-free ship.

From Tampa, *Carnival Miracle* launched seven-day "exotic" Caribbean cruises from the Port of Tampa beginning November 2004, becoming the newest and largest ship based year-round at that port, replacing *Inspiration* on trips to Grand Cayman, Costa Maya, Cozumel, and Belize. In turn *Inspiration* shifted to year-round four- and five-day cruises from Tampa.

Carnival Spirit began eight-day cruises from San Diego in late 2004 through April 2005 to the Mexican Riviera ports of Acapulco, Zihuatanejo/Ixtapa, and Manzanillo. Acapulco is known for its beaches, resorts, and cliff divers. Zihuatanejo is a quaint fishing village with beautiful beaches and crystal-clear waters teeming with colorful tropical fish, while nearby Ixtapa is a cosmopolitan resort area with excellent shopping and dining opportunities; Manzanillo is known for its white-sand beaches (where the hit movie *10* was filmed), as well as snorkeling and other water sports.

The first year-round cruise program from Mobile, Alabama, began in October 2004 when the 1,452-passenger *Holiday* began four- and five-day voyages to the western Caribbean. *Holiday* sailed four-day cruises to Cozumel and five-day cruises to Cozumel and Calica/Playa del Carmen or Costa Maya. The refurbished *Celebration* assumed *Holiday*'s previously announced schedule of four- and five-day cruises from Jacksonville, the first year-round cruise program from that port. *Celebration*'s four-day cruises headed to Freeport and Nassau in the Bahamas, while five-day cruises visit Key West and Nassau.

In 2004 Carnival chose to devote part of its vast fleet to the expanding short-cruise segment, offering thirty-nine different cruise itineraries of less than a week, including departures from two new homeports, Jacksonville, Florida, and Mobile, Alabama. Overall, thirteen of Carnival's twenty ships were due to operate short cruises from thirteen different North American home ports, the most of any cruise line.

Carnival's short cruise programs included *Carnival Miracle* sailing three-day Bahamas and five-day Key West/Bahamas cruises from Jacksonville, and two-day voyages from Baltimore and Tampa. *Jubilee* offered four-day Bahamas and fiveday Key West/Bahamas cruises from Jacksonville through the summer. *Celebration* offered year-round four-day Bahamas and five-day Key West/Bahamas cruises from Jacksonville beginning in October 2004. In that same month, *Holiday* was due to begin year-round four- and five-day Mexico cruises from Mobile.

From Miami, *Imagination* offered year-round four- and five-day western Caribbean cruises, while *Fascination* sailed three-day Bahamas and four-day western Caribbean cruises. *Ecstasy* was due to offer four- and five-day Mexico cruises from Galveston beginning in late October.

Paradise began its year-round assignment in Long Beach in September of 2004, sailing three- and four-day Baja cruises. *Sensation* was due to begin sailing year-round four- and five-day Mexico cruises from New Orleans beginning in late October; *Inspiration* is scheduled for four- and five-day cruises from Tampa year-round. And *Fantasy* is due to sail year-round three- and four-day Bahamas cruises from Port Canaveral.

In 2004 Carnival *Spirit* began using Whittier, Alaska, as its port of origin for southbound cruises; in prior years Carnival ships had departed from Seward when heading south. The change cuts the drive to the ship from the Anchorage airport in half, to about ninety minutes. Using Whittier also allows for a longer stay in Sitka, the first stop on the southbound itinerary. Week-long northbound cruises for the ship continued to depart from Vancouver.

■ THE CARNIVAL STORY

It all began with a small cruise charter company run by Ted Arison, an Israeli who had an air freight company in New York. In 1966, when financial difficulties by a shipowner forced the removal of a leased vessel, Arison was left with several loads of passengers but no ship. He contacted Knut Kloster, a Norwegian shipping company operator whose vessel the *Sunward* was laid up, and the two put the passengers together with a cruise ship. Thus was born Norwegian Caribbean Lines, the predecessor of today's Norwegian Cruise Line. The partnership of Arison and Kloster came to an end in 1972, and Arison went on to found Carnival.

The launch of what became the world's largest cruise company began in 1972 with just one ship, the aging classic *Empress of Canada,* renamed the *Mardi Gras.* In a much-reported example of an inauspicious start, the *Mardi Gras* ran aground off Miami Beach on her maiden voyage. But Carnival got past its beginning with a well-crafted marketing plan that turned 180 degrees away from the formal and stuffy image of the great ocean liners. Instead, Carnival's fleet was made up of the Fun Ships, featuring a near-continuous party atmosphere.

During the next twenty-five years, the line grew rapidly to become the largest cruise company in the world. In the mid-1980s Carnival launched an insistent series of television commercials that brought the cruise line into middle-class America with great success.

Carnival purchased Holland America Line and Windstar Cruises in 1989 and holds major interests in Seabourn Cruise Line, Cunard Line (including the QE2), and Costa Cruise Line.

In 1996 Carnival introduced the 2,642-passenger, 101,353-ton *Carnival Destiny,* which, for several years, was the largest passenger vessel afloat. *Carnival Conquest,* a 110,000-ton Megaship, joined the fleet in 2002; sister ship *Carnival Glory* arrived in summer 2003, and a third sister, *Carnival Valor,* arrived at the end of 2004. The fourth vessel in the Conquest class, *Carnival Liberty,* is due in late 2005.

The new Long Beach Cruise Terminal at the *Queen Mary,* about 25 miles south of Los Angeles, includes a single cruise berth capable of handling vessels up to 1,000 feet in length and a parking garage for approximately 1,250 vehicles. The embarkation/disembarkation facility is within a section of the existing geodesic dome, former home of Howard Hughes's *Spruce Goose* flying boat. Guests can stay in the hotel at the *Queen Mary* before and after their cruise.

Other vessels in the Carnival corporate family—Holland America Line, Costa Cruises, Cunard Line, Seabourn Cruise Line, and Windstar Cruises—may eventually use the terminal as well. Long Beach officials anticipate more than 500,000 annual departures and arrivals through the new terminal.

Guests can book one- to three-night pre- and postcruise land packages in one of 365 available Art Deco–inspired cabins within the *Queen Mary* hotel.

■ THE CARNIVAL EXPERIENCE

All Carnival vessels have at least three swimming pools, including a children's wading pool and water slide. Most staterooms can be adapted for use by families, with additional berths, rollaway beds, and cribs. There are children's playrooms on all vessels; two rooms on the six Fantasy-class vessels have toys, games, and activities for kids ages five to twelve. The *Carnival Destiny* includes a two-level 1,300-square-foot play area.

Camp Carnival has programs for four age groups: toddlers (ages two to four), intermediate (five to eight), juniors (nine to twelve), and teens (thirteen to seventeen). Kids can dine out under the stars on the lido deck with members of the youth staff.

In recent years, Carnival has introduced flexible dining on its larger ships, a combination of more assigned dining times and a wider range of alternative restaurants. You may be able to adjust your assigned time before you sail or once you are onboard the ship, or you can avail yourself of a number of alternative dining options.

For casual dining between 6:00 and 9:00 P.M., lido deck poolside eateries are converted to Seaview Bistros, where there are no assigned tables, seating times, or dress codes. Meals are served buffet-style most nights, with specialty stations serving made-to-order selections; an expanded salad bar is also offered. Full table service will occasionally be offered.

The newer ships in the Carnival fleet include a reservations-only gourmet restaurant, for which there is an additional charge.

Carnival has also adopted a prepaid gratuity system fleetwide. In 2004 a charge of $10.00 per person per day was automatically posted to shipboard charge accounts; the charges break down as follows: $5.50 per day for headwaiter and waiter, $3.50 per day for cabin steward, and $1.00 per day for the waiter and cooks in the bistro. According to the company, this system takes into account the fact that many guests are taking advantage of alternative dining and that the overall number of wait staff has been increased. Guests have the option of asking that tips be increased, decreased, or removed from their bill and can also make individual payments to staff.

In 2004 Carnival continued its "vacation guarantee," which offers a limited escape clause to guests who board a ship and find it not to their liking. Passengers who are in any way dissatisfied with their cruise can notify the ship's purser before arrival at the first port of call. They'll be able to disembark at the first non-U.S. port of call and receive a refund of the unused portion of the cruise fare and an airline ticket back to the port of departure.

Carnival Miracle unveiled a high-tech digital photo system in 2004 using computerized facial recognition technology to match a guest's likeness against thousands of digital images snapped by the ship's photographers. Guests can stand for a photograph at a kiosk, and the image is compared to all pictures in the computer's memory; all photos in which the guest appears show up on a computer monitor, and high-quality prints can be ordered.

■ WEB SITE

Everything is there for a knowledgeable and adventurous traveler: descriptions of the ships, itineraries, and cabin classes. Once you register for My Carnival on-line booking, you can choose from specific available cabins, cross-checking location against a deck-by-deck map. You can book your cruise with a credit card or ask for a Carnival representative to call you to answer questions and proceed with booking. You can also register and wait to receive "Fun Wave" e-mails with Carnival's latest cruise specials. ***Ease of use: excellent.***

Carnival Conquest, Carnival Glory, Carnival Valor, Carnival Liberty (2005) (CONQUEST CLASS)

Econoguide rating:	★★★★ 85 points
Ship size:	Colossus
Category:	Top of the Line
Price range:	Premium $$$
Registry:	Panama
Year built:	*Carnival Conquest,* 2002; *Carnival Glory,* 2003; *Carnival Valor,* 2004
Future ships:	*Carnival Liberty,* 2005
Information:	(305) 599–2600, (800) 227–6482
Web site:	www.carnival.com
Passenger capacity:	2,974 (double occupancy)
Crew:	1,160
Passenger-to-crew ratio:	2.5:1
Tonnage:	110,000
Passenger-space ratio:	38.6
Length:	952 feet
Beam:	116 feet
Draft:	27 feet

Cruising speed:	22.5 knots
Guest decks:	13
Total cabins:	1,487
Outside:	917
Inside:	570
Suites:	42
Wheelchair cabins:	N/A
Cuisine:	Contemporary and low-fat, low-calorie Nautica spa fare
Style:	Casual, with one or two semiformal nights
Price notes:	Single-occupancy premium, 150 to 200 percent
Tipping suggestions:	$10 pp/pd automatically posted to bill

Stretching more than three football fields in length, each of the $500 million Conquest-class ships has twenty-two lounges, nightspots, and bars. By the end of the voyage, most passengers have found pulsating dance clubs, three-deck-high 1,500-seat theaters showcasing lavish Las Vegas–style revues, piano bars, jazz clubs, sports bars, wine and caviar bars, and cigar bars.

All the ships in this class are too wide to transit the Panama Canal and are likely to spend all their time in the Caribbean and Europe.

In 2004 the number of children vacationing aboard Carnival Cruise Lines' ships was expected to reach 450,000, more than any other cruise line. "Camp Carnival" offers a full day-long schedule at indoor and outdoor facilities including arts and crafts centers, computer labs, and sports areas.

There are four swimming pools, including one with a 214-foot-long cascading water slide and another with a retractable dome. There is a 3,300-square-foot children's play area for the Camp Carnival program as well as a teen coffee bar and dance club and an outdoor recreation area featuring basketball and volleyball courts.

At the heart of the Camp Carnival program is "Children's World," which includes an arts and crafts center with spin and sand art and candy-making machines; an all-ages play room with a variety of toys, games, and puzzles, and kid-sized tables and chairs; a video room showing kids' favorite movies and cartoons; a children's library; a computer lab; and a set of video game machines. An onboard science education program gives children the chance to participate in science projects and experiments and a geography program focusing on the cultures and landmarks of the various ports of call.

The ships offer a golf program featuring professional instruction aboard ship and during golf excursions, along with netted driving ranges and teaching computers.

Of the 1,487 staterooms, 917 offer an ocean view and 556 feature private balconies.

Dining options begin with a pair of two-level full-service restaurants with traditional cruise ship dining for breakfast, lunch, and dinner. As an alternative, there's an expansive two-deck-high poolside eatery with full breakfast, lunch, and dinner buffets, including "Taste of the Nation," with traditional cuisine from a different country each day, a New York–style deli, a rotisserie serving broiled chicken and steak, and stations featuring traditional English-style fish-and-chips and Asian and American favorites. A twenty-four-hour pizzeria offers seven kinds of pies, calzones, Caesar salad, and garlic bread.

And then there is a patisserie featuring specialty coffees and sweets, a sushi bar, and a reservations-only steakhouse-style supper club serving prime aged beef along with crab claws from Miami Beach's famous Joe's Stone Crab Restaurant.

On the *Conquest,* the alternative restaurant is The Point, located at the top of the eleven-deck-high atrium; the eatery draws its name and design from the works of Impressionist Georges-Pierre Seurat, with colorful images inspired by his famous painting *Le Cirque* (The Circus), created in the artist's distinctive "pointillism" style, comprising thousands of tiny dots, or points. The Point comes with a hefty $25-per-person reservations fee. Specialties include large cuts of steak, broiled lobster tail, and stone crab claws.

Conquest's poolside restaurant is Restaurant Cezanne, incorporating design elements of that artist's post-Impressionist paintings. Evoking the atmosphere of a nineteenth-century French cafe, the two-level restaurant features handpainted ceramic wainscoting and authentic reproductions of the artist's works, including *Chateau Noir,* and *House of Pere Lacroix in Auvers.*

Carnival Glory takes colors as its central design theme, with each public room celebrating a different shade of the rainbow. The Conquest-class ship is scheduled to sail year-round from Port Canaveral.

It all begins in the lobby, home of the Color Bar and the main atrium, named Old Glory, featuring interpretative paintings of U.S. flags. Both the Kaleidoscope Boulevard promenade and the atrium are lit by fixtures subdivided into geometric modules that are backlit with LED lights, resulting in slow-moving kaleidoscopic effects.

Carnival Glory's main show lounge is Amber Palace. The Platinum and Golden Dining Rooms are inspired by Japanese temples; lights in concave ceiling fixtures provide color-changing effects.

The design of the White Heat Dance Club includes gigantic white candles in silver candelabra bases. The Ivory Club features replicas of elephant tusks, intricate wall coverings, and windows inset with mosaics of faux semiprecious stones. Cinn-A-Bar, a piano bar, is decorated in reddish-brown hues.

Bar Blue is the ship's jazz bar, festooned with giant peacock feathers that extend from the floor almost to the ceiling. The Ebony Cabaret has an African atmosphere, with dark ebony walls and ceilings and hand-carved and painted wooden African masks mounted in copperlike frames.

The Red Sail Restaurant, a casual poolside eatery, evokes a sailboat motif, with varnished pine masts, sails, chrome hardware, a wood-beam ceiling, teak railing, false portholes, and other touches. The reservations-only steakhouse-style supper club Emerald Room features cobalt-blue walls and lighting fixtures resembling giant emeralds.

In its first assignment, *Carnival Glory* will operate year-round from Port Canaveral in Florida, with alternating eastern and western Caribbean voyages departing every Saturday.

Carnival Valor offers its own version of the sister-ship design, with twin two-level main dining rooms, an expansive poolside restaurant with Asian and American specialty areas, New York–style deli, twenty-four-hour pizzeria, extensive salad and dessert bars, and a specialty seafood venue serving ceviche, bouillabaisse, and other delicacies. A sushi bar, a patisserie, and a reservations-only steakhouse-style supper club are also offered.

There are four swimming pools aboard, including one with a 214-foot-long water slide. Guests will find twenty-two lounges and bars, including a three-deck-high theater showcasing lavish Vegas-style productions, a wine bar, a sports bar, a two-level dance club, a piano bar, and numerous other live music venues. *Carnival Valor* continues the line's increased emphasis on the family cruise, featuring an enclosed 4,200-square-foot play area, as well as a variety of supervised activities for kids ages two to fifteen. Teens have their own space, as well, with Action Alley, featuring a dance club, coffee/soda bar, game room, and high-tech sound and lighting system. The line also offers just-for-teens shore excursions.

The new *Carnival Liberty* is due to begin service in the fall of 2005.

Carnival Destiny, Carnival Triumph, Carnival Victory (DESTINY CLASS)

Econoguide rating:	★★★★ 80 points
Ship size:	Colossus
Category:	Top of the Line
Price range:	Premium $$$
Registry:	Panama
Year built:	*Carnival Destiny,* 1999; *Carnival Triumph,* 1999; *Carnival Victory,* 2000
Information:	(305) 599–2600, (800) 227–6482
Web site:	www.carnival.com
Passenger capacity:	*Carnival Destiny,* 2,642; *Carnival Triumph,* 2,758; *Carnival Victory,* 2,758
Crew:	1,070
Passenger-to-crew ratio:	2.5:1
Tonnage:	*Carnival Destiny,* 101,353; *Carnival Triumph, Carnival Victory,* 102,000
Passenger-space ratio:	*Carnival Destiny,* 38.4; *Carnival Triumph, Carnival Victory,* 38.6
Length:	893 feet
Beam:	116 feet
Draft:	27 feet
Cruising speed:	22.5 knots
Guest decks:	12
Total cabins:	1,321
Outside:	758
Inside:	514

Suites:	48
Wheelchair cabins:	25
Cuisine:	Contemporary and low-fat, low-calorie Nautica spa fare
Style:	Casual, with one or two semiformal nights
Price notes:	Single-occupancy premium, 150 to 200 percent
Tipping suggestions:	$10 pp/pd automatically posted to bill

The **Carnival Destiny** was the first cruise ship to zoom past the 100,000-ton barrier; for a while it held the record as the largest passenger load afloat. The Destiny-class ships include the *Carnival Destiny, Carnival Triumph,* and *Carnival Victory.* Slightly smaller than the Conquest-class ships, these vessels are nevertheless also too wide to pass through the Panama Canal and will likely spend their lives sailing in the Caribbean and European waters.

The lifeboats and most other machinery are limited to Decks 3, 4, and 5, which are used for public rooms, including restaurants, lounges, and bars. This means there are hardly any outside cabins with obstructed views; the only exceptions are a scant nineteen cabins at the bow of the ship with forward-facing windows partially blocked by equipment there. More than 60 percent of the staterooms have ocean views, and 70 percent of those have private balconies.

Four upper decks offer private verandas. Up top on the Spa Deck are fourteen cabins with floor-to-ceiling windows.

These ships have an unusual feature that may appeal to extreme party animals: There are a handful of "Night Owl Staterooms" offered at deep discounts of 50 percent or more off the least-expensive rates. Of course, you'll have to be a night owl yourself, because these rooms are intended for guests who "love to party late into the night." In other words, these rooms, all inside twin/king cabins, are very close to the noisy late-night action.

At the other end of the spectrum is a set of "family staterooms" that give mom and dad a bit of privacy from the kids. Camp Carnival offers programs for children from ages five through twelve.

There are thirteen decks, numbered 1 to 14 (with an eye toward the superstitious, there's a numerical skip between the top decks). The Sky Deck contains a small observation platform and the entrance to the water slide down to the pool.

The **Triumph's** nine-story main atrium is the Capitol, with a spectacular sky dome showing the sky above a lobby bar way down below. There is a pair of bilevel dining rooms, London and Paris; you can also dine bistro-style in the laid-back South Beach Club Restaurant.

Las Vegas–style revues are presented in the three-level Rome Lounge. Drinks and cigars can follow at a cigar bar, or cappuccino and pastry at the Vienna Cafe. Underground Tokyo is a cavernlike video arcade. Youngsters can join Camp Carnival for daily activities.

Public rooms are inspired by the world's great cities, with decorations commissioned from a crew of international artists. Among the most spectacular is a series of three-dimensional maplike murals in glass created by renowned Venetian artist Luciano Vistosi. Depicting the planet's continents, the murals are positioned along the 525-foot-long World's Way promenade. Vistosi also created

Carnival *Triumph. Photo courtesy of Carnival Cruise Lines and CLIA*

Moebius, an expansive, tricolor glass sculpture that dominates the *Triumph*'s three-deck-high aft atrium. The 8-foot-high by 8-foot-long abstract sculpture, which took nearly a year to complete, is composed of intertwining blue, green, and white glass prisms woven together in a unique free-flowing pattern.

Adorning the *Triumph*'s elevator lobbies and passenger stair landings is a series of thirty-five original murals by Israeli artist Calman Shemi, whose works can also be seen aboard Carnival's *Sensation, Elation,* and *Paradise.* Citing influences ranging from Jules Vernes's *Around the World in Eighty Days* to twentieth-century French Impressionist Raoul Dufy, Shemi's vibrant, multihued murals depict such landmarks as Paris's Eiffel Tower, New York's towering skyscrapers, and India's ancient temples.

British artist Susanna Holt's four stone sculptures are located adjacent to the Universe Pool on the lido deck; the vaselike sculptures feature a variety of unique and exquisite materials from around the world, including small horn-shaped *Bullia vittata* shells from India, sea urchin spines from the Gulf of Mexico, and several varieties of star-shaped *Turritella terebra* shells from Taiwan and the Philippines.

The centerpiece of **Carnival Victory** is Oceanic Hall, a nine-deck atrium decorated in watery hues of turquoise, green, gold, and blue. Handmade glass-tile mosaics of mermaids, the sea god Neptune, and other aqueous themes are displayed; overhead, an illuminated dome is decorated in Tiffany-style glass.

The oceanic theme is continued in the names and decor of public rooms including the Coral Sea Cafe, laid out with displays of coral.

Ecstasy, Elation, Fantasy, Fascination, Imagination, Inspiration, Paradise, Sensation (FANTASY CLASS)

Econoguide rating:	★★★ 76 points
Ship size:	Megaship
Category:	Top of the Line
Price range:	Moderate $$
Registry:	Liberia
Year built:	Ecstasy, 1991; Elation, 1998; Fantasy, 1990; Fascination, 1994; Imagination, 1995; Inspiration, 1996; Paradise, 1998; Sensation, 1993
Information:	(305) 599–2600, (800) 227–6482
Web site:	www.carnival.com
Passenger capacity:	2,044 (double occupancy)
Crew:	920
Passenger-to-crew ratio:	2.2:1
Tonnage:	70,367
Passenger-space ratio:	34.4
Length:	855 feet
Beam:	103 feet
Draft:	25.9 feet
Cruising speed:	21 knots
Guest decks:	10
Total cabins:	1,022
Outside:	566
Inside:	402
Suites:	54
Wheelchair cabins:	22
Cuisine:	Contemporary and low-fat, low-calorie Nautica spa fare
Style:	Casual during the day; on one or two nights, formal dress or dark suit suggested
Price notes:	Single-occupancy premium, 150 to 200 percent
Tipping suggestions:	$10 pp/pd automatically posted to bill

Members of the Fantasy class, these ships include three dining areas, ten bars and lounges, a spa and health club, casino, three swimming pools, jogging tracks, and two children's playrooms. There are few places to get away from the bustle of a lively cruise, which may or may not appeal to you.

Elation was the first company ship to include the Azipod propulsion system, which pulls instead of pushes the vessel through the water, and eliminates the need for drive shafts, rudders, and stern thrusters. The system dramatically improves maneuverability and delivers higher operating speed, all at a significant savings in fuel.

Fantasy, delivered in 1990, was the first newly built cruise liner with a diesel-electric AC propulsion and power system and joystick-controlled navigation. Of more interest to most cruisegoers, *Fantasy* was also the first cruise ship to have a seven-deck central atrium, the Grand Spectrum.

Among her more unusual decorative features is Cleopatra's Bar, a great place to get mummified; the appointments are right out of Egypt by way of Las Vegas.

In 2000 *Fantasy* underwent a major refurbishment, emerging with a new Roman-themed promenade, Via Marina, leading to many of the ship's lounges and nightspots. The promenade's design includes a faux stone floor, electric torches, Doric columns, and terra-cotta urns. Aft of the promenade is a new Formality Shop, where guests can rent tuxedos and purchase specialty items. The former aft show lounge was converted to include a large conference facility and Children's World, a high-tech play area that includes toys and games, a bank of computers loaded with educational software and games, and a new teen center with video game machines, Foosball, and pool tables.

Fascination's public rooms pay homage to Tinseltown, with public rooms that include the Tara Library, modeled after a scene from *Gone with the Wind*, the Casino Royale, the Diamonds Are Forever dance club, and the Passage to India Lounge. The ship's main drag is Hollywood Boulevard on the promenade deck.

Geared toward sixteen- to eighteen-year-old guests, *Fascination*'s "Backstreet Club" features a CD jukebox stocked with the latest rock, R&B, rap and hip-hop hits, as well as a state-of-the-art sound and lighting system and a large dance

Carnival's *Paradise* in port. *Photo by Corey Sandler*

floor. The facility also houses a bank of Internet-connected Apple iMac computers, Sony PlayStation 2 video game units, and a "mocktail lounge" serving nonalcoholic versions of Carnival's popular frozen specialty drinks. A karaoke machine and a library featuring teen-oriented magazines are included as well.

Other "family-friendly" features aboard *Fascination* include three swimming pools (one with a 115-foot-long water slide), a video game room, special children's menus in the main dining rooms, and a turndown service offering chocolate chip cookies at bedtime. A nightly baby-sitting service is also available for a nominal fee.

Imagination's decor emphasizes some unusual corners of human fancy, from the Curiosity Library to the Shangri-La and Xanadu Lounges and the El Dorado Casino.

The *Inspiration*'s interior design pays tribute to the popular and fine arts, with rooms such as the Avant-Garde Lounge, featuring statues and wall designs reminiscent of the cubist art form, and the Shakespeare Library, whose ceiling is lined with some of the playwright's most famous quotations.

Paradise, which was launched in 1998 with much ballyhoo as the world's first smoke-free cruise ship—from cabins to dining rooms to the open decks—lost that distinction in 2004 with its reassignment to California for sailings to Baja, Mexico. According to the company, since the ship would be its only vessel on that itinerary it did not want to limit its appeal.

Elements of the ship's design are intended to echo the legendary *Queen Mary,* one of the most famous transatlantic ocean liners of all time. Located aft on the promenade deck, the Queen Mary Lounge is used for dancing, late-night comedy shows, and other live entertainment. Funnel shapes are used throughout the room: along the walls, framing the sofas, lining the bar front, and serving as table bases. Their lower portions are veneered in Nigerian satinwood, stained bright red to match the *Queen Mary*'s celebrated smokestacks; the upper sections are finished in black gloss lacquer. Where red meets black is a strip of lacquered ebony wood inlaid with a clear polycarbonate tube of twinkling Tivoli lights. Even the distinctive ribs that segment the funnels are re-created in ebony inlays. Set atop the large wall-mounted funnels are stylized brass-ringed "portholes," which house video monitors broadcasting vintage motion films of the celebrated *Queen Mary,* other classic liners, and life aboard the great ships of the former heyday of cruising.

Many of the vessel's interior designs are inspired by legendary ships of the past. In the case of the Rex Dance Club, the lounge takes its name from the *Rex,* a famed Italian liner of the 1930s.

Carnival plays off the name Rex, the Latin word for "king," with images of the king of the jungle and safari scenes. Floor-to-ceiling columns surrounding the lounge are stepped like the stones of ancient temples and covered with imitation animal hides that extend upward to the ceiling, creating a mosaic of zebra, leopard, and tiger skin patterns.

Sensation was one of Carnival's early breakthroughs into maritime glitz, and though it has been surpassed by more modern ships, it still has its flashy appeals, including the Roman architectural orgy of Michelangelo's Lounge and the ultracolorful Kaleidoscope Dance Club.

In July 1998 ***Ecstasy*** suffered a minor fire in crew areas at her stern soon after departing Miami and was forced to return. The ship has been refurbished and returned to service.

Carnival Spirit, Carnival Pride, Carnival Legend, Carnival Miracle (SPIRIT CLASS)	

Econoguide rating:	★★★ 79 points
Ship size:	Megaship
Category:	Top of the Line
Price range:	Budget to Moderate $–$$
Registry:	Panama
Year built:	*Carnival Spirit,* 2001; *Carnival Pride,* 2002; *Carnival Legend,* 2002; *Carnival Miracle,* 2004
Information:	(305) 599–2600, (800) 227–6482
Web site:	www.carnival.com
Passenger capacity:	2,124
Crew:	900
Passenger-to-crew ratio:	2.3:1

Carnival Legend in New York City. *Photo by Corey Sandler*

Tonnage:	86,000
Passenger-space ratio:	39.8
Length:	963 feet
Beam:	106 feet
Draft:	22 feet
Cruising speed:	22 knots
Guest decks:	12
Total cabins:	1,321
Outside:	792
Inside:	529
Suites:	None indicated
Wheelchair cabins:	None indicated
Cuisine:	Contemporary and low-fat, low-calorie Nautica spa fare
Style:	Casual during the day; on one or two nights, formal dress or dark suit suggested
Price notes:	Single-occupancy premium, 150 to 200 percent
Tipping suggestions:	$10 pp/pd automatically posted to bill

The Spirit-class ships include two decks of bars, lounges, and nightspots, one with an outdoor wraparound promenade. Some 80 percent of the staterooms offer ocean views; 87 percent of those cabins have private balconies. In addition to a two-level main restaurant, a topside alternative restaurant extends out over the uppermost section of the atrium.

Introduced in 2001, the Spirit class of ships included Carnival's first wedding chapel, a reservations-only supper club, and a wraparound outdoor promenade.

Carnival Spirit introduced the Nouveau Supper Club, an upscale steakhouse-style restaurant; soon after the ship took to the seas, Carnival announced with public relations fanfare that the restaurant was so popular that the reservations fee would be increased to $25 per person, including gratuity.

Diners are offered a choice of nine different starters and salads, prime aged beef, and stone crab claws from Miami Beach's legendary Joe's Stone Crab Restaurant, the first time the delicacies have been featured on a cruise ship menu. The claws, from crabs native to Florida waters, are traditionally served cold, accompanied by Joe's signature mustard sauce or drawn butter. The crab's hard shells are cracked with a wooden mallet immediately prior to serving.

Carnival reports serving upward of 300 pounds of stone crab claws per week. Other popular fare includes steaks, filet mignon, grilled lamb chops, broiled lobster tail with citrus butter, and Dover sole meunière.

The two-level restaurant is located at the top of a soaring nine-deck-high atrium and housed under a red-tinted glass dome that forms the forward portion of the ship's funnel. The room's design is based on the magnificent Hotel Tassel in Brussels, often cited as one of the finest examples of Art Nouveau design; there's a dance floor and nightly entertainment for diners.

The *Carnival Pride,* which joined the fleet in late 2001, introduced some elegant dining options to the fleet. The ship's main dining room, the Normandie, harkens back to the classic liner of the same name, decorated with Art Deco touches and dark wood accents. The ship's casual restaurant, Mermaids' Grille, includes Asian and American specialty areas, a pasta bar, and a twenty-four-hour pizzeria set in a world of mermaids, dolphins, and other sea creatures.

The showplace eatery is David's, an upscale New York–style steakhouse that offers steaks, chops, and seafood, including crab claws from Miami Beach's famous Joe's Stone Crab Restaurant. David's is dominated by a 12-foot replica of Michelangelo's famed statue of the same name, along with ornate wood patterns and other Renaissance-inspired touches. There's a dance floor, nightly entertainment, and $25 per person reservations fee.

Carnival Pride uses a typically eclectic cruise ship mix of decors. The lobby, atrium, and other public areas are based on the arts and craftsmanship of the Italian Renaissance in rich details of wood and bronze moldings, dominated by gold, sienna, and burnt red tones. Reproductions of murals by Botticelli, Raphael, and other Italian painters adorn the walls.

The Taj Mahal show lounge is filled with intricate Indian designs, elephant friezes, and stonework with small jewels pressed into decorative designs and illuminated from behind.

The casino salutes the atmosphere of the Jockey Club at the Kentucky Derby, with a mural of Churchill Downs and bas-relief statues of jockeys and paintings of horses in the walls and ceiling.

The Starry Night jazz club replicates Van Gogh's painting of the same name; a wall and ceiling mural are illuminated by tiny lights.

The Nobel Library, which also houses the Internet cafe, has a simple Swedish design that falls somewhere between classical and Art Deco. Portraits of Alfred Nobel and the award ceremonies conducted in his name adorn walls, which are painted Windsor blue and trimmed in light green.

At Beauties Dance Club, varicolored male and female torsos, reminiscent of *Venus de Milo,* line the walls, support the tables, and decorate the ceiling. Walls and ceilings are of antique-look one-way mirrors illuminated from behind with flashing and neon lights for a variety of effects. One wall is dominated by a two-deck-high video display that can mix live video, special effects, and prerecorded images to accompany the dance music.

The lido deck pool area features a grand mural of Botticelli's *Birth of Venus.* The pools are named after Apollo and Poseidon, and bronze sculptures of the Greek gods are on pedestals between the pools.

Included in a multimillion-dollar art collection are seventy decorative vases and candleholders by Czech glass artist Borek Sipek, who created similar works for the *Carnival Pride*'s sister ship, *Carnival Spirit.* For *Carnival Pride,* Sipek took a unique approach for his trademark glass pieces, incorporating Renaissance-inspired touches to create the ornate contemporary works, which are located in glass cases positioned in the ship's stair landings.

The classic/contemporary design concept is also carried out in a series of bronze statues of the mythical figures Venus, Apollo, and Poseidon created by

Italian sculptor Katia Tasselli. These 6-foot-high figures, each of which took several months to complete due to the complexity of their design, dramatically enhance the areas surrounding the pools that bear their names.

Carnival Legend has sixteen themed bars, lounges, and nightspots, with dramatic interiors inspired by famous legends and historical figures, as well as a 14,500-square-foot health and fitness facility, four swimming pools, a cascading water slide, an Internet cafe, a wedding chapel, and a children's play area, part of the line's Camp Carnival program.

Dining options include a 1,250-seat formal dining room, a patisserie with specialty coffees and sweets, twenty-four-hour room service, and a two-level poolside restaurant offering breakfast, lunch, and dinner alternatives as well as twenty-four-hour pizza and ice cream. Also featured is an intimate steakhouse-style supper club.

Carnival Miracle features a diverse selection of artwork, ranging from bronze sculptures and ornate glass vases to colorful bold paintings, all based around the ship's interior decoration theme of "fictional icons." Italian artist Augusto Vignali created eighteen original paintings of legendary fictional characters, including the Phantom of the Opera, Sherlock Holmes, Philip Marlowe, and Captain Ahab.

On the Lido pool deck is a trio of bronze statues of the mythical figures Orpheus, Ulysses, and the Sirens. On stairway landings are sixty Bohemian crystal pieces including elegant vases, candleholders, and other items.

As with other Spirit-class ships, *Carnival Miracle* offers indoor and outdoor promenades, four swimming pools, a cascading water slide, and an upscale reservations-only supper club on the uppermost level of the ship's eleven-deck-high atrium.

Sixteen lounges and bars celebrate fictional icons of film, music, and literature. Decor varies from the mythical muses of antiquity to the fictional hometowns of superheroes. The lobby and atrium are named after the Metropolis of Superman fame, the lobby lounge is called the Jeeves Lounge, after the fictional butler of P.G. Wodehouse's novels, the foyer is the Batman-inspired Gotham Lounge, and the lower promenade is called the Fountainhead, from the Ayn Rand book of the same name.

The main dining room is named Bacchus, for the Greek god of wine; the restaurant's walls have elements that look like giant silver goblets and chandeliers resembling bunches of grapes descend from the ceiling.

Carnival Miracle's casual dining lido deck area is Horatio's, from the C.S. Forester stories about the Napoleon-era British naval captain Horatio Hornblower. Around the room are large three-dimensional Horatio figureheads made to look like carved ivory sculptures. Between the banquettes are large models of eighteenth- and nineteenth-century sailing ships.

Nick and Nora's supper club salutes characters created by Dashiell Hammett; the room, located at the top of the atrium under a red skylight, has a sophisticated look of ebony paneling with a centerpiece of a large mural of New York in the 1930s.

As befits this huge ship, it just goes on and on. There's the Phantom Lounge, after Andrew Lloyd Webber's "The Phantom of the Opera"; the Mad Hatter's Ball show lounge; the gothic-style dance club, Dr. Frankenstein's Lab; the Mr. Lucky's casino, after the 1943 Cary Grant movie; and the Maguire's sports bar, named after the contemporary film *Jerry Maguire.*

And, of course, of all the gin joints in the world, *Carnival Miracle*'s piano bar just had to be named Sam's, after the movie *Casablanca.*

Celebration, Holiday
(HOLIDAY CLASS)

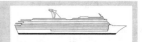

Econoguide rating:	★★★ 73 points
Ship size:	Large
Category:	Top of the Line
Price range:	Budget to Moderate $–$$
Registry:	Bahamas
Year built:	*Celebration,* 1987; *Holiday,* 1985
Information:	(305) 599–2600, (800) 227–6482
Web site:	www.carnival.com
Passenger capacity:	*Celebration,* 1,486; *Holiday,* 1,452
Crew:	660 to 670
Passenger-to-crew ratio:	2.2:1
Tonnage:	*Celebration,* 47,262; *Holiday,* 46,052
Passenger-space ratio:	31.7
Length:	727 feet
Beam:	92 feet
Draft:	24.7 feet
Cruising speed:	21 knots
Guest decks:	9
Total cabins:	726
Outside:	437
Inside:	279
Suites:	10
Wheelchair cabins:	15
Cuisine:	Contemporary and low-fat, low-calorie Nautica spa fare
Style:	Casual during the day; one or two nights, formal dress or dark suit suggested
Price notes:	Single-occupancy premium, 150 to 200 percent
Tipping suggestions:	$10 pp/pd automatically posted to bill

The two remaining Holiday-class sisters are still pretty flashy for a pair of older women. Early examples of the Carnival flash, they introduced the broad internal "boulevard" on the promenade deck. Less than half the tonnage of Carnival's Conquest- and Fantasy-class ships, Holiday-class ships don't offer many places to escape the lively onboard activities.

On *Celebration,* Bourbon Street runs down the length of the starboard side of the ship from the Islands in the Sky Lounge to the Astoria Lounge, passing by the Galax-Z Dance Club, the Rainbow Club Casino, and the dry-docked trolley parked nearby. The ship underwent an extensive refurbishment in 2003, emerging with a newly designed purser's lobby and promenade, remodeled staterooms, and cosmetic enhancements to a variety of lounges, bars, and restaurants.

Holiday's Broadway on the promenade deck features a bus parked outside the casino. The nightclub is the western-themed Doc Holiday's.

The third sister in the Holiday class, *Jubilee,* was due to leave the Carnival fleet in the fall of 2004 to join P&O Cruises Australia and sail as the *Pacific Sun.* The ship joins *Pacific Sky* in sailing year-round on seven- to fourteen-day cruises to the South Pacific islands of New Caledonia, Fiji, Vanuatu, and Tonga as well as cruises to New Zealand and Australia. The ship was due to receive a multimillion-dollar refurbishment.

On this class of ship, lifeboats sit way up high, resulting in very few obstructed views and affecting just four suites on the veranda deck.

CELEBRITY CRUISES

Address: 1050 Caribbean Way
   Miami, FL 33132-2096
Information: (800) 437–3111, (305) 262–6677
   www.celebritycruises.com
Econoguide's Best Cruise Lines
Econoguide's Best Cruise Values
Econoguide's Best Dining at Sea

The Celebrity Cruises Fleet

Constellation	2002	1,950 passengers	91,000 tons
Infinity	2001	1,950 passengers	91,000 tons
Millennium	2000	1,950 passengers	91,000 tons
Summit	2001	1,950 passengers	91,000 tons
Galaxy	1996	1,870 passengers	77,713 tons
Mercury	1997	1,870 passengers	77,713 tons
Century	1995	1,750 passengers	70,606 tons
Zenith	1992	1,375 passengers	47,255 tons
Horizon	1990	1,354 passengers	46,811 tons

X marks the spot for this upscale cruise line that sits somewhere between middle-of-the-market lines such as Royal Caribbean International (its parent company) and the small superluxury ships of companies such as Crystal and Seabourn.

The Celebrity *X* logo refers to the Greek character used to spell Chandris Group, the original founder of the company; Celebrity will also have you believe the symbol recalls the *X* ancient mariners used to mark their destinations.

The flagships of the line are the Millennium-class vessels. The 91,000-ton, 1,950-passenger ships, built at Chantiers de l'Atlantique in Saint-Nazaire, France, feature balconies for about 70 percent of staterooms, as well as some of the largest luxury suites afloat. Along with Royal Caribbean, they are the first cruise ships to use clean-burning gas turbines for propulsion.

The first ship in the class, *Millennium,* features a unique maritime treasure: the specialty dining room is decorated with the actual interior paneling of the RMS *Olympic,* sister ship to the RMS *Titanic.* The wood paneling in the 134-seat Olympic restaurant once graced the a la carte dining room onboard the glamorous *Olympic,* launched in 1911. The paneling was discovered in a private English residence and purchased at auction at Sotheby's.

The restaurant also offers the industry's first demonstration galley, along with a dine-in wine cellar. And speaking of wine, Celebrity was the winner of an auction at Christie's in New York for three rare bottles of 1907 Heidsieck Monopole champagne; the bottles of bubbly are displayed in the wine cellar. The champagne was salvaged in 1998 from the wreck of the *Jonkoping,* a Swedish merchant ship that was sunk in the Baltic Sea in 1916 by German sailors who believed the ship was carrying contraband: 5,000 bottles of top-quality French champagne destined for the czar of Russia. Wine experts say the champagne survived, with corks intact, in 35 degree water and total darkness. The same champagne was believed to be onboard the *Titanic* when it sank in 1912.

The Emporium is a high-tone shopping mall at sea, including outposts of DKNY, Versace, H. Stern, Fossil, La Perla, and Swarovski. The 14,460-square-foot mall also includes a shop selling cookware, kitchenware, and ingredients endorsed by chef Michel Roux.

The second ship in the class is the *Infinity,* which arrived in mid-2001. That ship includes a specialty restaurant that salutes the famed liner *United States.*

The third and fourth ships in the series are *Summit* and *Constellation.*

■ THE CELEBRITY STORY

Celebrity Cruises was founded in 1989 by the Athens-based Chandris Group as an upscale cruise line. The company's first vessel was the *Meridian,* formerly known as the *Galileo,* completely rebuilt and launched in 1990. That same year Celebrity brought onto the line a new ship, *Horizon.*

One of Celebrity's claims to fame is the quality of its food; among the company's first steps was the hiring of three-star Michelin chef and restaurateur Michel Roux to design the food service and train the executive restaurant staff. Roux continues as a consultant, sailing unannounced on the vessels and revising and updating menus every six months.

Roux also oversees the specifications for an elegant formal tea served weekly aboard all ships, elaborate midnight buffets featuring exquisite ice carvings, and theme meals.

The *Meridian* was sold to a Singapore company in 1997 when the sisters *Galaxy* and *Mercury* came on line. That same year, the Chandris family sold Celebrity to Royal Caribbean International.

Overall, Celebrity represents good value for the money, a reasonable step up in quality and price from the middle of the pack.

■ THE CELEBRITY EXPERIENCE

In the main dining room, the dress code is just a bit more formal than on other lines; jackets and ties are requested for men on formal and informal nights, with time off for good behavior on casual nights only.

At the same time, Celebrity has introduced more casual dining options most nights on every cruise, served in the Palm Springs Grill and pool area on *Mercury,* at the Oasis Grill and pool area on *Galaxy,* the Coral Seas Cafe on *Horizon,* the Windsurf Cafe on *Zenith,* and in the Sky Bar on *Century.* A typical casual menu would offer lasagna, broiled salmon steak, spit-roasted chicken, and grilled sirloin steak—simpler fare than offered in the main dining rooms.

Indulgences onboard include the AquaSpa program, which offers treatments and facilities from Middle Eastern, Asian, and European sources, including a 115,000-gallon thalassotherapy pool on the *Century;* hydrotherapy spa baths of seaweed, minerals, or aromatherapy oils; and aqua meditation. There's also the Rasul treatment that includes a seaweed soap shower, medicinal mudpack, herbal steam bath, and massage. Treatments can be booked individually or as part of packages extending over the course of a voyage.

The line's Family Cruising Program serves youngsters from age three through seventeen with events that include pool Olympics, scavenger hunts, video games, arts and crafts, ship tours, and pizza and ice-cream parties.

And then there are the occasional Celebrity Escape cruises, for adults only. We're not exactly talking about an X-rating at sea, but the line does offer a Valentine's Night, late-night comedy acts including an adult-themed show, poolside fashion shows, afternoon tea, and other entertainments. All guests on these cruises must be over the age of twenty-one.

Celebrity Cruises and world-famous entertainment oddity Cirque du Soleil have begun a cross-marketing relationship that includes Celebrity's sponsorship of some North American and European tours as well as a "unique entertainment concept" onboard some of the line's ships. Since its founding in Montreal in 1984, Cirque du Soleil has entertained more than 40 million people in ninety cities around the world.

The company also introduced a brand within its brand for exotic cruises in the Galapagos aboard *Celebrity Xpedition.* That small vessel, formerly the *Sun Bay I,* will offer seven- to ten-day cruises around the Galapagos chain. Celebrity Xpeditions, the brand, will also offer adventure travel on other ships including icebreakers in the Arctic and side trips to Antarctica on other cruises.

At Grand Cayman island in the western Caribbean, guests in a real hurry can try out a new rapid excursion. An 80-foot-long maxi-class yacht, renamed as

Celebrity Cruises will take guests on a three-hour high-speed sail from the pier to Cayman's Seven Mile Beach. The extreme racing yacht, built of carbon fiber, Kevlar, and titanium, can accommodate about twenty guests. On some days, the yacht will race against a nearly identical yacht named for sister cruise line Royal Caribbean.

ITINERARIES

In 2004 Celebrity offered cruises from eleven mainland U.S. cities, sailing to Alaska, Bermuda, California, the Caribbean, Hawaii, the Mexican Riviera, the Panama Canal, and South America. During the summer, three ships were dispatched to Europe for a series of cruises in the British Isles, Northern Europe, and the Mediterranean.

In 2004 *Zenith* and *Constellation* were homeported in New York for cruises to Bermuda and Canada/New England. *Horizon* sailed to Bermuda from Philadelphia and Norfolk.

Galaxy sailed from Baltimore to the Caribbean, Canada, and transatlantic to Europe. The ship also sailed from Galveston to the Panama Canal.

Celebrity operated sailings to the Caribbean from Jacksonville on the *Zenith* and Tampa for the *Horizon.* Fort Lauderdale was the port of embarkation for Caribbean cruises by *Century, Millennium, Summit,* and *Infinity.*

On the West Coast, San Diego and San Francisco were home ports for *Mercury* on cruises to the Mexican Riviera. *Mercury* also sailed to Alaska from San Francisco and Seattle.

In the summer of 2004, *Constellation* sailed in Europe from Dover, England, and Copenhagen; *Galaxy* left from Civitavecchia (Rome) and Nice; and *Millennium* from Barcelona and Venice.

Celebrity's Xpeditions exotic travel cruises in 2004 partnered with polar explorations leader Quark Expeditions. Celebrity planned to take guests to the isolated Arctic and Antarctic on twelve- and thirteen-night voyages. The platform for the latest Celebrity Xpedition is Quark Expeditions' 112-guest *Kapitan Khlebnikov,* a powerful, polar-class icebreaker with a 434-foot length considered ideal for navigating around icebergs and ice floes.

One such trip was a thirteen-night itinerary round-trip from Ottawa, Canada, sailing through dense ice to Resolute; Lancaster Sound, home to whales, polar bears, and Arctic seals; Coburg Island, circled by rocky ledges dotted with rare seabirds; Smith Sound, Kane Basin, and Ellesmere Island; northern Greenland's administrative capital, Qaanaaq (Thule); the migratory bird sanctuary of Bylot Island; and Beechy Island, where Sir John Franklin set out in the mid-1800s with 134 men and two ships to find the Northwest Passage and mysteriously disappeared.

At the other end of the earth was a twelve-night round-trip from Ushuaia, Argentina, past glaciers, icebergs, and rugged mountains to Drake Passage, known for numerous albatrosses and widely varied seabirds; Elephant Island, where legendary explorer Sir Ernest Shackleton's *Endurance* sank in 1915; the

South Shetland Islands, including the wildlife-rich Half Moon Island, Livingstone Island, and the active volcano of Deception Island; Cape Horn, the southernmost tip of South America and the legendary seafaring point where the Atlantic and Pacific Oceans meet.

■ WEB SITE

Celebrity's Web site provides a good collection of information, including a fleetwide calendar. Once you choose your trip, you can select from specific available cabins. The trip can be booked on-line, or you can hold the cabin and arrange for Celebrity to call you to complete the booking on the telephone. *Ease of use: very good.*

Millennium, Infinity, Summit, Constellation (MILLENNIUM CLASS)

Econoguide rating:	★★★★★ 93 points
Ship size:	Megaship
Category:	Top of the Line
Price range:	Premium $$$
Registry:	Liberia
Year built:	*Millennium,* 2000; *Infinity,* 2001; *Summit,* 2001; *Constellation,* 2002
Information:	(305) 262–6677
Web site:	www.celebritycruises.com
Passenger capacity:	1,950 (double occupancy)
Crew:	999
Passenger-to-crew ratio:	2:1
Tonnage:	91,000
Passenger-space ratio:	46.7
Length:	965 feet
Beam:	105.6 feet
Draft:	26.3 feet
Cruising speed:	24 knots
Guest decks:	11
Total cabins:	975
Outside:	780
Inside:	195
Suites:	50
Wheelchair cabins:	9
Cuisine:	Continental and international
Style:	Informal, with two or three formal evenings
Price notes:	Single-occupancy premium, about 125 percent
Tipping suggestions:	$9.00 pp/pd

The first of Celebrity's Millennium-class ships took to the seas in summer 2000 and was joined in coming years by three sisters.

The handsome ships employ environmentally friendly gas turbines and high-tech engine pods for maneuverability. The introduction of the cutting-edge *Millennium* was not without problems. The *Millennium* was delivered several months late, forcing the cancellation of its original maiden voyage. All four of the high-tech ships have suffered from various mechanical problems in their early years resulting in a number of canceled trips; in each case Celebrity took good care of disappointed guests, offering refunds, free trips, and discounts.

(You can read about a trip on the *Millennium* in Chapter 11: Cruise Diaries.)

Infinity, the second of four ships in Celebrity's Millennium class, began service in early 2001. The ship's two penthouse suites have marble floors, separate living and dining rooms, a baby grand piano, a high-tech flat-screen entertainment system, a fax machine, and a private veranda with a whirlpool for times when you absolutely need to get away from it all.

Infinity features the industry's first full conservatory at sea, created by prominent Paris-based floral designer Emilio Robba. Accenting the interior of the ship's SS United States specialty restaurant are actual glass panels from the liner *United States,* which launched in 1952 and gained fame for clocking the fastest transatlantic crossing from New York. Like the Olympic restaurant on her sister ship *Millennium,* the specialty restaurant on *Infinity* offers tableside cooking, carving, and flambé at sea. The dine-in wine cellar stocks more than 175 labels from around the world. The menu includes an entree first served in the dining room onboard the original SS *United States* in the 1950s: roast Long Island duckling à l'orange stuffed with fruit.

Like *Millennium,* the new ship presents exterior glass-enclosed elevators, offering guests panoramic ocean views as they move from deck to deck. The vessel also has an eighteen-workstation Internet cafe, accessible to all guests, and flat-screen PCs and printers in all suites. Every stateroom on the ship is also equipped with connections to the Internet for guests who bring their own computers.

Celebrity's advanced *Millennium* receives an old-fashioned christening in Southampton, England. *Photo by Corey Sandler*

The Emporium, *Infinity*'s 14,000-square-foot shopping area, offers elegant and trendy designer labels, including Swarovski, H. Stern, Donna Karan, and La Perla, in addition to shops featuring Michel Roux gourmet delicacies and Cova Cafe Milano confections.

Summit offers the same amenities, including an upper-deck conservatory, a botanical environment of flowers, plants, trees, and fountains. The specialty restaurant onboard *Summit* features original paneling and a variety of artifacts from the *Normandie,* considered the foremost ocean liner of the 1930s. The famed *Normandie* was the industry's first 1,000-foot liner; the first French Line vessel to win the coveted Blue Riband, the North Atlantic's prize for speed; and the first to take the chic *arts decoratifs*—now known as Art Deco—design style to sea.

The 134-guest specialty restaurant recalls the Art Deco design of the original *Normandie*'s scheme, with *Summit*'s dining venue divided by a circular colonnade that displays two sets of four large gold-lacquered panels from the stylish smoking room on the original *Normandie.* Celebrity obtained the panels at auction at Christie's.

The fourth sister, **Constellation,** joined the fleet in mid-2002.

Century

Econoguide rating:	★★★★★ 91 points
Ship size:	Megaship
Category:	Top of the Line
Price range:	Premium $$$
Registry:	Liberia
Year built:	1995
Information:	(305) 262–6677
Web site:	www.celebritycruises.com
Passenger capacity:	1,750 (double occupancy)
Crew:	858
Passenger-to-crew ratio:	2:1
Tonnage:	70,606
Passenger-space ratio:	40.3
Length:	815 feet
Beam:	105 feet
Draft:	25 feet
Cruising speed:	21.5 knots
Guest decks:	10
Total cabins:	875
Outside:	517
Inside:	306
Suites:	52

Wheelchair cabins:	8
Cuisine:	Continental and international
Style:	Informal, with two or three formal evenings
Price notes:	Single-occupancy premium, about 125 percent
Tipping suggestions:	$9.00 pp/pd

Celebrity's **Century** is a close sister to the handsome *Galaxy* and *Mercury* twins. The spectacular 1,080-seat two-level Grand Restaurant surrounds diners with the blue of the sea in a setting of old-world elegance.

Lifeboats on the handsome ship hang recessed into the entertainment and promenade decks, leaving very few obstructed views from passenger cabins above and below.

Galaxy, Mercury

Econoguide rating:	★★★★★ 91 points
Ship size:	Megaship
Category:	Top of the Line
Price range:	Premium $$$
Registry:	Liberia
Year built:	*Galaxy*, 1996; *Mercury*, 1997
Information:	(305) 262–6677
Web site:	www.celebritycruises.com
Passenger capacity:	1,870 (double occupancy)
Crew:	909
Passenger-to-crew ratio:	2.1:1
Tonnage:	77,713
Passenger-space ratio:	41.6
Length:	866 feet
Beam:	105.6 feet
Draft:	25.5 feet
Cruising speed:	21.5 knots
Guest decks:	10
Total cabins:	935
Outside:	419
Inside:	296
Suites:	220, with private balconies
Wheelchair cabins:	5
Cuisine:	Pacific Northwest cuisine for Alaska cruises
Style:	Informal, with two or three formal evenings
Price notes:	Single-occupancy premium, about 125 percent
Tipping suggestions:	$9.00 pp/pd

The lifeboats on **Galaxy** and **Mercury** are recessed into entertainment and promenade decks, all but eliminating obstructed views from passenger cabins that are all located above or below the boats. The promenade deck, though, does not allow a full circuit of the deck, blocked at the bow and stern by the Celebrity Theater and the Orion Restaurant, respectively.

The ships' shopping spaces resemble a European piazza. Recreation facilities include an indoor Palm Springs pool area, two outdoor La Playa pools, and four outdoor whirlpools. A sports deck offers basketball, a golf simulator, and volleyball; there's also trap shooting off the ship.

Horizon

Econoguide rating:	★★★★ 85 points
Ship size:	Large
Category:	Top of the Line
Price range:	Premium $$$
Registry:	Liberia
Year built:	1990 (refurbished 1998)
Information:	(800) 437–3111
Web site:	www.celebritycruises.com
Passenger capacity:	1,354 (double occupancy)
Crew:	642; Greek officers
Passenger-to-crew ratio:	2.1:1
Tonnage:	46,811
Passenger-space ratio:	34.6
Length:	682 feet
Beam:	95 feet
Draft:	24 feet
Cruising speed:	21.4 knots
Guest decks:	9
Total cabins:	677
Outside:	513
Inside:	144
Suites:	20
Wheelchair cabins:	4 ocean-view staterooms
Cuisine:	Continental and international
Style:	Informal, with two or three formal evenings
Price notes:	Single-occupancy premium, about 125 percent
Tipping suggestions:	$9.00 pp/pd

In relative terms, the **Horizon** is one of the more "intimate" ships in the Celebrity fleet, albeit still a rather large vessel, with more than 2,000 passengers and crew onboard most voyages. The *Horizon* is a near-twin to the *Zenith*. Most of the cabins on the Bermuda Deck have views obstructed by the lifeboats that hang outside the windows there.

In 1998 *Horizon* underwent a refurbishment that brought it up to the comfort and elegance specs of Celebrity's Century-class vessels. The Gemini Disco was gutted and redesigned to form a grand entrance area, with the intimate Michael's Club, a cigar and cognac club (complete with a high-tech fireplace). Also in the entrance area is a card room and library, complete with personal computers and printers; the former card room and library on Galaxy Deck was redesigned as a martini bar, art gallery, and boutique. A similar redesign was undertaken in late 1999 for Celebrity's *Zenith*.

Horizon's COVA Cafe, in the former Plaza Bar, is based on the famed Milan coffeehouse Pasticceria Confetteria COVA. The intimate cafe serves cappuccino, espresso, macchiato, a variety of teas, liqueurs, and chocolates.

The Fantasia bar on Sun Deck was remade as *Horizon*'s AquaSpa, including a beauty salon, five treatment rooms, and a fitness and aerobics area.

Zenith

Econoguide rating:	★★★★ 85 points
Ship size:	Large
Category:	Top of the Line
Price range:	Premium $$$
Registry:	Liberia
Year built:	1992 (refurbished 1999)
Information:	(800) 437–3111
Web site:	www.celebritycruises.com
Passenger capacity:	1,375 (double occupancy)
Crew:	670
Passenger-to-crew ratio:	2:1
Tonnage:	47,255
Passenger-space ratio:	34.4
Length:	682 feet
Beam:	95 feet
Draft:	24 feet
Cruising speed:	21.4 knots
Guest decks:	9
Total cabins:	687
Outside:	519
Inside:	146
Suites:	22
Wheelchair cabins:	4

Cuisine:	Continental and international
Style:	Informal, with two or three formal evenings
Price notes:	Single-occupancy premium, about 125 percent
Tipping suggestions:	$9.00 pp/pd

Near-twin to the *Horizon*, the **Zenith** received a major refurbishment in late 1999 along the lines of the remake of *Horizon*. The ship's observation lounge includes telescopes; the pool lies beneath a retractable sliding glass sunroof.

COSTA CRUISE LINES

⟨C Costa
CRUISING ITALIAN STYLE™

Address: 80 Southwest Eighth Street
 Miami, FL 33130-3097
Information: (800) 332–6782, (305) 358–7325
 www.costacruises.com
Econoguide's Best Party Ships

The Costa Cruise Lines Fleet

CostaMagica	2004	2,720 passengers	105,000 tons
CostaFortuna	2003	2,720 passengers	105,000 tons
CostaMediterranea	2003	2,154 passengers	86,000 tons
CostaAtlantica	2000	2,112 passengers	84,000 tons
CostaVictoria	1996	1,950 passengers	76,000 tons
CostaRomantica	1993	1,350 passengers	54,000 tons
CostaClassica	1991	1,350 passengers	54,000 tons
CostaEuropa	1986	1,494 passengers	53,872 tons
CostaTropicale	1982	1,022 passengers	36,674 tons
CostaAllegra	1992	820 passengers	28,500 tons
CostaMarina	1990	760 passengers	25,558 tons

FUTURE SHIPS

Unnamed ship	Summer 2006	3,004 passengers	112,000 tons

Costa puts the emphasis on its Italian roots, even though today it is best known to Americans for Caribbean itineraries. It is operated out of Miami by a Panamanian corporation with American ownership and management and a history that dates back to an Israeli founder.

Nevertheless, its ships do have a distinctive Italian flavor in their design, cuisine, and activities. And its distinctive appearance is enhanced with bright yellow smokestacks that bear the company's *C*.

Costa's history can be traced back to 1860 when Giacomo Costa began an olive oil business in Genoa, Italy. In 1916 his three sons inherited the family business; in 1924 they purchased the *Ravenna,* a 1,100-ton freighter, to reduce the transportation costs for their oil empire.

By 1935 seven more freighters had joined the fleet, with two more by 1942. World War II reduced the fleet back to a single ship, but by 1948 the company had rebounded to a twelve-ship fleet.

Passenger service began in 1948 with the 12,000-ton, 850-passenger *Anna C,* carrying passengers between Genoa and South America. The service was an immediate success, and within four years Costa had added three more vessels. In the late 1950s the company constructed its first brand-new ships.

Costa's year-round North American cruise operation began in 1959 with seven-day cruises into the Caribbean from Miami on the *Franca C.* The company continued to grow in North America and Europe, introducing in 1985 its North American flagship, the 984-passenger *CostaRiviera.*

After more than a century under Costa family ownership, the company was opened to outside investors in 1989, ushering in a new era of expansion. In 1997 Costa Crociere (Costa Cruises) was purchased by Carnival Corporation and Airtours PLC. In 2000 Carnival acquired the outstanding 50 percent interest in Costa from Airtours.

Costa has ordered a massive 112,000-ton ship to be delivered in summer 2006. The as-yet-unnamed ship, which will include 1,502 staterooms, a double-occupancy capacity of 3,004 passengers, will be the largest passenger ship in the history of Italian seafaring. It is expected to be deployed in the Mediterranean year-round.

As an all-new class of vessel for the line, it will offer innovative amenities and facilities including a wide range of formal and casual dining venues, one of the largest spas at sea, four swimming pools—two of which feature retractable domes–and state-of-the-art telecommunications capabilities that will enable guests to use their cellular telephones while at sea. Sixty-one percent of the ship's staterooms feature an ocean view with 62 percent of those offering private balconies.

The *CostaAtlantica,* a handsome 84,000-ton, 2,112-passenger ship, joined the fleet in spring 2000. *CostaMediterranea,* an 86,000-ton sister ship to the *CostaAtlantica,* entered the fleet in June of 2003; both are similar to Carnival's Spirit-class vessels.

CostaFortuna arrived in late 2003, and *CostaMagica* was due to arrive in November of 2004. Costa's largest current ships, at 105,000 tons and carrying 2,720 passengers, these two are expected to sail in Europe for the summer and move to the Caribbean for the winter.

In 2002 *CostaEuropa* was added to the fleet; the ship is the renovated and rebuilt *Westerdam,* formerly operated by sister company Holland America Line. The *CostaTropicale,* formerly Carnival's *Tropicale,* began sailing from Venice in mid-2002.

Costa Kreuzfahrten, a German subsidiary, operates year-round European and Caribbean sailings aboard the 760-passenger *CostaMarina.*

■ ITINERARIES

Costa operates in the Caribbean, the Mediterranean, and northern Europe. In a typical year, European cruises are concentrated from March through November, with most of the ships repositioning to the Caribbean for the winter months.

In the Caribbean, Costa's primary port of embarkation is Fort Lauderdale, with cruises to eastern and western parts of the basin.

Mediterranean ports of call typically include Spain, Portugal, Morocco, Greece, Croatia, Turkey, Tunisia, and Malta.

Costa operates transatlantic repositioning cruises from Europe late in the year and to Europe in the spring.

■ THE COSTA EXPERIENCE

Costa promotes "cruising Italian-style" with Italian theme nights, Italian language lessons, cooking lessons, and its famously quirky entertainments, including the Festa Italiana, which is billed as an Italian street festival at sea, with boccie ball tournaments, tarantella dance lessons, pizza dough–tossing contests, Italian karaoke, and the like.

Another theme night is Notte Tropical, when the evening's activities, which take place out on deck, include ice-carving demonstrations and a sumptuous midnight alfresco buffet.

But Costa is most famous for the "Roman Bacchanal" toga party on the last night of its Caribbean cruises; for the evening, passengers don togas and enjoy a bacchanal parade and other such preplanned debauchery. (By the way, passengers no longer have to create their own togas from bedsheets; ready-made off-the-shoulder models are available from the cruise staff.)

Costa added Ristorante Magnifico by Zeffirino to the *CostaVictoria* and *Costa-Atlantica*. Zeffirino has been a favorite restaurant in Genoa since 1939. Seating is by reservation, and a service charge of about $20 per person is applied.

The *CostaRomantica* and *CostaVictoria* offer the Golf Academy at Sea, with onboard golf clinics and seminars conducted by a PGA member golf instructor. Guests can also be accompanied by a PGA instructor as they play on some of the Caribbean's best golf courses, such as Mahogany Run in Saint Thomas, the Links at Safe Haven in Grand Cayman, Runaway Bay and Sandals Golf Resorts in Ocho Rios, Cable Beach Golf Course in Nassau, Key West Golf Course in Key West, and Teeth of the Dog or The Links at the Casa de Campo Resort in the Dominican Republic.

Costa's private beach is Catalina Island just off the coast of the Dominican Republic. Entertainment includes a beach barbecue, chaise longues, water floats, and land and water sports.

■ SPECIAL DEALS

Passengers who book at least 120 days in advance can take advantage of Costa's "Andiamo Rates" of about $500, which can work out to as much as one-third off per person on the less expensive cabins and still a decent break on more expensive accommodations.

Costa Cruise Savers offer additional savings for senior citizens, children, and single parents on selected ships and sailing dates. Savings are also available for passengers who combine two seven-night cruises.

■ WEB SITE

Costa provides a confusing and minimal site. Each of the ships in the fleet carries Web cams, and you can see the fore-aft views, current position, and speed of each ship. In mid-2003, there was no on-line booking capability, although the Web site appears to be set up to eventually permit reservations. *Ease of use: poor.*

CostaFortuna, CostaMagica

Econoguide rating:	★★★ 79 points
Ship size:	Colossus
Category:	Top of the Line
Price range:	Moderate to Premium $$–$$$
Registry:	Liberia
Year built:	*CostaFortuna,* 2003; *CostaMagica,* 2004
Information:	(800) 332–6782
Web site:	www.costacruises.com
Passenger capacity:	2,720 (double occupancy)
Crew:	1,100 (estimated)
Passenger-to-crew ratio:	2.5:1 (estimated)
Tonnage:	105,000
Passenger-space ratio:	38.6
Length:	885 feet
Beam:	123 feet
Draft:	27 feet (estimated)
Cruising speed:	19.5 knots
Guest decks:	14
Total cabins:	1,359
Cuisine:	Italian/continental
Style:	Informal, with two formal nights per cruise; one casual night is a Roman Bacchanal, with guests invited to wear togas
Price notes:	Single-occupancy premium, 150 to 200 percent
Tipping suggestions:	$8.50 pp/pd; $6.60 pp/pd in Europe
Best deal:	Andiamo advance rates, Costa Cruise Savers for seniors and singles

Costa Fortuna was the first large passenger ship to emerge from the shipyards in Sestri Ponente in Italy since the famed *Michelangelo* in 1965. The same yard also built a number of other famous Italian liners of yesteryear, including *Rex* in 1932, *Andrea Doria* in 1951, and *Leonardo da Vinci* in 1958.

The interior design (executed by parent company Carnival's architect Joe Farcus) salutes the legendary Italian liners that provided regular passenger services between Italy and the Americas. The ship's theater, which extends over three decks, is named after the *Rex*, two of the restaurants are Ristorante Raffaello and Ristorante Michelangelo, while the main bar is the Gran Bar Conte di Savoia.

Decorations include scale models of some of these transatlantic liners as well as copies of posters and advertisements from their times afloat. The ceiling of the main lobby, called *Atrio Costa* features large models of all the ships that have been at one time or another members of the Costa fleet.

Sister ship **Costa Magica** has a similar complement of facilities.

CostaAtlantica, CostaMediterranea

Econoguide rating:	★★★ 79 points
Ship size:	Megaship
Category:	Top of the Line
Price range:	Moderate to Premium $$–$$$
Registry:	Liberia
Year built:	CostaAtlantica, 2000; CostaMediterranea, 2003
Information:	(800) 332–6782
Web site:	www.costacruises.com
Passenger capacity:	CostaAtlantica, 2,112; CostaMediterranea, 2,154
Crew:	900
Passenger-to-crew ratio:	2.4:1
Tonnage:	86,000
Passenger-space ratio:	39.8
Length:	951 feet
Beam:	105 feet
Draft:	25 feet
Cruising speed:	24 knots
Guest decks:	12
Total cabins:	1,057
Outside:	787
Inside:	212
Suites:	58
Cuisine:	Italian/continental
Style:	Informal, with two formal nights per cruise; one casual night is a Roman Bacchanal, with guests invited to wear togas
Price notes:	Single-occupancy premium, 150 to 200 percent
Tipping suggestions:	$8.50 pp/pd; $6.00 pp/pd in Europe
Best deal:	Andiamo advance rates, Costa Cruise Savers for seniors and singles

The fast and splashy *CostaAtlantica* joined the fleet in summer 2000. Sister ship *CostaMediterranea* arrived three years later. Nearly three-quarters of the cabins on the $400 million ships have verandas. There are three pools, including one with a retractable magrodome, which allows swimming in all weather.

The twelve passenger decks of *CostaAtlantica* are named after motion pictures by famed Italian director Federico Fellini; deck names include La Dolce Vita, Amarcord, I Clowns, and La Strada.

The *CostaAtlantica* features a replica of the famed Caffé Florian, the landmark cafe located under the arcades of the Procuratie Nuove in Saint Mark's Square in Venice. The original cafe opened in 1720 and became the most famous *botega da caffé* of its time. Along the years, the Caffé Florian has entertained such notables as Casanova, who hung out there in search of beautiful women; composers Antonio Vivaldi and Igor Stravinsky; and author Charles Dickens.

In addition to the two-level Tiziano main restaurant, the Botticelli Buffet, and the Napoli Pizzeria, guests can also opt for an alternative dining experience at the Ristorante Magnifico by Zeffirino.

CostaClassica, CostaRomantica

Econoguide rating:	★★★ 75 points
Ship size:	Large
Category:	Top of the Line
Price range:	Moderate $$
Registry:	Liberia
Year built:	*CostaClassica,* 1991; *CostaRomantica,* 1993
Information:	(800) 332–6782
Web site:	www.costacruises.com
Passenger capacity:	*CostaClassica,* 1,350; *CostaRomantica,* 1,350
Crew:	610
Passenger-to-crew ratio:	2.2:1
Tonnage:	*CostaClassica,* 53,000; *CostaRomantica,* 54,000
Passenger-space ratio:	39
Length:	722 feet
Beam:	102 feet
Draft:	25 feet
Cruising speed:	18.5 knots
Guest decks:	10
Total cabins:	678
Outside:	428
Inside:	216
Suites:	34
Wheelchair cabins:	6

Cuisine:	Italian/continental
Style:	Informal, with two formal nights per cruise
Price notes:	Single-occupancy premium, 150 to 200 percent; single cabins available
Tipping suggestions:	$6.00 pp/pd
Best deal:	Andiamo advance rates, Costa Cruise Savers for seniors and singles

CostaRomantica offers a bit of European sophistication at sea, showcasing almost $20 million in works of art, including sculptures, paintings, murals, and wall hangings. There's a primarily Italian and international hotel and dining staff, and within is the Via Condotti, an elegant European shopping promenade.

The ship's decks are named after great cities of Europe: Monte Carlo, Madrid, Vienna, Verona, Paris, London, Copenhagen, and Amsterdam.

The Piazza Italia Grand Bar on the Verona Deck is one of the largest lounges afloat, with a capacity of 300; it has a teak dance floor and offers live entertainment. L'Opera Theatre is a 630-seat Renaissance-style amphitheater setting, extending to the Vienna Deck above. A disco atop the ship offers 360-degree views.

Oversize staterooms average 200 square feet, and thirty-four luxurious suites have as much as 580 square feet; there are only ten verandas, though. An inside standard room is a still-spacious 175 square feet.

CostaClassica is a near-twin sister.

CostaVictoria

Econoguide rating:	★★★ 77 points
Ship size:	Megaship
Category:	Top of the Line
Price range:	Moderate $$
Registry:	Liberia
Year built:	1996
Information:	(800) 332–6782
Web site:	www.costacruises.com
Passenger capacity:	1,950 (double occupancy)
Crew:	800
Passenger-to-crew ratio:	2.4:1
Tonnage:	76,000
Passenger-space ratio:	39
Length:	828 feet
Beam:	105.5 feet
Draft:	26 feet
Cruising speed:	23 knots
Guest decks:	10

CostaVictoria under sail. *Courtesy Costa Cruise Lines and CLIA*

Total cabins:	964
Outside:	555
Inside:	389
Suites:	20
Wheelchair cabins:	6
Cuisine:	Italian/continental
Style:	Informal, with two formal nights per cruise; one casual night is a Roman Bacchanal, with guests invited to wear togas
Price notes:	Single-occupancy premium, 150 to 200 percent
Tipping suggestions:	$8.50 pp/pd; $6.00 pp/pd in Europe
Best deal:	Andiamo advance rates, Costa Cruise Savers for seniors and singles

An unusual design in this day of Megaships; the **CostaVictoria** is almost squared off at the stern and pinched like a pumpkin seed at the bow, with a very steep forward slope. From the side it looks like a horizontal skyscraper.

Inside is the central Planetarium Atrium, seven decks high and covered by a large glass dome. Four panoramic elevators take passengers to the upper deck. The decks, named after classic operas, include Madame Butterfly, Rigoletto, Norma, Tosca, Othello, Carmen, Traviata, and Boheme.

CostaTropicale

Econoguide rating:	★★★ 68 points
Ship size:	Medium
Category:	Vintage
Price range:	Budget to Moderate $–$$
Registry:	Liberia
Year built:	1982
Information:	(800) 332–6782
Web site:	www.costacruises.com
Passenger capacity:	1,022 (double occupancy)
Crew:	550
Passenger-to-crew ratio:	1.9:1
Tonnage:	36,674
Passenger-space ratio:	35.9
Length:	660 feet
Beam:	85 feet
Draft:	23 feet
Cruising speed:	20 knots
Guest decks:	10
Total cabins:	511
Outside:	312

Inside:	187
Suites:	12
Wheelchair cabins:	11
Cuisine:	Contemporary and low-fat, low-calorie Nautica spa fare
Style:	Casual, with one or two semiformal nights
Price notes:	Single-occupancy premium, 150 to 200 percent
Tipping suggestions:	$8.50 pp/pd; $6.00 pp/pd in Europe
Best deal:	Andiamo advance rates, Costa Cruise Savers for seniors and singles

New to the Costa fleet in 2001, **CostaTropicale** had been the oldest and smallest ship in the Carnival fleet before it was transferred within the corporation.

The ship, formerly named *Tropicale,* underwent extensive refurbishment in Genoa before reemerging under Costa's colors. In addition to a refurbishment of all public areas and staterooms, the signature Carnival funnel was replaced with an upright yellow stack in Costa's style.

CostaTropicale is marketed as part of Costa's Best Value Collection, sailing mostly in the Mediterranean.

When the ship was commissioned in 1978, industry experts declared that she was too big and too expensive to ever make a profit; instead, the *Tropicale* blazed a path for the birth of the cruising industry and helped make Carnival a major success.

Tropicale entered service in 1982 as the first new cruise ship built in nearly a decade and served as the prototype on which Carnival's Holiday-class vessels were based.

CostaEuropa

Econoguide rating:	★★★ 76 points
Ship size:	Large
Category:	Top of the Line
Price range:	Premium $$$
Registry:	Liberia
Year built:	1986 (built as *Homeric,* lengthened by 130 feet in 1989, formerly *Westerdam* of Holland America Line)
Information:	(800) 332–6782
Web site:	www.costacruises.com
Passenger capacity:	1,494 (double occupancy)
Crew:	642
Passenger-to-crew ratio:	2.33:1
Tonnage:	53,872
Passenger-space ratio:	36
Length:	798 feet

Beam:	95 feet
Draft:	23.6 feet
Cruising speed:	20.5 knots
Guest decks:	9
Total cabins:	747
Outside:	489
Inside:	252
Suites:	6
Wheelchair cabins:	4
Cuisine:	Contemporary and low-fat, low-calorie Nautica spa fare
Style:	Casual, with one or two semiformal nights
Price notes:	Single-occupancy premium, 150 to 200 percent
Tipping suggestions:	$8.50 pp/pd; $6.00 pp/pd in Europe
Best deal:	Andiamo advance rates, Costa Cruise Savers for seniors and singles

New to the Costa fleet in 2002, **CostaEuropa** sailed for more than a decade as the *Westerdam* of Holland America Line. She changed her attitude from Dutch reserve to Italian *dolce vita* with a multimillion-dollar makeover that included the creation of the 450-seat Medusa Ball Room, the Delo Bar, and the Squok Club, reserved for Costa's youngest guests. An upright yellow Costa funnel was also installed.

One of the ship's two swimming pools is beneath a sliding roof for protection from the elements.

CostaEuropa was originally built in 1986 in West Germany as the *Homeric*, with a capacity of 1,000 passengers. After Holland America bought the ship in 1988, it was renamed the *Westerdam* and sent back to the shipyard for an $84 million expansion and redesign. The project included the insertion of a 130-foot section, increasing the ship's size by 13,872 tons. The capacity was increased to 1,494 passengers and the ship's length from 668 to 798 feet.

CostaAllegra, CostaMarina

Econoguide rating:	★★★ 66 points
Ship size:	Medium
Category:	Vintage
Price range:	Budget $

Costa operates two other ships, **CostaAllegra** and **CostaMarina,** primarily marketed in Europe and South America. Travel agents may be able to book space through international contacts, sometimes taking advantage of favorable international exchange rates for bookings made in a European currency. However, if you sail on one of these older, budget-priced ships, you might be the only English-speaking clientele.

Costa Cruises launched a cruise product aimed at the German market in spring 2002. Costa Kreuzfahrten will operate year-round European and Caribbean sailings aboard the 760-passenger *CostaMarina*.

While the *CostaMarina* will maintain its Mediterranean-style decor and Italian dining experiences, the ship will have a German-speaking crew with German the vessel's official language. Entertainment and onboard activities will also be geared toward German audiences.

CostaAllegra, refurbished in 2002, is an elegant smaller ship marketed mostly to French and Italian travelers. She sailed in the Mediterranean and the Greek Isles for the year.

The slightly larger *CostaAllegra*, built in 1992, is 28,500 tons in size, about 609 feet long and 84 feet wide. She has 410 cabins and a double-occupancy of 820 passengers and 400 crew members.

CostaMarina, built in 1990, is 25,558 tons in size, about 566 feet long and 84 feet wide. She has 385 cabins and a double-occupancy of 760 passengers and 397 crew.

CUNARD LINE — CUNARD

Address: 6100 Blue Lagoon Drive, Suite 400
Miami, FL 33126
Information: (800) 528–6273, (305) 463–3000
www.cunard.com

The Cunard Fleet

Queen Mary 2	2004	2,620 passengers	150,000 tons
Queen Elizabeth 2	1969	1,715 passengers	70,326 tons
Caronia	1973	677 passengers	24,492 tons

FUTURE SHIPS

Queen Victoria	early 2007	1,968 passengers	85,000 tons

Cunard is one of the most storied of passenger lines, dating back to 1839, when Samuel Cunard of Halifax, Nova Scotia, won the contract to deliver the mail across the Atlantic from Great Britain to North America. Today Cunard operates one of the best-known ships afloat, the *Queen Elizabeth 2,* as well as another fine old ship that carries on the name of another classic vessel, *Caronia.*

In 2004 Cunard regained much of her fame with the launch of the *Queen Mary 2.* At least for the moment she is the longest and widest cruise ship afloat, and in many ways the most technologically advanced and luxurious. The massive vessel—too big to fit through the Panama Canal—is 150,000 tons in size and 1,132 feet in length, with a beam of 135 feet. The Gargantuan ship will carry a relatively small passenger load of 2,620.

In April 2004 the new *Queen Mary 2* sailed eastbound from New York to

Southampton, departing in tandem with the *Queen Elizabeth 2,* which was making her last regular transatlantic crossing. The day in New York marked the first time two Cunard Queens were berthed in the port together since March 1940, when the new *Queen Elizabeth* escaped the war in Europe and arrived in Manhattan to dock alongside the *Queen Mary* for conversion as a troop carrier.

In her inaugural year *Queen Mary 2* sailed thirteen transatlantic crossings between England and New York. She also sailed a series of Caribbean cruises from New York and Fort Lauderdale; a voyage to Rio de Janeiro and back, timed for Carnival festival; five European itineraries; and two fall foliage cruises to ports in Canada and New England.

The *QE2*'s new role will be as a full-time cruise ship, based in Southampton but continuing with her annual world cruises.

The apparent success of the splashy *Queen Mary 2* caused Cunard and parent company Carnival to rethink plans to introduce a cookie-cutter cruise liner named *Queen Victoria* in 2005. That ship, which had originally been planned for Holland America was reassigned to Cunard while still in the shipyard. But in 2004 the plans for the partially Vista-class ship changed again and she was assigned to the P&O fleet to sail under the name *Arcadia.*

Instead, a new version of the same 85,000-ton Vista hull will be built in Italy, this time with much more luxurious appointments to complement her splashy older sister. The new, new *Queen Victoria,* now due for delivery in January of 2007, will share the "grand ocean liner" style of *Queen Mary 2,* according to the company. The ship will accommodate about 1,850 passengers and will include more luxury suites and minisuites, and more classic culinary experiences including Queens and Princess Grills, and an upscale Todd English alternative restaurant.

Like the *Queen Mary 2* and *Queen Elizabeth 2,* the *Queen Victoria* will be marketed to passengers in both the United States and United Kingdom, as well as to passengers in Australasia and Asia. This will mark the first time the Cunard fleet includes three Queens.

■ THE CUNARD STORY

Cunard, originally known as the British and North American Royal Mail Steam Packet Company, began service in 1840 with the 1,154-ton paddle-wheel steamer *Britannia* and three near-sister ships: *Arcadia, Caledonia,* and *Columbia.*

Cunard's ships could cross the Atlantic in fourteen days, and the four ships permitted weekly departures from Liverpool. Novelist Charles Dickens was an early passenger on the *Britannia;* his description of the sleeping and eating facilities was not of the sort that would be reprinted in a sales brochure.

From that beginning, Cunard went on to become one of the most successful transatlantic lines. Among its most famous liners were the *Lusitania* and the *Mauretania,* launched in 1906 and 1907; the *Mauretania* held the Blue Riband for twenty-two years.

Cunard carried more than a million troops and ten million tons of cargo during World War I; twenty vessels, including the *Lusitania,* were lost.

The *Queen Mary* and the *Queen Elizabeth* were requisitioned for use in World War II, carrying more than 1.5 million troops. From 1940 until 1996 the *Queen Elizabeth* held the title as the largest passenger ship ever built.

By the 1950s Cunard had twelve liners in service, carrying one-third of all transatlantic passengers. But after the first jet plane crossed the pond in 1959, the liners went into decline. When Cunard launched the *Queen Elizabeth 2* in 1969, it was the first major liner designed for both transatlantic and cruise service.

Today Cunard is the only cruise line to sail a regular schedule of transatlantic service, with nearly twenty crossings each year; at other times the company's fleet takes spectacular world cruises and special cruises in Europe, the Americas, and the Caribbean.

In recent years, Cunard has gone through a number of incarnations; in 1998 the company was acquired by Carnival Corporation and a group of Norwegian investors. Carnival then merged Cunard into its Seabourn Cruise Line division.

Cunard's *Vistafjord* was renamed *Caronia* in 2000, harkening back to one of the classic old liners of the heyday of the transatlantic ferry. *Caronia* is due to leave the fleet in late 2004, to sail for the U.K.-based Saga group.

The original *Queen Mary* of Cunard White Star Line entered transatlantic service in May 1936, first winning the Blue Riband for the fastest crossing in August of that year. In 1938 the ship won the Blue Riband again and held the award until 1952.

After serving as a troop transport during World War II, the *Queen Mary* was refitted and reentered the transatlantic liner service. But as air travel increased, that trade declined. In 1967 the ship was sold to the city of Long Beach, California, where she serves today as a floating hotel and conference center.

■ THE CUNARD EXPERIENCE

Travelers will find Cunard a bit more formal than some other cruise lines. On most transatlantic crossings, every night except the first and last calls for formal dress, and the guests like it that way very much, thank you.

At the start of 2005, *Queen Mary 2* is due to sail trips to the Caribbean from Fort Lauderdale, with one seven-day series of sailings calling at San Juan, Saint Thomas, and Saint Martin. In late February, she will sail to Curaçao, Barbados, and Martinique before heading north to New York. From March through early April the schedule calls for a set of four eight-day round-trips from New York to San Juan, Saint Kitts, and Saint Martin. Beginning in April through the end of 2005, she will sail transatlantic crossings from New York to Southampton, with a few Mediterranean cruises mixed in.

In January 2005, *Queen Elizabeth 2* is due to set out on a 108-day world cruise from New York; individual segments are also available. The trip will visit Fort Lauderdale, Curaçao, transit through the Panama Canal, Acapulco, Honolulu, Tahiti, Auckland, Sydney, Bali, Osaka, Hong Kong, Singapore, Mumbai, Cape Town, Barcelona, Southampton, and back across the Atlantic to New York. From the summer of 2005, *QE2* will mostly sail in the Mediterranean from Southampton.

Caronia operates mostly in the Mediterannean, with seasonal forays to northern Europe and the Arctic. In recent years, the ship has also visited the Middle East and Africa.

■ WEB SITE

Cunard's attractive Web site includes a great deal of information about Cunard and its ships, as well as destinations around the world. Cruising aficionados will appreciate a section that describes the history of dozens of ships that have sailed under the company's colors.

There is currently no provision for on-line booking, but visitors can fill out a form with their interests and request a phone call from a Cunard booking agent. *Ease of use: very good.*

Queen Mary 2

Econoguide rating:	★★★★★★ 95 points
Ship size:	Gargantuan
Category:	Luxury
Price range:	Premium $$$$
Registry:	Great Britain
Year built:	2004
Information:	(305) 463–3000
Web site:	www.cunard.com
Passenger capacity:	2,620 (double occupancy)
Crew:	1,250
Passenger-to-crew ratio:	2.1:1
Tonnage:	150,000
Passenger-space ratio:	57.25
Length:	1,131 feet
Beam:	131 feet
Draft:	32.6 feet
Cruising speed:	30 knots maximum
Guest decks:	17
Total cabins:	1,310
Outside:	1,010
Inside:	300
Suites:	93
Wheelchair cabins:	30
Cuisine:	International
Style:	Informal, with several formal nights per cruise
Price notes:	Single cabins available
Tipping suggestions:	$10–$13 pp/pd

Her Majesty's a pretty nice girl. *The Queen Mary 2,* the first true ocean liner to be built in more than three decades, is by most descriptions the longest, widest, tallest, most technologically advanced, and most luxurious passenger vessel afloat.

Queen Mary 2 features ten dining venues with acclaimed Chef Daniel Boulud serving as Cunard's culinary advisor and Chef Todd English operating a Mediterranean specialty restaurant aboard. The liner also has the world's first Canyon Ranch SpaClub at sea, the first planetarium at sea, the largest ballroom at sea, the largest library at sea, and the largest wine collection at sea, as well as a Veuve Clicquot Champagne bar, a two-story theater, a casino, five indoor and outdoor swimming pools, hot tubs, boutiques, and extensive children's facilities.

Harkening back to the designs of the grand liners, a promenade deck with a one-third-mile walkway completely circles the ship. Onboard are five swimming pools, including one beneath a retractable roof, as well as a large indoor pool in the spa.

A pair of exterior glass-walled elevators take passengers to the bridge deck, where they can look through windows at the operations of the ship's bridge.

In the style of the dining salons of classic grand liners, the 1,300-seat Britannia Restaurant, a three-deck-high main dining room, spans the full width of the ship. Guests can choose to make a grand entrance on a sweeping central staircase. The room is decorated with a large painting of the original *Queen Mary* and the skyline of Manhattan.

Although there is no formal class structure for dining rooms, assignments within the rooms are based on the class of guests' cabins.

Smaller, more intimate dining areas including buffets are located elsewhere on the ship. Included are Cunard's traditional Grill Rooms, reserved for the higher stateroom categories.

The Golden Lion Pub is a British pub with its own onboard microbrewery, a wine bar, a cocktail bar, and a wood-paneled smoking room.

Celebrity chef Todd English is responsible for an alternative restaurant, Todd English, that highlights his Mediterranean-style cuisine. The 216-seat room offers both indoor and poolside seating. Passengers must make advance reservations, but there is no additional gratuity or surcharge.

Chef's Galley, located in the ship's innovative King's Court dining pavilion, includes a mirrored workstation to allow diners to view meal preparation. Three other dining venues make up the King's Court, which by day serves as a casual-dining venue for breakfast and lunch but at night is transformed, through lighting and special screens, into four individual sit-down restaurants with distinctive china, menus, wine lists, and server uniforms. The smaller eateries include Lotus, serving Asian cuisine, including Chinese, Thai, Japanese, and Indian fare; La Piazza, a twenty-four-hour restaurant serving pasta, pizza, and other Italian specialities; and The Carvery, a nod to Cunard's rich British heritage. Here diners can enjoy carved beef, lamb, pork, and poultry.

A proper British afternoon tea can be taken in the Winter Garden or Queens

Grill Lounge. The tea, of course, is freshly brewed (no tea bags in sight), complete with scones, clotted cream, fresh pastries, finger sandwiches, and white-glove service.

And if you bring the kids, you can deposit them with real English nannies at the Play Zone (for children two to seven years old) or the Zone (for kids eight to twelve).

Illuminations, the full-scale onboard planetarium, offers an opportunity to view the stars, take a virtual ride into outer space, or take a course on celestial navigation. The facility also serves as a grand cinema, a 500-seat lecture hall, and even a broadcasting studio.

Cunard has engaged the London-based Royal Academy of Dramatic Art (RADA) to provide a company of actors to perform plays and lead onboard acting workshops. RADA, established in 1904, is one of the foremost acting training programs in the world. Graduates include a "who's who" of British actors, from Sir John Gielgud and Vivien Leigh to Anthony Hopkins, Joan Collins, Glenda Jackson, Peter O'Toole, Kenneth Branagh, and Ralph Fiennes. In addition to seminars led by graduate students, *Queen Mary 2* passengers will have the opportunity to see talented performers on the thresholds of their careers in plays seldom performed in the commercial theater.

An educational center is used for Cunard's College at Sea enrichment programs, offering classes in such subjects as computers, seamanship, cooking, wine, and art. The seven classrooms can be joined together for classes of as many as 230 persons.

A language program includes the option of total immersion in a foreign language, with instructors, waiters, butlers, and menus held to a particular language.

Satellite communications bring high-speed Internet connections to every stateroom as well as to an Internet cafe.

Standard cabins are about 194 square feet; suites are twice that size. Six 570-square-foot penthouses include butler and concierge services. Four deluxe penthouses, overlooking the bow, measure between 861 and 1,076 square feet and can be combined to create a luxurious living space of more than 5,000 square feet.

Finally, there are five duplex apartments overlooking the stern; the two-story spaces encompass more than 1,650 square feet and include a two-story glass wall, their own gymnasium, and butler and concierge services. And if that's not large enough, the duplexes can be combined and connected with two of the suites to create a private apartment of more than 5,000 square feet occupying the entire stern of the vessel.

With a passenger capacity of 2,620 (lower berths), *Queen Mary 2* boasts a space ratio per passenger of 57.25, making her among the roomiest of the world's larger passenger ships. Nearly three-quarters of the staterooms have a private balcony.

An unusual combination of four smokeless diesel engines and two gas turbines power the electrical plant of the ship to drive the motors of four podded propellers extending beneath the hull.

Constructed as a liner with a deep draft and more speed than most other cruise ships, the *Queen Mary 2* has a dramatic raked prow, with the hull painted matte black, a Cunard tradition dating back nearly 160 years. The ship's whistle is an exact replica of the one on the original *Queen Mary*. A giant single smokestack is painted in the historic Cunard red with black bands.

The ship was built at Chantiers de l'Atlantique in Saint-Nazaire, France, birthplace of such famous liners as *Normandie, France* (now *Norway*) and *Île de France.*

On December 22, 2003, Cunard took delivery of the ship with a ceremony that included the symbolic changing of the flag; the blue ensign and the Cunard house flag, a gold lion rampant on a red background, were raised. A month later she was christened in Southampton by Queen Elizabeth.

The ship includes seventeen decks, towering 200 feet above the waterline and just barely able to pass beneath the roadway of the Verrazano Narrows Bridge at the entrance to New York harbor. Her length and width make her too large to pass through the Panama Canal.

From the bottom of the keel to the top of the funnel, *Queen Mary 2* stands 236 feet tall. (By comparison, the same measure on the original *Queen Mary* is 181 feet, and the *Titanic* was 175 feet.) There are longer commercial ships, including the 1,513-foot supertanker *Jahre Viking.*

The ship is about 10 percent larger than Royal Caribbean's *Voyager of the Seas,* the previous holder of the largest passenger vessel record. The design of the ship takes into consideration the sometimes wild seas and weather of the North Atlantic, limiting the use of balconies at the front of the vessel and including an enclosed walkway at the bow for the promenade deck that circles the ship. The ship's hull is highly streamlined and angular, with a rounded stern, allowing for high speed through the water.

By the way, as large as the *Queen Mary 2* is, it would be dwarfed next to the *Jahre Viking,* the largest vessel afloat. That oil supertanker is 1,504 feet long, 226 feet wide, with a draft of 81 feet; its gross tonnage is 564,700 tons, about triple the size of *QM2*. But we bet the afternoon high tea is substandard.

Queen Elizabeth 2

Econoguide rating:	★★★★★ 90 points (ratings vary by class)
Ship size:	Megaship
Category:	Vintage/Luxury
Price range:	Premium $$$
Registry:	Great Britain
Year built:	1969 (changed from steam to diesel electric engines, 1987; refurbished in 1994, 1996, 1999)
Information:	(305) 463–3000

Web site:	www.cunard.com
Passenger capacity:	1,778 (double occupancy)
Crew:	921
Passenger-to-crew ratio:	1.9:1
Tonnage:	70,327
Passenger-space ratio:	39.5
Length:	963 feet
Beam:	105 feet
Draft:	32 feet
Cruising speed:	28.5 knots; 32.5 knots maximum
Guest decks:	12
Total cabins:	950
Outside:	671
Inside:	279
Suites:	187
Wheelchair cabins:	4
Cuisine:	International
Style:	Informal, with several formal nights per cruise
Price notes:	Single cabins available
Tipping suggestions:	$10–$13 pp/pd

With apologies to Her Majesty, the **QE2** is one of the grand old ladies of the sea. As she moves into her fourth decade, she's still an elegant, luxurious way to travel. She also offers one of the best glimpses back to the days of the great transatlantic liners; the QE2 was one of the last of the breed, launched after jets began flying over the route of the Atlantic Ferry.

The ship was designed as a replacement for the *Queen Mary* and *Queen Elizabeth.* In the face of competition from the jets, the designers chose to build a slightly smaller liner that could pass through the Panama and Suez Canals and combine service as a liner and as a cruise ship. She was originally intended to spend half the year on the Atlantic Ferry route between Southampton and New York and the other half in cruising. Today the QE2 still sails a dozen or more crossings, cruises in the Caribbean, and conducts one major around-the-world voyage each year.

The ship's impressive offerings include a thirteen-car garage, a florist, kennels, seven restaurants, a foreign exchange bank, twenty-channel television, e-mail, and financial fax service. The engines can deliver a top speed of 32.5 knots.

When the QE2 was requisitioned for service in the Falklands War in 1982, helicopter flight decks and a modern communications system were hurriedly added. In May of that year, the ship left Southampton for the Falklands with an infantry brigade of Scots and Welsh Guards and Gurkhas aboard. Arriving two weeks later, the ship took onboard the survivors of a sunken Royal Navy ship and quickly steamed out of harm's way.

The ship was out of service for approximately six months in 1986 and 1987 for the installation of modern diesel electric engines and propellers. Passenger accommodations were also upgraded at that time.

Queen Elizabeth 2 in Sydney. *Photo by Corey Sandler*

A major interior redesign was accomplished in 1994. Among the changes was a reduction in passenger cabins from 1,750 to 1,500, and a changeover of all restaurants to permit single seatings.

In late 1999 the ship emerged from a monthlong $18 million refurbishment program at Lloyd Werft Shipyard in Bremerhaven, Germany. From the Grand Lounge and the Queens Room to the renowned restaurants and the Golden Lion Pub, there were new furnishings, draperies, carpeting, and woodworking throughout. In addition, *QE2* added Harrods, the London-based luxury department store, to the shops of its Royal Promenade.

The Queens Grill received new furniture, carpeting, upholstery, and lighting, as well as etched-glass doors and a completely new galley. Following a complete makeover, the Caronia Restaurant displays the elegance and luster of an English country house, with rich mahogany paneling, new table lighting, crystal chandeliers, carpeting, curtains, and chairs, as well as a new stereo system. New etched-glass doors and a "rainfall" pattern air-conditioning system eliminate drafts.

The Queens Room received major treatment, including all new furniture and new royal blue carpeting interwoven with gold Tudor roses. The walls were repaneled in mahogany, and the famed bust of Her Majesty the Queen was relocated to the most prominent position within the room.

The 575-square-foot Caledonia Suite on the port side of Boat Deck, directly adjacent to and forward of the Queens Grill, features marble master and guest bathrooms, a separate dining area, and large picture windows. The 777-square-foot Aquitania Suite, forward of the midships lobby on the starboard side of Two Deck, offers similar luxury appointments.

Caronia

Econoguide rating:	★★★★ 83 points
Ship size:	Medium
Category:	Vintage/Luxury
Price range:	Premium $$$
Registry:	Great Britain
Year built:	1973 (formerly *Vistafjord*; refurbished 1997, 1999)
Information:	(305) 463–3000
Web site:	www.cunard.com
Passenger capacity:	677
Crew:	379 British
Passenger-to-crew ratio:	1.8:1
Tonnage:	24,492
Passenger-space ratio:	36.2
Length:	627 feet
Beam:	82 feet
Draft:	27 feet
Cruising speed:	20 knots
Guest decks:	9
Total cabins:	379
Outside:	325
Inside:	54
Suites:	13
Wheelchair cabins:	6
Cuisine:	International
Style:	Semiformal, with several formal nights per cruise
Price notes:	Single cabins available
Tipping suggestions:	$10–$13 pp/pd

The *Vistafjord* was renamed **Caronia** and reflagged under the Union Jack in Liverpool in 1999. In keeping with Cunard tradition, the ceremony was carried out not with champagne but with wine. Unlike the *Queen Mary, Queen Elizabeth,* and *QE2,* though, the *Caronia* was ceremonially doused not with Australian wine but with a bottle from the British Isle of Wight.

Prior to the ceremony, the ship underwent a multimillion dollar refurbishing. Today she's a well-kept middle-aged lady with some touches of Scandinavian elegance. The enlarged and redesigned dining room can accommodate all passengers in a single seating. Unusually large windows offer views of the sea from nearly all tables. There's also Tivoli, a forty-seat alternative Italian restaurant.

DISNEY CRUISE LINE

Address: 210 Celebration Place, Suite 400
   Celebration, FL 34747-4600
Information: (800) 326–0620
   www.disneycruise.com
Econoguide's Best Cruise Lines
Econoguide's Best Cruise Lines for Families

🏵 🏵 🏵 🏵

The Disney Cruise Line Fleet

Disney Wonder	1999	1,750 passengers	85,000 tons
Disney Magic	1998	1,750 passengers	85,000 tons

OK, let's get this out of the way right now: The Disney Cruise Line is a Mickey Mouse operation.

But this is the Mickey Mouse of *Fantasia,* the cultured gentleman in tuxedo and tails. The *Disney Magic* and her nearly identical sister ship, *Disney Wonder,* are two of the most stunning, beautifully realized cruise ships on the water today. From the moment they welcomed their first paying passengers in mid-1998 and summer 1999, respectively, the ships were instant classics.

The two ships sail from Port Canaveral in Florida to the Bahamas, the Caribbean, and the Gulf of Mexico on three-, four-, and seven-day trips. In 2004 the line experimented with a few longer voyages in the Caribbean.

And in 2005 the cruise line will dispatch the *Disney Magic* to the West Coast as part of the celebration of the fiftieth anniversary of Disneyland. The ship will sail twelve consecutive seven-night cruise vacations each Saturday from the Port of Los Angeles to Puerto Vallarta, Mazatlan, and Cabo San Lucas on the west coast of Mexico, between May 28 and August 19, 2005. The ship will also sail a transit from Florida through the Panama Canal in early May, and a return trip in late August 2005.

Demand for the West Coast trips is expected to be very high and cabins may be very hard to get. Meanwhile, rumors fly like Tinkerbell about plans for a third ship for the fleet.

Kids of all ages will love these ships, and adults will find an above-average cruise line that pays respects to the great ocean liners . . . and the world of Disney. (See Chapter 11 for a cruise diary about a voyage on the *Disney Magic.*)

Now let me say right up front that I had my misgivings about sailing on a Disney ship before I crossed the gangplank. I spend an inordinate amount of my time with Mickey Mouse and friends each year in keeping my travel books on Orlando and Anaheim up to date. It's not that I don't like Disneyland or Walt Disney World; it's just that I had a fear that too many parts of my world were coming together. I wanted the glamour, excitement, and sublime relaxation of a cruise, not the oh-too-popular hubbub of a theme park.

Well, I was 90 percent wrong—and 100 percent satisfied. Disney has done a wonderful job of creating a pair of cruise ships that, like a classic Disney film, bring together our dearest fantasies, an impressive display of artistry, and some welcome touches of the real world.

I have come to realize the following: Every other cruise line starts with the ship and tries to find the right mix of entertainment to help guests fill out their time. But Disney starts as one of the most successful entertainment companies of all time, adding a pair of handsome ships as home to their floating theme park.

Disney chose as its initial target the 90 percent or so of travelers who have never taken a cruise before, but even the most experienced cruise veteran will recognize how Disney has paid loving homage to the great ocean liners of the past. Today you're likely to find many Disneyphiles on their fourth or fifth or tenth sailing.

■ FANTASY AFLOAT

The fantasy begins with the exterior design of the twin ships, which consciously evokes the memory of the classic transatlantic liners of the prejet era, vessels like the *Queen Mary*. Their long, sleek hulls are painted jet black; atop the white upper half sit a pair of bright-red smokestacks. They look just about the way a child (of any age) would draw an ocean liner.

The black, white, and red colors of the ships, together with bright-yellow lifeboats, not only evoke the colors of the great liners but also match the color scheme for the admiral of the fleet, Mickey Mouse.

These are true Megaships, more than three football fields long, at 964 feet, from stem to stern; eleven decks tall; and 85,000 tons in size.

The artistry begins with those two smokestacks. The ultramodern power plant for the ships requires only one set of pipes, and those pipes run through the stack toward the stern. The forward smokestack is there because the ship looks better with one. And as long as you've got this big stack, why not make use of it? Disney's "Imagineers" installed a funky sports bar way up high and a dream-world club for teenagers (no adults allowed) at its base.

The Imagineers also took hold of the ships' design in myriad other wondrous ways—things like a truly spectacular central atrium with glass-walled elevators; a quartet of extraordinary and quirky restaurants that deliver fine food and more than a bit of Disney magic; a Broadway-quality theater that offers a different show every night; and a floor full of nightclubs for adults, including a comedy club, a country-western bar, a jazz club, and a sophisticated chrome-and-glass piano bar where Noel Coward would have felt right at home.

The interior design of the *Disney Magic* is based on an Art Deco vocabulary, with rounded chrome and brass, carved-wood details, and lovely oversize portholes along some of the interior promenade decks. The *Disney Wonder* is based on slightly different Art Nouveau flourishes.

The real world lies in the modern-day amenities, such as private verandas, relatively spacious family cabins that have nice touches like privacy curtains to separate the kids from the parents, and an overall sense of elegance. Disney has left neon flash to Royal Caribbean, Carnival, and others; the real competition to these ships, at least in terms of design, are the *Queens* of Cunard, present and past.

And finally, back to the fantasy. What kid wouldn't add a spiraling water slide to the top-deck kids-only swimming pool? (Adults have their own pond, and there's a third pool for families.) And how about nearly a full deck devoted to a kids' world of games, entertainment, and exploration, as well as a teens-only club up top and a state-of-the-art video arcade at sea?

And then there's Mickey. Disney is always quick to admit that it all started with a mouse. Mickey and his friends are there, making cameo appearances at the children's clubs and an occasional visit to the pools and restaurants. Goofy will sometimes appear on the dance floor in one of the clubs, or Minnie may visit the shopping district. But, in truth, the Disney characters have a relatively low-key presence aboard ship.

Within the massive ship are no fewer than four separate and distinct dining rooms, a huge theater for live productions, and an entire entertainment district for adults. The quality and presentation of the food is excellent, although some guests may find the offerings a bit on the safe side. There are a few adult touches if you want to amaze or frighten younger guests: escargots one night and an unusual side dish of braised parsnips in orange sauce.

Disney says its marketing target is the vast majority of Americans who have never taken a cruise. But experienced cruisers are likely to enjoy the many lovely touches onboard this elegant ship. A good deal of Disney's marketing is also aimed at tying a cruise into a visit to Walt Disney World; you can purchase a four-night cruise and a three-night stay at the park or a three-night cruise and a four-night stay. Or you can book a three-, four-, or seven-day cruise by itself.

Although Mickey, Minnie, Goofy, and others can be found onboard the ship, and the entertainment package features Disney characters in most productions, it is also possible to avoid most things Disney. The company offers Palo, a lovely adults-only restaurant, and also tries to place most families who have children in the early dining seating for the other restaurants. Then there is Beat Street, the nightclub area onboard *Disney Magic,* where there are lively jazz, comedy, and country-western clubs . . . and neither kids nor cartoon characters are expected after 9:00 P.M. The equivalent on the *Disney Wonder* is Route 66.

Only on a ship of this size owned by a company like Walt Disney would you reasonably expect to find most of an entire deck devoted to supervised children's activities: Disney's Oceaneer Lab and Disney's Oceaneer Club. There's even a kids-only buffet. And up top on the pool deck of *Disney Wonder* is Common Grounds, a coffee bar and hangout place just for teenagers; adults are carded at the door and asked to step outside. On *Disney Magic,* a rehab in 2003 moved the teen club into the ship's faux funnel, booting out the sports bar which was relocated to a multipurpose club called Diversions. A new adults-only space, Cove Cafe, took over the old Common Grounds area on that ship.

Disney's seven-day cruises include some special Disney magic with nightly shows and special presentations. The tony Palo restaurant is open during the day for a champagne brunch and afternoon tea.

Disney Magic tied up at Disney's private island, Castaway Cay. *Photo by Corey Sandler*

Guests can take backstage peeks at the extensive theater facilities on the ship, as well as tours of the bridge, galley, and other places not ordinarily open to the public. There is also a program that focuses on sea lore, from the days of the pirates to modern cruise ships.

■ THE DISNEY EXPERIENCE

Disney is a young cruise line without a grand history on the seas, and some purists will find fault with Goofy hanging on the stern or Mickey and Minnie lounging by the pool. But in some ways Disney has come up with a ship that is more true to our memories or dreams of grand ocean liners than are many of the larger vessels now being launched, ships that are more like floating vacation resorts or shopping malls.

Blessed with the deep pockets of Walt Disney Company, the Disney Cruise Line purchased a pair of stunning ships from one of the most advanced shipyards. Its ships are among the most elegant and polished afloat.

Among Disney's innovations is "rotation dining": Guests are assigned to one of the three main restaurants each day, and their servers and tablemates move with them from dining room to dining room.

Onboard the *Disney Magic*, the elegant continental Lumière's restaurant mixes a grand dining room of a classic ocean liner with chandeliers and candlesticks whimsically derived from Disney's *Beauty and the Beast*. The equivalent dining room on the *Wonder* is Triton's, based on *The Little Mermaid*. Parrot Cay, on both ships, is an informal eatery bedecked with palms and flowers and gingerbread-trimmed verandas—a Disney magnification of the mind's-eye perception of the Bahamas and the Caribbean.

Also on both ships is Animator's Palette, one of the most unusual settings for a restaurant at sea or on land. The very room itself is an actor in the evening's entertainment. The meal begins in a room that is entirely outlined in black and white—from the linens on the table and the uniforms on the serving staff to the line art sketches on the wall. As the meal progresses, dabs of color work their way into the drawings and onto the uniforms.

The fourth restaurant is Palo, an adults-only sophisticated Italian bistro perched high in the second smokestack. You'll need a reservation; Disney assesses a reasonable $5.00 service charge for dinner or $10.00 for the brunch, which includes a glass of bubbly.

About three-quarters of the 875 staterooms have outside views, and nearly half have verandas, a welcome modern touch. Most of the cabins offer a bath-and-a-half design; one bathroom holds a sink and toilet, the other a sink and bathtub/shower.

Disney's attention to detail begins at the handsome Art Deco–style terminal it constructed in Port Canaveral; it's all part of the company's packaging of its ships as a return to the golden era of cruising. Many guests arrive at the terminal by bus from Disney World, about an hour away; even the buses have been molded and painted in an artist's vision of a streamlined conveyance of the 1930s and 1940s.

■ DISNEY ENTERTAINMENT AT SEA

The Walt Disney Theatre is a 975-seat showplace that would be the envy of most Broadway producers. The stage is used for nightly performances of Disney-produced shows that are entertaining, but not to be confused with *Les Misérables*. Facilities include three elevators for special effects, indoor fireworks, and lasers.

On no other cruise line does the captain magically appear on stage in a cloud of fog, popping up on a hidden stage elevator.

A spectacular recent show is "The Golden Mickeys," which combines theater, song, dance, animated film, video, and special effects. Animated backdrops whisk guests from high above Notre Dame Cathedral in one scene to the inside of a young boy's toy-filled bedroom in another, and dramatic sets create a three-dimensional illusion as films race across stage-size screens. Special effects create a starlit African night for a scene from *The Lion King,* an under-the-sea setting from *Little Mermaid* and more.

Guests arriving at the theater walk along a red carpet, complete with paparazzi, a roving reporter and live "celebrity" interviews broadcast on giant video screens inside the theater.

Also onboard is the Buena Vista Theatre, a full-screen, 270-seat cinema that presents Disney classics and first-run films, including an occasional premiere at sea. Disney has offered theme cruises from time to time, such as a focus on movies, with appearances by noted critics.

There are no casinos onboard the ships, which Disney executives said would be at odds with the corporate mission. They point out, however, that if you've got the itch to gamble, the proprietors of the casinos in Nassau and Saint Martin will be happy to take your money.

Disney claims the largest dedicated area of children's space on any ship. Children ages three through eight have Disney's Oceaneer Club, a supervised playroom. Older youngsters through age twelve can spend their time at Disney's Oceaneer Lab, which includes giant video walls and computer activities. Parents can borrow a pager so that they can head off on their own while staying in touch aboard ship.

Our teenagers were thrilled to be granted admission to Common Grounds, a trendy coffee-bar setting where they could dance, listen to music, play video games, and generally hang out in a place that adults were politely encouraged not to visit.

■ ITINERARIES

Disney Wonder sails from Port Canaveral on three- or four-day cruises to Nassau and Castaway Cay, Disney's private Bahamas beach. On alternate four-day cruises, the itinerary trades a day at sea for a second stop in the Bahamas, at Freeport, Grand Bahama Island.

Disney Magic sails alternating weeklong itineraries to the eastern and western Caribbean. The eastern Caribbean trip departs each Saturday from Port Canaveral for Saint Martin, Saint Thomas, and Castaway Cay and includes three days at sea. The western trip departs on Saturday for Key West, Grand Cayman Island, Cozumel, and Castaway Cay, with two full days at sea.

And as noted earlier, *Disney Magic* is due to reposition to Los Angeles to sail week-long trips to the west coast of Mexico from May to September 2005 as part of the celebration of the fiftieth anniversary of Disneyland.

Guests with confirmed reservations can reserve shore excursions in advance through the cruise line.

Disney promotes its shorter cruises as part of a weeklong vacation that includes a few days at Walt Disney World in Orlando. You can, however, choose to book just a cruise.

■ DISNEY'S BAHAMIAN THEME PARK

Although the Walt Disney Company has created its own worlds in California, Florida, Japan, and France, the creation of the Disney Cruise Line offered the first opportunity for the Imagineers to design their own little country. In typical Disney style, they ended up creating a place that is more real than the real thing, an idealized island paradise with perfect white sand beaches, palm trees, and a huge Megaship parked at a dock around the corner.

Castaway Cay, a 1,000-acre island 50 miles north of Nassau and near Abaco, was reworked by Disney Imagineers in a massive $25 million effort that included construction of a dock for the ships and creation of beaches with some 50,000 truckloads of sand dredged from the floor of the Atlantic when the channel was dug.

In an interesting irony, Disney's island, formerly known as Gorda Cay, is reputed to have been used in recent years as a hideaway for drug smugglers. A short World War II–era runway on the island was believed to have been used by the smugglers.

Only about fifty-five acres of the island have been developed, with the remainder mostly open for hiking and biking paths. Saltwater desalination and sewage treatment plants, as well as a small village of housing for staff members, are well hidden from view.

The main beach is the snorkeling and swimming lagoon, which features a snorkeling "track" with underwater and marine objects to explore (you'll need to rent snorkels and a flotation vest). Nearby are Scuttle's Cove, a supervised children's water area, and the Teen Beach. Again, in keeping with Disney's promise to offer grown-ups an escape, the north side of the island has a somewhat isolated "quiet" beach for adults only.

Recent additions include parasailing on the open waters beyond the lagoon, wet and high-speed tours on a "banana boat," and tours of the surrounding reef on a glass-bottom boat.

■ THE BOTTOM LINE

All of this does not come cheap. Disney's list prices for cruises are approximately 15 to 30 percent higher than those for similar operations, placing the cruise line somewhere between moderate- and premium-priced classes. As with most other cruise lines, however, cruises with Disney are often available at deep discounts from travel agencies; Disney also books its cruises directly. There are advance booking discounts, and guests onboard one of the ships are offered substantial cuts for cruises engaged at sea.

■ WEB SITE

Disney offers a polished and informative Web site with details about the ships, itineraries, and onboard activities. You can check availability of cabins for individual cruises and make reservations online. *Ease of use: excellent.*

Disney Magic, Disney Wonder

Econoguide rating:	★★★★ 86 points
Ship size:	Megaship
Category:	Top of the Line
Price range:	Premium $$$
Registry:	Bahamas
Year built:	*Disney Magic,* 1998; *Disney Wonder,* 1999
Information:	(800) 326–0620
Web site:	www.disneycruise.com
Passenger capacity:	1,750 (double occupancy)

Crew:	915; European and American staff
Passenger-to-crew ratio:	1.9:1
Tonnage:	85,000
Passenger-space ratio:	48.6
Length:	964 feet
Beam:	106 feet
Draft:	25.3 feet
Cruising speed:	21.5 knots
Guest decks:	11
Total cabins:	875
Outside:	547
Inside:	246
Suites:	82
Wheelchair cabins:	14
Cuisine:	Continental, American; three restaurants in rotation
Style:	Casual, informal resort atmosphere
Price notes:	Single-occupancy premium, 175 to 200 percent; reduced rates for third through seventh occupant of cabins or suites
Tipping suggestions:	$11 pp/pd

The **Disney Magic** and **Disney Wonder** are spectacular ships that look back fondly on the grand old liners of the past. Disney's Imagineers worked with Italian designers to create a pair of thoroughly modern Megaships that come very close to our mind's-eye view of what a cruise ship should look like.

Disney's attention to detail includes wondrous parallel worlds for children and adults. There's an adults-only restaurant and an adults-only swimming pool and a kids-only buffet and pool. Most of an entire deck of the huge ship is devoted to kids' programs, and an adult entertainment district has a set of swinging nightspots.

The Walt Disney Theatre is a tribute to grand theatrical palaces, with a different live musical stage show each night of the cruise.

The art theme for *Disney Wonder* is Art Nouveau, differing from the *Disney Magic*'s Art Deco concept.

The showplace dining room on the *Wonder* is Triton's, derived from *The Little Mermaid* story. The menu, of course, emphasizes seafood. Animator's Palette and Parrot Cay are alternative restaurants on both ships.

The adult entertainment district on the *Wonder* is Route 66, and includes Cadillac's dance club, the Brew Ha Ha (themed like a brewpub) comedy club, and the Wave Bands jazz club.

A renovation of *Disney Magic* in late 2003 created a new teen club, called The Stack, in the forward funnel of the ship. The Stack replaced ESPN Skybox. The isolated space allows for a wider range of activities including dancing, watching multiple televisions, accessing the Internet, or snacking with friends.

In its former home was added Cove Cafe, open daily from 10:00 A.M. to midnight, providing a quiet spot on the pool deck for adults. It features comfortable furniture, large screen televisions, paperback books and magazines, four Internet stations, and a bar serving gourmet coffee, specialty teas, cocktails, sandwiches, and desserts.

The former Off-Beat club was recast as Diversions, a pub offering a broad range of evening entertainment options with the addition of nightly themed activities. The Pub Master hosts sporting events, trivia-based game shows, piano sing-along entertainment, and talent competitions. The decor includes multiple satellite television screens and specialty game tables for backgammon, checkers, and chess.

HOLLAND AMERICA LINE

Address: 300 Elliott Avenue West
Seattle, WA 98119
Information: (800) 227–6482, (800) 426–0327
www.hollandamerica.com
Econoguide's Best Cruise Lines
Econoguide's Best Cruise Values

Holland America Fleet

Westerdam	2004	1,848 passengers	85,000 tons
Oosterdam	2003	1,848 passengers	85,000 tons
Zuiderdam	2002	1,848 passengers	85,000 tons
Zaandam	2000	1,440 passengers	63,000 tons
Volendam	1999	1,440 passengers	63,000 tons
Amsterdam	2000	1,380 passengers	61,000 tons
Rotterdam	1997	1,316 passengers	60,000 tons
Veendam	1996	1,266 passengers	55,451 tons
Ryndam	1994	1,266 passengers	55,451 tons
Maasdam	1993	1,266 passengers	55,451 tons
Statendam	1993	1,266 passengers	55,451 tons
Prinsendam	1988	794 passengers	37,845 tons
Noordam	1984	1,214 passengers	33,930 tons

FUTURE SHIPS

Noordam	February 2006	1,848 passengers	85,000 tons

Holland America was the floating highway for nearly a million European immigrants who traveled to the New World in the late nineteenth and early twentieth centuries. Today it continues as one of the premier cruise lines, carrying Americans and others to holidays in the Caribbean, Alaska, and through the Panama Canal.

■ THE HOLLAND AMERICA STORY

The company was founded in 1873 as the Netherlands-America Steamship Company for shipping and passenger service. Because it provided service to the Americas, it became known as Holland America Line (HAL).

The company's first liner was the original *Rotterdam,* which made its maiden voyage from the Netherlands to New York in 1872. Within twenty-five years the company owned a fleet of six ships and also provided service between Holland and the Dutch East Indies via the newly constructed Suez Canal.

Today the company's Holland America–Westours is the largest cruise tour operator in Alaska and Canada's Yukon, with a fleet of 176 buses and several dozen tourism railroad cars. Westours owns Gray Line of Alaska, Gray Line of Seattle, and the Westmark Hotels and Inns group, with more than a dozen hotels in Alaska and the Yukon Territory. The company also owns both the *Ptarmigan,* a small ship that operates tours to the face of Portage Glacier, and the *Yukon Queen,* which travels the Yukon River between Dawson City in the Yukon Territory and Eagle, Alaska.

In January 1989 Holland America Line–Westours, Inc., became a wholly owned subsidiary of The Carnival Corporation. Holland America also owns Windstar Cruises, which operates four computer-directed luxury sailing cruise ships in the Mediterranean, the Caribbean, and Costa Rica.

Many Caribbean cruises include a stop at Half Moon Cay, a 2,500-acre private Bahamian island purchased in 1997 and lightly developed by Holland America Line. The crescent-shaped isle, just 2 miles long and a third of a mile across, was an uninhabited cay known as Little San Salvador. In 2004 HAL added new activities to the island, including horseback riding, a swimming tour, a stingray adventure program, a WaveRunner park, and an aqua park. The nation of the Bahamas honored the tourist dollars of HAL guests with a special postage stamp that has an image of the *Ryndam* and a small Holland America Line logo.

■ NEW SHIPS

The fourth new "Project Vista" ship, *Noordam,* will be added to the fleet in 2006. The 85,000-ton, 951-foot-long, 1,848-passenger ship marks the beginning of a new class of vessels for Holland America, introducing new features, including the first "exterior elevators" on a cruise ship. The lifts, located on the port and starboard sides, connect ten decks of the ship, offering panoramic sea views through glass walls. About 85 percent of the cabins on the new ship are outside; about 80 percent of those have private verandas. The first three ships are *Zuiderdam* (pronounced ZOO-der-dam), *Oosterdam* (OH-ster-dam), and *Westerdam.*

Other features include two interior promenade decks, an exterior covered promenade deck encircling the entire ship, and HAL's trademark lido area pool with a retractable dome. The ships also offer a new cabaret-style show lounge complementing a new three-deck main show lounge. Other new features include a sophisticated nightclub, the largest spa facilities in the fleet, Internet/e-mail dataports in all staterooms, an extensive Club HAL children's facility with inside and outside play areas, a concierge lounge for the exclusive use of Penthouse and Deluxe Veranda Suite guests, and two interior promenade decks.

The new vessels' propulsion system includes a full-scale diesel-electric power plant, backed up by a gas turbine as an additional power source. The ships also will use the Azipod propulsion system, allowing for greater maneuverability.

In April 2002 the sumptuous *Seabourn Sun* was transferred to Holland America Line from Seabourn Cruise Line. The ship was refurbished and renamed *Prinsendam* and is billed as the most luxurious vessel in the HAL fleet.

■ ITINERARIES

In 2004 Holland America offered nearly 500 sailings on thirteen ships from twenty-three home ports. New ports of embarkation included Norfolk and Baltimore, as well as Athens and Barcelona in Europe.

The new *Westerdam* joined the fleet in mid-2004, sailing in the spring and summer months in the Mediterranean Sea. At the end of the year, the ship moved to Florida for a winter season of Caribbean voyages from Fort Lauderdale.

The small and elegant 794-passenger *Prinsendam* made a Grand World Voyage that began in Los Angeles in January and concluded in New York City 108 days later, with stops in Hawaii, American Samoa, Fiji, New Zealand, Tasmania, and Australia. After stops in Indonesia, Malaysia, and India, the ship crossed the Suez Canal to visit ports in the Aegean and Mediterranean Seas before passing Gibraltar and heading across the Atlantic to Fort Lauderdale and on to New York.

Amsterdam called at Antarctica from Rio de Janeiro.

In 2004 Holland America Line sailed seven ships on 139 cruises in Alaska, adding more departures from Seattle and expanded glacier excursions; ships will make ninety-six visits to Glacier Bay National Park, more than any other cruise line. A naturalist sails on each trip to discuss wildlife and natural features. The "Artisans in Residence" program brings a native artist on board to demonstrate traditional crafts such as ivory or soapstone carving, basket weaving, and mask making.

Glacier visits include the imposing 5-mile wide, 40-stories-tall Hubbard Glacier, Tracy Arm with the Sawyer Glaciers, College Fjord, and Glacier Bay National Park. Alaska cruises are scheduled in conjunction with Holland America's Cruisetours program which offer a variety of land-based touring options to the Yukon and Alaska's most popular attractions, including Denali National Park, the gold rush towns of Whitehorse and Dawson, and Canada's Kluane National Park.

Oosterdam joined *Amsterdam* from a homeport in Seattle for twenty consecutive seven-day southeast Alaska cruises. From Vancouver *Statendam, Ryndam, Veendam, Volendam,* and *Zaandam* sailed seven-day itineraries to the Alaska Gulf including Glacier Bay National Park and port calls in Sitka and Seward.

Maasdam made late-spring, summer, and early-fall sailings along the New England and Canada coast, with stops along the way at Martha's Vineyard and

Halifax, Nova Scotia; some sailings continued in the Saint Lawrence River to Montreal. Most trips departed from Boston or Montreal. *Rotterdam* sailed a pair of Fall Foliage tours of Canada and New England from New York and Montreal.

Ten ships made 191 cruises to the Caribbean in 2004, an increase from 163 the year before. *Zuiderdam* sailed all year to the islands from its homeport in Fort Lauderdale. *Veendam* and *Oosterdam* offered weekly Caribbean cruises from Tampa and Fort Lauderdale, and the *Zaandam* sailed twenty-four week-long tours from Port Canaveral.

For the first time ever, Holland America offered departures to the Caribbean from Norfolk, Baltimore, and Philadelphia. *Maasdam* made fifteen departures from Norfolk, while *Rotterdam* sailed six trips from Baltimore, Philadelphia, and New York.

Hawaii was visited by *Statendam* on voyages round-trip from San Diego. *Amsterdam* paid a port call from Seattle.

Company ships made thirty-seven voyages to Mexico, including twenty-six departures by *Ryndam* from San Diego on itineraries that visited Cabo San Lucas, the Sea of Cortez, and Mexican Riviera ports of Mazatlán, Acapulco, and Puerto Vallarta. *Statendam* also made two tours to Mexico from San Diego.

Holland America sent seven ships to or through the Panama Canal in 2004 on twenty-eight trips. *Rotterdam* offered sixteen sailings from Fort Lauderdale. *Statendam, Veendam, Volendam, Zaandam,* and *Oosterdam* traversed the Canal twice each, and *Prinsendam* once, on repositioning and world tour itineraries.

Amsterdam conducted nine sailings to South America, calling at the ports of Rio de Janeiro, Valparaiso, Buenos Aires, and Stanley in the Falkland Islands. *Prinsendam* set sail from Fort Lauderdale on a month-long tour of the southern Caribbean and Amazon River.

Ships made nine transatlantic voyages in 2004. *Rotterdam* departed from New York to Amsterdam and London to New York. *Noordam* and *Prinsendam* each made two transatlantic crossings, from Tampa to Lisbon and Lisbon to Fort Lauderdale for *Noordam,* and New York to Lisbon and Lisbon to Fort Lauderdale for *Prinsendam.*

The company's European schedule of fifty sailings included tours to and from Athens, Greece, that bookended the 2004 Summer Olympic Games, on *Westerdam, Rotterdam,* and *Noordam.*

In mid-November 2004, Holland America ended service of its oldest ship, *Noordam.* That ship was due to be chartered to the U.K.'s Thomson Holidays to sail as *Thomson Celebration.* The next *Noordam,* a much larger and more modern vessel, is due to enter the Holland America fleet in early 2006.

■ THE HOLLAND AMERICA EXPERIENCE

Holland America cultivates an air of refinement aboard its ships, and its clientele has historically been slightly older and more experienced than that of other cruise lines. Fresh flowers, in some cases flown in from Holland, decorate the ship. An art and history tour is scheduled on each cruise to inform guests about the $2 million worth of art and artifacts aboard each ship.

For families traveling with children, Holland America's Club HAL youth program provides activities for youngsters ages five through seventeen. Additional youth counselors are onboard for Christmas and Easter cruises.

The ships also offer more traditional cruise activities: dance lessons, bingo, "horse" racing, trap shooting, a mileage pool, a passenger talent show, and karaoke. The show lounge features a Broadway or Las Vegas–style revue or variety entertainment.

Harking back to its Dutch roots, HAL employs mostly Indonesian and Filipino crew members, training them in its own school in Jakarta. In 2004 Holland America ended its attractive but confusing "no tipping required" policy, which left it entirely up to guests whether to leave gratuities and gave them no guidance on amounts; guests now see a $10 per day per person charge on their onboard accounts; the amount can be adjusted up or down on request.

Guests aboard all Holland America Line cruise ships are now offered a casual lido dining option for dinner on several nights of their cruise. Serenaded by a pianist, diners order from a set menu with choices including Caesar salad, shrimp cocktail, and such entrees as fillet of salmon, sirloin steak, roast chicken, and lasagna.

In 2004 work was well underway on a nearly $250 million upgrade to all of the existing Holland America ships. Every vessel will see the addition of a Pinnacle Grill, an alternative restaurant specializing in Pacific Northwest specialties including seafood and prime beef. The casual Lido restaurants were enhanced with made-to-order dinner entrees and waiter service at dinner.

In the staterooms, beds are now outfitted with premium plush mattresses and high-end Egyptian cotton bed linens. Suites were upgraded with VCRs or DVD players and access to a library of films. Guests in suites also have access to a private concierge area, the Neptune Lounge.

The sister ships *Volendam* and *Zaandam* are the first of a new generation of luxury cruise ships. The interior decor of the *Volendam* features a flower theme, while the *Zaandam* is based around musical themes. The two ships have the same length and width as the *Rotterdam,* but their gross tonnage is larger (about 63,000 tons versus 59,652 tons) because they have more passenger staterooms.

In 2000 Holland America added a new ship with an old name. The *Amsterdam* also has the same length and beam as the *Rotterdam* but has a slightly larger gross tonnage (61,000 gross tons) because of an increase in the number of staterooms to 690. The new ship's all-suite deck was extended, and the number of suites that have verandas increased. The new ship also features 120 deluxe minisuites with verandas, 385 large outside staterooms, and 133 large inside staterooms, for a total of 690 staterooms.

In early 2002 Holland America began implementing a new ban against smoking in all dining areas, including main dining rooms and the enclosed portion of lido restaurants. Alternative restaurants have been nonsmoking since their introduction and continue as such under the new policy. All ships will continue to have designated smoking areas in public spaces.

Holland America offers early booking fares at a 25 percent discount for a limited number of staterooms.

■ WEB SITE

Holland America's Web site includes full information about ships and itineraries and offers the option to book a cruise on-line or request a call from the company's reservations department to answer questions and make reservations. Although the organization of the Web site is a bit confusing, a strong point is the cruise calendar, which makes it easy to see where the ships are at any time of the year. *Ease of use: good.*

Zuiderdam, Oosterdam, Westerdam, Noordam (2006)

Econoguide rating:	★★★★ 86 points
Ship size:	Megaship
Category:	Top of the Line
Price range:	Premium $$$
Registry:	Netherlands
Year built:	*Zuiderdam,* 2002; *Oosterdam,* 2003; *Westerdam,* 2004; *Noordam,* scheduled for 2006
Information:	(206) 283–2687, (800) 426–0327
Web site:	www.hollandamerica.com
Passenger capacity:	1,848 (double occupancy)
Crew:	800
Passenger-to-crew ratio:	2.3:1
Tonnage:	85,000
Passenger-space ratio:	46
Length:	951 feet
Beam:	105.8 feet
Draft:	22 feet
Cruising speed:	23 knots
Guest decks:	10
Total cabins:	720
Outside:	552
Inside:	139
Suites:	29
Wheelchair cabins:	23
Cuisine:	International
Style:	Elegantly casual to formal in the evening
Price notes:	Single-occupancy premium, 150 to 190 percent; Single Partners Program (agree to share a stateroom with another nonsmoking guest of the same sex, and pay only the per-person, double-occupancy rate)
Tipping suggestions:	$10 pp/pd
Best deal:	Early-booking savings

Noordam, Zuiderdam, Westerdam, and *Oosterdam,* named for dams at the northern, southern, western, and eastern points of the Dutch compass, are technologically advanced ships, each powered by a full-scale diesel-electric power plant backed up by a gas turbine as an additional power source. The turbines reduce exhaust emissions and can be used together with the diesels when cruising in particularly sensitive environments such as Glacier Bay in Alaska or the Baltic Sea. Azipods also reduce consumption—and therefore emissions—by as much as forty tons of fuel per week.

Fully 85 percent of the staterooms have an ocean view, with 80 percent of those offering private verandas. Two interior promenade decks and a covered exterior promenade deck circle the ship.

Exterior elevators traverse ten decks, with panoramic views out over the water. Other features include a Cabaret-style show lounge and a three-level main show lounge. Computer users will find an Internet cafe and data ports in all staterooms.

The ships include extensive facilities for children. The Club HAL program features KidZone for younger cruisers ages five to twelve, with inside play areas with safety matting. Professional youth coordinators supervise daily activities such as games, arts and crafts, computer fun, candy-bar bingo, movies, and special kids-only parties.

WaveRunner is a place for teenagers, complete with a dance floor where they can dance to a booming sound system and special lighting effects. There is also a video game room and large-screen TV.

Vista ships also feature a new stateroom category, Deluxe Veranda Outside, which feature verandas approximately twice the size of the regular verandas for the category. A concierge lounge is for the exclusive use of Penthouse and Deluxe Veranda Suite guests. The *Oosterdam* offers 461 of these staterooms.

The fourth ship in the series, *Noordam,* is due to arrive in early 2006. The first ship with that name joined the Holland America Line fleet in 1902, sailing the Rotterdam–New York run until being damaged by a mine during World War I. In 1938 the name was given to a new passenger-cargo ship which offered exclusively first-class accommodations for 148 passengers. The most recent *Noordam,* delivered in 1984, was due to leave the fleet at the end of 2004.

Volendam, Zaandam

Econoguide rating:	★★★★ 85 points
Ship size:	Large
Category:	Top of the Line
Price range:	Premium $$$
Registry:	Netherlands
Year built:	*Volendam,* 1999; *Zaandam,* 2000
Information:	(206) 283–2687, (800) 426–0327
Web site:	www.hollandamerica.com

Passenger capacity:	1,440 (double occupancy)
Crew:	561
Passenger-to-crew ratio:	2.6:1
Tonnage:	63,000
Passenger-space ratio:	43.8
Length:	781 feet
Beam:	105.8 feet
Draft:	23 feet
Cruising speed:	23 knots
Guest decks:	10
Total cabins:	720
Outside:	552
Inside:	139
Suites:	29
Wheelchair cabins:	23
Cuisine:	International
Style:	Elegantly casual to formal in the evening
Price notes:	Single-occupancy premium, 150 to 190 percent; Single Partners Program (agree to share a stateroom with another nonsmoking guest of the same sex, and pay only the per-person, double-occupancy rate)
Tipping suggestions:	$10 pp/pd
Best deal:	Early-booking savings

Holland America's *Volendam. Courtesy Holland America Line*

Sister ships **Volendam** and **Zaandam** have the same basic layout as *Rotter-dam*. Slightly larger, the new design moves the oudoor swimming pool one deck higher to the lido deck and extends the navigation deck aft to accommodate forty-eight additional minisuites with verandas.

Volendam, the third ship in the company's 125-year history to bear that name, cruises in the winter in the Caribbean out of Fort Lauderdale. In spring she repositions to Vancouver, British Columbia, via the Panama Canal, for a season of sailings in Alaska's Inside Passage before returning to Florida for the winter.

The predominant theme of *Volendam*'s interior decor is flowers, from the seventeenth to the twenty-first centuries. Flowers are featured in the ship's artwork, doors, and other design elements. The three-deck-high central atrium features a monumental crystal sculpture titled *Caleido* by Italian artist Lucian Vistosi, who also created the towering glass sculptures onboard the *Maasdam* and *Veendam*.

The *Volendam*'s Marco Polo Restaurant, an alternative to the dining room, is a re-creation of a classic European "artist's bistro," a place where the walls are lined with works of art traded by artists for plates of spaghetti. The walls are a pastiche across time, with works by unknown contemporary artists as well as etchings by Rubens and Rembrandt and works by Henry Moore, Matisse, and Picasso.

Diners at the eighty-eight-seat restaurant are offered "California-style" Italian cuisine for lunch or dinner; there is no extra charge, but advance reservations are required. Typical pasta menu items include fettuccine with rock shrimp, chopped tomato, spinach, garlic, and toasted pine nuts; and linguine with Italian sausage, peppers, onions, tomato, and sangiovese wine sauce. Entrees include marinated chicken breast in garlic puree and rosemary, veal chop grilled with sage and rosemary, and pan-roasted lamb loin with red wine sauce.

Luncheon offerings include pizza rustica with goat cheese, salami, mushrooms, kalamata olives, crisp pancetta, tomato sauce, fontina cheese, and oregano; and a poached salmon niçoise salad with potatoes, eggs, green beans, tomato, red onions, cucumber, capers, and a light mustard dressing.

The casino bar, in addition to being the ship's sports bar, features such cinematic memorabilia as costumes, props, photos, and posters of movies and the stars who made them.

The ship's main show lounge features colorful colonnades against satiny dark wood walls, harkening back to the Art Deco era, with a design inspired by the famed Tuschinski Theater in Amsterdam.

On both the *Volendam* and *Zaandam,* the navigation deck was extended aft to accommodate the additional staterooms, moving the outdoor swimming pool to the lido deck, one level above its location on the Rotterdam- and Statendam-class ships. This design change permits direct access between the indoor and outdoor swimming pools and the Lido Restaurant.

Zaandam joined the Holland America fleet in spring 2000. The interior theme is music, featured throughout public rooms but most prominently in the Casino Bar, which showcases music memorabilia from jazz and blues to rock and roll and the classics. The centerpiece of the *Zaandam*'s grand atrium is a towering pipe organ that has mechanical figures of dancing musicians.

Amsterdam, Rotterdam

Econoguide rating:	★★★★ 85 points
Ship size:	Large
Category:	Top of the Line
Price range:	Premium $$$
Registry:	Netherlands
Year built:	Amsterdam, 2000; Rotterdam, 1997
Information:	(206) 283–2687, (800) 426–0327
Web site:	www.hollandamerica.com
Passenger capacity:	Amsterdam, 1,380; Rotterdam, 1,316 (double occupancy)
Crew:	644
Passenger-to-crew ratio:	2.1:1
Tonnage:	Amsterdam, 61,000; Rotterdam, 60,000
Passenger-space ratio:	47.1
Length:	Amsterdam, 780 feet; Rotterdam, 778 feet
Beam:	105.8 feet
Draft:	25.5 feet
Cruising speed:	25 knots
Guest decks:	10
Total cabins:	658
Outside:	381
Inside:	117
Suites:	160
Wheelchair cabins:	20
Cuisine:	International
Style:	Elegantly casual to formal in the evening
Price notes:	Single-occupancy premium, 150 to 190 percent; Single Partners Program (agree to share a stateroom with another nonsmoking guest of the same sex, and pay only the per-person, double-occupancy rate)
Tipping suggestions:	$10 pp/pd
Best deal:	Early-booking savings

The **Rotterdam** is the sixth company ship to bear the name. The onboard art collection includes artifacts related to the voyages of seventeenth-century mariners for the Dutch East and West Indies Companies.

The two-deck, 747-seat La Fontaine Dining Room features a giant mural reminiscent of the wall treatment of the previous *Rotterdam*'s much loved Ritz Carlton room.

The **Amsterdam** is slightly larger than her sister. HAL quietly reintroduced a bit of the old class system with the Neptune Lounge on the *Amsterdam*; the room is open only to guests in suites. The flashy star of the lobby is the Astrolabe Clock, a three-story thingamabob. One of the four faces of the clock displays twenty-four-hour ship's time; a second is a calendar with a zodiac. Another face shows the constellations as they appear in the night sky of Amsterdam, and a fourth shows the time in cities around the world.

The ship's eighty-eight-seat alternative restaurant, Odyssey, features Italian cuisine. Typical entrees may include *costelleta di vitello al carbone,* a sage and rosemary broiled veal chop served on sautéed eggplant and peppers; *petto de pollo rustico,* grilled chicken breast with mushroom, tomato concasse, and Gorgonzola; and *osso buco alla Milanese,* braised veal shank in red wine sauce with saffron risotto and asparagus.

Maasdam, Ryndam, Statendam, Veendam

Econoguide rating:	★★★★ 84 points
Ship size:	Large
Category:	Top of the Line
Price range:	Premium $$$
Registry:	Netherlands
Year built:	*Maasdam,* 1993; *Ryndam,* 1994; *Statendam,* 1993; *Veendam,* 1996
Information:	(206) 283–2687, (800) 426–0327
Web site:	www.hollandamerica.com
Passenger capacity:	1,266 (double occupancy)
Crew:	588
Passenger-to-crew ratio:	2.2:1
Tonnage:	55,451
Passenger-space ratio:	43.8
Length:	720 feet
Beam:	101 feet
Draft:	24.6 feet
Cruising speed:	22 knots
Guest decks:	10
Total cabins:	633
Outside:	336
Inside:	148
Suites:	149
Wheelchair cabins:	6
Cuisine:	International
Style:	Elegantly casual to formal in the evening
Price notes:	Single-occupancy premium, 150 to 190 percent; Single Partners Program (agree to share a stateroom with another nonsmoking guest of the same sex, and pay only the per-person, double-occupancy rate)
Tipping suggestions:	$10 pp/pd
Best deal:	Early-booking savings

The fifth Holland America Line ship to carry the name, the **Maasdam** features a $2 million collection of art and artifacts, a company trademark. A three-deck grand atrium, featuring a monumental glass sculpture by Italian artist Luciano Vistosi, extends from lower promenade deck to upper promenade. An escalator provides access upward from the main deck to staterooms on lower promenade deck.

Located on promenade and upper promenade decks, the Rotterdam Dining Room seats 657 on two levels connected by a pair of grand curved staircases. An antique marble fountain from Argentina is the centerpiece of the lower level. Windows on two sides and at the stern offer panoramic views of the sea, accented by murals by Danish ceramic artist Bjorn Wiinblad.

A 2004 renovation made *Maasdam* the latest vessel in its fleet to feature a Pinnacle Grill restaurant, as well as the concierge-level Neptune Lounge.

At the opposite end of the ship, the two-deck, 600-seat Rembrandt Show Lounge features Broadway-style entertainment. The room is decorated with delft ceramic tiles from Holland as well as plush brocaded fabrics, gold-tinted mirrors, and mahogany panels to recall the era of seventeenth-century Dutch master Rembrandt van Rijn, whose portrait is etched into the glass doors. (A cruise diary about a trip on the *Maasdam* is included in Chapter 11.)

The **Ryndam,** third in the company's history to carry the name, shares most of the same interior features. The Rotterdam Dining Room, with side and stern windows, is decorated with four large murals by a Dutch artist depicting elaborately costumed seventeenth-century Dutch noblemen against a backdrop of period sailing ships. The Vermeer Show Lounge has a tulip motif throughout, in light fixtures, wall panels, and carpeting.

On the **Statendam,** the atrium features the ornate, 26-foot-high *Fountain of the Sirens,* extending from the lower promenade deck to upper promenade. At the opposite end of the ship, the two-deck, 600-seat Van Gogh Show Lounge presents Broadway-style entertainment. The show room is themed to Dutch artist Vincent van Gogh's paintings *The Starry Night* and *Irises.*

On the **Veendam,** the Rotterdam Dining Room, seating 657 on two levels connected by a pair of grand curved staircases, is decorated with enormous paintings of flowers based on details from seventeenth-century Dutch still lifes. The Rubens Show Lounge, named for Flemish master painter Peter Paul Rubens, is done in copper brown and gray tones with accents of gold leaf and brass. Glass cutouts of dancers' forms radiate from large columns. (You can read a cruise diary about the *Veendam* in Chapter 11.)

Noordam

Econoguide rating:	★★★ 74 points
Ship size:	Medium
Category:	Top of the Line
Price range:	Premium $$$

Registry:	Netherlands
Year built:	1984
Information:	(206) 283–2687, (800) 426–0327
Web site:	www.hollandamerica.com
Passenger capacity:	1,214 (double occupancy)
Crew:	605
Passenger-to-crew ratio:	2:1
Tonnage:	33,930
Passenger-space ratio:	27.9
Length:	704.2 feet
Beam:	89.4 feet
Draft:	24.2 feet
Cruising speed:	21 knots
Guest decks:	10
Total cabins:	605
Outside:	391
Inside:	194
Suites:	20
Wheelchair cabins:	4
Cuisine:	International
Style:	Elegantly casual to formal in the evening
Price notes:	Single-occupancy premium, 150 to 190 percent; Single Partners Program (agree to share a stateroom with another nonsmoking guest of the same sex, and pay only the per-person, double-occupancy rate)
Tipping suggestions:	$10 pp/pd
Best deal:	Early-booking savings

This venerable ship, oldest in the HAL fleet, ended its service with the company in November 2004 and chartered to the U.K.'s Thomson Holidays to sail as *Thomson Celebration*. Thomson also operates *Thomson Spirit*, *Noordam's* sister ship, which sailed for many years as the *Nieuw Amsterdam* and for a short period of time as the *Patriot* of United States Lines.

Noordam's theme is the Dutch East India Company, established in Amsterdam in 1603 for trade between Holland and the Far East and East Indies. The art collection is composed of priceless vases and statues from China, Japan, and Indonesia.

Prinsendam

Econoguide rating:	★★★★★ 91 points
Ship size:	Medium
Category:	Ultraluxury
Price range:	Beyond Opulent $$$$$
Registry:	Netherlands

Year built:	1988 (formerly *Royal Viking Sun, Seabourn Sun*; refurbished 1995, 1999, 2002)
Information:	(206) 283–2687, (800) 426–0327
Web site:	www.hollandamerica.com
Passenger capacity:	794 (double occupancy)
Crew:	460
Passenger-to-crew ratio:	1.6:1
Tonnage:	37,845
Passenger-space ratio:	48.5
Length:	669 feet
Beam:	95 feet
Draft:	23 feet
Cruising speed:	21.4 knots
Guest decks:	9
Total cabins:	397
Outside:	372
Inside:	25
Suites:	19
Wheelchair cabins:	4
Cuisine:	International
Style:	Elegantly casual to formal in the evening
Price notes:	Single-occupancy premium, 150 to 190 percent; Single Partners Program (agree to share a stateroom with another nonsmoking guest of the same sex, and pay only the per-person, double-occupancy rate)
Tipping suggestions:	$10 pp/pd
Best deal:	Early-booking savings

The **Prinsendam** is an understatedly elegant ship, designed for the Royal Viking Line, then part of the Cunard fleet. She was transferred to Seabourn as the *Seabourn Sun* in 2000 and, most recently, to Holland America in 2002. The line plans to promote her as the "Elegant Explorer."

The ship's public rooms were completely refitted in 1999, and a Roman-style health spa and expanded golf facilities were added. Improvements to the spa on the Scandinavia Deck began at the entrance to the beauty salon, which was enlarged to add a reception area; an outdoor pool there was covered and enclosed to become a gymnasium. The center of the deck was extended to accommodate a new lap pool and two whirlpools.

The ship's two pools are filled with heated salt water; the pool on the Bridge Deck includes a swim-up bar. Four modern catamaran tenders have sloping bows for beach landings.

Renaming the ship *Prinsendam* brings back one of the cherished names of HAL's history. The original ship of that name sailed Far East and Alaska itineraries from 1973 through 1980. The name translates to "prince's" ship, with "dam" being the familiar Holland America passenger ship name suffix.

One of the most spacious larger ships in the cruise industry, the *Prinsendam* offers eight passenger decks plus fifteen public rooms and boutiques. Among

Holland America's classic Dutch art and ambience, passengers will discover an Explorer's Lounge, Crow's Nest, Java Cafe, Rotterdam Dining Room, an Italian alternative restaurant, and other familiar features.

Starting from the thirteenth deck, the passenger decks were renamed Sky, Sports, Lido, Verandah, Upper Promenade, Promenade, Lower Promenade, Main, and Dolphin. Other enhancements include a reconfigured La Fontaine dining room to accommodate two dinner sittings, a new concierge lounge for the exclusive use of suite guests, conversion of the Compass Rose Room to an Explorer's Lounge, upgraded furnishings in the Wajang movie theater, a new windscreen at the bow, and a specially commissioned sculpture for the central atrium.

The Sky Deck houses a Holland America trademark Crow's Nest lounge. The intimate lounge has floor-to-ceiling windows, a piano, and spectacular views from high atop the ship.

The *Prinsendam* introduces a new type of stateroom with its ten "lanai" cabins. These staterooms, constructed in space formerly used as a lounge on promenade deck aft, have private lanais and share a private covered deck and a hot tub.

The Queen's Lounge show room on promenade deck forward was redesigned for Holland America's customary two nightly shows with state-of-the-art lighting and sound equipment.

The port side of the forward portion of the dining room was converted into an alternative Odyssey Restaurant, featuring Italian cuisine and Mediterranean decor. Opposite the Odyssey is a traditional Ocean Bar, with bandstand and dance floor.

The ship also has a golf simulation center on the main deck. This virtual-reality golf game allows golfers to "play" several famous courses around the world as well as practice their golf swing and putting stroke. It is identical to simulators to be installed on Holland America's new Vista series of ships.

During its first year under the HAL flag, the 38,000-ton, 794-passenger *Prinsendam* sailed on twenty-three cruises ranging in length from ten to twenty-two days.

NORWEGIAN CRUISE LINE

NORWEGIAN CRUISE LINE

Address: 7665 Corporate Center Drive
Miami, FL 33126
Information: (800) 327–7030
    www.ncl.com
Econoguide's Best Cruise Lines
Econoguide's Best Cruise Values

The Norwegian Cruise Line Fleet

Norwegian Dawn	2002	2,200 passengers	91,000 tons
Norwegian Star	2001	2,200 passengers	91,000 tons
Norwegian Sun	2001	2,400 passengers	77,104 tons

Pride of Aloha	2004	2,400 passengers	77,104 tons
(formerly Norwegian Sky)			
Norwegian Spirit	2000	1,996 passengers	76,800 tons
(formerly SuperStar Leo)			
Norwegian Wind	1993	1,748 passengers	50,760 tons
Norwegian Dream	1992	1,748 passengers	46,000 tons
Norwegian Sea	1988	1,518 passengers	42,000 tons
Norwegian Majesty	1992, to NCL in 1997	1,460 passengers	38,000 tons
Norwegian Crown	1988	1,050 passengers	34,250 tons

FUTURE SHIPS

Pride of America	2005	2,144 passengers	81,000 tons
Unnamed	Fall 2005	2,400 passengers	93,000 tons
Unnamed	Spring 2006	2,400 passengers	93,000 tons

Norwegian Cruise Line is a fleet on the move, growing rapidly and expanding its reach from its Caribbean roots to include Alaska, Hawaii, the Mexican Riviera, and a subsidiary operation out of Australia. Owned by Star Cruises, a growing line based in Malaysia, NCL has been adding new ships at a rapid rate; some vessels have been transferred into the fleet from parent company Star Cruises.

NCL lived in interesting times in 2004. Even as it continued to grow—placing orders for two more Megaships and launching its American-flagged subsidiary to sail in Hawaiian waters without the need to sail thousands of miles away to touch a foreign port—it was forced to deal with setbacks on one old and one brand-new ship.

The company's *Pride of America*, under construction at Bremerhaven, Germany, and expected to join the fleet in July 2004, suffered extensive damage in March of that year when it rolled over and sank in an unexpected gale. Several of the lower decks were submerged for weeks, causing tens of millions of dollars in damage and a delay in the launching of the ship until sometime in 2005.

As a result of the mishap, the company quickly shifted the *Norwegian Sky*— renamed as *Pride of Aloha*, given a major refurbishment, and reflagged into the U.S. Registry—to assume *Pride of America*'s itinerary.

NCL also announced that the venerable SS *Norway* would not return to the North American cruise market. The ship had been towed to Germany for repairs after a disastrous explosion of one of its engines at port in Miami in 2003. The future of the ship remains uncertain. Also unclear is the company's intended use for the former *United States*, which NCL purchased in 2003.

Meanwhile, parent company Star Cruises announced it had finalized orders for two new "Freestyle Cruising" vessels for delivery in fall 2005 and spring 2006. The two ships will be built at Meyer Werft in Germany, the same shipyards that constructed *Superstar Leo* (now *Norwegian Spirit*), *Superstar Virgo*, *Norwegian Star,* and *Norwegian Dawn*.

The new ships will be based on the successful *Norwegian Dawn/Norwegian Star* design, built slightly larger at an estimated tonnage of 93,000 and including 2,400 berths at double occupancy.

Norwegian Sea is due to leave the fleet in the spring of 2005, transferred to Star Cruises.

■ THE NORWEGIAN STORY

NCL, originally named Norwegian Caribbean Lines, began in 1966 as a partnership between the Norwegian shipping company Klosters and entrepreneur Ted Arison. That arrangement lasted until 1972 when Arison left to form Carnival Cruise Lines.

NCL's first vessel was the *Sunward.* Part ocean liner and part ferryboat, the ship was built to take British vacationers and their cars to Spain. That itinerary became less attractive because of political issues, and the ship was transferred to the then obscure port of Miami. A company named Norwegian Caribbean Lines was formed.

The *Sunward* was an instant success, contributing to Miami's tremendous growth as a cruise ship port. NCL brought out a line of new "white ships," beginning with the *Starward* in 1968.

In 1979 NCL rescued the nearly forgotten *France* from retirement for $18 million; the ship was towed to Bremerhaven, Germany, and rebuilt for Caribbean cruising at a cost of $130 million. The flagship of the NCL fleet, renamed the *Norway,* it was the longest cruise ship afloat. But an explosion while at dock in Miami in May 2003 severely damaged the ship and killed seven crewmen; *Norway* was eventually towed to Europe with its future unknown.

In 1984 the line's parent company purchased another Norwegian company, the Royal Viking Line, integrating it into NCL operations. Five years later, Royal Cruise Line was also brought into NCL.

In 1997 and 1998 the *Windward* and *Dreamward* were stretched, with the insertion of a 130-foot midsection, increasing each vessel's capacity by 40 percent. The ships were reborn as the *Norwegian Wind* and *Norwegian Dream.*

In summer 1998, NCL completed the acquisition of Orient Lines, including the 845-guest cruise ship *Marco Polo.* Orient Lines continues as an independent premium brand, offering five- to twenty-five-day itineraries onboard the *Marco Polo* to exotic destinations in Africa, Antarctica, Australia, Egypt, India, Southeast Asia, and the Mediterranean, including the Greek Isles. In 1999 Malaysia-based Star Cruises acquired a controlling interest in NCL.

NCL's Great Stirrup Cay is a speck of coral and limestone 120 nautical miles due east of Fort Lauderdale in the Berry Islands of the Bahamas. When the 2.5-by-1.5-mile island was purchased in 1977 the cruise line was the first to own a private island; in subsequent years NCL has added several buildings, extended the beach, and erected a sea wall to reduce erosion.

Historians and archeologists say that long before tourists brought their blankets and video cameras to the island, the first settlers were Lucayan Indians around 600 A.D. Christopher Columbus and the Spanish arrived in 1492, and the British were active in the area in the early 1600s.

The principal lure of Great Stirrup Cay is its protected cove, and for that reason the island was regularly used by pirates who laid in wait for Spanish ships returning to Europe with gold and other treasure from South America. During the U.S. Civil War, Federal troops stored provisions there; in World War II American troops were stationed there as part of the defense of the East Coast. In more modern times, a small satellite tracking station was installed there.

ITINERARIES

NCL boosted its presence in "homeland cruising" in 2005, deploying three ships in Hawaii to sail seven-, ten-, and eleven-day cruises out of Honolulu; four ships in Alaska; departures from three eastern seaboard cities to Bermuda; and sailings to the Caribbean from five nearby ports.

NCL will deploy three ships in the Aloha state year-round. *Pride of Aloha* offers seven-day inter-island cruises round-trip from Honolulu. The new *Pride of America* ship will also sail in Hawaiian waters once it arrives sometime in 2005. *Norwegian Wind* will continue ten- and eleven-day cruises from Honolulu to the American islands, as well as a call at Fanning Island in the Republic of Kiribati.

In Alaska the company will feature its largest deployment ever with four ships in service—three from Seattle (*Norwegian Star, Norwegian Spirit,* and *Norwegian Dream*) and one from Vancouver (*Norwegian Sun*). The Alaska season runs from mid-May through mid-September.

NCL will sail fifty-two seven-day trips from Boston, Philadelphia, and New York to Bermuda, visiting three ports in the island nation; NCL is the only company with regular sailing from Boston. *Norwegian Crown* will sail from Philadelphia from late April to mid-May and again from late September to late October; the same ship will sail from New York from mid-May through mid-September. *Norwegian Majesty* is due to sail from Boston from May through the end of October 2005.

Ships will sail to the Caribbean from five American ports: Charleston, Houston, Miami, New Orleans, and New York. *Norwegian Dawn* is assigned year-round for sailings, including week-long trips to Port Canaveral, Miami, and the Bahamas, as well as a series of eleven-day trips deeper into the Caribbean with calls including Saint Thomas, Antigua, Barbados, Saint Martin, Tortola, and Grenada.

Norwegian Majesty was due to sail from Charleston to Grand Cayman, Cozumel, and Key West from January through mid-April 2005 and again from mid-November through mid-April 2006. *Norwegian Sun* was scheduled to sail from Miami to Grand Cayman, Honduras, Belize, and Cozumel from January through mid-April; the ship was due to sail a similar itinerary from New Orleans from mid-October 2005 through the end of April 2006.

The renamed and renovated *Norwegian Spirit* was assigned to sail round-trip from Miami from January through late April 2005 and again from mid-October through mid-April 2006. Itineraries were to alternate between nine-day trips to

Barbados, Grenada, Saint Lucia, Antigua, and Tortola, and five-day cruises to Grand Cayman and Honduras.

Norwegian Sea is due to sail Texaribbean cruises from Houston to Cozumel, Honduras, Belize, and Cancun from January through the end of April. During that same period of time, *Norwegian Dream* is scheduled to sail from New Orleans to the same set of ports. *Norwegian Dream* will sail from Houston on the same schedule from mid-October 2005 through the end of April 2006.

Norwegian Star will return to Los Angeles to sail to the Mexican Riviera, including Acapulco, Zihuatanejo, Puerto Vallarta, and Cabo San Lucas; the itineraries run from early January through the end of April, and again from late September 2005 through the end of April 2006.

Norwegian Crown will offer a series of fourteen-day cruises around Cape Horn in South America, alternating homeports between Valparaiso, Chile, and Buenos Aires, Argentina; the ship will include calls in the Falkland Islands and cruise the Darwin Canal, Chilean Fjords, and the Strait of Magellan. The trips are scheduled for January and February 2005, late November and from December through February 2006.

■ PROJECT AMERICA

On July 4, 2004, NCL became the first company in nearly fifty years to hoist the Stars and Stripes above a new oceangoing passenger ship. This represents no easy accomplishment: It took an act of Congress and—truth be told—the failure of another company's effort to bring it about.

In late 2002 NCL purchased from Northrop Grumman Ship Systems the partially completed hull of the first Project America ship, which had been under way for United States Line, an offshoot of the former owner of Delta Queen Steamboat Company. United States Line had planned to build and launch a pair of 1,900-passenger vessels that would have been the first new American-built and -operated cruise ships in half a century. Unfortunately the company went out of business and the ships were never completed.

NCL arranged for the towing of one hull and associated materials for a second vessel from the Northrup shipyard in Pascagoula, Mississippi, to a shipyard in Bremerhaven, Germany. The company also successfully managed to get some fancy legal language into the 2003 federal appropriations act that allows NCL to use Project America vessels in the Hawaiian Islands for interisland cruise service. The vessels will be U.S. flagged and 100 percent U.S. crewed, allowing NCL to avoid the necessity of visiting a foreign port, such as the long haul from Hawaii to Fanning Island in the Republic of Kiribati. The exemption also gives NCL an exclusive license for interisland cruising. Congress did add a requirement that the Hawaii ships could not be repositioned for revenue service in Alaska or the Gulf of Mexico.

Pride of America will offer open-seating main dining rooms, multiple dining choices at eight restaurants, three pools, an expansive spa and health and fitness center, and extensive children's facilities. Eighty percent of the staterooms will have an ocean view, with 85 percent of those including private balconies.

▓ WEB SITE

The NCL Web site includes all you need to know about ships and itineraries, and its on-line booking engine permits you to view the location of available cabins. You can also select pre- and postcruise accommodations and tours and selected shore excursions. Travelers have the option to book online, direct their information to a travel agent of their choice, or seek the assistance of an NCL reservationist. *Ease of use: excellent.*

Pride of America

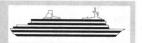

Econoguide rating:	★★★★ 82 points (estimated)
Ship size:	Megaship
Category:	Top of the Line
Price range:	Premium to Opulent **$$$–$$$$**
Registry:	United States
Year built:	*2005*
Information:	(800) 327–7030
Web site:	www.ncl.com
Passenger capacity:	2,144 (double occupancy)
Crew:	900
Passenger-to-crew ratio:	2.4:1
Tonnage:	81,000
Passenger-space ratio:	37.8
Length:	919 feet
Beam:	106 feet
Draft:	26 feet
Cruising speed:	22 knots
Guest decks:	15
Total cabins:	1,072
Outside:	791
Inside:	229
Suites:	52
Wheelchair cabins:	22
Cuisine:	American, Asian, French, Italian
Style:	Informal, with one optional formal night per cruise
Price notes:	Single surcharge, 150 to 200 percent
Tipping suggestions:	$10 pp/pd
Best deal:	Early-bird fares; group discounts with minimum of eight guests

Pride of America, the first completely new oceangoing cruise ship to fly the U.S. flag in nearly fifty years, salutes the many regions of the country with Stars & Stripes artwork on the hull and design elements within. Public rooms include the Alaskan Gold Rush Saloon, a New Orleans–style Mardi Gras Cabaret Lounge, a French restaurant inspired by Thomas Jefferson's Monticello, and a Waikiki Bar.

All told, there are eight restaurants and ten bars and lounges aboard ship. The eateries are the Skyline and Liberty main restaurants, Jefferson's Bistro, Little Italy, East Meets West, the Steakhouse, Cadillac Diner, and the Aloha Cafe. Also available to guests are three swimming pools and four hot tubs, a tennis court, a conservatory, and art gallery.

Norwegian Star, Norwegian Dawn

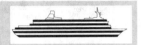

Econoguide rating:	★★★★ 84 points
Ship size:	Megaship
Category:	Top of the Line
Price range:	Premium to Opulent **$$$–$$$$**
Registry:	Bahamas
Year built:	*Norwegian Star,* 2001; *Norwegian Dawn,* 2002
Information:	(800) 327–7030
Web site:	www.ncl.com
Passenger capacity:	2,200 (double occupancy)
Crew:	1,122
Passenger-to-crew ratio:	2:1
Tonnage:	91,000
Passenger-space ratio:	41.4
Length:	965 feet
Beam:	105 feet
Draft:	23 feet
Cruising speed:	25 knots
Guest decks:	15
Total cabins:	1,122
Outside:	761
Inside:	361
Suites:	147
Wheelchair cabins:	20
Cuisine:	Italian, Asian, continental
Style:	Informal, with two formal nights per cruise
Price notes:	Single surcharge, 150 to 200 percent
Tipping suggestions:	$10 pp/pd
Best deal:	Early-bird fares; group discounts with minimum of eight guests

NCL's fastest and largest ships, **Norwegian Star** and **Norwegian Dawn** were originally planned for Star Cruises, but the parent company transferred them as they were being built.

Designed with the freestyle cruising concept in mind, there are ten different restaurants aboard. On the *Norwegian Star,* Versailles is an ornate main restau-

The *Norwegian Dawn* in Port Canaveral, Florida. *Photo by Corey Sandler*

rant with a French-inspired design offering traditional six-course dining. Aqua is a contemporary-styled main restaurant featuring a lighter, modern menu. It has an open galley displaying the preparation of pastries and desserts. Ginza, a Japanese/Chinese/Thai restaurant, includes a sushi tempura bar, a teppanyaki room, and a sake bar. The show kitchen in the entrance area introduces passengers to the traditional styles of Asian preparation.

The Soho Room, a Pacific Rim restaurant, serves a fusion of a la carte Californian, Hawaiian, and Asian dishes. The restaurant has a modern art gallery with a collection of pop art. Passengers can pick a lobster from a large tank. Le Bistro is an upscale French Mediterranean restaurant with an a la carte menu of traditional gourmet French cuisine in Art Nouveau style. Market Cafe has buffet-styled "food action stations" with prepared-to-order breakfast, lunch, and themed dinners. Endless Summer is a Hawaiian-themed restaurant offering such delicacies as roast suckling pig and Lomi Lomi salmon.

La Trattoria is an evening-only offering at the Market Cafe serving pasta, pizza, and other traditional Italian fare, and Blue Lagoon is an indoor/outdoor food court featuring hamburgers, hot dogs, stir-fry dishes, and traditional fish-and-chips with malt vinegar.

The artwork of *Norwegian Dawn* begins on the hull. Paintings on the starboard side feature dolphins playing in colorful waves, a salute to Caribbean itineraries. The port side shows New York's Statue of Liberty, signifying the ship's Bahamas and Florida itinerary from the port of New York. The ship's hull also features reproduced signatures of nineteenth- and twentieth-century masters Renoir, Matisse, Van Gogh, and Monet and pop icon Andy Warhol. NCL installed a collection of original oil paintings by Impressionist artists in its signature Le Bistro restaurant and a collection of original signed works by Warhol around the ship. The interior paintings are on loan from the personal collection of the chairman of Star Cruises, parent company of Norwegian Cruise Line.

Norwegian Star underwent a major refurbishment in May 2004, including the addition of a steakhouse, a 10,000-square foot casino, and dramatic hull artwork. NCL said it intends to treat the hulls of its newer Freestyle Cruising vessels as blank canvases to reflect the personality of the ships.

The green, red, yellow, purple and aqua art on the side of *Norwegian Star* is intended as a whimsical interpretation of the long-time cruise tradition of passengers throwing streamers from the bow of a ship as the vessel pulled away from the dock at the beginning of a sailing.

The restaurant space on Deck 13 formerly used as Las Ramblas restaurant was converted into Cagney's Steakhouse, a 1930s-style American steakhouse decorated in a Western theme. A similar restaurant on *Norwegian Dawn* has proven very successful. *Norwegian Star*'s Endless Summer restaurant, located on Deck 8 overlooking the Atrium, was changed to a Tex-Mex and tapas style restaurant with offerings including sangria, tamales, black bean soup with chorizo, enchiladas, quesadillas, and Mexican chocolate mascarpone cheesecake.

A new casino was installed in the place of the former Dazzles Nightclub. The Star Club Casino offers standards including slot machines, blackjack, baccarat, roulette, poker, and craps, as well as more exotic games including pai-gow poker and pai-gow tiles. Players can also use an electronic player tracking system that logs play and offers rewards, including onboard amenities, credit applied to their onboard accounts, reduced rates for future cruises, and even a complimentary cruise if the level of play is high enough.

The former Teen Club was transformed into the hip Pearl Martini lounge; a new Teen Club and Video Arcade were moved to Deck 12 in the Market Cafe.

Norwegian Spirit

Econoguide rating:	★★★★ 84 points
Ship size:	Megaship
Category:	Top of the Line
Price range:	Premium to Opulent $$$–$$$$
Registry:	Bahamas
Year built:	Built as *Superstar Leo* in 2000
Information:	(800) 327–7030
Web site:	www.ncl.com
Passenger capacity:	1,996 (double occupancy)

Crew:	920
Passenger-to-crew ratio:	2.2:1
Tonnage:	76,800
Passenger-space ratio:	38.5
Length:	880 feet
Beam:	106 feet
Draft:	26 feet
Cruising speed:	25.5 knots
Guest decks:	11
Total cabins:	1,120
Outside:	602
Inside:	400
Suites:	18
Wheelchair cabins:	n/a
Cuisine:	Italian, Asian, continental
Style:	Informal, with two formal nights per cruise
Price notes:	Single surcharge, 150 to 200 percent
Tipping suggestions:	$10 pp/pd
Best deal:	Early-bird fares; group discounts with minimum of eight guests

Superstar Leo was the largest and flashiest new cruise ship in Asian waters when she was added to the Star Cruises fleet in 2000. In her new incarnation, as **Norwegian Spirit,** the ship is flashier than ever. Following a first season in Alaska, the ship was due for a major renovation before beginning regular Caribbean service for the winter of 2004 and 2005.

The main eatery is the Windows Restaurant, which serves international fare. Shogun offers Japanese items; Tai Pan, despite its name, is a French bistro; Maxim's is a gourmet room; and there are informal places to eat at the Raffles Buffet and the Blue Lagoon. In 2004 there was an extra charge of $20.00 for Maxim's, $15.00 for Tai Pan, and $12.50 for Shogun.

Entertainment options include the 1,000-seat Moulin Rouge showroom, the Celebrity Disco, and The Picture House cinema. You'll also find karaoke at The Bund, a casino, and a mahjong room.

Pride of Aloha, Norwegian Sun

Econoguide rating:	★★★★ 82 points
Ship size:	Megaship
Category:	Top of the Line
Price range:	Premium to Opulent $$$–$$$$
Registry:	Bahamas
Year built:	*Norwegian Sun*, 2001; *Pride of Aloha (Norwegian Sky)*, 1999
Information:	(800) 327–7030

Web site:	www.ncl.com
Passenger capacity:	2,002 (double occupancy)
Crew:	800
Passenger-to-crew ratio:	2.5:1
Tonnage:	77,104
Passenger-space ratio:	39
Length:	853 feet
Beam:	108 feet
Draft:	26 feet
Cruising speed:	23 knots
Guest decks:	12
Total cabins:	1,001
Outside:	574
Inside:	407
Suites:	14
Wheelchair cabins:	6
Cuisine:	French, Italian, Chinese, continental
Style:	Resort casual
Price notes:	Single supplement, 150 to 200 percent
Tipping suggestions:	$10 pp/pd
Best deal:	Early-bird fares; group discounts with minimum of eight guests

The *Norwegian Sun* and her near-twin the *Norwegian Sky* (now sailing as *Pride of Aloha*) were the Freestyle Cruising flagships of the NCL fleet, elegant and comfortable Megaships. The **Norwegian Sky** entered service in August 1999, sailing from the shipyard to Boston to begin her service with a series of cruises to Canada. Unfortunately, the spectacular new ship made a most spectacular debut on her first passage in the Saint Lawrence River—running aground at the juncture with the Saguenay River. The mishap damaged one of the rudders and a propeller and cut a large gash in her side. There were no reported injuries (except perhaps to the résumé of the captain and the two river pilots aboard), but the brand-spanking-new ship had to limp back to Quebec City and enter into dry dock for more than a month of repairs.

NCL acquired an unfinished hull in 1997 when the Bremer Vulkan shipyard in Germany went bankrupt. Intended as the *CostaOlympia* flagship of the Costa line, the ship was recast as the *Norwegian Sky.* Most of the cabins are on Decks 8, 9, and 10, well above the lifeboats on Deck 7; a bit more than 200 others are spread among the lower decks. About a quarter of the ship's staterooms have a private teak-floored balcony; four owners' suites also have private outdoor hot tubs. Up top are three pools, including one with a waterfall.

The focus of the interior is a pair of glass-domed atria. Aft, there's Neptune's Court with a grand stair tower; midships is the Atrium, eight decks high with four panoramic lifts.

There are two major restaurants on the Atlantic Deck: the Four Seasons and Seven Seas dining rooms. The Horizons Restaurant on the Atlantic Deck offers intimate dining for eighty-four. The Stardust Lounge on the promenade and international decks seats about 1,000 guests in a two-story show lounge that has a proscenium stage. The Sports Bar on the pool deck serves as a teen disco during the day; also onboard is The Zone teenage disco, which has a soft-drink bar.

In May 2004 *Norwegian Sky* was recast once more, this time as *Pride of Aloha* as part of NCL's Project America fleet.

The ship will join the new *Pride of America* with an all-American crew sailing among the islands of Hawaii. Operating under U.S. registry, *Pride of Aloha* will be able to sail between domestic ports without the need for a visit to a foreign country.

Norwegian Sun was based on the same hull design, but NCL modified its internal design to work with the freestyle cruising concept. Among the many new features on the ship are no less than nine different restaurants and slightly larger staterooms than those on her near-sister. Dining choices include two main dining rooms; a formal Italian restaurant; Le Bistro gourmet French cafe; a Pacific Rim restaurant complex featuring a sushi bar, teppanyaki room, and a California/Hawaii/Asian fusion restaurant; a tapas bar; a twenty-four-hour indoor-outdoor cafe; and a "healthy living" restaurant with spa menus.

The *Norwegian Sun* offers more than a hundred additional outside staterooms than the *Pride of Aloha,* and cabins with verandas are slightly larger. You can read a cruise diary about the *Pride of Aloha* in Chapter 11.

NCL's *Pride of Aloha* docked in Haines, Alaska. *Photo by Corey Sandler*

Norwegian Dream

Econoguide rating:	★★★ 76 points
Ship size:	Large
Category:	Top of the Line
Price range:	Premium to Opulent $$$–$$$$
Registry:	Bahamas
Year built:	1992 (as *Dreamward;* stretched by 130 feet in 1998 and renamed)
Information:	(800) 327–7030
Web site:	www.ncl.com
Passenger capacity:	1,760 (double occupancy)
Crew:	614
Passenger-to-crew ratio:	2.9:1
Tonnage:	50,760
Passenger-space ratio:	26.1
Length:	754 feet
Beam:	94 feet
Draft:	22 feet
Cruising speed:	18 knots
Guest decks:	10
Total cabins:	874
Outside:	585
Inside:	158
Suites:	118
Wheelchair cabins:	13
Cuisine:	Italian, continental, French, international
Style:	Resort casual
Price notes:	Single supplement, 150 to 200 percent
Tipping suggestions:	$10 pp/pd
Best deal:	Early-bird fares; group discounts with minimum of eight guests

The **Norwegian Dream** and her sister ship *Norwegian Wind* were reborn in 1998 after they were stretched and refurbished, growing from nice Medium-size vessels to even nicer Large ships.

You don't really "stretch" a ship. Instead, each ship was cut in half and a matching 130-foot midsection was installed. As a result, passenger capacity was increased by 40 percent, with the addition of 502 new berths, several new public rooms, and a few interesting amenities, including a swim-up pool bar.

On the *Dream,* the Stardust Lounge is a two-story main show lounge that has a proscenium stage, used for a full production of Broadway shows.

In August 1999 the *Norwegian Dream* inexplicably collided with a large freighter in the English Channel, sustaining major damage and shaking up passengers, though none was seriously injured. The ship continued to England under her own power but was disabled for more than a month.

Norwegian Wind

Econoguide rating:	★★★ 76 points
Ship size:	Large
Category:	Top of the Line
Price range:	Moderate to Premium $$–$$$
Registry:	Bahamas
Year built:	1992 (as *Windward*; stretched by 130 feet and renamed in 1998)
Information:	(800) 327–7030
Web site:	www.ncl.com
Passenger capacity:	1,760 (double occupancy)
Crew:	689
Passenger-to-crew ratio:	2.6:1
Tonnage:	50,760
Passenger-space ratio:	28.8
Length:	754 feet
Beam:	94 feet
Draft:	23 feet
Cruising speed:	21 knots
Guest decks:	10
Total cabins:	874
Outside:	623
Inside:	139
Suites:	101
Wheelchair cabins:	11
Cuisine:	Italian, continental, French, international
Style:	Resort casual
Price notes:	Single supplement, 150 to 200 percent
Tipping suggestions:	$10 pp/pd
Best deal:	Early-bird fares; group discounts with minimum of eight guests

As with the *Norwegian Dream*, the *Windward* was stretched by 130 feet in 1998 and renamed the **Norwegian Wind.** The two sisters are now nearly identical.

In 2001 the ship underwent another renovation, resulting in the enlargement of the Sports Bar and Grill and a remodeling of the casino. Open, restaurant-style seating and extended hours are now offered in the ship's dining rooms and alternative restaurants. *Norwegian Wind* has five dining venues each night: two main dining rooms; the Sun Terraces, converted to an Italian Trattoria offering traditional Italian fare; Le Bistro; and the Sports Bar and Grill, serving buffet-style breakfast, lunch, dinner, and snacks throughout the day. In addition to the five permanent full-service restaurants, *Norwegian Wind* also has an on-deck Caribbean Night barbecue with jerk chicken, pork, ribs, and fish.

The Sports Bar and Grill on the Sports Deck contains a wall of multiple televisions that display videotaped and live broadcasts of major sports events. The Stardust Lounge on the Star Deck is a two-story main show lounge used for full-scale productions of Broadway shows.

Norwegian Sea

Econoguide rating:	★★★ 76 points
Ship size:	Large
Category:	Vintage
Price range:	Premium $$$
Registry:	Bahamas
Year built:	1988 (formerly the *Seaward*)
Information:	(800) 327–7030
Web site:	www.ncl.com
Passenger capacity:	1,518 (double occupancy)
Crew:	630
Passenger-to-crew ratio:	2.4:1
Tonnage:	42,000
Passenger-space ratio:	27.7
Length:	700 feet
Beam:	93 feet
Draft:	22 feet
Cruising speed:	20 knots
Guest decks:	9
Total cabins:	759
Outside:	536
Inside:	212
Suites:	7
Wheelchair cabins:	4
Cuisine:	Italian, continental, French, international
Style:	Resort casual
Price notes:	Single supplement, 150 to 200 percent
Tipping suggestions:	$10 pp/pd
Best deal:	Early-bird fares; group discounts with minimum of eight guests

A veteran of the Caribbean (and on a comparative basis, a relatively homely member of the NCL fleet), the **Norwegian Sea** nevertheless has some nice touches in public areas, enhanced by redecoration. The ship's name was changed from *Seaward* to add a reference to its owner's Scandinavian heritage. The Cabaret Lounge is used for full-scale Broadway productions.

The ship underwent another round of refurbishment in early 2003, adding a new restaurant and upgrades to public rooms. The forty-seat Pasta Cafe serves traditional Italian fare. The refurbished Stardust Lounge features a rich burgundy-and-gold theme with new carpet, drapes, and upholstery. Le Bistro, NCL's signature restaurant, was also redecorated.

Junior cruisers have their own playroom, The Porthole, for NCL's "Kids Crew" activities.

In the spring of 2005, *Norwegian Sea* is due to transfer to the Star Cruises fleet. Her new name and assignment were not yet announced at press time.

Norwegian Majesty

Econoguide rating:	★★★ 76 points
Ship size:	Large
Category:	Top of the Line
Price range:	Moderate to Premium $$–$$$
Registry:	Bahamas
Year built:	1992 (formerly *Royal Majesty*; stretched by 112 feet in 1999)
Information:	(800) 327–7030
Web site:	www.ncl.com
Passenger capacity:	1,462 (double occupancy)
Crew:	550
Passenger-to-crew ratio:	2.65:1
Tonnage:	40,876
Passenger-space ratio:	26
Length:	680 feet
Beam:	91 feet
Draft:	20 feet
Cruising speed:	20 knots
Guest decks:	9
Total cabins:	731
Outside:	466
Inside:	239
Suites:	22
Wheelchair cabins:	4
Cuisine:	Italian, continental, French, international
Style:	Resort casual
Price notes:	Single supplement, 150 to 200 percent
Tipping suggestions:	$10 pp/pd
Best deal:	Early-bird fares; group discounts with minimum of eight guests

The *Norwegian Majesty* was stretched by 112 feet in early 1999; addition of the new midsection increased the capacity from 1,056 to 1,462 guests and boosted the crew size by 25 percent.

The new midsection contains a second swimming pool and dining room, a new casino, the intimate fifty-eight-seat Le Bistro restaurant, more deck space, and 203 new staterooms. Also included in the section were two new elevators and a third set of stairs to improve movement throughout the ship.

An entirely new space, the Sky Deck, was added above the lengthened Sun Deck to add sunning areas and to create a ring of shaded areas around the two pools and whirlpools below.

Existing staterooms on the ship will be upgraded to match the new staterooms in upcoming refurbishments.

Installation of the new midsection took about three months. According to engineers, the new midsection actually helped the ship's underwater profile, allowing it to maintain its 21 knot speed without changes to the power plant. And added buoyancy from the new midsection reduced the vessel's draft about 18 inches.

Norwegian Crown

Econoguide rating:	★★★ 79 points
Ship size:	Medium
Category:	Vintage
Price range:	Premium $$$
Registry:	Bahamas
Year built:	1988 (as the *Crown Odyssey* of the Royal Viking Line and Royal Cruise Line; renamed *Norwegian Crown* for NCL in 1996; renamed *Crown Odyssey* in 2000 for Orient Lines; renamed again as *Norwegian Crown* for NCL in 2003)
Information:	(800) 327–7030
Web site:	www.ncl.com
Passenger capacity:	1,050 (double occupancy)
Crew:	470
Passenger-to-crew ratio:	2.3:1
Tonnage:	34,250
Passenger-space ratio:	32.6
Length:	614 feet
Beam:	92.5 feet
Draft:	24 feet
Cruising speed:	22 knots
Guest decks:	10
Total cabins:	526
Outside:	322
Inside:	114

Suites:	90
Wheelchair cabins:	4
Cuisine:	Contemporary
Style:	Informal with two formal nights per cruise
Price notes:	Single supplement, 150 to 200 percent
Tipping suggestions:	$10 pp/pd
Best deal:	Early-bird fares; group discounts with minimum of eight guests

Built as an upper-ranks cruise ship, the **Norwegian Crown** has held up well over the years through several reinventions. She was transferred from NCL to sister company Orient Lines in 2000 but was brought back to NCL for 2003 and beyond.

In anticipation of her return to NCL, the ship was remodeled in 2003 in keeping with the line's freestyle cruising scheme for dining. The Seven Seas Restaurant is built on two levels, with a central sunken section beneath a domed Tiffany-style glass ceiling. New eateries added during the remodeling include Cafe Italia, an alfresco Italian kitchen; Le Bistro, an upscale French restaurant; Pasta Cafe, an informal pasta restaurant; and Chopsticks, a modern combination of Pacific Rim and Asian fusion offerings.

The ship also gained a state-of-the-art fitness center and children's activity area.

PRINCESS CRUISES

PRINCESS CRUISES 🐾.

Address: 24844 Avenue Rockefeller
Santa Clarita, CA 91355
Information: (800) 421–0522, (800) 774–6237
www.princess.com
Econoguide's Best Cruise Lines

Princess Cruises Fleet

Caribbean Princess	2004	3,110 passengers	116,000 tons
Diamond Princess	2004	2,600 passengers	113,000 tons
Sapphire Princess	2004	2,600 passengers	113,000 tons
Star Princess	2002	2,600 passengers	110,000 tons
Golden Princess	2001	2,600 passengers	110,000 tons
Grand Princess	1998	2,600 passengers	109,000 tons
Island Princess	2003	1,970 passengers	88,000 tons
Coral Princess	2003	1,970 passengers	88,000 tons
Sea Princess	1998	1,950 passengers	77,000 tons
Dawn Princess	1997	1,950 passengers	77,000 tons

Sun Princess	1995	1,950 passengers	77,000 tons
Regal Princess	1991	1,590 passengers	70,000 tons
Royal Princess	1984	1,200 passengers	45,000 tons
Pacific Princess	1997	680 passengers	30,277 tons
Tahitian Princess	1997	680 passengers	30,277 tons

FUTURE SHIPS

| Unnamed | May 2006 | 3,110 passengers | 116,000 tons |

Princess continues to expand and update its fleet at a remarkable pace. The company added three new Megaships in 2004, expanding its Grand class to six well-designed floating cities. The line also welcomed the return of Sea Princess, which had been sailing for sister company P&O Cruises; at the same time, the older, smaller Royal Princess will go to P&O. The net effect of the latest moves increases the capacity of Princess by about 16 percent while the average age of the company fleet goes down to less than five years and the percentage of the fleet's total number of cabins with balconies increases to about 54 percent.

And under the stewardship of its new owner, Carnival Corporation, Princess has ordered a sister ship to the new Caribbean Princess.

In 2003 the line added Pacific Princess and Tahitian Princess, newly repolished gems purchased from the assets of much-loved but very bankrupt Renaissance Cruises.

Princess, of course, is the cruise line that made its name as the home of the "Love Boat." Today Princess sails to six continents and calls at more than 260 ports around the world. Princess owns a big piece of Alaska, too, dispatching at least six cruise ships to those waters and operating four riverside wilderness lodges, a fleet of deluxe motor coaches, and an armada of Midnight Sun Express luxury railcars.

The flagships of the fleet are the Grand class, which includes Grand Princess, Golden Princess, Star Princess, Diamond Princess, and Sapphire Princess. The 2,600-passenger ships are 951 feet long and 118 feet wide, a few feet wider than the Panama Canal.

■ THE PRINCESS STORY

Princess itself was founded in 1965 with a single chartered ship cruising from Los Angeles to Mexico; within a few years, Princess Cruises had a small fleet of ships on the West Coast. London-based Peninsular and Orient Steam Navigation Company (P&O) came to the same waters in the early 1970s; although it could not compete against Princess's head start, P&O later purchased the cruise line.

P&O dates back to 1822 to a fleet of small sailing ships; among their destinations was a link between Great Britain and Spain and Portugal, the Iberian Peninsula. To demonstrate their appreciation for the services provided during the Portuguese and Spanish civil wars of the early 1830s, the Royal Houses of both countries granted the company the right to fly their colors: the Portuguese blue and white, and the Spanish red and gold. Those colors continue to this day in the P&O flag.

In 1836 the company began a regular steamer service to the Iberian Peninsula under the name Peninsular Steam Navigation Company. Within a few years, the steamer company added routes to India and Egypt (with an overland route across Egypt until the opening of the Suez Canal in 1869). P&O began offering leisure cruises in 1844 and eventually became known for its "big white ships." By 1845 the steamers reached to Malay and China, and *Orient* was added to the company's name.

P&O purchased Princess in 1974. A year later, a television producer approached Princess Cruises with an idea for a series about cruising; *The Love Boat* was the result. The successful show became a weekly prime-time advertisement for cruising in general, and Princess in particular. The cruise company continued to market itself as The Love Boat well after the original series left the airwaves. *Pacific Princess,* the original Love Boat of the TV series, was retired from the Princess fleet at the end of 2002 after more than three decades of service.

In 1988 P&O bought out another competitor, Sitmar Cruises of Los Angeles, and merged its operations and ships with the Princess fleet. Today P&O Princess Cruises operates Princess Cruises, P&O Cruises and Swan Hellenic in the United Kingdom, Aida Cruises and Seetours, which offer vacations for the German market, and P&O Cruises in Australia.

In 2003 the Carnival Corporation successfully acquired P&O Princess, outmaneuvering Royal Caribbean Cruise Line, which also sought to buy the company.

■ THE PRINCESS EXPERIENCE

The Love Boat lives on in the hearts and minds of Princess executives and many of the company's passengers. In 1998 another go-round of the television show took to the airwaves. *Love Boat: The Next Wave* was filmed in part aboard the $300 million 77,000-ton *Sun Princess.*

The original *Love Boat* series was set aboard the smaller 20,000-ton *Pacific Princess,* which left the fleet in 2002; its twin sister, the *Island Princess,* departed in 1999. Both names have since returned to the fleet on new ships.

Love Boat aside, Princess actually offers a pretty refined experience, with continental cuisine and a mostly Italian dining room staff. There are sushi restaurants on all ships in the fleet during lunch hours, and you can expect a full regime of parties, games, and other cruise entertainment.

The company operates the 353-room Denali Princess Wilderness Lodge just outside Denali National Park in Alaska. The company also owns the Kenai Princess Wilderness Lodge, the Mount McKinley Princess Wilderness Lodge, and the Fairbanks Princess Lodge.

Princess also has the eighty-four-room Copper River Princess Wilderness Lodge on land bordering Wrangell–Saint Elias National Park and Preserve in south-central Alaska. Public areas include a signature two-story Great Room fea-

Golden Princess verandas. *Photo by Corey Sandler*

turing a stone fireplace, 25-foot ceilings, and stunning views of awe-inspiring Mounts Wrangell, Drum, and Blackburn.

Tours include an opportunity to fly over Wrangell–Saint Elias National Park en route to the historic towns of McCarthy and Kennicott. A guide takes participants on a tour of main street Kennicott and tells the incredible story of this mining boomtown. This is followed by a short trip to McCarthy, which served as a supply post for prospectors, hunters, and trappers. Also offered is an airplane tour to view three of the tallest peaks in Wrangell–Saint Elias National Park and one of the tallest in North America, Mount Sanford, with its 9,000-foot vertical rock wall. The Klutina River Whitewater Adventure offers Class III rapids and continuous splashy white water as it cascades over large boulders left behind from the last major glaciation period.

Personal Choice Dining on Princess ships allows travelers to choose from a traditional two-seating, fixed-time dining schedule with assigned seats and tablemates, or a flexible option to choose when, where, and with whom to dine during an expanded dining period from 5:30 P.M. to midnight. A special dining desk is open throughout the day to accept reservations; guests can also dine without reservations.

Partly to deal with the fact that guests may not have the same servers through the course of a trip, the line now includes an automatic gratuity program to cover all service staff; a daily charge of $10 per person is placed on the passenger's shipboard account. The tip can be adjusted up or down or removed by request.

Princess struck a blow for the environment with a program to turn off the engines of its ships when they dock in Juneau. Instead they use surplus hydroelectric power supplied by the local utility to run the ship's systems while it is in port.

Princess Kids, the line's expanded children's program, includes activities for three age groups as well as complimentary in-port programming. The program also includes activities developed with the California Science Center and the National Wildlife Federation. Activity groups are Princess Pelicans (ages three to seven), Princess Pirateers (ages eight to twelve), and Off Limits (ages thirteen to seventeen). Group baby-sitting services for children ages three to twelve are also available for $5.00 per hour per child. Junior cruisers can participate in two special dinner evenings designed for each age group. Teens can also take advantage of Princess's new Teen Spa program, which has an exclusive selection of specialized spa packages.

■ ITINERARIES

The expanding Princess fleet is all over the place, with a concentration in Alaska in the summer and the Caribbean in the winter.

Africa: *Pacific Princess* sails a 30-day trip from Bangkok to India and East Africa.

Alaska: From July through September 2005 *Royal Princess, Diamond Princess,* and *Sapphire Princess* sail round-trip from Seattle on Inside Passage cruises. The

Island Princess, Dawn Princess, Sun Princess, and *Coral Princess* sail seven-day cruises from Vancouver or Whittier, Alaska, on the Voyage of the Glaciers.

Asia: *Pacific Princess* sails in September from South Africa to Australia on a twenty-eight-day itinerary. *Sapphire Princess* travels from Sydney to Bangkok in March, and on to Beijing and Osaka before crossing over to Alaska at the end of April. *Diamond Princess* crosses from Seattle to Osaka in September, on to Beijing in mid-October, and finishes the year sailing from Singapore to Sydney in December.

Australia and New Zealand: *Sapphire Princess* sails in January and February from Sydney to Auckland.

Canada and New England: *Sea Princess* sails from Quebec City in October. *Golden Princess* sails round-trip from New York in September and October.

Caribbean: Princess ships sail all over the crystal waters. The *Caribbean Princess* sails year-round from Fort Lauderdale to the Eastern Caribbean. *Star Princess* sails in the Western Caribbean from January to April and October to December from Galveston; *Dawn Princess* sails a similar itinerary from May to September from Galveston. *Grand Princess* heads west from Fort Lauderdale from November 2004 through April 2005.

Golden Princess sails south as far as Antigua and Saint Lucia or Grenada and Aruba from San Juan from January to April and October to December.

Europe: *Star Princess* sails between Venice and Barcelona for much of the summer, also mixing in a few Northern European cruises round-trip from Cophenhagen to Scandinavia and Russia. *Grand Princess* will sail in the Greek Isles and the Mediterranean between Venice and Rome. *Royal Princess* sails round-trip from London to Northern Europe.

Tahiti and Hawaii: *Island Princess* sails round-trip from Los Angeles to Hawaii on fifteen-day trips from September through April. *Tahitian Princess* cruises from Hawaii to Tahiti in May; in the same month, *Pacific Princess* sails the reverse itinerary.

Mexican Riviera: From January through April 2005 *Diamond Princess* sails round-trip from Los Angeles. *Regal Princess* cruises round-trip from San Diego from September to November on ten-day cruises. *Dawn Princess* sails round-trip from San Francisco from September 2005 to May 2006. And *Sapphire Princess* picks up the Los Angeles round-trip service from October 2005 through April 2006.

Panama Canal: *Coral Princess* will sail round-trip into the canal from Fort Lauderdale from January to April, and from October 2005 through April 2006. Trips that go fully through the canal include *Regal Princess* from Fort Lauderdale to Los Angeles in January and February, and *Sun Princess* on the same itinerary in April. *Regal Princess* sails from Fort Lauderdale to San Diego in March, returning to Florida in April. Repositioning cruises from Fort Lauderdale to San Francisco include *Coral Princess, Dawn Princess,* and *Regal Princess* in April.

South America: *Royal Princess* will sail from Buenos Aires in January and February, and from Valparaiso, Chile, in March. *Regal Princess* will sail similar itineraries in 2006.

■ WEB SITE

Visitors to the Princess Web site can find information about the ships and itineraries but can not book staterooms directly. Princess was the first major cruise
line to add live bridgecams on most of its ships. *Ease of use: very good.*

Grand Princess, Golden Princess, Star Princess, Diamond Princess, Sapphire Princess, Caribbean Princess

Econoguide rating:	★★★★ 85 points
Ship size:	Colossus
Category:	Top of the Line
Price range:	Opulent $$$$
Registry:	Bermuda
Year built:	Caribbean Princess, 2004; Sapphire Princess, 2004; Diamond Princess, 2004; Star Princess, 2002; Golden Princess, 2001; Grand Princess, 1998
Information:	(800) 774–6237
Web site:	www.princess.com
Passenger capacity:	3,110
Crew:	1,100
Passenger-to-crew ratio:	2.4:1
Tonnage:	Diamond Princess, 113,000; Sapphire Princess, 113,000; Golden Princess, 110,000; Star Princess, 110,000; Grand Princess, 109,000; Caribbean Princess, 116,000
Passenger-space ratio:	41.9
Length:	951 feet
Beam:	118 to 123 feet; 159 feet including bridge wing
Draft:	26 to 28 feet
Cruising speed:	22 knots; 24 knots maximum
Guest decks:	18
Total cabins:	1,300 to 1,337
Outside:	928 to 960
Inside:	372 to 377
Suites:	208 to 216
Wheelchair cabins:	28 (18 outside, 10 inside)
Cuisine:	International
Style:	Formal, semiformal, and casual
Price notes:	Single-occupancy premium, 160 to 200 percent
Tipping suggestions:	$10 pp/pd
Best deals:	Advance-booking "Love Boat Savers" fares

For a short time, the **Grand Princess** was the Colossus of the Oceans, the
largest cruise ship afloat. (She was trumped by Royal Caribbean's *Voyager of the
Seas* and her sisters.) But the Grand-class Princess ships are still huge floating

Golden Princess docked in Saint Martin. *Photo by Corey Sandler*

cities; in a cruise diary in Chapter 11, we point out how successfully designers subdivide these ships into comfortable neighborhoods.

How big are these ships? More than three football fields long, they're too wide to fit through the Panama Canal; and at 201 feet tall, the ships are 50 feet taller than the Statue of Liberty and higher than Niagara Falls. They're home to 3,700 or so close friends and crew members. The entire *Pacific Princess,* the original "Love Boat," could fit within the Horizon Court dining and lido areas on the *Grand Princess.*

The hallmark lounge on each of the Grand-class ships is Skywalker's Disco, which is suspended 150 feet above the water at the stern of the ship, accessible by a glass-enclosed, moving "skywalk." The new ***Diamond Princess*** expands the disco, adding a balcony that gives views over the stern of the ship from way up high. Each of the ships in this class sports five swimming pools, including a lap pool that allows you to swim against the current. Princess Links offers simulated play on the world's greatest courses as well as a nine-hole putting green.

As appropriate for the queen of the "Love Boat" line, the *Grand Princess* featured the first oceangoing wedding chapel, including a program that allows passengers to be married by the ship's captain—something that despite the common conception is not often permitted. Chapels have also been added to a number of other ships in the fleet, and live "Wedding Cams" allow friends, relatives, and complete strangers to observe the goings-on in the chapel while the ship is at sea.

These ultra-modern ships were the first passenger vessels built with fully redundant operational and technical systems. There are two separate engine rooms. Power supplies are duplicated, and cooling systems are split into two separate circuits, with pumps and coolers in separate spaces.

The Horizon Court on the lido deck is a twenty-four-hour cafe with 620 seats. On the promenade deck are two of the three main dining rooms, each with about 500 seats, and a smaller specialty restaurant. A third 500-seat restaurant is on plaza deck, nearby an Italian trattoria. As an example, *Sabatini's,* one of two specialty restaurants aboard *Grand Princess,* serves informal Italian fare, specializing in seafood. A selection of Italian antipasti, Sevruga caviar, fresh-baked pizza, pastas, soups, and breads are offered. Entrees include lobster, langoustines, tiger prawns, Chilean sea bass, scallops, and meat dishes. Guests at Sabatini's are assessed an additional charge; in 2004 the fee was $20 per person.

On the *Grand Princess,* the Painted Desert Southwestern restaurant and the Bistro offer intimate settings with seating by prior reservation and require a $8.00 per person service charge. *Sun, Dawn, Sea,* and *Ocean* feature the Sterling Steakhouse, also for an $8.00 per person service charge.

On the health front, the Grand-class ships include a "telemedicine" setup that allows the ship's doctors to consult electronically with emergency physicians on shore.

The **Caribbean Princess,** assigned to sail full-time in her namesake waters, includes a Caribbean-themed alternative restaurant and nearly 900 cabins with balconies, more than on any other cruise ship.

One interesting new feature of the *Caribbean Princess* is "Movies Under the

The *Grand Princess* arrives in New York City. *Courtesy Princess Cruises*

Stars," a form of dive-in movie. Current films are played on a giant Times Square–style high-intensity LED screen built into the superstructure of the vessel at the midship pool. (The premiere film, of course, was *Pirates of the Caribbean.*) The screen will also be used to present special sports events and for Caribbean Island Night parties held on each cruise.

Complimentary chaise longue reservations, special movie theme cocktails, and casual dining will be offered to round out the ultimate poolside experience. The million-dollar 300-square-foot screen is bright enough to be seen clearly at midday and the 69,000-watt sound system is powerful enough to be heard clearly even while the ship is moving at full speed. The movie system is expected to be added to the other Grand-class ships in coming years.

Cafe Carib, exclusive to the *Caribbean Princess,* features the flavors of the Caribbean in a casual setting, reminiscent of an island hot spot. A blend of buffet and made-to-order service from a changing menu feature such local specialties as grilled Caribbean rock lobster, whole roast suckling pig, jerk chicken, and Guiana pepperpots and curries. The cafe is open for dinner each night, with a bistro menu offered after 10:00 P.M.

Also new on the *Caribbean Princess* is the "Ultimate Balcony Dinner," an all-inclusive evening featuring cocktails, fresh flowers, champagne, and a four-course meal including Caribbean lobster tail served by a member of the Princess dining staff on passengers' private balcony; an extra charge of $25 is added to accounts for the special. You can also order a balcony breakfast featuring Cuban specialty pastries, tropical fruit salad in a pineapple boat, chilled marinated shrimp with papaya relish, warm egg and tomato pie with cheese gratin, and a split of French champagne.

Caribbean Princess also debuted a new stage show, "Caribbean Caliente" with music from the islands, Mexico, and Latin America. It features contemporary music from Latin artists including Ricky Martin, Enrique Iglesias, Gloria Estefan, Tito Puente, and Bob Marley. For some "reality" entertainment, there is a "makeover" show videotaped onboard as two passengers go through a day of spa treatments and shopping.

The ship that was to have been christened the *Diamond Princess* was severely damaged in a shipyard fire in Japan in late 2002; as a result, the shipyard arranged to move forward the completion of **Sapphire Princess,** under construction nearby, and the two ships swapped names in the shipyard.

Diamond Princess and *Sapphire Princess* offer guests five main dining rooms: one traditional seating dining room and four smaller restaurants for those choosing Princess's Anytime Dining option. In the Vivaldi dining room, which specializes in Italian fare, diners can enjoy dishes such as *farfalle alla scoglio* or *ossobuco.* In the Sterling dining room menu items include prime rib, New York steak, and apple pie. The Pacific Moon dining room features a variety of Asian favorites including sushi, five-spice Mandarin duckling, and bamboo steamer baskets with dim sum, pot stickers, and spring rolls. In the Santa Fe dining room, guests can choose tableside-prepared guacamole, sizzling fajitas, fried catfish with roasted corn relish and Kahlua rice pudding.

These new ships, like others in the class, also include Trattoria Sabatini, the alternative Italian restaurant that offers a special eight-course menu for an additional charge of $20.

The line also debuted a computerized restaurant reservations system, called Princess Concierge Service, on the *Diamond Princess*.

Diamond Princess was delivered to Princess at the Mitsubishi shipyard in Japan, the first Princess vessel built in Asia. The event included a traditional dragon dance, a drum demonstration, and a sake barrel-smashing ceremony.

Caribbean Princess was christened by "Love Boat" actress Jill Whelan, who played Captain Stubing's daughter; after the christening, Whelan also became the first bride to be married aboard the ship.

Coral Princess, Island Princess

Econoguide rating:	★★★★ 85 points
Ship size:	Megaship
Category:	Top of the Line
Price range:	Opulent $$$$
Registry:	Bermuda
Year built:	*Coral Princess,* 2003; *Island Princess,* 2003
Information:	(800) 774–6237
Web site:	www.princess.com
Passenger capacity:	1,970 (double occupancy)
Crew:	900
Passenger-to-crew ratio:	2.2:1
Tonnage:	88,000
Passenger-space ratio:	44.6
Length:	964 feet
Beam:	106 feet; 122 feet including bridge wing
Draft:	27 feet
Cruising speed:	22 knots; 24 knots maximum
Guest decks:	11
Total cabins:	987
Outside:	879
Inside:	108
Suites:	208
Wheelchair cabins:	28 (18 outside, 10 inside)
Cuisine:	International
Style:	Formal, semiformal, and casual
Price notes:	Single-occupancy premium, 160 to 200 percent
Tipping suggestions:	$10 pp/pd
Best deals:	Advance-booking "Love Boat Savers" fares

Coral Princess, the line's first 88,000-ton 1,950-passenger ship from French builder Chantiers de l'Atlantique, launched in January 2003. Sister ship *Island Princess* arrived in July 2003, reprising the name of one of the original "Love Boats." The ships use diesel and gas turbine engines, and the design will have only 10 percent of staterooms inside; 80 percent of the outside cabins will have balconies. There are three pools, three show rooms, and five restaurants onboard.

The two ships are the largest of the line's ships to be able to transit the Panama Canal.

Both ships offer a pair of main dining rooms, Provence and Bordeaux, as well as Sabatini's Trattoria, the Bayou Cafe New Orleans Restaurant, and the Princess Theater main show room. The two-story interactive aft lounge is equipped to offer full television production capabilities and high-definition projection. Known as the Universe Lounge, this special area features decor inspired by Jules Verne's classic tale *20,000 Leagues Under the Sea,* and offers three revolving stages. The lounge will also be home to a new "ScholarShip at Sea" program, including enrichment courses on cooking, photography, ceramics, visual arts, computers, and other fun and informative classes.

The Bayou Cafe—the $10 lunch and dinner cover charge includes a complimentary Hurricane cocktail—offers platters of Mardi Gras shrimp piquante, sausage grillades, oysters Sieur de Bienville, and crawfish "mud bug" bisque as entrees. Traditional Creole favorites include Seafood Gumbo Ya-Ya, Toulouse chicken, and chorizo jambalaya. Grill options feature such spicy delicacies as smothered gator ribs, flambeaux grilled jumbo prawns, cornmeal-fried catfish, blackened chicken brochette, Carpetbagger's Trinity Smothered Filet of Beef, and red pepper–butter broiled lobster. If you've got room left for dessert, consider buttermilk bread pudding, sweet potato pie, fried yellow peach pie, or banana whiskey pound cake.

Both vessels use innovative power generation technology: a gas turbine/diesel engine combination, with the gas turbines placed in the ships' funnels. This configuration is not only environmentally advantageous but also allows for additional space inside the ships for passenger facilities.

Pacific Princess, Tahitian Princess

Econoguide rating:	★★★★ 83 points
Ship size:	Medium
Category:	Top of the Line
Price range:	Premium $$$
Registry:	Gibraltar
Year built:	*Pacific Princess* (built as Renaissance *R3* in 1999); *Tahitian Princess* (built as Renaissance *R4* in 1999)
Information:	(800) 774–6237

Web site:	www.princess.com
Passenger capacity:	680 (double occupancy)
Crew:	373
Passenger-to-crew ratio:	1.8:1
Tonnage:	30,277
Passenger-space ratio:	44.1
Length:	592 feet
Beam:	83.5
Draft:	19.5 feet
Cruising speed:	20 knots maximum
Guest decks:	9
Total cabins:	342
Outside:	317
Inside:	25
Suites:	10
Wheelchair cabins:	14
Cuisine:	International
Style:	Formal, semiformal, and casual
Price notes:	Single-occupancy premium, 160 to 200 percent
Tipping suggestions:	$10 pp/pd
Best deals:	Advance-booking "Love Boat Savers" fares

Renaissance Cruise Lines had a devoted following for its eight medium-size cruise ships, vessels that bridged the gap between the best of the major ships and the small boutique luxury vessels. When Renaissance went out of business in late 2001, most of the company's young fleet of nearly identical ships were purchased by existing or new companies.

Pacific Princess sails out of Sydney harbor in Australia. *Photo by Corey Sandler*

Princess added *R3* and *R4* to its fleet, renaming them *Pacific Princess* and *Tahitian Princess,* respectively. The ships will offer sailings in Tahiti and the wider Pacific Ocean region. The vessels include a wide variety of dining options, including a twenty-four-hour Lido and alternative dining programs with both an Italian restaurant (Sabatini's Trattoria) and an American steakhouse (Sterling Steakhouse). Ninety-two percent of the staterooms offer outside views, with more than two-thirds of these having a private balcony.

Plans call for the ***Tahitian Princess*** to sail year-round in Tahiti and the South Pacific. Three unique itineraries, with a total of fifty round-trip departures from Papeete, Tahiti, include calls at the tropical paradises of Bora Bora, Moorea, and Raiatea. Passengers can choose one of the thirty-four French Polynesia/Cook Islands sailings that explore such ports as mystic Huahine and Raratonga, trips with stops at Pago Pago and Apia, or Marquesas islands such as Nuku Hiva and Hiva Oa.

The ***Pacific Princess*** will operate on a split deployment, sailing half the year throughout French Polynesia and the wider Pacific region for Princess Cruises and the other half for the P&O Cruises Australia brand, serving the growing Australian market in the South Pacific region.

Dawn Princess, Sea Princess Sun Princess

Econoguide rating:	★★★★ 85 points
Ship size:	Megaship
Category:	Top of the Line
Price range:	Premium to Opulent $$$–$$$$
Registry:	Great Britain
Year built:	*Sun Princess,* 1995; *Dawn Princess,* 1997; *Sea Princess,* 1998
Information:	(800) 774–6237
Web site:	www.princess.com
Passenger capacity:	1,950 (double occupancy)
Crew:	900; Italian officers
Passenger-to-crew ratio:	2.2:1
Tonnage:	77,000
Passenger-space ratio:	39.5
Length:	856 feet
Beam:	106 feet
Draft:	26 feet
Cruising speed:	21 knots
Guest decks:	14
Total cabins:	975
Outside:	603
Inside:	372
Suites:	38
Wheelchair cabins:	19

Cuisine:	International
Style:	Formal, semiformal, and casual nights
Price notes:	Single-occupancy premium, 160 to 200 percent
Tipping suggestions:	$10 pp/pd
Best deals:	Advance-booking "Love Boat Savers" fares

The ships in the Grand class are modern favorites, with more than 400 veranda staterooms and high-tech theaters. A teak promenade deck encircles the entire ship. Within is a $2.5 million art collection.

Sea Princess sailed with the line for five years before being transferred to sister company P&O Cruises in 1998 to sail under the name *Adonia*. In May 2005 she is due to return to Princess and regain her name. She will be primarily marketed to the British cruise market, operating from the United Kingdom in the summer and fourteen-day Caribbean cruises in the winter.

A fourth member of this class of ships, *Ocean Princess*, was transferred to P&O in 2002 and sails as *Oceana*.

Regal Princess

Econoguide rating:	★★★★ 80 points
Ship size:	Megaship
Category:	Top of the Line
Price range:	Premium to Opulent **$$$–$$$$**
Registry:	Great Britain
Year built:	1991
Information:	(800) 774–6237
Web site:	www.princess.com
Passenger capacity:	1,590 (double occupancy)
Crew:	696
Passenger-to-crew ratio:	2.3:1
Tonnage:	70,000
Passenger-space ratio:	44
Length:	811 feet
Beam:	105.8 feet
Draft:	26.5 feet
Cruising speed:	21 knots
Guest decks:	12
Total cabins:	795
Outside:	624
Inside:	171
Suites:	50
Wheelchair cabins:	10
Cuisine:	International

Style:	Formal, semiformal, and casual nights
Price notes:	Single-occupancy premium, 160 to 200 percent
Tipping suggestions:	$10 pp/pd
Best deals:	Advance-booking "Love Boat Savers" fares

Older but still elaborate and elegant, with her original dolphin profile intact, the **Regal Princess** received a "Millennium Makeover" in 2000, with new decor in public rooms, a new children's and teens' center, and an expanded twenty-four-hour bistro in addition to a pizzeria and patisserie. The ship now sports the Bacchus Bar, a handsome wine-and-caviar watering hole.

Near-identical sister *Crown Princess* left the line in early 2002 to join the fleet of Princess's German subsidary.

Royal Princess

Econoguide rating:	★★★★ 84 points
Ship size:	Large
Category:	Golden Oldie
Price range:	Moderate $$
Registry:	Great Britain
Year built:	1984
Information:	(800) 774–6237
Web site:	www.princess.com
Passenger capacity:	1,200 (double occupancy)
Crew:	520; British officers
Passenger-to-crew ratio:	2.3:1
Tonnage:	45,000
Passenger-space ratio:	38.3
Length:	757 feet
Beam:	106 feet
Draft:	26 feet
Cruising speed:	20 knots
Guest decks:	9
Total cabins:	600
Outside:	600
Inside:	0
Suites:	66
Wheelchair cabins:	4
Cuisine:	International
Style:	Formal, semiformal, and casual nights
Price notes:	Single-occupancy premium, 160 to 200 percent
Tipping suggestions:	$10 pp/pd
Best deals:	Advance-booking "Love Boat Savers" fares

A gracefully aging pioneer of cruising, **Royal Princess** earned her name when she was christened by Princess Diana. Among the first ships to offer verandas on many of her cabins, her 600 staterooms are in prime outside, upper-deck locations; public rooms are located on lower decks. (Some of the outside cabins, however, have restricted views because of low-hanging lifeboats.)

Royal Princess is due to leave the Princess fleet in May 2005, transferred to sister company P&O and renamed *Artemis*. The rename includes a complex tip of the hat to her original godmother; Artemis was goddess of the moon in Greek mythology, also known as Diana in Roman myth.

ROYAL CARIBBEAN INTERNATIONAL

RoyalCaribbean®
INTERNATIONAL

Address: 1050 Caribbean Way
Miami, FL 33132-2096
Information: (800) 327–6700
www.royalcaribbean.com
Econoguide's Best Cruise Lines for Families

The Royal Caribbean Fleet

Mariner of the Seas	2003	3,114 passengers	142,000 tons
Navigator of the Seas	2003	3,114 passengers	142,000 tons
Adventure of the Seas	2001	3,114 passengers	142,000 tons
Explorer of the Seas	2000	3,114 passengers	142,000 tons
Voyager of the Seas	1999	3,114 passengers	142,000 tons
Jewel of the Seas	2004	2,100 passengers	90,090 tons
Serenade of the Seas	2003	2,100 passengers	90,090 tons
Brilliance of the Seas	2002	2,100 passengers	90,090 tons
Radiance of the Seas	2001	2,100 passengers	90,090 tons
Vision of the Seas	1998	2,435 passengers	78,491 tons
Rhapsody of the Seas	1997	2,435 passengers	78,491 tons
Enchantment of the Seas	1997	2,446 passengers	74,140 tons
Grandeur of the Seas	1996	2,446 passengers	74,140 tons
Majesty of the Seas	1992	2,744 passengers	73,941 tons
Monarch of the Seas	1991	2,744 passengers	73,941 tons
Sovereign of the Seas	1988	2,850 passengers	73,192 tons
Splendour of the Seas	1996	2,076 passengers	69,130 tons
Legend of the Seas	1995	2,076 passengers	69,130 tons
Empress of the Seas	1990	2,020 passengers	48,563 tons

FUTURE SHIPS

Unnamed Ultra-Voyager	2006	3,600 passengers	88,000 tons

Think Royal Caribbean and think large. The line owns and operates five of the largest cruise ships afloat: the 142,000-ton *Adventure of the Seas, Explorer of the Seas, Mariner of the Seas, Navigator of the Seas,* and *Voyager of the Seas.* Each of these ships is about twice the size of the average cruise ship. The ships lost their spot as the hugest of the huge in 2004 with the arrival of Cunard's *Queen Mary 2,* which put 150,000 tons afloat.

But not to worry: The company has placed an order for an even larger ship, the first of the Ultra-Voyager class. Expected to arrive in 2006, the ship will be more than 160,000 tons in size, with space for 3,600 passengers at double occupancy, plus 1,400 crew. The ship, under construction at Kvaerner-Masa Yards in Finland, will be about 1,112 feet long and 126 feet wide, about 15 percent larger than the Voyager ships. The yard also granted the company an option for a second Ultra-Voyager, with a 2007 delivery date.

The new *Jewel of the Seas* arrived in April 2004, to spend her first summer in Europe, sailing twelve-night Scandinavia/Russia and British Isles/Norwegian Fjords itineraries from Harwich, England. In the fall, she was due to cross the Atlantic to offer ten-night Canada/New England journeys from Boston before repositioning to Fort Lauderdale for the winter, where she was scheduled to sail alternating eight-night Eastern Caribbean and six-night Western Caribbean itineraries.

Nordic Empress, Royal Caribbean's oldest and smallest vessel, received a makeover in 2004 and a new name to fit in with the other ships in the fleet: *Empress of the Seas.*

Royal Celebrity Tours, the land-tour company of Royal Caribbean Cruises, has expanded its Wilderness Express train cars in Alaska. The double-deck dome coaches offer 360-degree viewing platforms, extra-wide seats that recline and rotate, and onboard dining. The cars are also equipped with dome-level ADA-compliant seating, allowing physically challenged travelers to access both levels. Royal Celebrity Tours has also expanded operations into the Canadian Rockies, in conjunction with Rocky Mountaineer Railtours.

■ THE RCI STORY

Royal Caribbean Cruise Line was founded in 1969 by three Norwegian shipping companies: Anders Wilhelmsen and Company, I. M. Skaugen and Company, and later, Gotaas Larsen. The cruise company pioneered air/sea vacations, flying cruise guests to meet the ships in their first port, Miami.

The company's first ship, *Song of Norway,* entered service in 1970; the *Nordic Prince* followed the next year and the *Sun Viking* a year later. Promoted as the first passenger ship built specifically for warm-weather cruising rather than point-to-point transport, the *Song of Norway* was also the first ship to have a cocktail lounge cantilevered from its smokestack; the Viking Crown Lounge has since become the hallmark of every Royal Caribbean vessel.

In 1978 the *Song of Norway* became the first major passenger cruise ship to be "stretched"; it was cut in two and an 85-foot midsection was added, increasing guest capacity from 700 to just over 1,000. The *Nordic Prince* underwent a similar conversion in 1980. The *Nordic Prince* and the *Song of Norway* were sold in 1995 and 1997, respectively, to the British leisure company Airtours PLC.

In 1988 Royal Caribbean merged its operations with Admiral Cruises, and Anders Wilhelmsen and Company bought out its original partners. That same year the massive *Sovereign of the Seas* debuted, introducing a five-deck atrium—the Centrum—with glass elevators, sweeping staircases, and fountains in marble pools; this marked the first time such a central atrium had been constructed on a passenger ship.

Royal Caribbean became a publicly traded company in 1993. The line sold *Song of America* in early 1999 to Airtours. The 1,400-passenger ship, introduced in 1982, most recently sailed seven-night Mexican Riviera cruises in the winter and Bermuda itineraries in the summer.

■ THE RCI EXPERIENCE

Royal Caribbean goes for headlines: an ice-skating rink on *Voyager of the Seas,* an eighteen-hole miniature golf course on *Splendour of the Seas* and *Legend of the Seas,* and cantilevered cocktail lounges up high on the smokestacks.

In 2003 the company committed to installing rock-climbing walls on all of its ships by the end of the year. First introduced on *Voyager of the Seas,* the climbing walls have proven very popular—and distinctive. Designed for both beginners and advanced climbers, the walls are perched on the top decks; participants are rewarded with an unparalleled bird's-eye view of the ship, sea, and sky. On Voyager-class vessels, the top of the walls are nearly 200 feet above the ocean. Lessons are offered.

RCI delivers a high-quality product aimed at the middle of the cruise market. A corporate goal is to make the experience pretty much the same on all of its ships, even though they may differ in size and configuration.

Royal Caribbean offers two private spots just for its guests in the Caribbean and the Bahamas. Labadee is a 260-acre wooded peninsula at Pointe Sainte Honoré, about 6 miles from Cap Haitien on the mountainous and secluded north coast of Haiti. There are five beaches, an outdoor performance area, an open-air dining area, nature trails, shaded hammocks, and a coral reef that includes a sunken airplane. Recreational highlights include paddleboats, water cycles, parasailing, sailboats, and snorkeling with underwater cameras. The line was forced to temporarily suspend visits to the beach in 2004 because of unrest elsewhere on Haiti.

Coco Cay is a 140-acre island in the Bahamas' Berry Island chain between Freeport and Nassau; its offerings are similar to those of Labadee. Recent additions at Coco Cay include new facilities for snorkeling and personal watercraft. With equipment from the Snorkel Shack, guests can check out a sunken plane wreck, explore the coral reef, or attend a fish-feeding frenzy. For deeper explorations, the Diver's Den offers certified divers an opportunity to experience the crystal-clear waters of the Bahamas on a one-tank, shallow-water beach dive that takes them 40 feet below, where a PADI scuba instructor will help identify the varied marine life and coral formations.

Guests can also rent a personal watercraft to head out on a guided, fifty-minute tour of Great Stirrup Cay Lighthouse, Slaughter Harbor, Star Fish Alley, and the abandoned island community of Cistern Cay. Back on land, guests can explore the island's attractions on a new 3-mile-long nature trail.

The Adventure Ocean children's program organizes activities for Aquanauts (ages three to five), Explorers (six to eight), Voyagers (nine to twelve), and Navigators (thirteen to seventeen). Programs include finger painting and dress-up for the very young, arts and crafts, sports and pool activities, karaoke, talent shows, and special parties. Island activities include beach parties and games, sand castle building, seashell collecting, and more. During summer and holidays, Adventure Science classes are conducted by specially trained science staff. The program blends science with entertainment—rockets, slime, and bubbling potions included.

Royal Caribbean operates what is claimed as the world's largest passenger cruise terminal at its home base in Miami. The building has to be large; on turn-around day as many as 8,400 guests may be getting off or on the ship, at more or less the same time. The roof sports a replica of Royal Caribbean's signature Viking Crown Lounge as an observation point.

■ ITINERARIES

In 2004 the new *Jewel of the Seas* was due to spend the summer in Europe, sailing twelve-night Scandinavia/Russia and British Isles/Norwegian Fjords itineraries from Harwich, England. In the fall, she crossed the Atlantic to offer ten-night Canada/New England journeys from Boston before repositioning to Fort Lauderdale for the winter, where she was scheduled to sail alternating eight-night eastern Caribbean and six-night western Caribbean itineraries.

The Big Apple saw the big *Voyager of the Seas* in 2004, with the ship offering alternating five-night Canada/New England and nine-night western Caribbean itineraries from May through October 2004. Voyager joined Empress of the Seas in New York; that ship offered six- and eight-night alternating Bermuda cruises, making ports of call at King's Wharf and Hamilton, as well as St. George's on the longer itineraries.

Grandeur of the Seas sailed out of Baltimore from July through October in 2004, a new homeport for the company; trips departed to the Bahamas, the Caribbean, and fall-season Canada and New England itineraries.

In November 2004 *Splendour of the Seas* was due to take up residence in Tampa to offer seven-night western Caribbean cruises with stops in George Town, Grand Cayman; Costa Maya; Belize City, Belize; and Cozumel. From New Orleans, *Grandeur of the Seas* was dispatched to offer western Caribbean cruises throughout the 2004/2005 winter seasons.

Three Royal Caribbean ships sailed seven-night Alaska voyages throughout the summer of 2004. *Radiance of the Seas* and *Serenade of the Seas* are designed to bring the sea, sun, and coastal scenery of Alaska indoors with nearly 3 acres of exterior glass. Both ships sailed round-trip Hubbard Glacier itineraries. A third ship, *Vision of the Seas,* offered open-jaw cruises between Vancouver and Seward with stops including Icy Strait Point, a historic area located on a picturesque Alaskan bay ideal for wildlife spotting.

Royal Caribbean dispatched three ships to Europe in the summer of 2004. The new *Jewel of the Seas* began its service with twelve-night Scandinavia/Russia cruises, as well as two special British Isles/Norwegian Fjords sailings. *Brilliance of the Seas* sailed alternating twelve-night Mediterranean and Mediterranean/ Greek Isles itineraries. *Splendour of the Seas* sailed seven-night Mediterranean vacations from Barcelona.

On the West Coast, *Legend of the Seas* sailed a summer season of seven-night Mexican Riviera cruises from San Diego, plus ten- and eleven-night Hawaii and fourteen-night Panama Canal itineraries. *Vision of the Seas* offered seven-night Mexican Riviera escapes from Los Angeles in the spring, fall, and winter, while *Monarch of the Seas* sailed three- and four-night Baja Mexico getaways year-round.

A total of fifteen Royal Caribbean ships cruised the Caribbean in the winter of 2004, departing from Miami, Fort Lauderdale, Port Canaveral, Tampa, New Orleans, Galveston, and San Juan. Ten of those ships were due to cruise the Caribbean/Bahamas year-round throughout 2004.

Brilliance of the Seas offered ten-night, round-trip cruises from Miami that included a partial transit of the Panama Canal in the spring, fall, and winter.

Empress of the Seas sailed a new itinerary from San Juan at the end of 2004, visiting Saint Martin, Saint Bart's, Saint Kitts, Saint Lucia, Barbados, Grenada, Margarita Island, Aruba, and Curaçao.

Royal Caribbean Cruises signed a letter of agreement with the Bayonne Local Redevelopment Authority to construct and operate a new cruise port facility at the former Bayonne Military Ocean Terminal in New Jersey. The new facility, named Cape Liberty Cruise Port, will serve as a seasonal homeport to two Royal Caribbean International ships, including the huge *Voyager of the Seas.*

The former Bayonne Military Ocean Terminal is a 430-acre, man-made peninsula that extends into New York Harbor. Future plans for the peninsula call for a vibrant mixed-use waterfront development composed of residential, light industrial and office space, film studios, a riverwalk, and extensive recreational and park areas. The new cruise port will be located at the northeast corner of the peninsula, offering unobstructed views of the Statue of Liberty and the Manhattan skyline.

The peninsula is located just off the New Jersey Turnpike, approximately fifteen minutes from Newark airport. A nearby Light Rail service connects to both PATH and Amtrak train lines. In addition Royal Caribbean is considering offering ferry service from Manhattan to the cruise port.

■ WEB SITE

Royal Caribbean's Web site allows selection of a cruise and browsing specific available staterooms. Visitors can also learn about and book more than 1,500 shore excursions in 260 ports of call. *Ease of use: excellent.*

Adventure of the Seas, Explorer of the Seas, Mariner of the Seas, Navigator of the Seas, Voyager of the Seas (VOYAGER CLASS)

Econoguide rating:	★★★★ 84 points
Ship size:	Gargantuan
Category:	Top of the Line
Price range:	Premium $$$
Registry:	Liberia
Year built:	Adventure of the Seas, 2001; Explorer of the Seas, 2000; Mariner of the Seas, 2003; Navigator of the Seas, 2003; Voyager of the Seas, 1999
Information:	(305) 539–6000, (800) 327–6700
Web site:	www.royalcaribbean.com
Passenger capacity:	3,114 (double occupancy)
Crew:	1,181
Passenger-to-crew ratio:	2.6:1
Tonnage:	142,000
Passenger-space ratio:	45.6
Length:	1,021 feet
Beam:	157.5 feet
Draft:	29 feet
Cruising speed:	22 knots
Guest decks:	14
Total cabins:	1,557
Outside:	939
Inside:	618, including 138 Promenade View staterooms

Explorer of the Seas backs out of her berth in Saint Thomas, USVI. *Photo by Corey Sandler*

Suites:	119
Wheelchair cabins:	Call (305) 539–4440 for special assistance
Cuisine:	International
Style:	Resort casual, with occasional formal nights
Price notes:	Single-occupancy premium, 150 to 200 percent; Single Guarantee Program guests add $250 or $500; Special Share Program pairs people of same sex and smoking preference
Tipping suggestions:	$9.00 pp/pd

The **Voyager of the Seas** took the mantle as the largest cruise ship when she debuted in November 1999 at 1,019 feet long, 157.5 feet wide, and 206.5 feet above the waterline. The behemoth is thus about 20 feet too long and 50 feet too wide to fit through the Panama Canal. It has to be that big, you see, to fit the skating rink, twin eleven-story atria, and the Royal Promenade shopping district with its own version of Mardi Gras onboard.

On its May 28, 2000, cruise *Voyager of the Seas* set a world record, carrying 3,608 guests, including 380 honeymooners. The theoretical limit for the vessel, if all of its third and fourth berths were filled, is 3,838.

These are not your typical cruise ships: They include an ice-skating rink with its own Zamboni machine, a rock-climbing wall, and a wedding chapel in the sky. The Peek-a-Boo Bridge above the wheelhouse allows guests to watch the team that is "driving" and navigating the ship.

The Royal Promenade runs most of the length of each of the ships, four decks high, punctuated by two atria (the Centrums). The promenade offers shops, restaurants, and entertainment areas fronting on a winding "street." Special lighting effects allow the promenade to change in ambience from day to night.

On *Voyager*, the Royal Promenade has street festivities and performers, including *Voyager*'s own version of Mardi Gras. Arching over the promenade is the Captain's Balcony, a podium the captain uses to welcome guests on formal nights.

The Royal Promenade also features inside staterooms that offer a view of the atrium and street scene. The cabins, which represent about 10 percent of the staterooms on the ship, have bay windows—the first such inside views on a cruise ship. Almost half the cabins offer balconies, and rooms are generally larger than those on other ships.

Voyager of the Seas includes a three-level main dining room with separate and distinct themed dining areas—Carmen, La Boheme, and Magic Flute—all connected by a dramatic three-deck grand staircase. Smaller dining rooms, Seville and Granada, adjoin the Carmen area. Casual eateries include the SeaSide Diner, a 1950s-style, twenty-four-hour spot; Island Grill, a casual restaurant; and Portofino, an upscale Euro-Italian restaurant.

Entertainment areas include the La Scala Theater, a 1,350-seat theater that spans five decks and offers a hydraulic orchestra pit and stage area and above-stage fly space for full productions.

Studio B is a 900-seat arena for variety shows, ice shows, game shows, and rock and roll performances. The seating and floor can be retracted, allowing the area to be used as an ice-skating rink for guests.

The *Voyager*'s outdoor sports deck includes a golf course, driving range, and golf simulator. Also onboard is a rock-climbing wall, an in-line skating track, and regulation-size basketball, paddleball, and volleyball courts.

A full range of youth facilities for Aquanauts (ages three to five), Explorers (six to eight), and Voyagers (nine to twelve) include Mission Control, with interactive virtual rockets and a space theater. A computer lab has games and educational software, and there's a large arcade. Optix is a clubhouse for teens that has computers, a soda bar, and a dance area with a DJ.

Explorer of the Seas is the first cruise ship to boast a state-of-the-art atmospheric and marine laboratory, with an interactive environmental classroom.

Navigator of the Seas introduced the company's first wine bar, a Latin jazz bar, the Royal Caribbean's Chops Grille steakhouse, and a new Asian fusion restaurant, Jade. In addition, *Navigator* features expanded kids activities areas, with three new teen-only hangouts: an ultrahip nightclub, a laid-back lounge, and a private sundeck. *Navigator* also has a slightly different look than her sister ships, with more exterior glass offering even grander views from balcony staterooms.

The fifth and final member of the Voyager class, **Mariner of the Seas,** joined the fleet in late 2003. Brazilian pop artist Romero Britto decorated the ship's pool deck with whimsical figures and playful patterns.

The Vintages wine bar, first introduced on *Navigator of the Seas,* features sixty-one selections from premier wine-growing regions around the globe, available by the half glass, glass, or bottle. In addition to the main restaurants, *Mariner of the Seas* includes two specialty restaurants: Portofino and the Chops Grille steakhouse. The Windjammer Cafe and Jade Asian-fusion buffet serve international choices in a more casual atmosphere, while Johnny Rockets offers all-American fare. A Ben & Jerry's ice cream shop features sixteen flavors.

Radiance of the Seas, Brilliance of the Seas, Serenade of the Seas, Jewel of the Seas (RADIANCE CLASS)

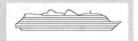

Econoguide rating:	★★★★ 85 points
Ship size:	Megaship
Category:	Top of the Line
Price range:	Premium $$$
Registry:	Liberia
Year built:	*Radiance of the Seas,* 2001; *Brilliance of the Seas,* 2002; *Serenade of the Seas,* 2003; *Jewel of the Seas,* 2004
Information:	(305) 539–6000, (800) 327–6700
Web site:	www.royalcaribbean.com

Passenger capacity:	2,100 (double occupancy)
Crew:	859
Passenger-to-crew ratio:	2.4:1
Tonnage:	90,090
Passenger-space ratio:	42.9
Length:	961 feet
Beam:	105 feet
Draft:	26.7 feet
Cruising speed:	25 knots
Guest decks:	12
Total cabins:	1,050
Outside:	813
Inside:	237
Suites:	80
Wheelchair cabins:	Call (305) 539–4440 for special assistance
Cuisine:	International
Style:	Resort casual with occasional formal nights
Price notes:	Single-occupancy premium, 150 to 200 percent; Single Guarantee Program guests add $250 or $500; Special Share Program pairs people of same sex and smoking preference.
Tipping suggestions:	$9.00 pp/pd

On **Radiance of the Seas,** the indoor-outdoor Windjammer Cafe provides sweeping views of the ocean from floor-to-ceiling windows, a sail-like tent roof, and a yachting decor that includes scale models of famed yachts. At pool's edge, a bronze statue of a lion cub dips its paw into the water; nearby, an elephant waterfall is surrounded by live jungle vegetation.

Active sports include a rock-climbing wall, in-line skating track, basketball and volleyball courts, a miniature golf course, a jogging track, and a golf simulator. In the gymnasium, a bank of treadmills faces a wall of windows overlooking the sea.

Brilliance of the Seas includes similar sports and recreation facilities. After you've worked up an appetite, five dining venues await you: the Chops Grille steakhouse, Portofino Italian restaurant, Minstrels main dining room, the casual Windjammer and Seaview cafes, and pizza, cappuccino, and pastry offerings at Books Books & Coffee.

Jewel of the Seas is Royal Caribbean's fourth and final Radiance-class ship. The ship includes a spectacular, two-story main dining room; an exotic Thailand-themed, adults-only Solarium with a retractable glass roof; two intimate specialty restaurants; and the full-service ShipShape Day Spa, equipped with a thermal suite, which includes heated tile loungers facing the ocean, an aromatherapy steam room, a sauna, and tropical rain showers.

Jewel of the Seas also has a playful side, including active options such as Royal Caribbean's signature rock-climbing wall, a jogging track, a basketball and volleyball court, table tennis, a nine-hole miniature golf course, and two self-leveling, gyroscopic pool tables.

The Adventure Ocean Youth Program offers guests ages three to seventeen activities ranging from scavenger hunts and sports tournaments to art and science workshops. Teens have their own exclusive hangout, Fuel nightclub, complete with a soda bar, dance floor, and DJ music.

The sometimes slow and sultry, sometimes quick and foot-pounding rhythms of the tango will arrive onboard *Jewel of the Seas* with a new show, "Tango Buenos Aires." When the ship began service in the spring of 2004, popular Argentine tango couple Ruben and Sabrina Veliz took passengers through the history of the dance, from the athletic "Apache" to the "Elegant Tango," reminiscent of the age of Valentino.

The ship's full dance troupe join in a salute to *gauchos,* complete with *bolos,* the legendary lasso-like tool of the famed South American cowboy. Argentine musicians join the Royal Caribbean orchestra and featured vocalists in arrangements including "Don't Cry for Me, Argentina" from *Evita.*

The ship's 915-seat Coral Theater was also due to be home to two Broadway-style spectaculars: "City of Dreams," with tunes from top artists such as Billy Joel, Elton John, and Celine Dion; and "From West End to Broadway," with show-stoppers from Cole Porter classics to favorites from blockbuster musicals like "Les Miserables."

The Safari Club lounge features dance bands, karaoke nights, and theme parties, while the line's signature, nautical-themed Schooner Bar is a gathering place to enjoy sing-along piano music. Guests can head to the Viking Crown Lounge to dance the night away at the Vortex nightclub, or enjoy a more intimate evening with jazz performances or solo artists in the Hollywood Odyssey lounge.

Rhapsody of the Seas, Vision of the Seas (VISION CLASS)

Econoguide rating:	★★★★ 84 points
Ship size:	Megaship
Category:	Top of the Line
Price range:	Moderate to Premium $$$–$$$$
Registry:	Norway
Year built:	*Rhapsody of the Seas,* 1997; *Vision of the Seas,* 1998
Information:	(305) 539–6000, (800) 327–6700
Web site:	www.royalcaribbean.com
Passenger capacity:	2,435 (double occupancy)
Crew:	765
Passenger-to-crew ratio:	2.6:1
Tonnage:	78,491
Passenger-space ratio:	39.2
Length:	915 feet
Beam:	105.6 feet
Draft:	25 feet
Cruising speed:	22 knots

Guest decks:	11
Total cabins:	1,000
Outside:	496
Inside:	407
Suites:	97
Wheelchair cabins:	14
Cuisine:	International
Style:	Resort casual, with occasional formal nights
Price notes:	Single-occupancy premium, 150 to 200 percent; Single Guarantee Program guests add $250 or $500; Special Share Program pairs people of same sex and smoking preference
Tipping suggestions:	$9.00 pp/pd

Rhapsody of the Seas and *Vision of the Seas* are twins, close sisters to *Enchantment, Grandeur, Legend,* and *Splendour of the Seas.*

Enchantment of the Seas, Grandeur of the Seas (VISION CLASS)

Econoguide rating:	★★★★ 84 points
Ship size:	Megaship
Category:	Top of the Line
Price range:	Premium $$$
Registry:	Norway
Year built:	*Enchantment of the Seas,* 1997; *Grandeur of the Seas,* 1996
Information:	(305) 539–6000, (800) 327–6700
Web site:	www.royalcaribbean.com
Passenger capacity:	1,950 (double occupancy)
Crew:	760
Passenger-to-crew ratio:	2.6:1
Tonnage:	74,140
Passenger-space ratio:	38
Length:	916 feet
Beam:	105.6 feet
Draft:	25 feet
Cruising speed:	22 knots
Guest decks:	11
Total cabins:	975
Outside:	554
Inside:	399
Suites:	22
Wheelchair cabins:	14
Cuisine:	International
Style:	Resort casual, with occasional formal nights

Price notes:	Single-occupancy premium, 150 to 200 percent; Single Guarantee Program guests add $250 or $500; Special Share Program pairs people of same sex and smoking preference
Tipping suggestions:	$9.00 pp/pd

Enchantment of the Seas and her near-identical older sister, **Grandeur of the Seas,** are members of Royal Caribbean's six-ship Project Vision series, a group of vessels that are aflood with light from acres of windows. Their seven-deck-high central atrium is topped off with a glass skylight, and nearly every other public room is open to the sunsets, sunrises, daylight, and moonlight of a voyage at sea.

In April 2000 *Enchantment of the Seas* moved her base to Port Everglades near Fort Lauderdale, sailing alternating eastern and western Caribbean itineraries. The move opened space at the Port of Miami for Royal Caribbean's two new 142,000-ton Eagle-class vessels.

The Vision series, which also includes *Legend of the Seas, Rhapsody of the Seas, Splendour of the Seas,* and the namesake *Vision of the Seas* are big ships, but well below the size of the Megaships and Colossuses that are now becoming common.

Royal Caribbean is known for its shipboard entertainment as well, presenting Broadway-style revues, musicals, comedians, movies, discos, limbo competitions, country line dancing, and just about anything to draw a crowd.

The free Adventure Ocean program for children from ages three through seventeen includes a professional staff, play facilities, science demonstrations, a video game room, arts and crafts, and a teen disco.

Royal Caribbean's *Grandeur of the Seas* arrives in Charlotte Amalie, Saint Thomas. *Photo by Corey Sandler*

Majesty of the Seas, Monarch of the Seas, Sovereign of the Seas (SOVEREIGN CLASS)

Econoguide rating:	★★★ 76 points
Ship size:	Megaship
Category:	Top of the Line
Price range:	Moderate $$
Registry:	Norway
Year built:	Majesty of the Seas, 1992; Monarch of the Seas, 1991; Sovereign of the Seas, 1988
Information:	(305) 539–6000, (800) 327–6700
Web site:	www.royalcaribbean.com
Passenger capacity:	2,744 (double occupancy)
Crew:	822
Passenger-to-crew ratio:	2.9:1
Tonnage:	Majesty of the Seas, Monarch of the Seas, 73,941; Sovereign of the Seas, 73,192
Passenger-space ratio:	31.5
Length:	880 feet
Beam:	106 feet
Draft:	25 feet
Cruising speed:	22 knots
Guest decks:	14
Total cabins:	1,177

Royal Caribbean's *Majesty of the Seas* under way. *Courtesy Royal Caribbean International*

Outside:	669
Inside:	445
Suites:	63
Wheelchair cabins:	4
Cuisine:	International
Style:	Resort casual, with occasional formal nights
Price notes:	Single-occupancy premium, 150 to 200 percent; Single Guarantee Program guests add $250 or $500; Special Share Program pairs people of same sex and smoking preference
Tipping suggestions:	$9.00 pp/pd

The design of **Majesty of the Seas, Monarch of the Seas,** and **Sovereign of the Seas** puts most of the cabins forward and the public rooms aft, allowing passengers to move vertically by elevator or stairs from lounge to restaurant or show room without having to traverse hallways of cabins. On the five lowest decks— Tween, Showtime, Main, A, and B—there are as many as nine cabins shoehorned across the beam of the ship. There is a pair of outside cabins, of course, with five or more cross-width hallways serving rows of seven inside cabins. Put another way, on this class of ship, some inside cabins are as far as four cabins away from the nearest outside window; that's *really* inside.

The *Monarch of the Seas* suffered an unpleasant encounter with an underwater shoal off the coast of Saint Martin in December 1998 and began taking on water. Her captain was able to steer the ship back to port where it was beached; all 2,557 passengers were evacuated from the ship in the middle of the night without injury. After a few weeks of repairs, the ship was returned to service.

The *Sovereign of the Seas* is an older, slightly smaller sister.

In 2003 *Monarch of the Seas* underwent major renovations in preparation for reassignment to her new homeport of Los Angeles to sail three- and four-night cruises year-round to Baja California in Mexico.

The first floor of the casual two-story Windjammer Cafe gained an Asian fusion restaurant; the eatery was also reconfigured with buffet "islands" for better traffic flow. Upstairs, guests can try the exotic offerings at the upscale sushi bar, Jade Sushi, or check out the creations at the gourmet pizza station.

The ship's main dining rooms were renamed and refurbished with new carpet, chairs, tables, and decor. The dining rooms—now called Claude's and Vincent's—feature color palettes inspired by the works of Monet and Van Gogh. Between meals, guests can enjoy specialty drinks from Seattle's Best Coffee or indulge their sweet tooth with Ben & Jerry's ice cream.

The midship lounge on Deck 7 now offers Boleros, a Latin-themed bar that dispenses specialty tequilas and cocktail favorites like mojitos, as well as live entertainment that includes jazz bands and dueling pianos. The secondary lounge on Deck 8 was transformed into a disco, The Circuit.

The renovations also tripled the space dedicated to Monarch's Adventure Ocean Youth Program, including a video arcade; the Living Room coffee bar and hangout, complete with Club Cafe Internet center; Fuel nightclub; and the Back Deck, a private outdoor area.

Other refurbishments include updates to all staterooms. Up top, the ship gained a rock-climbing wall, part of the line's fleetwide program.

Legend of the Seas, Splendour of the Seas (VISION CLASS)	

Econoguide rating:	★★★★ 83 points
Ship size:	Large
Category:	Top of the Line
Price range:	Moderate to Premium **$$–$$$**
Registry:	Liberia
Year built:	_Legend of the Seas,_ 1995; _Splendour of the Seas,_ 1996
Information:	(305) 539–6000, (800) 327–6700
Web site:	www.royalcaribbean.com
Passenger capacity:	1,800 (double occupancy)
Crew:	720
Passenger-to-crew ratio:	2.5:1
Tonnage:	69,130
Passenger-space ratio:	38.4
Length:	867 feet
Beam:	105 feet
Draft:	24 feet
Cruising speed:	24 knots
Guest decks:	11
Total cabins:	902
Outside:	488
Inside:	327
Suites:	87
Wheelchair cabins:	17
Cuisine:	International
Style:	Resort casual, with occasional formal nights
Price notes:	Single-occupancy premium, 150 to 200 percent; Single Guarantee Program guests add $250 or $500; Special Share Program pairs people of same sex and smoking preference
Tipping suggestions:	$9.00 pp/pd

Among the **Legend of the Seas'** claims to fame is the first miniature golf course at sea, a nine-hole challenge ten decks up on the Compass Deck, just below the cruise line's signature Viking Crown Lounge.

In recent years, _Legend of the Seas_ has pioneered Royal Caribbean's Exotic Destinations itineraries in Australasia, the Middle East, India, Asia, and the South Pacific.

Splendour of the Seas offers a nine-hole miniature golf course, circled by the jogging track on the Compass Deck.

Empress of the Seas

Econoguide rating:	★★★ 72 points
Ship size:	Large
Category:	Top of the Line
Price range:	Moderate $$
Registry:	Liberia
Year built:	1990. Formerly *Nordic Empress,* renovated and renamed 2004
Information:	(305) 539–6000, (800) 327–6700
Web site:	www.royalcaribbean.com
Passenger capacity:	2,020 (double occupancy)
Crew:	671
Passenger-to-crew ratio:	2.4:1
Tonnage:	48,563
Passenger-space ratio:	30.4
Length:	692 feet
Beam:	100 feet
Draft:	25 feet
Cruising speed:	19 knots
Guest decks:	12
Total cabins:	800
Outside:	467
Inside:	329
Suites:	4
Wheelchair cabins:	4
Cuisine:	International
Style:	Resort casual, with occasional formal nights
Price notes:	Single-occupancy premium, 150 to 200 percent; Single Guarantee Program guests add $250 or $500; Special Share Program pairs people of same sex and smoking preference
Tipping suggestions:	$9.00 pp/pd

Empress of the Seas, the smallest and one of the oldest ships in the RCI fleet, received major renovations and a new name in 2004. The elegant ship, which entered service in 1990 and sailed as *Nordic Empress,* was given additional dining, entertainment, and fitness areas.

The ship now features a new specialty restaurant, Portofino, serving Italian cuisine, in addition to an upgraded Windjammer Cafe and refurbished main dining room. In between meals, guests can enjoy specialty coffee drinks from Seattle's Best Coffee or indulge a sweet tooth at the new, combined Latte'tudes coffee bar and ice cream scoop shop.

An expanded spa and gym complex is on two levels, including a fitness center overlooking the Viking Crown Lounge, perched at the top of the ship and offering spectacular, panoramic sea views. In addition the ship features RCI's signature rock-climbing wall. The former High Society Lounge on Deck 6 was recast as Boleros, a Latin-themed bar, offering live entertainment and specialty tequilas and cocktail favorites such as mojitos. The Schooner Bar, a nautical-themed lounge with sing-along piano entertainment, replaced the mid-ship Carousel Bar on Deck 5. The ship's casino was moved to Deck 6, and a new card room was created off the Centrum.

Guest staterooms in all categories received new and upgraded bathrooms, and cabins accommodating third and fourth guests were fitted with modified wardrobes offering increased storage.

The renovations of the *Empress of the Seas* preceded the ship's redeployment to New York harbor, where it began a series of six- and eight-night Bermuda cruise itineraries from the Cape Liberty Cruise Port in Bayonne, New Jersey. The new name brings the ship into line with the remainder of Royal Caribbean's fleet, all of which feature names that end with "of the Seas."

CHAPTER FOURTEEN

ECONOGUIDE'S BEST LUXURY CRUISE LINES

🏵️🏵️🏵️🏵️🏵️🏵️ Crystal Cruises   🏵️🏵️🏵️🏵️🏵️ Seabourn Cruise Line
🏵️🏵️🏵️🏵️🏵️ Radisson Seven Seas   🏵️🏵️🏵️🏵️🏵️ Silversea Cruises
Cruises

CRYSTAL CRUISES

Address: 2049 Century Park East, Suite 1400
Los Angeles, CA 90067
Information: (800) 820–6663, (310) 785–9300
www.crystalcruises.com
Econoguide's Best Luxury Cruise Lines

🏵️🏵️🏵️🏵️🏵️

The Crystal Cruises Fleet

Crystal Serenity	2003	1,080 passengers	68,000 tons
Crystal Symphony	1995	940 passengers	51,044 tons
Crystal Harmony	1990	940 passengers	49,400 tons

Crystal Cruises is a luxury cruise line that has a most unusual pedigree. Founded in 1988, Crystal offers a world of attendants in white gloves, leaded crystal wineglasses filled with the contents of a world-class wine cellar at sea, Wedgwood bone china, teak deck furniture, goose down pillows, and mohair lap blankets.

The line's youngest ship, *Crystal Serenity*, entered the fleet in June 2003. The 1,080-guest, 68,000-ton cruise ship is a large ship by any measure; it joins a set of 50,000-ton twins. But these ships are less than half the size of the current heavyweight champions, and they carry only about one-third the number of passengers, resulting in a very large amount of space per passenger. On the new ship, 635 crew members serve about 1,080 passengers; the *Crystal Harmony* and *Crystal Symphony* carry a crew of about 545 for about 940 passengers. (It's an unusual mix for the crew, too: A Norwegian captain commands Norwegian and Japanese officers, a European hotel and dining staff, and an international crew.)

All this from a company that is much more used to hauling around grain and auto parts. Crystal Cruises is owned by the Japanese company Nippon Yupen Kaiska (NYK), the largest freighter shipping company in the world, with more than 500 vessels in its fleet.

■ ITINERARIES

Crystal Serenity begins 2005 with a Mexican Riviera cruise before embarking on a101-day world cruise from Los Angeles to London, encompassing a passage of the Suez Canal and sailings in the Mediterranean; shorter segments of the cruise are also available for booking. In the spring and summer, *Crystal Serenity* will offer sixteen Mediterranean cruises; in the fall, the ship heads back to North America, from Lisbon to Fort Lauderdale.

In late November, *Crystal Serenity* makes a ten-day Caribbean cruise round-trip from Fort Lauderdale with an inaugural call at Grand Turk in the Turks and Caicos. A Panama Canal cruise positions *Crystal Serenity* back on the West Coast for a Christmas/New Year voyage to the Mexican Riviera, round-trip from Los Angeles.

Crystal Harmony will spend the winter cruising the Panama Canal and Mexican Riviera, including an option departing from San Diego. In the spring the ship is due to return to Asia for a series of fourteen-day cruise and land programs in China and Japan. The summer of 2005 will bring *Crystal Harmony* back to Alaska, sailing round-trip from San Francisco for most of the season. In the fall the ship will cruise the Mexican Riviera, repositioning in December through the Panama Canal to New Orleans to conclude the year with a twelve-day Christmas/New Year cruise round-trip to the Caribbean from New Orleans.

Crystal Symphony begins 2005 with a unique Panama Canal cruise from Fort Lauderdale down the West Coast of Peru and Chile to Valparaiso, a cruise that offers excursions to the Galapagos Islands and Machu Picchu. The ship will remain in South America through February for two cruises around Cape Horn and through the Chilean Fjords, including an eighteen-day voyage that features three days cruising around the Antarctica Peninsula.

In March and April *Crystal Symphony* is due to cruise through the Caribbean and Panama Canal. Following a transatlantic repositioning, the ship will spend May in the Mediterranean and then head north for a series of Baltic, North Cape, and British Isles cruises. In September the ship will head west across the Atlantic to begin a fall foliage series in New England and Canada. In November and December 2005, *Crystal Symphony* heads south for tropical cruises in the Panama Canal and Caribbean, rounding out the year with a Christmas/New Year cruise in the Caribbean round-trip from Fort Lauderdale.

For the year, thirty-two of the ninety-five cruises sail round-trip from domestic ports, and twenty-three more begin or end at an American port.

■ THE CRYSTAL EXPERIENCE

Crystal's two older ships are very similar, although they were built oceans apart: the *Crystal Harmony* in Nagasaki, Japan, in 1990 and the *Crystal Symphony* in Turku, Finland, in 1995. They shared the same lead designer. The newer *Crystal Symphony* includes a larger atrium and restaurants.

The *Crystal Serenity* was built at Chantiers de l'Atlantique in France. About 85 percent of the staterooms on the new ship offer private verandas. Other features include a full outside promenade, a grand observation lounge, a variation of Crystal's popular Palm Court lounge, multiple dining rooms, and a state-of-the-art theater.

On all three ships, most of the cabins have private verandas, and the most spectacular suites are, well, spectacular. The Penthouse Suites are nearly a thousand square feet in size, including a private Jacuzzi with an ocean view. The *Crystal Harmony* has a small number of inside cabins, while the *Crystal Symphony* offers outside accommodations for all. The lobby of each ship showcases a "crystal" piano (made of lucite, actually, but still an impressive objet d'art).

Shipboard dining is a high priority. The elegant Crystal Dining Room never repeats a menu, even on three-month world cruises, although guests can order past favorites. The *Crystal Harmony* offers Japanese cuisine in the Kyoto dining room, and *Crystal Symphony* offers Asian specialties at Jade Garden. A third choice, the Italian bistro Prego, is offered on both ships. The small alternative restaurants can accommodate only a portion of the total number of guests, though.

While *Crystal Harmony* and *Crystal Symphony* have two alternative specialty restaurants, *Crystal Serenity* has three: the Italian restaurant Prego, reminiscent of northern Italy and offering a seasonally changing "Valentino at Prego" menu alongside its own, featuring the cuisine and wine offerings of the revered Los Angeles Valentino restaurant; Silk Road, an elegant pan-Asian restaurant, and the Sushi Bar, which will exclusively feature menu selections by chef Nobu Matsuhisa.

On *Crystal Serenity,* casual international fare is offered throughout the day at Tastes, a hot food counter aft of the second pool.

On select evenings during a cruise, Crystal offers casual dining on deck at the Trident Grill around the Neptune Pool, which features a retractable roof. Unusual for Crystal, the dress code at the grill is casual.

Onboard entertainment ranges from *Some Enchanted Evening,* the first licensed shipboard production show of Rodgers and Hammerstein music, to a performance by a concert pianist, to a nightclub comedian. And if you haven't spent enough money already, you can go to a Caesars Palace casino at sea.

The Crystal Visions Enrichment Program features authors, journalists, historians, and famed chefs.

A handful of cruises each year are designated as Value Collection offerings, with discounts of as much as 50 percent. Membership in the Crystal Society (for previous customers) brings with it a 5 percent discount on future sailings.

■ WEB SITE

Crystal's Web site presents an attractive and detailed view of the line's ships, itineraries, and activities. Once you register, you can request a booking by telephoning Crystal, requesting a callback through the Web site or going through a travel agent. *Ease of use: very good.*

Crystal Serenity

Econoguide rating:	★★★★★★ 95 points
Ship size:	Large
Category:	Ultraluxury
Price range:	Beyond Opulent $$$$$
Registry:	Bahamas
Year built:	2003
Information:	(800) 820–6663
Web site:	www.crystalcruises.com
Passenger capacity:	1,080 (double occupancy)
Crew:	635; Norwegian and Japanese officers
Passenger-to-crew ratio:	1.7:1
Tonnage:	68,000
Passenger-space ratio:	63.0
Length:	820 feet
Beam:	106 feet
Draft:	24.9 feet
Cruising speed:	22 knots
Guest decks:	9
Total cabins:	548
Outside:	550 (468 with verandas)
Inside:	0
Suites:	100
Wheelchair cabins:	8
Cuisine:	Continental and American; two specialty restaurants: Japanese, Italian
Style:	Casual, with at least three formal evenings per cruise
Price notes:	Single-occupancy supplement, 125 to 200 percent of advance-booking fares; discounts available for bookings made six months or more in advance, and cruises booked onboard a previous cruise; an adult or child age twelve or older in a third berth pays minimum fare, children ages eleven and younger pay 50 percent of the minimum fare when accompanied by two full-fare adults
Tipping suggestions:	$10.50 pp/pd
Best deal:	Value Collection cruises discounted as much as 50 percent

Crystal Serenity boasts an even greater space-per-guest ratio than her sister ships *Crystal Harmony* and *Crystal Symphony,* two of the most spacious ships afloat. The ship's one hundred penthouse accommodations include four 1,345 square-foot Crystal Penthouses, thirty-two Penthouse Suites, and sixty-four penthouses. All but 80 of the ship's 548 cabins offer verendas.

Guests have five evening dining choices, beginning with the Crystal Dining Room and extending to Italian and Asian specialty restaurants, a casual evening deck menu, and a sushi bar. Other new features on Crystal's third ship are a pair of paddle tennis courts, a Creative Learning Center for interactive educational classes, and an expanded Computer University@Sea classroom with an Internet center and private area for computer use.

Additional daytime dining venues, which have been favorites on *Crystal Harmony* and *Crystal Symphony,* include the Bistro, a popular social coffee and wine bar, for morning and afternoon snacks; the Trident Grill, for casual poolside lunches throughout the afternoon; plus lavish themed luncheon buffets on selected days by the ship's second pool.

Entertainment venues include the Galaxy Lounge, with improved sight lines for the Broadway-style production shows; the Stardust Club for dancing and cabaret; the Caesars Palace at Sea casino; the Hollywood Theatre cinema and conference center; a Bridge Lounge for card players; and the line's signature Avenue Saloon cocktail and piano bar. Young passengers can visit the Fantasia children's playroom or the Waves teen center.

The Caesars Palace at Sea Casino continues the exclusive alliance between Crystal Cruises and the Las Vegas gaming establishment and is one of the largest luxury casinos afloat. Fantasia is home to the supervised Junior Activities Program, while Waves offers a teen center and video arcade.

The ship's second pool is covered by a sliding dome for inclement weather. A full promenade extends around the exterior of the ship, and the sports deck offers a golf driving range, shuffleboard court, and table tennis area.

Crystal Harmony

Econoguide rating:	★★★★★★ 95 points
Ship size:	Large
Category:	Ultraluxury
Price range:	Beyond Opulent $$$$$
Registry:	Bahamas
Year built:	1988
Information:	(800) 820–6663
Web site:	www.crystalcruises.com
Passenger capacity:	940 (double occupancy)
Crew:	545; Norwegian and Japanese officers

Passenger-to-crew ratio:	1.7:1
Tonnage:	49,400
Passenger-space ratio:	52.6
Length:	790 feet
Beam:	105 feet
Draft:	24.6 feet
Cruising speed:	22 knots
Guest decks:	8
Total cabins:	480
Outside:	461 (260 with verandas)
Inside:	19
Suites:	62
Wheelchair cabins:	4
Cuisine:	Continental and American; two specialty restaurants: Japanese, Italian
Style:	Casual, with at least three formal evenings per cruise
Price notes:	Single-occupancy supplement, 125 to 200 percent of advance-booking fares; discounts available for bookings made six months or more in advance, and cruises booked onboard a previous cruise; an adult or child age twelve or older in a third berth pays minimum fare, ages eleven and younger pay 50 percent of the minimum fare when accompanied by two full-fare adults
Tipping suggestions:	$10.50 pp/pd
Best deal:	Value Collection cruises discounted as much as 50 percent

Offering high-tone elegance and service on one of the largest of the luxury ships, the **Crystal Harmony** has eight guest decks; cabins with verandas include four 948-square-foot Crystal Penthouses, fifty-eight other suites, and 198 outside deluxe staterooms. The smallest cabins are nineteen inside staterooms, a not-too-tiny 183 square feet in size.

Entertainment includes the Caesars Palace at Sea casino with 115 slot machines, seven tables, and a roulette wheel. The domed Vista Observation Lounge up forward offers three levels of seating and a 270-degree view.

The Crystal Dining Room serves international cuisine and a world-class wine list. Crystal also offers a pair of alternative restaurants: The Kyoto restaurant features a Japanese menu, not surprising for a ship line owned by a Japanese freight line. Typical menu items include tempura, Pacific salmon with shiitake mushrooms, and traditional sukiyaki dinner with filet mignon. The Prego restaurant offers intimate Italian dining.

Recreation facilities include a full-length lap pool and an indoor/outdoor pool, a paddle tennis court, golf driving ranges and putting greens, and a sumptuous spa.

The ship underwent a multimillion dollar renovation at the end of 2003. The Connoisseur Club, modeled after a similar improvement to *Crystal Symphony,* brings an intimate cigar and cognac lounge with private club atmosphere.

Located adjacent to the ship's existing Avenue Saloon, the club features a dedicated ventilation system and a well-stocked island humidor complete with imported cigars and individual compartments for guest's cigar storage during a cruise.

The 450-seat Galaxy Lounge was redesigned with ceiling and wall finishes, window treatments, carpet, seating, and cocktail tables. The Crystal Spa & Salon and Fitness Center was completely reconstructed, recast in accordance with the principles of *feng shui,* the ancient philosophy of balance and harmony.

Crystal Symphony

Econoguide rating:	★★★★★★ 95 points
Ship size:	Large
Category:	Ultraluxury
Price range:	Beyond Opulent $$$$$
Registry:	Bahamas
Year built:	1992
Information:	(800) 820–6663
Web site:	www.crystalcruises.com
Passenger capacity:	940 (double occupancy)
Crew:	545; Norwegian and Japanese officers
Passenger-to-crew ratio:	1.7:1
Tonnage:	51,044
Passenger-space ratio:	54.3
Length:	781 feet
Beam:	99 feet
Draft:	24.9 feet
Cruising speed:	22 knots
Guest decks:	8
Total cabins:	480
Outside:	416 (278 with verandas)
Inside:	0
Suites:	64
Wheelchair cabins:	7
Cuisine:	International; two specialty restaurants: Italian, Asian
Style:	Casual, with three formal nights per cruise
Price notes:	Single-occupancy supplement, 125 to 200 percent of advance-booking fares; reduced rates for third in cabin
Tipping suggestions:	$10.50 pp/pd
Best deal:	Value Collection cruises discounted as much as 50 percent

Crystal Symphony, the younger and near-identical sister to the *Crystal Harmony,* includes a larger Caesars Palace at Sea casino and a different alternative

Crystal Symphony under way. *Photo by Corey Sandler*

restaurant in addition to the Crystal Dining Room. The Jade Garden restaurant features a broad Asian menu and offers such items as Peking duck with plum sauce; spicy coconut chicken with eggplant, lemongrass, and basil; and orange-glazed beef with red chilies and basil. There's also the Prego restaurant for classic Italian cuisine served in a Venetian atmosphere.

On both of these Crystal ships, dance concerts and lessons are presented regularly in the Club 2100. Each ship's library has more than 2,000 books, plus a collection of videotapes that can be borrowed for play on VCRs in the staterooms.

In 2004 the ship underwent another upgrade, including a new spa and fitness center (designed, according to the company, using the principles of *feng shui*), an expanded Computer University@Sea, and a new Vintage Room—a boardroom that just happens to have access to the ship's extensive wine cellar. The Crystal Dining Room was redesigned with rich dark paneling and new carpeting, chairs, and window treatments. More than 750 shipyard workers, contractors, and designers from all over the world, supported by more than 400 of Crystal's international shipboard crew, worked on the renovation during a twenty-one-day drydock in Lisbon.

RADISSON SEVEN SEAS CRUISES

RADISSON SEVEN SEAS
CRUISES

Address: 600 Corporate Drive, Suite 410
Fort Lauderdale, FL 33334
Information: (800) 333–3333, (800) 285–1835
www.rssc.com
Econoguide's Best Luxury Cruise Lines
Econoguide's Best Dining at Sea

The Radisson Seven Seas Fleet

Radisson Seven Seas Voyager	2003	700 passengers	50,000 tons
Radisson Seven Seas Mariner	2001	700 passengers	50,000 tons
Radisson Seven Seas Navigator	1999	490 passengers	33,000 tons
Radisson Diamond	1992	350 passengers	20,295 tons
Paul Gauguin	1998	320 passengers	18,800 tons

Radisson Seven Seas Cruises has an eclectic collection of small luxury cruise ships and a pair of sybaritic adventure ships. The tony ships are managed by the upscale hotel chain of the same name; plans call for the gradual removal of the "Radisson" label in coming years in favor of "Seven Seas Cruises." Radisson claims to be the only cruise line whose vessels reach all seven continents, as well as the polar regions.

The line's largest ships, the *Radisson Seven Seas Mariner* and the *Radisson Seven Seas Voyager,* are home to the first permanent Le Cordon Bleu restaurant at sea, the 110-seat reservations-only Signatures. The all-suite, all-balcony ships accommodate 700 passengers and offer four dining venues, including a main dining room that is capable of seating the entire passenger load at once.

Also in the fleet are *Radisson Seven Seas Navigator, Radisson Diamond,* and *Paul Gauguin.* Radisson charters the 12,500-ton 198-passenger *Explorer II* for a pair of cruises to Antarctica from Ushuaia, Argentina, in January 2005. *Song of Flower* left the fleet in 2003.

The company is part of Carlson Hospitality Worldwide, which includes among its holdings the Radisson and Regent hotel chains, Country Inns and Suites by Carlson, and TGI Friday's.

The ship's staff is made up of Norwegian officers and Scandinavian stewardesses, and gratuities are neither expected nor accepted.

The cruise line has moved away from its previous position, which ignored and sometimes banned children. Radisson has brought the Club Mariner children's program to selected Alaskan and European sailings of the *Seven Seas Mariner, Seven Seas Voyager,* and *Seven Seas Navigator.* Club Mariner offers a program of events in two tiers: for ages six to eleven and ages twelve to seventeen. Counselor-supervised activities are organized onboard and ashore, focusing on the destination's nature, heritage, and crafts.

■ ITINERARIES

Seven Seas Voyager will begin 2005 arriving in Los Angeles on a repositioning cruise from Fort Lauderdale. On January 5 the ship begins a world cruise from Los Angeles with segments from Auckland, Sydney, Hong Kong, Singapore, Dubai, with the final leg from Civitavecchia (Rome) back across the Atlantic to Fort Lauderdale at the end of April. The ship turns around immediately in May to sail back to Europe for a series of cruises in the western Mediterranean.

From June through late August *Seven Seas Voyager* sails from Le Havre, Stockholm, and Copenhagen to the Baltic Sea. From August through the end of October, the ship sails in Western Europe, the Black Sea, the Greek Isles, and the Mediterranean. In November *Seven Seas Voyager* sails transatlantic from Funchal, Madeira, to Fort Lauderdale to complete the year sailing to the eastern and western Caribbean.

Seven Seas Navigator sails to the Caribbean from Fort Lauderdale and San Juan in the winter of 2005 through May when she begins a series of cruises from New York to Bermuda that continues through mid-June. On June 15 the ship is due to sail from New York through New England and on to Reykjavik, then Copenhagen and the Baltic Sea. *Seven Seas Navigator* reverses the itinerary at the end of July, returning to New York for more cruises to Bermuda in August.

From September through the end of October, *Seven Seas Navigator* sails through New England, alternating home ports between New York and Montreal. Beginning October 22, 2005, the ship departs New York heading south and then west through the Panama Canal to reposition to Los Angeles. For much of November, *Seven Seas Navigator* will sail round-trip from Los Angeles on a twenty-six-day itinerary to Hawaii and Tahiti. In December the ship returns from Los Angeles through the Panama Canal to Fort Lauderdale to begin service in the Caribbean.

Seven Seas Mariner will sail from Fort Lauderdale on a circle of South America from the end of December 2004 through the end of February. In March the ship will sail a fourteen-day trip from Fort Lauderdale through the Panama Canal to Los Angeles, and then return to Florida to sail in the Caribbean, to the Bahamas, and a single cruise to Bermuda at the end of April.

At the beginning of May, *Seven Seas Mariner* travels from Fort Lauderdale to Los Angeles to be in position for sailings in Alaska through the end of August; home ports will be Vancouver, Seward, and Whittier. At the beginning of September, the ship begins a "Circle Pacific" trip with segments beginning in Vancouver, Whittier, Tokyo, Hong Kong, Singapore, Sydney, and Auckland; the ship returns to Los Angeles to sail a series of Mexican Riviera cruises in December.

The unusual *Radisson Diamond* will sail from San Juan to the eastern Caribbean from early January through late April when the ship will reposition to Barcelona. From May through the end of October, the ship will sail in the Mediterranean, the Greek Isles, and the Adriatic from Barcelona, Civitavecchia (Rome), Venice, Istanbul, Piraeus, and Monte Carlo. *Radisson Diamond* will sail across the Atlantic from Barcelona to San Juan at the end of October to resume sailings in the Caribbean. In mid-December the ship will sail from San Juan through the Panama Canal to Puerto Caldera in Costa Rica, and then return to San Juan at the end of the month.

Paul Gauguin sails from Papeete in Tahiti all year long, mostly to the Society Islands; several cruises also visit the Marquesas and Tuamotus.

Explorer II sails a pair of eleven-day cruises to Antarctica from Ushuaia, Argentina, on January 14 and 25, 2005.

■ WEB SITE

Radisson Seven Seas' Web site provides good information about cruises and itineraries. All bookings are directed to travel agents—either one you specify or one that the cruise line suggests in your area. *Ease of use: very good.*

Radisson Seven Seas Mariner
Radisson Seven Seas Voyager

Econoguide rating:	★★★★★★ 94 points
Ship size:	Large
Category:	Ultraluxury
Price range:	Beyond Opulent $$$$$
Registry:	France
Year built:	*Radisson Seven Seas Mariner,* 2001; *Radisson Seven Seas Voyager,* 2003
Information:	(800) 333–3333
Web site:	www.rssc.com
Passenger capacity:	700
Crew:	445
Passenger-to-crew ratio:	1.6:1
Tonnage:	50,000
Passenger-space ratio:	71.4
Length:	670 feet
Beam:	90 feet
Draft:	21 feet
Cruising speed:	20 knots
Guest decks:	8
Total cabins:	350
Outside:	350
Inside:	0
Suites:	All
Cuisine:	Inventive international cuisine; open, single-seating dining in main restaurant
Style:	Jackets required for men on occasion; suitable resort wear or dresses for women
Price notes:	Single-occupancy premium, expected to be up to 200 percent

Tipping suggestions:	Gratuities included in cruise fare; no tips expected onboard
Best deal:	Advance-booking discounts and onboard credits

The *Seven Seas Mariner* was Radisson's first all-balcony, all-suite vessel and the first in the line with a pod propulsion system. Slung below the ship are a pair of pods with forward-facing propellers that can be turned 360 degrees to drive the ship in any direction.

The main dining room is the Compass Rose, where guests are free to come at any time that suits them. Latitudes is the smallest restaurant onboard, a reservations-only hideaway featuring tableside preparation. By night, the ship's breakfast and lunch buffet eatery becomes La Veranda, a Mediterranean bistro. Finally, there is Signatures, where chefs wear the white toque and blue riband of the Cordon Bleu of Paris. In addition to reservations-only dining at Signatures, passengers may enroll in intensive cooking classes on selected cruises.

The nearly identical sister ship, *Radisson Seven Seas Voyager,* features the same single-corridor design, with standard ocean-view suites offering more than 300 square feet of living space (including balconies), with separate living areas, walk-in closets, and full bathrooms that have separate showers and full bathtubs.

Paul Gaugin

Econoguide rating:	★★★★★ 90 points
Ship size:	Medium
Category:	Ultraluxury
Price range:	Beyond Opulent $$$$$
Registry:	France
Year built:	1998
Information:	(800) 333–3333
Web site:	www.rssc.com
Passenger capacity:	320 (double occupancy)
Crew:	206; European officers
Passenger-to-crew ratio:	1.6:1
Tonnage:	18,800
Passenger-space ratio:	58.8
Length:	513 feet
Beam:	71 feet
Draft:	17 feet
Cruising speed:	18 knots
Guest decks:	7
Total cabins:	161
Outside:	142
Inside:	0
Suites:	19

Wheelchair cabins:	1
Cuisine:	Inventive international cuisine by two-star Michelin chef Jean-Pierre Vigato
Style:	Resort casual, with occasional semiformal nights
Price notes:	Single-occupancy premium, up to 200 percent
Tipping suggestions:	Gratuities included
Best deal:	Advance-booking discounts and onboard credits

An elegant resident of Polynesia, among **Paul Gauguin**'s recreational facilities is a retractable platform that brings guests to sea level for windsurfing, kayaking, waterskiing, snorkeling, and more. Original works by Gauguin from the 1890s and a gallery of vintage black-and-white photographs of French Polynesia are part of the ship's decor.

Radisson Diamond

Econoguide rating:	★★★★ 87 points
Ship size:	Medium
Category:	Ultraluxury
Price range:	Opulent and Beyond $$$$–$$$$$
Registry:	Bahamas
Year built:	1992
Information:	(800) 333–3333
Web site:	www.rssc.com
Passenger capacity:	354 (double occupancy)
Crew:	192
Passenger-to-crew ratio:	1.8:1
Tonnage:	20,295
Passenger-space ratio:	57.3
Length:	420 feet
Beam:	103 feet
Draft:	23 feet
Cruising speed:	12.5 knots
Guest decks:	12
Total cabins:	177
Outside:	177
Inside:	0
Suites:	2 master suites
Wheelchair cabins:	2
Cuisine:	Inventive international cuisine; single, open-seating dining; indoor/outdoor specialty restaurant and lounge offering Northern Italian cuisine
Style:	Resort casual, with occasional semiformal evenings
Price notes:	Single-occupancy premium, 125 to 200 percent

Tipping suggestions:	Gratuities included
Best deal:	Advance-booking discounts and onboard credits

The 20,295-ton **Radisson Diamond** is one of the most readily identifiable ships afloat, with its one-of-a-kind twin-hull design intended to cut down on pitch and roll movements. Of her 177 outside staterooms, 123 have private balconies, and her space ratio of 57.3 is among the highest of any cruise ship in its class.

A luxury hotel afloat, the *Radisson Diamond* is the world's first major cruise ship to use a submerged twin hull; there are only a handful of other passenger-carrying twin-hull vessels, all considerably smaller.

The SWATH (Small Waterplane Area Twin Hull) design utilizes a narrow hull area in contact with the waves and computer-controlled fins to counteract the effects of the sea. According to the company, the resulting degree of vessel roll is only one-fifth that of a monohull cruise vessel, and the vibration level is one-tenth that of a conventional ship.

In a traditional single-hull ship, stabilizers are only effective in reducing side-to-side rolling. By contrast, the *Radisson Diamond* has stabilizer fins on the front and back of each submerged hull, thus reducing both pitching and rolling.

By placing the propulsion machinery in the hulls beneath the waterline, the ship's 26-foot draft adds to the stability and greatly reduces engine noise and vibration. The ship has a wind-resistant nose cone on the bow and a computerized control center.

About the only downside to the design (besides its most untraditional profile, which makes it look like an overgrown houseboat) is the relatively poky speed of the ship. The *Diamond* can eke out a top speed of approximately 12.5 knots.

The five-story entry atrium contains a grand staircase and glass-enclosed elevators. The 230-seat Windows Lounge, located at the bow of the ship on Deck 8, provides a breathtaking view. The elegant Grand Dining Room offers individualized seating at times convenient to passengers.

Recreational facilities include a jogging track, swimming pool, a golf driving range with nets and a putting green, and a hydraulic marina for such activities as windsurfing and personal watercraft.

(You can read a cruise diary about the *Radisson Diamond* in Chapter 11.)

Radisson Seven Seas Navigator

Econoguide rating:	★★★★★ 91 points
Ship size:	Medium
Category:	Ultraluxury
Price range:	Beyond Opulent $$$$$
Registry:	Bahamas
Year built:	1999
Information:	(800) 333-3333

Web site:	www.rssc.com
Passenger capacity:	490
Crew:	325; Italian officers
Passenger-to-crew ratio:	1.5:1
Tonnage:	33,000
Passenger-space ratio:	67.3
Length:	560 feet
Beam:	81 feet
Draft:	21 feet
Cruising speed:	20 knots
Guest decks:	12
Total cabins:	245
Outside:	245
Inside:	0
Suites:	All
Cuisine:	International; open single-seating dining in main restaurant
Style:	Jackets required for men on occasion; suitable resort wear or dresses for women
Price notes:	Single-occupancy premium, expected to be up to 200 percent
Tipping suggestions:	Gratuities included in cruise fare; no tips expected onboard
Best deal:	Advance-booking discounts and onboard credits

The *Seven Seas Navigator* gives 490 passengers an all-suite 33,000-ton luxury cruise ship with 245 ocean-view suites, 90 percent of which have private balconies. The ship cruises the world, with a regular circuit including the Americas and a series of Panama Canal transits. The ship's ice-strengthened hull permits operation around the world.

The smallest accommodations on the ship comprise a spacious 301 square feet, about twice the size of a typical small cabin on a cruise ship. The passenger-space ratio is 67.3, among the highest of any cruise ship afloat.

There is open seating in the main restaurant, which has sufficient space for the entire passenger complement. There is also an alternative Italian restaurant.

The ship was finished at the renowned Fincantieri yard in Italy; the hull was built in Saint Petersburg, Russia, but never completed there.

SEABOURN CRUISE LINE

Address: 6100 Blue Lagoon Drive, Suite 400
Miami, FL 33126

Information: (800) 929–9391
www.seabourn.com

Econoguide's Best Luxury Cruise Lines

Seabourn Cruise Line Fleet

Seabourn Legend	1993	200 passengers	10,000 tons
Seabourn Spirit	1989	200 passengers	10,000 tons
Seabourn Pride	1988	200 passengers	10,000 tons

Seabourn is a floating home for the rich and famous, the rich and private, and others for whom price is of little object. The only real question is whether these are very large yachts or relatively small cruise ships. There are ways, though, to save big dollars on Seabourn cruises: Look for repositioning cruises, advance booking, and last-minute deals.

Seabourn, with its sister operation Cunard line, is one of the anchors of the luxury cruise ship business. Seabourn operates three sister ships: the *Seabourn Pride, Seabourn Spirit,* and *Seabourn Legend.* Each is a 200-passenger all-suite vessel, with a crew of 150. All three of the ships were refurbished in 2000 to replace picture windows with French balconies—sliding doors and minibalconies—in thirty-six suites.

The company's first vessel, the *Seabourn Pride,* set sail in 1988 and today includes itineraries that enter North American waters and the Caribbean. The other ships cruise the Mediterranean, western Europe, Scandinavia, the British Isles, South America, Southeast Asia, India, Africa, and the Red Sea.

In mid-2001, the line unloaded the *Seabourn Goddess I* and *Seabourn Goddess II* to a start-up cruise line, SeaDream Yacht Club; the ships were renamed *Sea Dream I* and *Sea Dream II.* The new venture was started by some of the founders and former executives of Seabourn and Cunard.

THE SEABOURN EXPERIENCE

The basic idea of Seabourn can be summed up quite simply: This is about as close as you can get to owning your own luxury yacht without having to go out and hire yourself a captain and crew.

The three Seabourn sisters, cut from the same pattern and nearly identical inside, feature large outside suites with all the amenities. Passengers can dine when they please, with whom they please, and pretty much where they please: in the formal dining room, the indoor/outdoor Veranda Cafe, the Sky Grill on deck, or in their cabins. Where appropriate, you can even bring some takeout with you to shore. You'll travel in no ordinary tender, either; guests are chauffeured from anchorage to shore in a mahogany-paneled water taxi. Somewhere on the beach, the staff will also set up a catered barbecue, served on fine china and crystal. Guests lounging on deck are likely to be offered a complimentary "massage moment" by spa staffers.

The 440-foot-long vessels carry about half the number of passengers of comparably sized ships. Standard suites offer 277 square feet of space, with walk-in closets, marble-clad bathrooms, and large picture windows. Each suite includes a Bose stereo radio/CD, with a library of music and audio versions of best-selling books available to guests. The cuisine on the ships is described as a mixture of classic and eclectic offerings. Dishes are prepared "a la minute" (as they are ordered) as they would be in a fine restaurant. The Veranda Cafe offers alternative casual dining; the dining area on all three ship was redecorated, offering an "open kitchen" ambiance. The cafes are open for dinner nightly, welcoming guests dressed in casual elegant attire (jacket, no tie) on evenings when the dress suggestion in the Restaurant is formal.

There is complimentary bar service of fine wines and spirits throughout the ship. Guests' in-suite bars are stocked with their choice of internationally known wines and spirits as well. There's also a more specialized wine cellar for those who just have to spend more.

The crew is drilled to learn the names of all passengers and keep up to speed on their preferences in food, entertainment, and comfort.

Each ship has a marina at the stern that opens out into the ocean to provide a dock for water sports. An enclosed steel mesh pool allows passengers to swim without fear of interruption by unpleasant marine creatures.

All this comes at a price, of course. Per person rates for Seabourn's suites average about $761 per day; there is a strict no-tipping policy aboard ship. According to the company, on any cruise as many as half the passengers are repeat customers, which says a lot about satisfaction with the product. If you become a regular, the Seabourn Club offers a complimentary cruise of up to 14 days after you have sailed 140 days.

Renowned American chef-restaurateur Charlie Palmer developed more than 200 new recipes to be served in the exclusive, single-seating restaurants aboard the line's ships. Palmer's Progressive American Cuisine is featured at his restaurants: Aureole, Alva, and Métrazur in New York City; Aureole at Mandalay Bay Resort and Casino and Charlie Palmer Steak at The Four Seasons Hotel in Las Vegas; and Dry Creek Kitchen, located in the Palmer-owned boutique Hotel Healdsburg in Sonoma, California. The three-year agreement calls for Palmer to create a wide array of signature dishes consisting of hot and cold appetizers, soups, and entrees, as well as vegetarian entrees, low-fat low-calorie options for the line's celebrated Simplicity offerings, and desserts. These signature dishes will supplement the existing favorites to provide dinner menus rich with variety. The ship's chefs will be trained in Palmer's shoreside restaurants, and Palmer will then provide shipboard training on each of Seabourn's three ships.

Among the Charlie Palmer recipes that will be added to the Seabourn repertoire are butter braised lobster and sweet pea leaf ravioli with carrot-ginger emulsion; herb grilled quail and French green lentils; roasted Vidalia onion consommé with sherry-braised oxtail and bone marrow; olive-oil-poached rock shrimp gazpacho with lime, avocado, and cumin; sautéed pheasant with crisp spring rolls and red onion marmalade; rabbit saddle with truffle sauce, snap peas, and pea shoots; grilled venison chops with fifty-year-old balsamic vinegar and foie gras sauce; and grilled lamb loin with roasted morels, Parmesan flan, and sweet peas.

Seabourn provides a complimentary shoreside experience in at least one port on every cruise. These invitation-only events use local expertise and insights to allow an exceptional, personalized experience of the port of call.

In 1998 Seabourn became a division of Cunard Line Limited, which also owns and operates Cunard Line. Cunard is, in turn, owned by Carnival Corporation and a consortium of Norwegian investors.

■ ITINERARIES

Seabourn Pride sails the Inca Coast, from Fort Lauderdale to Valparaiso, Chile. Other cruises include an eighteen-day Patagonian Passage from Valparaiso, Chile, to Buenos Aires, Argentina.

In mid-February, the ship is scheduled to offer a thirteen-day trip from Rio de Janeiro to Manaus, Brazil, including a bit of the Amazon, with stops in Salvador de Bahia, Natal, Fortaleza, Alter do Chao, and the Anavilhanas Archipelago. At the end of the month, *Seabourn Pride* prepares to reposition with a sixteen-day cruise from Manaus, Brazil, to Fort Lauderdale with stops including Parintins, Brazil; Devil's Island, French Guiana; Bridgetown, Barbados; Gustavia, Saint Bart's; and Charlotte Amalie, Saint Thomas.

On March 15, 2005, the ship is due to sail across the Atlantic from Fort Lauderdale to Lisbon. From the end of March through early June, *Seabourn Pride* will sail in the Mediterranean from Lisbon and Barcelona; ports of call on various trips include Funchal, Madeira; Santa Cruz de Las Palmas, Las Palmas, Fuerteventura, Canary Islands; Casablanca, Morocco; Gibraltar; Cadiz, Spain; Mahon, Menorca; Porto Vecchio, Corsica; Palermo, Sicily; Valetta, Malta; Syracuse, Sicily; Pylos, Monemvasia, Greece; Antalya, Bodrum, Turkey; Patmos, Greece; and Kusadasi, Turkey.

In mid-May, the ship sails a fourteen-day trip from Lisbon to London, including port calls at major ocean and river ports including Santander, Spain; Bayonne/Biarritz, Bordeaux, La Pallice/La Rochelle, Saint Malo, France; Saint Peter Port, Guernsey; Rouen, France; and Oøstend, Belgium.

From June through the end of August, *Seabourn Pride* will sail from London in the British Isles and the Baltic. The initial trip circles the British Isles with stops in England, Ireland, and Scotland. Later in the summer, the ship will make several trips from London to the Kiel Canal, Warnemunde, Germany; Tallinn, Estonia; a three-day stay in St. Petersburg, Russia; and two days in Stockholm, Sweden.

Other summer trips include Norway and Northern Capitals with stops in Edinburgh, Scotland; Gudvangen, Flaam, Bergen, Ulvik, Eidfjord, Oslo, Norway; Copenhagen, Denmark; and Amsterdam, Netherlands.

At the end of August *Seabourn Pride* is due to head back to North America, sailing from London to Falmouth, England; Waterford, Dublin, Ireland; Douglas, Isle of Man; Londonderry, Northern Ireland; St. John's, Newfoundland; Halifax, Nova Scotia; Newport, Rhode Island; and New York.

From mid-September through mid-October, the ship will sail from New York and Quebec City on leaf-peeper cruisers. The next trip takes the ship from New York to Fort Lauderdale by way of historic ports in Newport, Rhode Island; Philadelphia; Baltimore; Alexandria and Norfolk, Virginia; Charleston, South Carolina; Savannah, Georgia; and Amelia Island, Florida.

Beginning in mid-November and continuing through the end of 2005, *Seabourn Pride* will sail in the Caribbean from Fort Lauderdale and Barbados, with some itineraries heading as far south as the Grenadines and Venezuela.

Plans for 2006 include a return to South America through mid-March when *Seabourn Pride* is due to reposition to Lisbon to begin its European season.

Seabourn Legend begins 2005 with a series of sailings from Fort Lauderdale to Costa Rica through the Panama Canal. Four fourteen-day trips include visits to Belize City and Hunting Caye, Belize; Roatan, Honduras; Puerto Moin, Costa Rica; Gamboa and Fuerte Amador, Panama; Puerto Quepos, Costa Rica; and San Juan del Sur, Nicaragua.

At the end of February, the ship begins service from Fort Lauderdale and Charlotte Amalie, Saint Thomas to the Caribbean. Ports of call on a series of cruises include Tortola, BVI; Basseterre, Saint Kitts; Charlestown, Nevis; Cruz Bay, Saint John, USVI; Pointe-á-Pitre, Guadeloupe; Saint John's, Antigua; Gustavia, Saint Bart's; Virgin Gorda, BVI; Marigot, Saint Martin; Fort-de-France, Martinique; Gustavia, Saint Bart's; and Virgin Gorda, BVI.

At the end of March, *Seabourn Legend* crosses the Atlantic from Saint Thomas to Lisbon to begin a summer in the Mediterranean with a series of trips that continues until November. The schedule includes mostly seven- and ten-day trips in Spain, Portugal, Monaco, Italy, and France. Unusual calls on some of the trips include Calvi, Corsica; Portovenere and Portoferraio on Elba island; Costa Smeralda, Sardinia; and La Goulette (Carthage), Tunisia.

In early November the ship crosses the Atlantic from Santa Cruz de Tenerife in the Canary Islands to Fort Lauderdale. From the end of November through mid-December, *Seabourn Legend* sails from Florida to Costa Rica through the Panama Canal and back. After a sixteen-day holiday trip from Fort Lauderdale deep into the Caribbean, the ship resumes alternating trips from Florida to Costa Rica through the end of March, transitioning into Caribbean cruises before crossing back to Europe from Saint Thomas to Lisbon at the end of April.

Seabourn Spirit begins 2005 in southeast Asia, sailing from Hong Kong to Singapore with stops in Haiphong (Hanoi), Halong Bay, Danang, and Ho Chi Minh City in Vietnam; and Ko Kood and Bangkok in Thailand. A series of six fourteen-day trips from January through April include Vietnam, Thailand, Burma, and Singapore.

In mid-April the ship sails from Singapore to Dubai with port calls in Penang, Malaysia; Colombo, Sri Lanka; Cochin, Mumbai (Bombay), India; Muscat and Oman in Dubai. The next cruise, at the end of April, moves the ship from Dubai to Alexandria, Egypt, with stops in Khasab and Salalah, Oman; Aqaba (Petra), Jordan; Sharm el Sheikh, Egypt and through the Suez Canal.

From mid-May through the end of July, *Seabourn Spirit* sails in the Greek and Aegean isles with cruises that start in Alexandria, Egypt; Istanbul, Turkey; Athens, Greece; and Rome (Civitavecchia), Italy.

In mid-July the ship visits the Black Sea, sailing to Venice, Italy, with port calls in Yalta, Sevastopol, and Odessa in Ukraine; Nesebur, Bulgaria; Istanbul, Turkey; Mycenae (Navplion), Santorini, Corinth Canal, Delphi (Itea), and Corfu in Greece; and Korcula, Croatia.

After then, from the end of July through mid-October, *Seabourn Spirit* sails in the Greek and Italian isles, the Aegean and Adriatic from Venice, Rome, Athens, and Istanbul.

On October 16, 2005, the ship repositions from Athens to Alexandria, Egypt, and then continues with a sixteen-day Red Sea and Africa cruise with stops in Sharm el Sheikh (Sinai), Egypt; Aqaba (Petra), Jordan; Safaga (Luxor), Egypt; Djibouti; and Mombasa, Kenya.

In November, *Seabourn Spirit* continues from Kenya to Singapore. At the end of the month, the ship sails from Singapore to Kuala Lumpur, Malaysia. A Christmas holiday cruise extends fourteen days from Singapore to Hong Kong, China with stops including Bangkok, Thailand; Ho Chi Minh City, Danang, and Haiphong/Hongai (Hanoi), Vietnam.

The ship will begin 2006 sailing a seventeen-day cruise from Hong Kong to Cairns, Australia. After then *Seabourn Spirit* will sail a series of cruises in Australia, New Zealand, and South Pacific waters.

■ WEB SITE

The Seabourn Web site includes basic information about the cruise line and ships. Booking requests are forwarded to a telephone callback service or a travel agent. *Ease of use: good.*

Seabourn Legend, Seabourn Pride, Seabourn Spirit

Econoguide rating:	★★★★★★ 97 points
Ship size:	Medium
Category:	Ultraluxury
Price range:	Beyond Opulent $$$$$
Registry:	Norway
Year built:	*Seabourn Legend,* 1993; *Seabourn Pride,* 1988; *Seabourn Spirit,* 1988
Information:	(800) 929–9391
Web site:	www.seabourn.com
Passenger capacity:	208 (double occupancy)
Crew:	150
Passenger-to-crew ratio:	1.3:1
Tonnage:	10,000
Passenger-space ratio:	50
Length:	440 feet
Beam:	63 feet
Draft:	16.4 feet
Cruising speed:	18 knots
Guest decks:	4
Total cabins:	104

Outside:	104
Inside:	0
Suites:	104
Wheelchair cabins:	4
Cuisine:	International cuisine and eclectic offerings; alternative casual dining in Veranda Cafe; the onboard wine cellar with boutique wines from the vineyards of Italy, France, and the United States
Style:	Semiformal to formal
Price notes:	Single-occupancy premium, 175 to 200 percent, some special offers available
Tipping suggestions:	Strict no-tipping policy

After a renovation, the **Seabourn Legend, Seabourn Pride,** and **Seabourn Spirit** now feature thirty-six suites per vessel with step-out French balconies, each with floor-to-ceiling glass doors, in addition to the six full verandas on each ship's premium category suites.

Every stateroom is a suite, each with a large picture window that has an electrically operated blackout curtain. A marina opens out into the ocean from the stern of the ship, providing a launch for water sports. An enclosed steel mesh pool allows for swimming right in the ocean (weather permitting).

SILVERSEA CRUISES

Address: 110 East Broward Boulevard
  Fort Lauderdale, FL 33301
Information: (800) 722–9955, (954) 522–4477
  www.silversea.com
Econoguide's Best Luxury Cruise Lines

The Silversea Cruises Fleet

Silver Shadow	2000	396 passengers	25,000 tons
Silver Whisper	2001	396 passengers	25,000 tons
Silver Cloud	1994	296 passengers	16,800 tons
Silver Wind	1994	296 passengers	16,800 tons

Guests are greeted by white-gloved attendants offering perfectly chilled flutes of champagne; they are then escorted to their suites where a private bottle awaits. Need we say more?

Life aboard the *Silver Cloud* and *Silver Wind* or the younger and slightly larger *Silver Shadow* and *Silver Whisper,* two pairs of near-identical luxury twins, is pretty rarified: Limoges china, Christofle silverware, Frette linens, and soft down pillows.

Silversea also makes a big deal about wine onboard its vessels, offering selected wines as part of a cruise package and carrying a seagoing wine cellar and a staff of sommeliers for guests who insist on spending even more. So, too, with caviar and other gastronomic specialties.

The dining room is simply called The Restaurant, although it is less than simple. There's a single sitting with open seating. On formal nights the ship's orchestra provides dance music. If gentlemen don't feel like wearing a tuxedo, dinner jacket, or suit, you can have dinner served in your cabin, course by course.

In coming years, Silversea intends to emphasize headliner concerts, local performers, and guest artists on each cruise. In 2003 renowned Italian mezzo-soprano Cecilia Bartoli sailed on four voyages in the Mediterranean and Black Sea, giving intimate recitals for the guests and conducting discussions of music and opera.

■ PERSONALIZED VOYAGES

You say you'd rather not fly to Barbados to pick up a Caribbean cruise that ends in Fort Lauderdale but would rather catch up with the ship after it passes Morro Castle in San Juan harbor? And while you're at it, you'd rather stay on board past Fort Lauderdale and disembark in Virgin Gorda? No problem . . . with Silversea's unusual Personalized Voyages plan.

In 2003 Silversea extended the plan to all four of its ships, permitting guests to choose the length of their voyage and to embark and disembark from their choice of a wide selection of ports.

The Silversea Cruise Atlas lists available ports and daily rates. Guests can cruise for as long as they want, with a minimum of five consecutive nights.

■ THE SILVERSEA STORY

Silversea is owned by the Lefebvre family of Rome, former owners of Sitmar Cruises. The company was founded in the early 1990s with a concept for "ultra-luxury" ships with the largest passenger-space ratio of any ship at sea. All cabins are outside, and most have private verandas. There's an open, single-seating dining room and a show lounge for nightly entertainment.

Silver Shadow and *Silver Whisper* joined the fleet in 2000 and mid-2001, and the company has an option for two additional ships in following years. The younger 25,000-ton vessels have 194 outside suites for 388 passengers. The resulting passenger-space ratio of 63 places the ships among the most spacious afloat.

Cruise fares include all gratuities, all beverages including select wines and spirits, and port charges. Passengers can make their own air reservations to connect with the ships or use Silversea's travel department to arrange for flights and pre- or postcruise hotel stays.

Guests who have sailed for one hundred days or more are eligible for membership in the Silversea Venetian Society; they are also eligible to receive a 5 percent discount. At 250 days or more the discount rises to 10 percent, and guests will also receive a free 7-day cruise; at the 500-day milestone, the company offers a complimentary 14-day cruise.

■ ITINERARIES

Silver Cloud begins the winter 2005 season in the warm waters of the South Pacific, offering three cruises to Australia and New Zealand, ranging from ten to sixteen days, continuing to the Far East and Africa. In the spring *Silver Cloud* is due to head for the Mediterranean, offering a series of eight cruises to destinations in Spain, Portugal, France, and Italy. In the summer the ship cruises to Northern Europe before crossing the Atlantic to end the year with cruises to South America and the Amazon.

Silver Wind begins its year in South America, before crossing the Atlantic to embark on a series of cruises to Africa, featuring stopovers in Walvis Bay, Namibia, and Cape Town and Richard's Bay in South Africa. The ship's schedule continues with more than twenty Mediterranean sailings, ranging from five to fifteen days. In the fall the *Silver Wind* cruises to Egypt, the Seychelles, and South Africa.

Silver Shadow is scheduled to spend the winter navigating the warm waters of the Mexican Riviera and South America before repositioning to the Mediterranean. In the spring and summer of 2005, the ship is due to offer more than twenty-five varied cruises visiting the western and eastern Mediterranean. In the autumn, *Silver Shadow* offers a collection of voyages to the Far East and South Pacific.

Silver Whisper begins the winter sailing to the islands of the Caribbean on nine different voyages ranging from five to ten days. After then the ship repositions to the Mediterranean for a series of cruises to Spain, Italy, France, and Northern Europe including several three-day stopovers in the celebrated city of Saint Petersburg. In the fall *Silver Whisper* sets a course for Canada, the Colonial Coast of New England, and then sails south to the Caribbean.

■ GETTING THE PRIORITIES RIGHT

We were sailing just south of Greenland on the way from Reykjavik, Iceland to Newfoundland aboard *Silver Shadow*. The winds were howling and the seas moderately rough, a harbinger of the storm we were going to meet in Saint John's in a few days. However, the modern *Silver Shadow* handled the seas well, her stabilizers smoothing out most of the side-to-side rolls.

It was dinner time, and we were ensconced at our usual private table at the Terrace on Deck 7. We had just finished our appetizer of *conchiglie ai gamberoni* (shell-shaped pasta with prawns) and expecting the serving of *costata di manzo alla griglia con salsa al barolo* (grilled prime rib with Italian vegetable compote). The table was set with a panettiere of grissini and focaccia breads, a tub of bresaola butter, and elegant crystal stemware for Vernaccia di San Gimignano and Dolcetto DOC, the white and red wines of the evening.

The ship heeled all the way over to starboard in a slow roll. Plates and glasses and wine bottles flew off the tables. From the back of the room, we heard a cacophony of crashes as hundreds of additional plates and glasses fell to the floor in the galley. Waiters, sommeliers, and deck crew appeared from every direction to help a few guests who had undergone a slow-motion fall.

The ship returned to its steady upright position. The captain later told us that the ship's computer-controlled stabilizer suffered a once-in-a-lifetime hiccup.

The room was quiet as we all surveyed the thousands of dollars in broken glass and dishes, the overturned wine coolers, and the crumbled grissini. We then heard a weak little voice from a table by the window: "Excuse me? More wine please."

All was back to luxurious normalcy on the *Silver Shadow*.

Silver Shadow, Silver Whisper

Econoguide rating:	★★★★★★ 97 points
Ship size:	Medium
Category:	Ultraluxury
Price range:	Beyond Opulent $$$$$
Registry:	Bahamas
Year built:	*Silver Shadow*, 2000; *Silver Whisper*, 2001
Information:	(800) 722–9955
Web site:	www.silversea.com
Passenger capacity:	388 (double occupancy)
Crew:	295; Italian officers
Passenger-to-crew ratio:	1.3:1
Tonnage:	25,000
Passenger-space ratio:	64.4
Length:	597 feet
Beam:	81.8 feet
Draft:	19.6 feet
Cruising speed:	21 knots
Guest decks:	11
Total cabins:	194
Outside:	194
Inside:	0
Suites:	194
Wheelchair cabins:	4
Cuisine:	Regional, American, continental; select wines, spirits, and champagnes from around the world included
Style:	Casual to formal; two formal nights on sailings of eight days or less, three or four formal nights on longer cruises
Price notes:	Single-occupancy premium, 110 to 200 percent
Tipping suggestions:	All gratuities included
Best deal:	Special promotions on some cruises

Silver Shadow was christened in Civitavecchia, Italy, in September 2000, using a salmanazar of Moët & Chandon champagne. (A salmanazar is the equivalent of twelve bottles, or six magnums.)

The restaurant on the fourth deck is appropriately sumptuous. Beneath three grand chandeliers, Frette tablecloths are set with Christofle silverware and European stemware.

(See Chapter 11 for a cruise diary about a *Silver Shadow* voyage from New Zealand to Australia.)

Silver Whisper joined the fleet in mid-2001; during its construction Silversea changed its name from *Silver Mirage*.

Silver Cloud, Silver Wind

Econoguide rating:	★★★★★★ 96 points
Ship size:	Medium
Category:	Ultraluxury
Price range:	Beyond Opulent $$$$$
Registry:	Bahamas
Year built:	*Silver Cloud,* 1994; *Silver Wind,* 1994
Information:	(800) 722–9955
Web site:	www.silversea.com
Passenger capacity:	296 (double occupancy)
Crew:	209; Italian officers
Passenger-to-crew ratio:	1.4:1
Tonnage:	16,800
Passenger-space ratio:	56.8
Length:	514 feet
Beam:	70 feet
Draft:	18 feet
Cruising speed:	20.5 knots
Guest decks:	6
Total cabins:	148
Outside:	148
Inside:	0
Suites:	148
Wheelchair cabins:	2
Cuisine:	Regional, American, continental; select wines, spirits, and champagnes from around the world included
Style:	Casual to formal; two formal nights on sailings of eight days or less, three or four formal nights on longer cruises
Price notes:	Single-occupancy premium, 110 to 200 percent; Venetian Society discounts of 5 to 15 percent for past customers
Tipping suggestions:	All gratuities included
Best deal:	Special promotions on some cruises

Silver Wind arrives in London. *Courtesy of Silversea Cruises*

Silver Cloud and **Silver Wind** provide a luxurious cruising experience, with opulent appointments and service within and a wide range of interesting ports of call without, helped by the shallow draft of the yachtlike ships.

This is a classy, pricey world of Limoges china, Christofle silverware, Frette bed linens monogrammed with the Silversea logo, down pillows, and brand-name bath amenities.

The restaurant offers open seating for the entire passenger complement; on select formal nights, there's an orchestra for dancing. Terrace Cafe offers alternative dining with Italian regional specialties on a reservation basis. Items from the restaurant menu can be delivered to your suite. On select sailings, visiting chefs from Le Cordon Bleu Culinary Academy prepare delicacies to complement the menu selections, including regional, American, and continental cuisine.

Silver Wind entered its scheduled dry dock in October 2001 for a comprehensive refurbishment and sat out the 2002 calendar year until its return in mid-2003. *Silver Cloud* was taken out of service in October 2003 and was to be brought back to the fleet in April 2004.

Upgrades to *Silver Cloud* include new furniture, linens, and artwork in all suites. The ship will also feature an intimate new wine bar, echoing the innovative and highly popular Le Champagne wine bars aboard Silversea's newer ships. Guests will also find an expanded spa facility featuring a new Tranquility Room—a blissful, between-treatment sanctuary. The ship will also receive a new Internet cafe, and an expanded fitness center, relocated to the observation deck and providing a panoramic view of the ocean.

Econoguide Ship Classifications

Gargantuan	130,000 or more tons
Colossus	100,000 to 130,000 tons
Megaship	70,000 to 100,000 tons
Large	40,000 to 70,000 tons
Medium	10,000 to 40,000 tons
Small	Less than 10,000 tons

CHAPTER FIFTEEN

OTHER CRUISE LINES

ΩΩΩ Discovery World Cruises   ΩΩΩ MSC Italian Cruises
ΩΩ   Imperial Majesty Cruise Line   ΩΩΩ Oceania Cruises

DISCOVERY WORLD CRUISES

DISCOVERY WORLD CRUISES

Address: 1800 S.E. 10th Avenue, Suite 205
Fort Lauderdale, FL 33316
Information: (866) 623–2689, (954) 761–7878
www.discoveryworldcruises.com

Ω Ω Ω

The Discovery World Cruises Fleet

Discovery	1972	650 passengers	20,216 tons

The Discovery World Cruises fleet consists of the *Discovery,* an older ship brought up to modern standards, and though it is much smaller than a Megaship, it is one of the largest ships sailing in exotic waters. The 650-passenger vessel was formerly the *Island Princess,* sister ship to the *Pacific Princess,* which was the "love boat" of television fame.

There's hardly an "ordinary" port of call on any of the itineraries of Discovery World Cruises. From December through April of each year, the company sails in the Southern Hemisphere, from Argentina and Chile to the Falklands and Antarctica. Other trips head to the South Pacific and New Zealand.

For the rest of the year, *Discovery* operates under charter to Voyages of Discovery, a tour operator based in the United Kingdom, offering cruises of the British Isles, the Baltic, Greenland, Iceland and the Faroe Islands, Scandinavia, the Mediterranean, the Black Sea, Red Sea, Suez Canal, and North Africa.

The line, which began sailing in 2003, includes management that came out of niche cruise operators including Orient Lines, Ocean Cruise Lines, and Pearl Cruises.

▓ ITINERARY

Discovery's 2004 to 2005 season begins in Southampton, England, on December 4 with a twenty-five-day cruise that crosses the Atlantic to Buenos Aires, with port calls including Lisbon, Gibraltar, Cape Verde, Rio de Janeiro, and Montevideo, Uruguay. On December 28, the ship departs Buenos Aires for the Antarctic and the Falkland Islands, ending at Ushuaia, Argentina, ten days later.

On January 10, 2005, the ship sails to Antarctica round-trip from Ushuaia, transiting the Drake Passage and Lemaire Channel. The next cruise, departing January 18, returns to the Antarctic and Chilean fjords, arriving at Valparaiso, Chile, on February 1.

From Chile *Discovery* heads to the South Pacific, following some of the paths of the *Bounty*. Ports of call include Robinson Crusoe Island, Easter Island, and Pitcairn Island, arriving in Papeete, Tahiti, on February 15. From Tahiti, the next cruise heads to Auckland, New Zealand, with stops at the islands of Raitea, Raratonga, Vavau, Suva, and Darvuni, and the Bay of Islands in New Zealand, arriving March 2.

The next cruise circles New Zealand, sailing round-trip from Auckland with port calls at Tauranga, Napier, Dunedin, Christchurch, and Wellington. On March 18, *Discovery* heads east from Auckland across the International Date Line with stops at Norfolk Island, Port Vila, Suva, Apia, Pago Pago, Bora Bora, and Raiatea, ending in Papeete, Tahiti, on April 3.

From Tahiti *Discovery* heads down to South America on April 3, with port calls including Pitcairn Island and Easter Island, arriving in Callao, Peru, seventeen days later. On April 20, the ship heads up the west coast of South America to Panama to cross through the canal, continuing on to Fort Lauderdale on May 2.

The final cruise of the year is a repositioning from Fort Lauderdale to Harwich, England, with port calls in Nassau, Bermuda, and Horta in the Azores, arriving May 16.

Discovery

Econoguide rating:	★★ 65 points
Ship size:	Medium
Category:	Adventure
Price range:	Premium $$$
Registry:	Bermuda
Year built:	1972, as *Island Venture* of Flagship Cruises. Sailed as *Island Princess* for Princess Cruises from 1974–2001. Refurbished 2003
Information:	(866) 623–2689
Web site:	www.discoveryworldcruises.com
Passenger capacity:	650 (double occupancy)
Crew:	305

Passenger-to-crew ratio:	2.1:1
Tonnage:	20,216
Passenger-space ratio:	30.1
Length:	553 feet
Beam:	80 feet
Draft:	27 feet
Cruising speed:	18 knots
Guest decks:	8
Total cabins:	351
Outside:	280
Inside:	71
Suites:	19
Wheelchair cabins:	2
Cuisine:	International
Style:	Casual, with scheduled formal nights
Price notes:	Repositioning and early booking discounts.
Tipping suggestions:	$7.50 pp/pd
Best deal:	Early-booking discounts reduce rates by almost 50 percent

With a profile looking more like a classic ocean liner than a floating hotel/cruise ship, *Discovery* was updated in 2003 to include most of the modern amenities of today's vessels. There are three restaurants, five lounges, a library, casino, and health club aboard. One of the two small swimming pools is covered with a retractable dome to protect bathers from the elements.

Most itineraries are offered as cruise-tour packages that include extended stays and sightseeing in ports of embarkation or disembarkation, local cultural performances on board, and an enrichment program of lectures and workshops at sea.

IMPERIAL MAJESTY CRUISE LINE

Address: 2950 Gateway Boulevard
Pompano Beach, FL 3306
Information: (954) 956–9505
www.imperialmajesty.com

The Imperial Majesty Cruise Line Fleet

Regal Empress	1953	900 passengers	21,909 tons

Imperial Majesty retired the *Ocean Breeze* in June 2003, replacing her with the more technologically current *Regal Empress*. Built in 1953 as the flagship of the Greek Line, she offers a very similar design and accommodations.

Per person rates run from as low as $150 for a minimal inside cabin to $400 for a suite for two nights. Prices more than double for peak-season cruises in holiday periods.

This is a party ship, with all the basic trappings of the early days of cruising: happy hours, karaoke bars, late night buffets, a casino, and bingo. You can play shuffleboard, shake the captain's hand and pose for a picture at a reception, and enter a table tennis tournament.

■ ITINERARY

The ship leaves Fort Lauderdale at 5:00 P.M. and sails overnight directly to Nassau. She stays in port there from about 9:00 A.M. to 6:00 P.M. before heading back to home port. The short cruises are marketed to first-time cruisers, families, and those looking for a quick getaway.

■ WEB SITE

Visitors to the Imperial Majesty Web site find a very detailed description of the ship and her history. The site includes an online request for booking but no prices. Travelers will be contacted by phone to book a voyage. *Ease of use: very good.*

Regal Empress

Econoguide rating:	★★ 61 points
Ship size:	Medium
Category:	Vintage
Price range:	Budget $
Registry:	Bahamas
Year built:	1953 (formerly *Olympia, Caribe I*; refurbished 1993, 1999)
Information:	(800) 511–5737
Web site:	www.imperialmajesty.com
Passenger capacity:	900 (double occupancy)
Crew:	396
Passenger-to-crew ratio:	2.3:1
Tonnage:	21,909
Passenger-space ratio:	24.3
Length:	612 feet
Beam:	79 feet
Draft:	27.5 feet
Cruising speed:	17 knots
Guest decks:	8
Total cabins:	457
Outside:	201
Inside:	227

Suites:	29
Wheelchair cabins:	2
Cuisine:	International
Style:	Semiformal and casual
Price notes:	Single-occupancy premium, 150 percent
Tipping suggestions:	$9.00 pp/pd
Best deal:	Early-booking discounts reduce rates by almost 50 percent

The **Regal Empress** is a fine old ship, a bit worn around the edges, but very appropriate for cruise virgins and travelers looking for an excellent deal and some less-visited ports of call. A renovation in 1999 added a new small and casual restaurant, a computer cafe, and other amenities. The ship has been brought up to date with most SOLAS regulations, including fire safety sprinklers.

Note that, as with many older liners, many of the "outside" cabins actually look out on an open or enclosed promenade along the rail.

MSC ITALIAN CRUISES

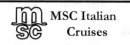

MSC Italian Cruises

Address: 250 Moonachie Road
Moonachie, NJ 07074
Information: (800) 666–9333
www.msccruises.com

The MSC Italian Cruises Fleet

Armonia	2001	1,566 passengers	58,700 tons
Opera	2004	1,756 passengers	58,600 tons
Lirica	2003	1,586 passengers	58,600 tons
Melody	1982	1,076 passengers	36,500 tons
Monterey	1952	576 passengers	20,040 tons
Rhapsody	1977	768 passengers	16,852 tons

FUTURE SHIPS

Unnamed	June 2006	2,550 passengers	70,000 tons (estimated)
Unnamed	Spring 2007	2,550 passengers	70,000 tons (estimated)

MSC Italian Cruises (formerly Mediterranean Shipping Cruises) operates a small fleet of cruise ships around the world.

The company more than doubled its capacity in 2003 and 2004 with the arrival of two new Megaships. In spring 2003 the company added *Lirica,* a new 1,586-passenger ship. The 58,600-ton vessel has 795 cabins, including 132 suites with private verandas. A sister ship, *Opera,* arrived in spring 2004. Both vessels will sail Mediterranean itineraries. And in May 2004, the company purchased the nearly-new *European Vision* from Festival Cruises, renaming it as

Armonia and assigning it to sail in the Mediterranean.

And the company plans to add two or three more large ships in coming years. Work has begun in France on the construction of a pair of 2,550-passenger cruise ships for delivery in June 2006 and the spring of 2007, with an option for a third sister ship.

The ships will be about 964 feet long and 106 feet wide, just barely able to squeeze through the Panama Canal. Designed for cruises in the Mediterranean and Caribbean seas, about 80 percent of the 1,275 cabins will have outside views, and three-quarters of these will also have balconies.

MSC's older fleet includes *Melody,* which sails in the Caribbean in winter and in Europe for the remainder of the year. Melody is the former *Star/Ship Atlantic,* one of the Big Red Boats of the former Premier Cruise Line.

Also in the fleet are the *Rhapsody,* formerly the *Cunard Princess, a*nd the *Monterey,* formerly the U.S. flag freighter the *Free State Mariner.* They serve European, South American, and South African ports.

The line began as Flotta Lauro, an Italian carrier little known outside its home waters until the 1985 terrorist attack on its cruise ship *Achille Lauro* off Egypt. The *Achille Lauro* later sank off Africa in 1994.

The company was purchased in 1990 by Mediterranean Shipping Cruises, part of the Swiss-based Mediterranean Shipping Company, the second-largest container shipping company in the world with a fleet of over 250 ships operating worldwide.

ITINERARIES

In 2004 *Lirica* sailed in the Caribbean from Port Everglades in the spring, crossing over to the Mediterranean in June to sail from Barcelona and Genoa to begin a summer in Europe. Summer and fall cruises include trips from Genoa and Venice to Malta, Greece, Croatia, Istanbul, and elsewhere in Italy through November, setting up for a return to the Caribbean.

The new *Opera* sailed from Genoa to Tunisia, Spain, France and Italy, beginning in May 2004 and continuing through November. In December she was due to make a transatlantic crossing to sail in the Caribbean for the winter.

Armonia joined the fleet at the end of May 2004, with her first assignment to sail week-long cruises from Venice to Corfu, Santorini, Athens, Katakolon, Dubrovnik, and Venice through mid-November.

In 2004 *Melody* sailed along the coast of Brazil from Rio de Janeiro from January to March before crossing the Atlantic to Barcelona and Genoa. *Melody* sailed in the Mediterranean with itineraries that visited Italy, Tunisia, Spain, and France from April through October; late in the season, the ship moves eastward to include visits to Greece, Turkey, Malta, and Egypt.

Rhapsody sailed from Genoa to Greece, Turkey, Cyprus, and Egypt beginning April 2004 through the fall. Other trips visited Yalta and Odessa in the Ukraine, and Morocco, Gibraltar, Spain, and Portugal.

Monterey sailed from Genoa to Naples, Piraeus, Yalta, Odessa, Istanbul, Catania, and Capri in the summer of 2004. In past years the ship has spent the winter sailing South African waters.

■ WEB SITE

The MSC Web site presents basic information about ships and detailed itineraries. You can research prices for cruises and request that a reservations agent call you to book a trip. *Ease of use: good.*

Lirica, Opera

Econoguide rating:	★★★★ 83 points
Ship size:	Large
Category:	Top of the Line
Price range:	Premium $$$
Registry:	Panama
Year built:	*Lirica,* 2003; *Opera,* 2004
Information:	(800) 666–9333
Web site:	www.msccruisesusa.com
Passenger capacity:	*Lirica,* 1,586; *Opera,* 1,756 (double occupancy)
Crew:	*Lirica,* 760; *Opera,* 800
Passenger-to-crew ratio:	*Lirica,* 2.1:1; *Opera,* 2.2:1
Tonnage:	58,600
Passenger-space ratio:	*Lirica,* 36.9; *Opera,* 33.4
Length:	763 feet
Beam:	84 feet
Draft:	N/A
Cruising speed:	21 knots
Guest decks:	14
Total cabins:	*Lirica,* 795; *Opera,* 878
Outside:	*Lirica,* 521; *Opera,* 687
Inside:	*Lirica,* 272; *Opera,* 186
Suites:	*Lirica,* 132; *Opera,* 200
Wheelchair cabins:	4
Cuisine:	Italian, international
Style:	Casual, with two or more semiformal evenings
Price notes:	Single-occupancy premium, 150 percent
Tipping suggestions:	$8.00 pp/pd
Best deals:	Advance-booking discounts

These two modern ships offer all the amenities contemporary cruisers expect. Spread over the fourteen decks are two swimming pools, a spa with a Turkish bath and sauna, and an Internet cafe. The main dining rooms on *Lirica* are La Bussola and Ippocampo; informal eateries include La Pergola and La Canzone del Mare on the pool deck plus a pizzeria. Entertainment offerings include the Blue Disco, the Rossini Music Hall, the Puccini Theatre, and the Broadway Theatre.

Opera has the same exterior dimensions as her sister ship *Lirica,* but gives up a bit of internal public space to gain eighty-three more cabins.

Armonia

Econoguide rating:	★★★★ 83 points
Ship size:	Large
Category:	Top of the Line
Price range:	Premium $$$
Registry:	Italy
Year built:	As *European Vision,* 2001
Information:	(800) 666–9333
Web site:	www.msccruisesusa.com
Passenger capacity:	1,566
Crew:	700
Passenger-to-crew ratio:	2.2:1
Tonnage:	58,700
Passenger-space ratio:	37.5
Length:	823 feet
Beam:	94 feet
Draft:	N/A
Cruising speed:	21 knots
Guest decks:	9
Total cabins:	783
Outside:	460
Inside:	323
Suites:	132
Wheelchair cabins:	N/A
Cuisine:	Italian, international
Style:	Casual, with two or more semiformal evenings
Price notes:	Single-occupancy premium, 150 percent
Tipping suggestions:	$8.00 pp/pd
Best deals:	Advance-booking discounts

A thoroughly modern ship, built for service in Europe and the Caribbean by Festival Cruises and sailing as *European Vision.* After Festival ran onto financial shoals in 2004, the vessel was purchased by MSC, renovated and renamed as *Armonia.*

Melody

Econoguide rating:	★★★ 69 points
Ship size:	Medium
Category:	Vintage
Price range:	Budget $

Registry:	Panama
Year built:	1982 (formerly Star/Ship *Atlantic;* refurbished 1996)
Information:	(800) 666–9333
Web site:	www.msccruisesusa.com
Passenger capacity:	1,076 (double occupancy)
Crew:	535
Passenger-to-crew ratio:	2:1
Tonnage:	36,500
Passenger-space ratio:	33.9
Length:	671 feet
Beam:	90 feet
Draft:	25.5 feet
Cruising speed:	21 knots
Guest decks:	8
Total cabins:	627
Outside:	392
Inside:	157
Suites:	78
Wheelchair cabins:	4, but not up to modern standards for handicapped access
Cuisine:	Italian, international
Style:	Casual, with two or more semiformal evenings
Price notes:	Single-occupancy premium, 150 percent
Tipping suggestions:	$8.00 pp/pd
Best deals:	Advance-booking discounts

The **Melody** is a sturdy but undistinguished vessel that manages to pack a large number of guests onboard. There's a nice pool area with a retractable cover that allows use in any weather.

There are only three of the lowest-price staterooms on the ship, two on the bottommost Bahamas Deck and one on the Restaurant Deck. The most plentiful outside cabins are Class 8 staterooms, primarily on the Oceanic Deck, with some additional cabins scattered about the ship.

Monterey

Econoguide rating:	★★ 61 points
Ship size:	Medium
Category:	Vintage
Price range:	Budget $
Registry:	Panama
Year built:	1952 (formerly *Free State Mariner*; refurbished 1997)
Information:	(800) 666–9333
Web site:	www.msccruisesusa.com
Passenger capacity:	576 (double occupancy)

Crew:	200; Italian
Passenger-to-crew ratio:	2.9:1
Tonnage:	20,040
Passenger-space ratio:	34.8
Length:	563 feet
Beam:	80 feet
Draft:	29.5 feet
Cruising speed:	20 knots
Guest decks:	8
Total cabins:	294
Outside:	163
Inside:	127
Suites:	4
Cuisine:	Italian, international
Style:	Casual, with two or more semiformal evenings
Price notes:	Single-occupancy premium, 150 percent
Tipping suggestions:	$8.00 pp/pd
Best deals:	Advance-booking discounts

Monterey is a sturdy old ship, built as the fast freighter *Free State Mariner* during the Korean War. After the war, the ship was converted for use as a passenger liner, sailing for many years from the West Coast to Australia, New Zealand, and Hawaii. Although most cabins are relatively small and simple, there's a lot of space per passenger throughout.

Rhapsody

Econoguide rating:	★★★ 65 points
Ship size:	Medium
Category:	Vintage
Price range:	Budget $
Registry:	Panama
Year built:	1977 (formerly *Cunard Princess, Cunard Conquest*)
Information:	(800) 666–9333
Web site:	www.msccruisesusa.com
Passenger capacity:	768 (double occupancy)
Crew:	250; Italian
Passenger-to-crew ratio:	3:1
Tonnage:	16,852
Passenger-space ratio:	21.9
Length:	541 feet
Beam:	76 feet
Draft:	18.5 feet
Cruising speed:	19 knots

Guest decks:	8
Total cabins:	406
Outside:	257
Inside:	127
Suites:	22
Cuisine:	Italian, international
Style:	Casual, with two or more semiformal evenings
Price notes:	Single-occupancy premium, 150 percent
Tipping suggestions:	$8.00 pp/pd
Best deals:	Advance-booking discounts

A relatively simple ship, **Rhapsody** is one of the last two ships built for the original Cunard Line. The ship sailed mostly in the Caribbean from San Juan in her early years, moving on to the Mediterranean. During the Persian Gulf War she was chartered by the U.S. government to serve as a troop recreation vessel in Bahrain.

The cabins are on the small side. The ship underwent an $8 million renovation in 2004.

OCEANIA CRUISES

Address: 8120 Northwest 53rd Street
Miami, FL 33166
Information: (800) 531–5658, (305) 514–2300
www.oceaniacruises.com

The Oceania Cruises Fleet

Insignia	1997	680 passengers	30,277 tons
Regatta	1997	680 passengers	30,277 tons
Nautica	2000	680 passengers	30,277 tons

Renaissance Cruise Lines is dead, but some of its many fans now hope: "Long live Oceania."

Two of Renaissance's nearly identical sister ships, *R3* and *R4*, along with several former top executives of the bankrupt line, returned to service in mid-2003 and early 2004 with a new company. A third ship, the former *R5*, is due to join the fleet in May 2005. The elegant midsize vessels, which bridge the gap between the top end of the mass market and the ultraluxury cruise lines, have been spruced up a bit and their formerly black hulls repainted white—but former customers will recognize them immediately. (Two other former Renaissance ships are now in the fleet of Princess Cruises, and another now sails for Swan Hellenic, part of the P&O family.)

Aside from the appeal of the ships themselves, Renaissance also prided itself on its itineraries, which put the emphasis on extended port calls. In previous editions of *Econoguide Cruises,* we described the operation as providing a floating five-star hotel that delivers pampered guests from one spectacular destination to another, while delivering one of the best deals in the cruise industry.

▮ ITINERARIES

Regatta is due to begin 2005 sailing from Miami on January 2 through the Panama Canal to Los Angeles on a sixteen-day cruise, returning to Miami on a trip that departs January 18. After then, the ship will sail four round-trip cruises from Miami; the first two, on February 8 and 20, are twelve-day itineraries that head into the eastern Caribbean with stops in-

The formal central stairs of *Insignia. Photo by Corey Sandler*

cluding the Dominican Republic, Virgin Gorda, Nevis, Dominica, Saint Lucia, Antigua, and Saint Bart's. On March 4 the ship sails a fourteen-day trip westward in the Gulf of Mexico from Miami to ports including Cozumel, Mexico; Guatemala; Honduras; Puerto Limon, Costa Rica; a partial transit of the Panama Canal; Jamaica; and back to Miami. On March 18 the ship sails one last twelve-day cruise to the eastern Caribbean.

Regatta repositions to Europe with a twelve-day direct crossing from Miami on March 30, beginning with seven days at sea before making a call at Funchal in the Madeira Islands and then two more sailing days to Barcelona. Plans call for the ship to sail from Genoa, Barcelona, and Venice for cruises in the Mediterranean in April and mid-May.

From early June through the end of August, *Regatta* is due to sail in the Baltic from Stockholm or Dover. In September and October the ship returns to the western Mediterranean for sailings from Civitavecchia, Barcelona, and Venice. The ship is due to return to the Caribbean with a repositioning on November 5 from Barcelona to Miami.

In the fall of 2005 through the end of the year, *Regatta* will sail from Miami on trips to the eastern and western Caribbean.

Insignia sails in South America at the start of 2005. A fifteen-day cruise beginning January 3 takes the ship from Buenos Aires to Valparaiso; *Insignia* sails the return itinerary to Buenos Aires on January 18. The next cruise, February 2, is a twelve-day trip to Rio de Janeiro.

A fifteen-day cruise departs February 14 from Rio de Janeiro to Manaus; *Insignia* visits a number of Brazilian ports and makes an entrance into the Amazon River. On March 1, the ship heads north from Manaus to Bridgetown, Barbados, on a fourteen-day cruise that includes Brazilian ports; entrance into the Amazon River; Devil's Island, French Guiana; and the Orinoco River.

Insignia crosses the Atlantic beginning March 15 with a sixteen-day cruise from Bridgetown to Barcelona. Port calls include Antigua; Funchal, Madeira; Lisbon; Gibraltar; and Majorca.

Plans for the summer in Europe include cruises in the Mediterranean and the Greek Isles, sailing from ports including Barcelona, Piraeus, Civitavecchia, and Venice from April through mid-June. From mid-July through mid-August, the ship sails from Southampton on trips around the British Isles, the Baltic, and Norwegian fjords. *Insignia* returns to the Mediterranean at the end of August, continuing through the end of October with departures from Civitavecchia, Venice, and Barcelona.

The ship is due to return to the Caribbean in early November, with a sailing from Lisbon to Bridgetown. *Insignia* heads into South America in mid-November, from Bridgetown to Manaus. Other cruises at the end of the year include Manaus to Rio de Janeiro; Rio de Janeiro to Buenos Aires, and Buenos Aires to Valparaiso.

On most European itineraries, Oceania Cruises calls on a minimum of eight ports. In 2004 the initial schedule for *Regatta* included ten- to sixteen-day sailings from Barcelona to London (with stops in France, Portugal, and Majorca), London to Stockholm (including visits to Denmark, Estonia, Russia, and Finland); Barcelona to Venice, Barcelona to Istanbul, Istanbul to Rome, and Rome to Barcelona.

When *Nautica* joins the fleet in May 2005, it will begin service from Piraeus, sailing in the eastern Mediterranean and the Greek Isles on a twelve-day trip ending in Istanbul; the next cruise reverses the itinerary, ending in Piraeus at the end of the month. In early June the ship sails one more time in the Greek Isles, ending in Istanbul.

In mid-June the ship sails round-trip from Istanbul to eastern Europe with stops including Yalta, Sevastopol, and Odessa in Ukraine; Constanta in Romania; and Nessebur in Bulgaria. From late June through early July, *Nautica* includes visits to the Greek Isles and Croatia, ending in Venice on July 6.

A fifteen-day trip departs Venice on July 6 with visits to Sorrento, Amalfi, Civitavecchia (Rome), Livorno, and Portofino in Italy; Dubrovnik, Croatia; Bonifacio, Corsica; Monte Carlo; and Marseille before ending in Barcelona. On July 20 *Nautica* sails the reverse itinerary to Venice.

In early August, *Nautica* sails a fifteen-day itinerary from Venice to Istanbul, followed by a thirteen-day trip to Civitavecchia with stops in Turkey, Greece, and

Italy enroute. The ship reverses the itinerary at the end of August through mid-September, ending in Istanbul.

From September 10 through 22, *Nautica* will travel once again from Istanbul to Piraeus; a reverse itinerary ends in Istanbul in early October. The next two cruises, from early October through November 1 sail from Istanbul to Venice and return.

■ WEB SITE

Oceania's Web site includes all the basic information for researching the ships; the listing of itineraries is a bit difficult to use. Would-be travelers are asked to contact a travel agent to book passage. *Ease of use: good.*

Regatta, Insignia, Nautica

Econoguide rating:	★★★★ 81 points
Ship size:	Medium
Category:	Top of the Line
Price range:	Premium $$$
Registry:	Marshall Islands
Year built:	1997 (as *R3* and *R4;* refurbished 2003); 2000 (as *R5,* refurbished 2003)
Information:	(800) 531–5658
Web site:	www.oceaniacruises.com
Passenger capacity:	680
Crew:	373
Passenger-to-crew ratio:	1.8:1
Tonnage:	30,277
Passenger space ratio:	44.1
Length:	594 feet
Beam:	83.5 feet
Draft:	19.5 feet
Cruising speed:	18 knots
Guest decks:	9
Total cabins:	342
Outside:	317
Inside:	25
Suites:	10
Wheelchair cabins:	14
Cuisine:	International
Style:	Country club casual
Price notes:	Advance booking discounts
Tipping suggestions:	$10.50 pp/pd

The main restaurant on all three ships is the Grand Dining Room, offering continental cuisine designed by celebrity French chef Jacques Pepin.

Up top is a pair of intimate ninety-seat reservations-only restaurants: Toscana offers gourmet Italian fare; the Polo Grill serves beef, chops, and fresh seafood. (There is no extra charge for reservations.)

The Tides Cafe offers casual buffet breakfast or lunch. In the evening the same room is transformed into "Tapas at Tides" for cocktails, live entertainment, and a menu featuring a wide array of tapas and authentic dishes from Spain and around the world.

Oceania has upgraded the bedding, carpeting, and upholstery throughout the ships and added new teak decking on all 233 verandas.

Econoguide Ship Classifications

Gargantuan	130,000 or more tons
Colossus	100,000 to 130,000 tons
Megaship	70,000 to 100,000 tons
Large	40,000 to 70,000 tons
Medium	10,000 to 40,000 tons
Small	Less than 10,000 tons

CHAPTER SIXTEEN

ADVENTURE CRUISE LINES

♔♔♔ American Canadian
Caribbean Line
♔♔♔ American Cruise Lines
♔♔♔ Clipper Cruise Lines
♔♔♔ Cruise West
♔♔♔ Delta Queen Steamboat
Company

♔♔♔ Glacier Bay Cruise Line
♔♔♔ Lindblad Special
Expeditions
♔♔♔ RiverBarge Excursion Line
♔♔♔ Society Expeditions

AMERICAN CANADIAN CARIBBEAN LINE

AMERICAN
CANADIAN
CARIBBEAN
LINE, INC

Address: 461 Water Street
Warren, RI 02885
Information: (800) 556–7450
www.accl-smallships.com

♔ ♔ ♔

The American Canadian Caribbean Line Fleet

Grande Caribe	1997	100 passengers	761 tons
Grande Mariner	1998	100 passengers	781 tons
Niagara Prince	1994	84 passengers	687 tons

American Canadian Caribbean Line is a multinational name for a small but ambitious American-flagged cruise line. The line's three vessels sail a grand tour of the Americas, including the Mississippi, Great Lakes, Erie Canal, Newfoundland, and Labrador, as well as the Caribbean and Central America to ports including the Virgin Islands, Antigua, Nassau, Trinidad and Tobago, Panama, Venezuela, Belize, Guatemala, and Honduras. Another interesting itinerary travels from Rhode Island to Buffalo, through New York City and Albany, and across the Erie Canal.

Open Space on Small Ships

Many of the ships in this chapter do not have a passenger-space ratio listed; some use a different formula for calculating tonnage. In any case, smaller ships are usually configured differently from sprawling cruise ships, doing without open atriums and making multiple use of dining rooms, theaters, and outdoor areas.

The twin flagships of the line are the *Grande Mariner* and the *Grande Caribe,* each having a capacity of one hundred passengers. The third ship is the slightly smaller *Niagara Prince,* which carries eighty-four passengers.

■ THE ACCL STORY

ACCL was founded in 1966 by shipbuilder Luther Blount; all the vessels are constructed at Blount Industries in Warren, Rhode Island. The company is one of the last working shipyards in New England building midsize metal boats; it has produced more than 300 ships since it began in 1949. Blount finally retired in 2001 at the age of eighty-four and was succeeded by his daughter, Nancy.

One of the goals of ACCL is to explore smaller waterways and ports. The vessels are custom designed for that purpose, with shallow drafts and other features, such as bow ramps for easy unloading of passengers directly to shore, an innovative retractable pilot house that permits the ships to sail under low bridges on waterways such as the Erie Canal, and glass-bottom launches on most trips. According to the company, Blount "seeks out unusual places and then builds the ships to take us there."

Cabins and public areas are simple and functional. There's no room service, no frills, no glitz, and a bring-your-own-bottle bar policy. The company's emphasis is much more on the destinations sailed by its ships than on the ships themselves.

■ ITINERARIES

The ACCL fleet began 2004 in the Caribbean, sailing to the Virgin Islands, the Caicos, and the Bahamas in January and February.

Cruises from March to May included itineraries in Belize and Roatan, along the Intracoastal Waterway on the U.S. East Coast, and from New Orleans to Chicago. Later in the spring the ships expanded north to Baltimore to sail to Chesapeake Bay and Alexandria.

In June cruises began on the Erie Canal and the Saguenay River. Other summer cruises include visits to Lake Michigan, Lake Superior, the Finger Lakes, and New England islands. Erie Canal and fall foliage cruises begin in late September. Cruises on the Intracoastal Waterway return in November, setting the stage for a return to the Caribbean for the winter.

■ WEB SITE

ACCL's site provides only basic information and a clumsy listing of itineraries. There is no provision to check availability on-line. Visitors can request a callback from the cruise line for booking or can telephone directly. ***Ease of use: good.***

Grande Caribe

Econoguide rating:	★★ 60 points
Ship size:	Small
Category:	Adventure
Price range:	Premium $$$
Registry:	United States
Year built:	1997
Information:	(800) 556–7450, (401) 247–0955
Web site:	www.accl-smallships.com
Passenger capacity:	100 (double occupancy)
Crew:	17
Passenger-to-crew ratio:	6:1
Tonnage:	761
Length:	183 feet
Beam:	40 feet
Draft:	6.6 feet
Cruising speed:	10 knots
Guest decks:	3
Total cabins:	50
Outside:	50
Inside:	0
Suites:	0
Wheelchair cabins:	None indicated
Cuisine:	American
Style:	Always casual
Price notes:	Single-occupancy premium, 175 percent in certain cabin classifications; certain cabins on each vessel accommodate a third passenger at a 15 percent discount for each occupant
Tipping suggestions:	Gratuities are left to the discretion of guests

A comfortable soft-adventure ship, **Grande Caribe** has some special features that are well suited to small harbors and landings. The ship's small draft enables access to shallow rivers, canals, and waterways; a retractable pilot house allows ships to maneuver under low bridges and locks. By using its bow ramp, the ship can make its own landings on beaches and river banks.

ACCL brings along experts on wildlife, marine biology, flora and fauna, and local indigenous cultures. Like the other vessels in the ACCL fleet, this is a no-frills operation. You will not find room service, casinos, swimming pools, or formal dinners. One dining room on main deck accommodates all passengers for single-seating dining. The Vista View Lounge has a bring-your-own-bottle policy.

Grande Mariner

Econoguide rating:	★★ 60 points
Ship size:	Small
Category:	Adventure
Price range:	Premium $$$
Registry:	United States
Year built:	1998
Information:	(800) 556–7450, (401) 247–0955
Web site:	www.accl-smallships.com
Passenger capacity:	100 (double occupancy)
Crew:	17
Passenger-to-crew ratio:	6:1
Tonnage:	781
Length:	183 feet
Beam:	40 feet
Draft:	6.6 feet
Cruising speed:	10 knots
Guest decks:	3
Total cabins:	50
Outside:	50
Inside:	0
Suites:	0
Wheelchair cabins:	None indicated
Cuisine:	American
Style:	Always casual
Price notes:	Single-occupancy premium, 175 percent in certain cabin classifications; certain cabins on each vessel accommodate a third passenger at a 15 percent discount for each occupant
Tipping suggestions:	Gratuities are left to the discretion of guests

The **Grande Mariner**'s philosophy and set of offerings are similar to those of the *Grande Caribe*.

Niagara Prince

Econoguide rating:	★★ 60 points
Ship size:	Small
Category:	Adventure
Price range:	Premium $$$
Registry:	United States
Year built:	1994
Information:	(800) 556–7450, (401) 247–0955

Web site:	www.accl-smallships.com
Passenger capacity:	84 (double occupancy)
Crew:	17
Passenger-to-crew ratio:	5:1
Tonnage:	687
Length:	175 feet
Beam:	40 feet
Draft:	6.3 feet
Cruising speed:	10 knots
Guest decks:	3
Total cabins:	42
Outside:	42
Inside:	0
Suites:	0
Wheelchair cabins:	None indicated
Cuisine:	American
Style:	Always casual
Price notes:	Single-occupancy premium, 175 percent; certain cabins accommodate a third passenger at a 15 percent discount for each occupant
Tipping suggestions:	Gratuities are left to discretion of guests

The oldest, simplest, and most casual of the ACCL fleet, the **Niagara Prince** is still a favorite with passengers who find their entertainment as they move along.

AMERICAN CRUISE LINES

Address: One Marine Park
Haddam, CT 06438
Information: (860) 345–3311
www.americancruiselines.com

The American Cruise Lines Fleet

American Eagle	2000	49 passengers	1,200 tons
American Glory	2002	49 passengers	1,200 tons

FUTURE SHIPS

American Spirit	2005	92 passengers	1,900 tons

In June 2005 the company plans to add *American Spirit*, its largest vessel. The new ship will include fifty-two staterooms, some with private verandas.

American Eagle began her coastal cruiser career in April 2000, journeying up and down the eastern seaboard. Sister ship *American Glory* joined the fleet in July 2002.

ITINERARIES

The new *American Spirit* is due to begin service in June 2005 with a pair of Chesapeake Bay cruises from Baltimore. For the summer the ship will sail to New England islands from New London, Connecticut. In October 2005 *Spirit* is due to return to Baltimore and sail a series of Inland Passage cruises from Norfolk, Virginia, and Charleston, South Carolina. In December the ship is scheduled to sail from Jacksonville, Florida, on river cruises.

American Eagle begins 2005 sailing from Jacksonville and Fort Myers, Florida, on Okeechobee and southern waterways, moving on to alternating Jacksonville and Charleston, South Carolina, for Antebellum South cruises from March through May. From mid-May through mid-June, *Eagle* is due to sail Chesapeake Bay cruises from Baltimore, and then move to New London for New England Island cruises that continue until the end of September. In October the ship reverses direction and heads to Baltimore for a month, and then from mid-November to the end of the year sails from Charleston, Jacksonville, and Fort Myers.

American Glory's 2005 schedule begins in Jacksonville through mid-March, adding round-trips from Jacksonville and Charleston from April through the end of May. After a pair of cruises in the Chesapeake Bay from Baltimore in June, *American Glory* moves north to Bangor, Maine, to sail a summer of coastal itineraries including visits to Bar Harbor, Rockland, Bath, and Belfast, Maine. In October the ship heads south to New London for Hudson River fall foliage cruises, and then works its way down through Baltimore to conclude the year sailing from Jacksonville and Charleston.

WEB SITE

Basic information on the ships and itineraries of the line is presented on the Web site. Visitors must call the cruise line or a travel agent to book a trip. There is no provision to check availability on-line. ***Ease of use: good.***

American Spirit

Econoguide rating:	★★ 60 points
Ship size:	Small
Category:	Adventure
Price range:	Premium $$$
Registry:	United States
Year built:	2005
Information:	(860) 345–3311
Web site:	www.americancruiselines.com
Passenger capacity:	92 (double occupancy)
Crew:	32
Passenger-to-crew ratio:	2.9:1

Tonnage:	1,900
Passenger-space ratio:	20.7
Length:	220 feet
Beam:	52 feet
Draft:	7 feet
Cruising speed:	14 knots
Guest decks:	3 passenger decks, 1 sundeck
Total cabins:	53
Outside:	53
Inside:	0
Suites:	0
Wheelchair cabins:	1
Cuisine:	American
Style:	Casual
Tipping suggestions:	$14.25 pp/pd
Best deal:	Savings up to $400 for bookings five months or more in advance

American Eagle, American Glory

Econoguide rating:	★★ 50 points
Ship size:	Small
Category:	Adventure
Price range:	Premium $$$
Registry:	United States
Year built:	*American Eagle,* 2000; *American Glory,* 2002
Information:	(860) 345–3311
Web site:	www.americancruiselines.com
Passenger capacity:	49 (double occupancy)
Crew:	22
Passenger-to-crew ratio:	2.2:1
Tonnage:	1,200
Passenger-space ratio:	24.5
Length:	*American Eagle,* 162 feet; *American Glory,* 168 feet
Beam:	*American Eagle,* 39 feet; *American Glory,* 43 feet
Draft:	7 feet
Cruising speed:	11 knots
Guest decks:	3 passenger decks, 1 sundeck
Total cabins:	31
Outside:	31
Inside:	0
Suites:	1
Wheelchair cabins:	0

Cuisine:	American
Style:	Casual
Tipping suggestions:	$14.25 pp/pd
Best deal:	Savings up to $1,000 for bookings five months or more in advance

Each of American Cruise Lines' young sister ships has thirty-one outside cabins. The newer **American Glory** offers fourteen staterooms with private balconies; **American Eagle** has six with balconies. Both have a glass-enclosed dining room that accommodates all passengers in one seating.

CLIPPER CRUISE LINE

❖ *CLIPPER*

Address: 11969 Westline Industrial Drive
Saint Louis, MO 63146
Information: (800) 325–0010, (314) 727–2929
www.clippercruise.com

The Clipper Cruise Line Fleet

Clipper Adventurer	1975	122 passengers	4,364 tons
Clipper Odyssey	1989	120 passengers	5,050 tons
Nantucket Clipper	1984	102 passengers	1,471 tons
Yorktown Clipper	1988	138 passengers	2,354 tons

The Clipper ships emphasize expeditions to unusual destinations; there are no casinos, Las Vegas–type shows, or glitzy gift shops aboard. The accommodations and public rooms are comfortable but hardly posh.

The small ships travel to places as diverse as the hidden fjords of Alaska, Caribbean coves, the Intracoastal Waterway of the U.S. South, the coast of New England, the Guadalquivir River of Spain, and the icescapes of Antarctica.

The line's two U.S.-flagged ships, the *Nantucket Clipper* and the *Yorktown Clipper,* were designed with shallow drafts and easy maneuverability for coastal trips along the mainland United States, Alaska, Canada, Mexico, the Caribbean, and Central and South America.

The *Clipper Adventurer* was built in 1975 as the Russian research vessel *Alla Tarasova;* it has a hardened hull that allows her to navigate in rugged natural environments, including ice fields. It was completely converted in 1998 for use as a small oceangoing cruise ship, with a remake of all of the cabins and public rooms; stabilizers were added later in the year. She includes a fleet of ten Zodiac landing craft.

■ ITINERARIES

The company's ships sail to nearly every corner of the world; gaps in the schedule represent private charters or scheduled dry dock or refurbishment stops.

In 2005 the *Nantucket Clipper* sails through the Antebellum South along the Intracoastal Waterway on six cruises between mid-March and the end of April, alternating home ports of Jacksonville, Florida, and Charleston, South Carolina. On April 24 the ship begins to work its way north, sailing from Savannah, Georgia, to Alexandria, Virginia, with ports of call including Charleston; Norfolk and Richmond, Virginia; and Baltimore.

A May 4 departure takes the ship from Alexandria to New York, with calls including Annapolis and Baltimore. Beginning May 11 the ship sails four week-long round-trips from New York up the Hudson River with calls at Kingston, Troy, West Point, and Yonkers in New York. On June 8 *Nantucket Clipper* begins trips in Canada; the first eight-day trip from New York includes stops in Newport, Rhode Island; Vineyard Haven and Nantucket, Massachusetts; Bar Harbor, Maine; and ends in Halifax, Nova Scotia. A repositioning cruise takes the ship from Halifax to Quebec City by way of Prince Edward Island and the Saint Lawrence River. Three subsequent cruises sail in the Saint Lawrence and the Great Lakes from Quebec City to Montreal, the Thousand Islands; Kingston, Toronto; the Welland Canal; and Buffalo.

For the next month, from July 21 through mid-August, *Nantucket Clipper* follows the route of the traders in Lake Huron and Georgian Bay, with week-long cruises between Buffalo and Sault Sainte Marie. On August 18 the ship sails from Buffalo to Quebec City.

On September 7, 2005, *Nantucket Clipper* begins to head south, traveling from Halifax to New York on a fifteen-day itinerary with stops including Campobello Island, Saint Andrews, and Bar Harbor in Maine; Boston, Nantucket, and Martha's Vineyard in Massachusetts; and Newport, Rhode Island. Two week-long trips from New York to New England follow; on October 5 and 12 the ship sails a pair of trips up the Hudson River from New York.

An autumn tour begins on October 19 in New York, heading north up the Hudson River as far as West Point and then heading south to Annapolis, Norfolk, and Alexandria, Virginia. From there, on October 29, *Nantucket Clipper* begins a series of Intracoastal Waterway cruises, sailing first from Alexandria to Jacksonville, Florida, and then making a series of cruises in the Antebellum South, alternating between home ports of Jacksonville and Charleston through the end of November.

The *Yorktown Clipper* begins 2005 sailing in the "yachtsman's" Caribbean, round-trip from Saint Thomas with stops in Jost van Dyke, Tortola, Virgin Gorda, Salt Island, Norman Island, and Saint John. At the end of January and again in early February, the ship sails along the coast of Central America with ports of call including Belize City, Cocoa Plum Cay, Lime Cay, Puerto Barrios, Rio Dulce, Roatan Island, Utila, and Puerto Cortes.

From February 23 through March 23, the ship sails four trips along the Mexican Coast of Baja California and the Sea of Cortez on whale-watching expeditions. Beginning April 12, *Yorktown Clipper* sails six California wine and cuisine cruises with ports of call including Redwood City, Sausalito, Vallejo, and San Francisco.

On May 16 the ship heads north to sail from Seattle to Juneau with calls at

Victoria, Nanaimo, and Vancouver, British Columbia; and Alaskan ports including Misty Fjords, Ketchikan, Petersburg, Glacier Bay National Park, Sitka, and Tracy Arm. After then the vessel sails a series of fifteen week-long cruises from Juneau to the fjords and glaciers of Alaska's Inside Passage.

At the end of the summer, *Yorktown Clipper* sails three week-long cruises between Seattle and Vancouver with stops at some of the obscure, undeveloped islands and ports in the area. The ship repeats the California wine and cuisine cruises with four six-day cruises beginning October 16.

From November 17 through December 1, the ship sails eight-day cruises in Costa Rica and Panama, including a transit of the canal. The ship returns to the yachtman's Caribbean on December 15 for a series of cruises from Saint Thomas.

Clipper Adventurer begins 2005 with three cruises to Antarctica and the Falkland Islands; the seventeen-day trips include calls at Port Stanley, Carcass Island, West Point Island, Antarctic Peninsula, the Drake Passage, Ushuaia, and Buenos Aires. On March 16 and 30, the ship sails fifteen-day trips into some of the jungle rivers of South America, with visits to the Port of Spain, Orinoco River, Essequibo River, Suriname River, Paramaribo, Amazon River, and Belem.

After a repositioning to Europe, *Clipper Adventurer* sails an unusual pair of trips on May 7 and 17 from Lisbon into northern Africa, with calls including Tangier, Morocco; Tunis and Sousse, Tunisia; Tripoli and Leptis Magna in Libya; and Valetta, Malta. Beginning May 27 the ship sails three trips on the route of the old wine traders in Portugal, Spain, and France, between Lisbon and Bordeaux.

The ship moves on to the United Kingdom beginning June 17, sailing from Bordeaux stopping at a number of medieval French seaports before crossing the English Channel to Portsmouth and London. On June 24 the ship sails from London around the United Kingdom to Dublin, with port calls including Portsmouth, Penzance, Tresco, Cork, Waterford, Fishguard, and Holyhead. The next two cruises, on July 1 and 8, sail between Dublin and Greenock, Scotland.

Clipper Adventurer begins its repositioning to North America with a thirteen-day cruise from Dublin to Reykjavik on July 17, with calls including Portrush and Giant's Causeway in Northern Ireland and Dunvegan/Isle of Skye, Stornoway, Handa Island, Kirkwall, Torshavn, Mykines, Hofn, Heimaey, and Surtsey in Scotland. The ship continues on to eastern Greenland on July 27. After then it sails a seventeen-day exploration of Greenland; on August 10, the ship cruises Iceland and then continues on to Ottawa, Canada.

The ship sails round-trip from Ottawa beginning August 24, visiting Greenland and Baffin Island. On September 7 *Clipper Adventurer* sails from Ottawa to Newfoundland, Labrador, and Nova Scotia, ending in Halifax. The next cruise, September 18, continues south from Halifax to Charleston, with calls including Boston, Newport, New York, Philadelphia, Baltimore, and Norfolk.

On October 5 the ship returns to Central America for a cruise that includes Mexico's Yucatan, Belize, Costa Rica, and the Panama Canal. On November 9 the ship returns to South America for a series of trips to Antarctica and the Falkland Islands.

Clipper Odyssey begins 2005 with a series of explorations of New Zealand's North and South Islands. On February 7 the ship sails from Auckland, New Zealand, to Sydney, Australia, on a seventeen-day trip that includes visits to some of the less-visited ports and islands of both countries.

On March 28 the ship sails from Sydney to some of the sites of bloody battles and events of World War II in the South Pacific, including Port Moresby, Guadalcanal, Purvis Bay, Tokyo Bay, Gavutu, Tulagi, Savo Island, Viru Harbor (New Georgia), Lubaria Island (Renoova), Kennedy Island, Vella Lavela Island, Rabaul (New Britain), Admiralty Island, and Apra (Guam).

An April 30 cruise calls at ports in Japan and South Korea. After a scheduled dry dock, the ship sets sail for Alaska's Outer Islands and Russia on July 7 and 19, with ports of call including Anchorage, Nome, Little and Big Diomede Island, Cape Dezhnev, Lorino Village, Itygram, Campbell, Hall Island, Saint Matthew Island, Saint Paul Island, Saint George Island, Dutch Harbor, Baby Island, Unga Island, Semidi Island, Geographic Harbor, Kodiak Island, and Homer.

On July 31 the ship travels from Northwest Alaska to Russia's Kamchatka Peninsula, returning to Anchorage; the next cruise, on August 11, heads into a different set of isolated islands, ending up in Japan. A fifteen-day cruise beginning August 23 travels from Japan to Hong Kong and Vietnam, ending in Hanoi; two subsequent cruises on September 2 and 12 sail round-trip from Hanoi to ports in Vietnam including Haiphong, Cat Ba Island, Vinh Moc, Cua Thaunan, Da Nang, Gui Nhon, Port Dayot, Nha Trang, and Ho Chi Minh City.

On November 1 the ship sails in the South Pacific, crossing the Coral Sea and visiting Sydney en route to Melbourne, Australia. *Clipper Odyssey* returns to New Zealand for a circle of the two major islands beginning November 27 and December 22, 2005.

▮ THE CLIPPER STORY

Clipper Cruise Line was founded in 1982 in Saint Louis. In 1996 Clipper was purchased by Intrav, a deluxe-tour operator that was a sister company. In 1999 Clipper and Intrav were, in turn, purchased by a Swiss company, Kuoni Travel Holding Ltd.

All of Clipper's voyages feature guest speakers, including naturalists, historians, and other experts. On cruises through the South, a Civil War historian gives lectures. On Alaskan cruises, guests are accompanied by a park ranger and naturalist.

▮ WEB SITE

The Web site presents basic information about the cruise line and itineraries. There is no on-line provision to check availability. Visitors can either request a callback to book a cruise or go through a travel agent. *Ease of use: good.*

Clipper Adventurer

Econoguide rating:	★★ 64 points
Ship size:	Small
Category:	Adventure
Price range:	Premium $$$
Registry:	Bahamas
Year built:	1991 (formerly Russian research vessel *Alla Tarasova;* rebuilt 1997–98)
Information:	(800) 325–0010
Web site:	www.clippercruise.com
Passenger capacity:	122 (double occupancy)
Crew:	72
Passenger-to-crew ratio:	1.7:1
Tonnage:	4,364
Passenger-space ratio:	35.8
Length:	330 feet
Beam:	53.5 feet
Draft:	16 feet
Cruising speed:	14 knots
Guest decks:	4
Total cabins:	61
Outside:	61
Inside:	0
Suites:	3
Cuisine:	American regional
Style:	Casual and comfortable; no formal clothing or evening wear required
Price notes:	Single-occupancy premium, approximately 150 percent
Tipping suggestions:	$9.00 pp/pd

A relatively new vessel, especially after its 1998 conversion from its former life as a Russian research ship, the *Clipper Adventurer* in some ways harks back in style to the heyday of the steamship era in the 1930s and 1940s.

Public rooms are small and clublike, including the Clipper Club and Bar, and an intimate library/card room. The ship includes a covered promenade, sheltered from the weather. The windowed dining room accommodates all passengers at a single seating. The Main Lounge and Bar will accommodate a full passenger load.

I toured the ship soon after her arrival in America when she set anchor outside the harbor of Nantucket Island. Most of her load of passengers clambered onto the ship's ten Zodiacs for a choppy ride through October seas into town; others stayed onboard to listen to a lecture by a local artist. The bridge was open to visitors.

An important part of the entertainment is educational: Historians, naturalists, and other experts are often on the cruises or come aboard in port. They replace variety shows and bingo. There's no gambling and no disco, and there are no television sets in the staterooms.

The cabins and public rooms are airy and well appointed with Scandinavian furnishings. An attractive dining room has windows on three sides.

In March 2002 the ship, with 118 passengers aboard, ran aground on a sandbank in the Essequibo River in Guyana. No injuries were reported, and the ship was freed several days later. *Clipper Adventurer* was on a tour to Brazil, French Guiana, and Suriname.

Clipper Odyssey

Econoguide rating:	★★★★ 80 points
Ship size:	Small
Category:	Adventure
Price range:	Premium $$$
Registry:	Bahamas
Year built:	1989
Information:	(800) 325–0010
Web site:	www.clippercruise.com
Passenger capacity:	128 (double occupancy)
Crew:	72
Passenger-to-crew ratio:	1.8:1
Tonnage:	5,218
Passenger-space ratio:	40.8
Length:	338 feet
Beam:	51 feet
Draft:	15 feet
Cruising speed:	15 knots
Guest decks:	5
Total cabins:	64
Outside:	64
Inside:	1
Suites:	1
Wheelchair cabins:	None listed
Cuisine:	American regional
Style:	Casual and comfortable; no formal clothing or evening wear required
Price notes:	Single-occupancy premium, approximately 150 percent
Tipping suggestions:	$9.00 pp/pd

The *Clipper Odyssey* was built in Japan to the specifications of a master Dutch yacht designer specifically for year-round itineraries in the Pacific that range from New Zealand and Australia's Great Barrier Reef to Japan, the Kuril Islands, and the Russian Far East, including the Kamchatka Peninsula.

Unusual for a smaller ship, amenities include an outdoor swimming pool, dedicated jogging track, and two sundecks.

Nantucket Clipper

Econoguide rating:	★★★ 67 points
Ship size:	Small
Category:	Adventure
Price range:	Premium $$$
Registry:	United States
Year built:	1984
Information:	(800) 325–0010
Web site:	www.clippercruise.com
Passenger capacity:	102 (double occupancy)
Crew:	32
Passenger-to-crew ratio:	3.2:1
Tonnage:	1,471
Length:	207 feet

Clipper Cruise Line's *Nantucket Clipper. Photo by Wolfgang Kaehler, courtesy of Clipper Cruise Line*

Beam:	37 feet
Draft:	8 feet
Cruising speed:	8 knots
Guest decks:	4
Total cabins:	51
Outside:	51
Inside:	0
Suites:	0
Wheelchair cabins:	0
Cuisine:	American
Style:	Casual and comfortable; no formal clothing or evening wear required
Price notes:	Single-occupancy premium, 150 percent of category 2
Tipping suggestions:	$9.00 pp/pd

Nantucket Clipper is a basic small ship for a cruise line that focuses more on ports of call and sights along the way than on interior flash. Historians, naturalists, and other experts often are on the cruises, replacing variety shows, disco dancing, bingo, and gambling. In some ports, local musicians or artisans come aboard.

The young chefs are recruited from the Culinary Institute of America in upstate New York; the cabin and restaurant staff are bright-faced young (mostly) Americans who serve with casual friendliness.

Yorktown Clipper

Econoguide rating:	★★★ 68 points
Ship size:	Small
Category:	Adventure
Price range:	Premium $$$
Registry:	United States
Year built:	1988
Information:	(800) 325–0010
Web site:	www.clippercruise.com
Passenger capacity:	138 (double occupancy)
Crew:	40
Passenger-to-crew ratio:	3.4:1
Tonnage:	2,354
Length:	257 feet
Beam:	43 feet
Draft:	8 feet
Cruising speed:	10 knots
Guest decks:	4
Total cabins:	69

Outside:	69
Inside:	0
Suites:	0
Wheelchair cabins:	0
Cuisine:	American regional
Style:	Casual and comfortable; no formal clothing or evening wear required
Price notes:	Single-occupancy premium, 150 percent
Tipping suggestions:	$9.00 pp/pd

The **Yorktown Clipper** provides a relaxed country-club atmosphere on an unpretentious small ship. The excitement comes from the ports of call and waterways. Again, historians, naturalists, and other experts often are on the cruises, and local musicians, artisans, and representatives come aboard in some ports.

CRUISE WEST

Address: 2401 Fourth Avenue, Suite 700
  Seattle, WA 98121
Information: (800) 426–7702
  www.cruisewest.com

The Cruise West Fleet

Spirit of Oceanus	1990	114 passengers	4,200 tons
Spirit of '98	1984	96 passengers	1,472 tons
Spirit of Alaska	1980	78 passengers	529 tons
Spirit of Columbia	1979	78 passengers	514 tons
Spirit of Discovery	1976	84 passengers	910 tons
Spirit of Endeavour	1983	102 passengers	1,425 tons
Pacific Explorer	1995	100 passengers	438 tons

Chuck West, a World War II pilot who returned home to start a bush flying service in Alaska, founded a small cruise company that eventually became Westours. That company was sold to Holland America Line, and he later began Alaska Sightseeing/Cruise West.

The company began with day cruises in the Inside Passage and by 1990 had added overnight cruises on the *Spirit of Glacier Bay.* In 1991 the company introduced cruises from Seattle to Alaska, restoring a long-suspended U.S.-flagged route.

Today the company is run by West's son and has seven small cruise ships. It has a legitimate claim to knowing Alaska from the insider's point of view, and the small vessels allow guests to get up close and personal with whales and other aquatic life and the occasional bear on shore.

ITINERARIES

Cruise West ships are small enough to be allowed unrestricted access to Glacier Bay; larger vessels must vie for a limited number of permits. As American-flagged vessels, they can sail from Seattle to Alaska without making a stop in Canada.

Other journeys include Tracy Arm for an up-close visit with South Sawyer Glacier, LeConte Bay, and narrow inlets off Glacier Bay. The line claims it has the only ships that regularly sail through Wrangell Narrows, rarely visited El Capitan, and Sea Otter Sound.

The company's longer tours—fourteen to nineteen days—begin in Fairbanks or Anchorage and include rail, bus, and boat tours in central Alaska, then a flight to Juneau for a five-day cruise in the southeast portion of the state.

Alaska itineraries generally run from about April through October, after which time the ships migrate south to California and down to Mexico for explorations of Baja California. California trips include San Francisco to the Napa-Carneros-Sonoma wine region and a visit to Old Sacramento.

In recent winters, the company has based the *Spirit of Endeavour* in Cabo San Lucas to explore the Sea of Cortés in Mexico, home to many species of wildlife, including visits to remote desert beaches. Available shore excursions include a visit to Copper Canyon with a trip on the South Orient Express; the railroad, which took almost a century to build, travels from sea level to almost 8,000 feet, across thirty-six bridges and through eighty-six tunnels, including a 360-degree spiral through a mile-long tunnel.

THE CRUISE WEST EXPERIENCE

Four vessels have bow landing platforms, permitting the ships to offload passengers in many locations without having to use tenders. (This harks back to the stern-wheeler riverboats of the American heartland.)

Passengers are generally permitted to visit the bridge while the ships are under way, which allows guests to chat with the captain and consult charts and radar screens.

The dining room emphasizes the cuisine of the Pacific Northwest. Orders for dinner entrees are often taken the night before the meal; special requests can often be met.

These are decidedly casual cruises, with an open seating for meals and little in the way of entertainment—except for the spectacular passing scenery. And aside from your cabin, there are not many quiet hideaways away from the other guests. When the ship overnights in a port, the concierge will make dinner reservations and provide transportation to shore points.

One interesting plus on some Cruise West trips: a Kodak Ambassador to assist guests in getting the perfect photo. The ambassadors are retired photo professionals with a wide range of technical backgrounds.

Cruise West has introduced a program that reduces the cost of single supplements; the plan guarantees double-occupancy rates for single cruise guests who agree to share a cabin with another single traveler. If a roommate is unavailable, there is no extra charge for a single cabin.

And if your vacation time is very flexible–able to travel with about thirty days notice—you can sign up for a "stowaway" fare with a 25 percent discount. Would-be travelers make a deposit for an itinerary and stateroom category within a particular time window and are notified if your offer has been accepted with at least thirty days advance notice.

■ WEB SITE

The Web site presents basic information about the cruise line and itineraries. There is no on-line provision to check availability. Visitors can either request a callback to book a cruise or go through a travel agent. *Ease of use: good.*

Spirit of Oceanus

Econoguide rating:	★★★ 67 points
Ship size:	Small
Category:	Adventure
Price range:	Opulent $$$$
Registry:	Bahamas
Year built:	1990 (formerly *Megastar Sagittarius, Renaissance V*)
Information:	(800) 426–7702
Web site:	www.cruisewest.com
Passenger capacity:	114 (double occupancy)
Crew:	65
Passenger-to-crew ratio:	1.75:1
Tonnage:	1,263
Length:	295 feet
Beam:	50 feet
Draft:	13 feet
Cruising speed:	15.5 knots
Guest decks:	5
Total cabins:	57
Outside:	57
Inside:	0
Suites:	0
Wheelchair cabins:	None indicated
Cuisine:	Regional American
Style:	Casual
Price notes:	Single supplement, 125 to 175 percent
Tipping suggestions:	$10 pp/pd
Best deal:	Early-booking discount

Launched in 1990, **Spirit of Oceanus** has fifty-seven oversize staterooms ranging in size from 215 to 353 square feet, as much as twice the size of standard cabins on other ships. Twelve cabins have private teak verandas.

The ship, originally built for Star Cruises, sailed as *Megastar Sagittarius* and was later renamed *Renaissance V* for upscale Renaissance Cruises. *Spirit of Oceanus* splits its time between Alaska in summer and the South Pacific in winter, with forays into Asia between seasons.

Renovations by Cruise West included the removal of the casino and hair salon; both have been replaced with more public and lounge space. The ship flies the Bahamas flag and has a predominantly foreign crew.

Spirit of '98

Econoguide rating:	★★ 56 points
Ship size:	Small
Category:	Adventure
Price range:	Opulent $$$$
Registry:	United States
Year built:	1984 (formerly *Pilgrim Belle, Colonial Explorer,* and *Victorian Empress*; refurbished 1995)
Information:	(800) 426–7702
Web site:	www.cruisewest.com
Passenger capacity:	96 (double occupancy)
Crew:	26
Passenger-to-crew ratio:	3.7:1
Tonnage:	96
Length:	192 feet
Beam:	40 feet
Draft:	9.3 feet
Cruising speed:	13 knots
Guest decks:	4
Total cabins:	49
Outside:	48
Inside:	0
Suites:	1
Wheelchair cabins:	1
Cuisine:	Regional American; single, open seating
Style:	Casual
Price notes:	Two single cabins available, 125 to 175 percent supplement
Tipping suggestions:	$10 pp/pd
Best deal:	Early-booking discount

A modern-day re-creation of a Victorian-era riverboat, with nice attention to detail, the **Spirit of '98** was built to resemble old-time coastal cruising vessels; her Gay Nineties interior includes carved cabinetry, etched glass, and plush upholstery.

The *Spirit of '98* travels the Inside Passage between Seattle and Juneau in the summer, moving to the California Wine Country in the fall. In 1997 the ship helped lead a centennial celebration of the Klondike Gold Rush.

In the summer of 1999 the *Spirit of '98* suffered an unpleasant encounter with a rock about 16 miles into Tracy Arm in Alaska's Inside Passage. There were no reports of injuries or fuel spills, and all ninety-three passengers were transferred to another boat by inflatable rafts. The ship was about 100 yards from shore in the passage when it struck the rock and began taking on water. Some of the ship's crew members remained aboard to operate pumps, and with the aid of the U.S. Coast Guard and another cruise ship, the *Regal Princess,* the flooding was controlled and the ship was rescued.

Spirit of Alaska

Econoguide rating:	★★ 52 points
Ship size:	Small
Category:	Adventure
Price range:	Opulent $$$$
Registry:	United States
Year built:	1980 (formerly *Pacific Northwest Explorer*)
Information:	(800) 426–7702
Web site:	www.cruisewest.com
Passenger capacity:	78 (double occupancy)
Crew:	21
Passenger-to-crew ratio:	3.7:1
Tonnage:	97
Length:	143 feet
Beam:	28 feet
Draft:	7.5 feet
Cruising speed:	12 knots
Guest decks:	4
Total cabins:	39
Outside:	27
Inside:	12
Suites:	3
Wheelchair cabins:	0
Cuisine:	American; single, open seating
Style:	Casual
Tipping suggestions:	$10 pp/pd
Best deal:	Early-booking discount

The **Spirit of Alaska** cruises Prince William Sound in summer and the Columbia and Snake Rivers in spring and fall. Guests are accommodated in staterooms that range from lower-deck inside cabins that have two single beds to upper-deck cabins that have double beds or two single beds, as well as windows. *Spirit of Alaska* is the near-twin sister to the *Spirit of Columbia.*

Spirit of Columbia

Econoguide rating:	★★ 52 points
Ship size:	Small
Category:	Adventure
Price range:	Opulent $$$$
Registry:	United States
Year built:	1979 (formerly *New Shoreham II*; refurbished 1995)
Information:	(800) 426–7702
Web site:	www.cruisewest.com
Passenger capacity:	78 (double occupancy)
Crew:	21
Passenger-to-crew ratio:	3.7:1
Tonnage:	98
Length:	143 feet
Beam:	28 feet
Draft:	6.5 feet
Cruising speed:	9 knots
Guest decks:	3
Total cabins:	38
Outside:	27
Inside:	11
Suites:	4
Wheelchair cabins:	0
Cuisine:	American; single, open seating
Style:	Casual
Tipping suggestions:	$10 pp/pd
Best deal:	Early-booking discount

The **Spirit of Columbia** sails weekly in the summer between Ketchikan and Juneau. In spring and fall, the ship cruises Canada's Inside Passage round-trip from Seattle.

The ship, sister to the *Spirit of Alaska*, carries seventy-eight guests.

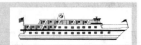

Spirit of Discovery

Econoguide rating:	★★ 52 points
Ship size:	Small
Category:	Adventure
Price range:	Opulent $$$$
Registry:	United States
Year built:	1976 (formerly *Independence, Columbia*; refurbished 1992)

Information:	(800) 426–7702
Web site:	www.cruisewest.com
Passenger capacity:	84 (double occupancy)
Crew:	21
Passenger-to-crew ratio:	4:1
Tonnage:	94
Length:	166 feet
Beam:	37 feet
Draft:	7.5 feet
Cruising speed:	13 knots
Guest decks:	3
Total cabins:	43
Outside:	43
Inside:	0
Suites:	0
Wheelchair cabins:	0
Cuisine:	American; single, open seating
Style:	Casual
Price notes:	Two single cabins available, 125 to 175 percent premium
Tipping suggestions:	$10 pp/pd
Best deal:	Early-booking discount

The *Spirit of Discovery* sails within Alaska between Ketchikan and Juneau in summer and in fall cruises the Columbia and Snake Rivers.

Spirit of Endeavour

Econoguide rating:	★★ 52 points
Ship size:	Small
Category:	Adventure
Price range:	Opulent $$$$
Registry:	United States
Year built:	1983 (formerly *Newport Clipper, Sea Spirit*; refurbished 1996, 1999)
Information:	(800) 426–7702
Web site:	www.cruisewest.com
Passenger capacity:	102 (double occupancy)
Crew:	28
Passenger-to-crew ratio:	3.6:1
Tonnage:	95
Length:	217 feet
Beam:	37 feet
Draft:	8.5 feet
Cruising speed:	12 knots
Guest decks:	4

Total cabins:	51
Outside:	51
Inside:	0
Suites:	0
Wheelchair cabins:	0
Cuisine:	American; single, open seating
Style:	Casual
Price notes:	Single supplement, 125 to 175 percent
Tipping suggestions:	$10 pp/pd
Best deal:	Early-booking discount

The *Spirit of Endeavour* cruises the Inside Passage between Seattle and Juneau in summer, moving to California Wine Country in fall, and on to Baja Mexico's Sea of Cortés in winter.

Pacific Explorer

Econoguide rating:	★★ 53 points
Ship size:	Small
Category:	Adventure
Price range:	Premium $$$
Registry:	Panama
Year built:	1995 (as *Temptress Explorer*); remodeled 1998
Information:	(800) 426–7702
Web site:	www.cruisewest.com
Passenger capacity:	100 (double occupancy)
Crew:	25; Costa Rican
Passenger-to-crew ratio:	4:1
Tonnage:	438
Length:	185 feet
Beam:	40 feet
Draft:	12.5 feet
Cruising speed:	12 knots
Guest decks:	4
Total cabins:	50
Outside:	50
Inside:	0
Suites:	4
Wheelchair cabins:	0
Cuisine:	International; with Central American specialties
Style:	Casual
Price notes:	Single cabins, 125 to 175 percent premium
Tipping suggestions:	$10 pp/pd
Best deal:	Early-booking discount

The neat *Pacific Explorer* looks like a pocket version of a major cruise ship, with fifty outside cabins and an open top deck for sightseeing. The ship visits Panama, Belize, Honduras, Guatemala, and Costa Rica year-round.

DELTA QUEEN STEAMBOAT COMPANY

THE DELTA QUEEN STEAMBOAT CO.

Address: Robin Street Wharf
1380 Port of New Orleans Place
New Orleans, LA 70130-1890
Information: (800) 543–1949
www.deltaqueen.com
Econoguide's Best Adventure Cruise Lines

The Delta Queen Steamboat Fleet

American Queen	1995	436 passengers	3,707 tons
Delta Queen	1927	174 passengers	3,360 tons
Mississippi Queen	1976, refurbished 1996	414 passengers	3,364 tons

The Delta Queen Steamboat Company, the oldest U.S. flag cruise line, returned to the rivers of America in summer 2002, a season after it went aground when an overly ambitious expansion program foundered.

New owner Delaware North Companies bought the company in a bankruptcy sale and has returned its three ships—the *Delta Queen,* the *Mississippi Queen,* and the *American Queen*—to year-round schedules on the rivers of America.

American Classic Voyages Company, the former parent company of the Delta Queen Steamboat Company, had attempted to expand in three other directions in 2001: American Hawaii Cruises, operating the *Independence* and the *Patriot* (the reflagged *Nieuw Amsterdam* of Holland) on cruises in Hawaii; the new Delta Queen Coastal Voyages, which built a pair of small coastwise packet boats, the *Cape Cod Light* and the *Cape May Light;* and the new United States Line, which commissioned the first new American-built cruise ships in forty years—a pair of 1,900-passenger, 72,000-ton ships, one of which was about half-finished when the company went under.

Delaware North, a hospitality and food service provider, is one of the largest privately held companies in the United States with more than $1.6 billion in annual revenue.

■ THE DELTA QUEEN STEAMBOAT COMPANY STORY

The cruise line traces its lineage back to 1890 when a young riverboat captain bought his first paddle wheeler. The fleet, founded by Captain Gordon Greene and his wife, Mary Becker Greene, also a licensed steamboat captain, eventually included thirty boats.

The flagship of the current fleet is the *Delta Queen,* a National Historic Landmark. She was launched in 1927, built with the finest woods available, including teak, oak, birch, and Oregon cedar; within she features Tiffany-style stained-glass windows and gleaming brass fixtures. The larger *Mississippi Queen* was launched in 1976.

These are real paddle wheelers; the main source of propulsion is that large red contraption at the stern. (They are updated a bit, with bow thrusters located below the waterline for maneuvering, and modern navigational devices.)

■ STEAMBOATIN'

At the peak of the steamboat era, from about 1811 to the early 1900s, there were more than 10,000 of these vessels on U.S. rivers. Onboard an old-style steamboat, the master of ceremonies is the "Interlocutor"; on the ships in the Delta Queen fleet, he oversees a cast of musicians and singers that pays tribute to American music, from Stephen Foster to Dixieland jazz to bluegrass to Broadway.

For many, the meal service onboard the steamboats is worth the trip, even though it would not qualify as haute cuisine. The boats feature regional American specialties such as bayou stuffed catfish, Cincinnati five-way chili, Minnesota wild rice soup, fried green tomatoes, and other down-home cooking.

The line also has an interesting mix of theme cruises, from Big Band to '50s rock to Elvis and Mark Twain (not together). Several voyages are "tramping" itineraries; on these, the boat will stop at the whim of the captain.

The annual Great Steamboat Race between the *Delta Queen* and *Mississippi Queen,* a most casual event, is usually scheduled for the last week of June, finishing on or about the Fourth of July.

Lewis & Clark Vacations take travelers to areas of interest to aficionados of Meriwether Lewis, William Clark, and their stalwart Corps of Discovery in the early 1800s. Guest historians provide lectures on cruises in the upper Mississippi River.

■ ITINERARIES

Today the Delta Queen Steamboat Company's boats explore the inner passage of America on ten major waterways. The main road is the Mississippi, which meanders some 2,350 miles from its mouth below New Orleans to Saint Paul in Minnesota.

Delta Queen begins her 2005 schedule on January 31, after a month-long refurbishment, sailing round-trip from New Orleans or one-way trips from New Orleans to Pensacola, Galveston, or Memphis—or the other direction—until the end of April. Included in those first trips of the year are five Spring Pilgrimage cruises.

Beginning April 29 the ship moves from home port to home port, starting with a Memphis to Cincinnati itinerary that includes the *Belle of Louisville* Race. Over the next several months, the ship sails from Cincinnati, Nashville, Chattanooga, Memphis, New Orleans, Pensacola, and Saint Louis. In mid-July *Delta*

Queen sails several round-trips from Pittsburgh and Cincinnati, moving on to Saint Louis in August for Mississippi trips to or from Saint Paul, Minnesota.

In late August 2005 the ship begins to head south once again, sailing from Saint Paul to Saint Louis to set up a series of cruises from that city as well as Mobile, Chattanooga, Cincinnati, and Pittsburgh through early November. From the middle of that month until the end of the year, *Delta Queen* is once again primarily based in New Orleans, with Thanksgiving and Christmas holiday cruises. Several trips to or from Galveston are also scheduled for December.

Mississippi Queen sails round-trip from New Orleans from late December 2004 through mid-March 2005; in the middle of that period the ship is scheduled for a twenty-three-day refurbishment in February. From mid-March the ship sails a combination of one-way trips between New Orleans and Memphis or return and a set of round-trips from New Orleans until late June; special trips in that period include Gardens of the River.

On June 24 the ship heads from New Orleans to Saint Louis and then sails three round-trips from that port. In late July *Mississippi Queen* moves on to sail mostly week-long cruises from St. Louis, Nashville, Chattanooga, Memphis, Nashville, Cincinnati, and Pittsburgh before returning to Saint Louis at the end of September; included in that period are Big Band and Bluegrass theme cruises.

After six cruises between Saint Louis and Saint Paul, or return, from late September through early November, the ship sails back to New Orleans, sailing mostly round-trips from that port for the Thanksgiving and Christmas holidays.

American Queen begins 2005 in lay-up, starting service on February 4. The ship will sail almost exclusively from New Orleans for the entire year, mostly on three- and four-day excursions departing Fridays and Mondays. In the summer the ship will sail a series of week-long trips between New Orleans and Memphis, or return.

■ WEB SITE

Delta Queen's Web site presents basic information about the cruise line and itineraries. There is no on-line provision to check availability. Visitors must call the cruise line to book a cruise or go through a travel agent. ***Ease of use: good.***

American Queen

Econoguide rating:	★★★ 75 points
Ship size:	Small
Category:	Adventure
Price range:	Premium $$$
Registry:	United States
Year built:	1995
Information:	(800) 543-1949
Web site:	www.deltaqueen.com

American Queen. Photo courtesy of Delta Queen Steamboat Company

Passenger capacity:	436 (double occupancy)
Crew:	180
Passenger-to-crew ratio:	2.4:1
Tonnage:	3,707
Passenger-space ratio:	19.3
Length:	418 feet
Beam:	89.4 feet
Draft:	8.6 feet
Cruising speed:	13 knots
Guest decks:	6
Total cabins:	222
Outside:	72
Inside:	150
Suites:	24
Wheelchair cabins:	9
Cuisine:	American regional
Style:	Casual by day, semiformal at night
Price notes:	Single-occupancy premium, 150 to 175 percent
Tipping suggestions:	$11.50 pp/pd
Best deal:	Early-booking incentives

This re-creation of an opulent nineteenth-century floating palace is the largest steamboat ever built. The *American Queen* stands 97 feet tall when her twin fluted stacks are fully extended; the stacks and the pilot house can be lowered to 55 feet to pass beneath low bridges.

The ship is furnished largely with antique furniture, vintage artwork, photographs, and books. Her J. M. White Dining Room has filigree woodwork, stunning chandeliers, and a full view of the riverside. The two-story Grand Saloon has private box seats in the mezzanine, in the style of an 1890s opera house. Other public rooms include the delicate Ladies' Parlor, the leather-upholstered Gentlemen's Card Room, and the Engine Room Bar. The ship's library has more than 600 volumes, including many classic, late-nineteenth-century accounts of river lore.

The *American Queen* still uses steam to propel its 30-foot-wide, forty-five ton paddle wheel; the builders refurbished a pair of 1930s-era steam engines that once drove a U.S. Army Corps of Engineers dredge.

Nearly every cruise has a theme; examples include Dixie Fest, Gardens of the River, the Civil War, Rockin' on the River, Fall Foliage, and Southern Christmas.

"Riverlorians" and naturalists present talks about the history, culture, and lore of the river.

The *American Queen* underwent a $2.3 million restoration in 2003 that included refurbishing public rooms, elevator lobbies, hallways and staterooms, and overhauling the boat's engine and mechanical systems.

Delta Queen

Econoguide rating:	★★★ 75 points
Ship size:	Small
Category:	Adventure
Price range:	Premium $$$
Registry:	United States
Year built:	1927
Information:	(800) 543–1949
Web site:	www.deltaqueen.com
Passenger capacity:	174 (double occupancy)
Crew:	75
Passenger-to-crew ratio:	2.32:1
Tonnage:	3,360
Passenger-space ratio:	19.3
Length:	285 feet
Beam:	60 feet
Draft:	9 feet
Cruising speed:	9 knots
Guest decks:	4
Total cabins:	87

Outside:	87
Inside:	0
Suites:	4
Wheelchair cabins:	0
Cuisine:	American regional
Style:	Casual by day, semiformal at night
Price notes:	Single-occupancy premium, 150 to 175 percent
Tipping suggestions:	$11.50 pp/pd
Best deal:	Early-booking incentives

Here's a chance to sail aboard a floating National Historic Landmark. The **Delta Queen** was launched in Stockton, California, in 1928 at a then impressive cost of $1 million. She boasts a fully welded steel hull; her superstructure and paddle wheel are made of various woods, reinforced with steel. The plates for the hull were fabricated in Scotland and then shipped to California for assembly.

The ship operated as a coastal steamboat between San Francisco and Sacramento from 1927 through 1940. During World War II, painted Navy gray, the *Delta Queen* was operated as a U.S. Navy ferry in San Francisco Bay. After the war, the *Delta Queen* was auctioned off for $46,250 (a fraction of its original cost) by the government and purchased by Tom Greene, president of the Cincinnati-based Greene Line Steamers.

The next problem: getting the ship from California to the inland rivers. A huge watertight crate was constructed to protect the *Delta Queen* from the ocean, and she set off on a 5,000-mile voyage from San Francisco—under tow through the Panama Canal, north into the Gulf of Mexico, and finally up the Mississippi River to New Orleans—arriving May 21, 1947. There she was uncrated before setting off to Pittsburgh under steam for a major face-lift.

The interior was restored and reconfigured for new staterooms and dining rooms. The *Delta Queen*'s steam calliope was recovered from the sunken showboat *Water Queen* and installed on the paddle wheeler in 1947.

The forty-four-ton paddle wheel is driven by a pair of steam engines with a combined 2,000 horsepower, capable of producing a top speed of nearly 10 miles per hour.

The ship's wooden superstructure was almost her undoing in the late 1960s, but the steamboat was granted an exemption from federal safety legislation by Congress. The boat also does not have elevators and is not especially easy to navigate for mobility-impaired passengers; the *Mississippi Queen* and *American Queen* are more accommodating in this regard.

Most cruises include a historian, "riverlorian," or naturalist. Theme cruises in recent years have included Mardi Gras, Spring Pilgrimage, Kentucky Derby, Cajun Culture, Mark Twain, Dickens on the Strand, and Old-Fashioned Holidays. There are no childrens' programs on the steamboats.

The *Delta Queen*'s twin, the *Delta King*, is a floating hotel in Sacramento.

Mississippi Queen

Econoguide rating:	★★★ 75 points
Ship size:	Small
Category:	Adventure
Price range:	Premium $$$
Registry:	United States
Year built:	1976 (refurbished 1996)
Information:	(800) 543–1949
Web site:	www.deltaqueen.com
Passenger capacity:	416 (double occupancy)
Crew:	156
Passenger-to-crew ratio:	2.6:1
Tonnage:	3,364
Passenger-space ratio:	8.0
Length:	382 feet
Beam:	68 feet
Draft:	9 feet
Cruising speed:	9.5 knots
Guest decks:	7
Total cabins:	208
Outside:	135
Inside:	73
Suites:	26
Wheelchair cabins:	1
Cuisine:	American regional
Style:	Casual by day, semiformal at night
Tipping suggestions:	$11.50 pp/pd
Best deal:	Early-booking incentives

The **Mississippi Queen** is a modern re-creation of a classic steamboat, built in 1976 and refurbished in 1996 in Victorian style. The boat was built at the former Howard Shipyard in Jeffersonville, Illinois, where, beginning in 1834, more than 4,800 steamboats were built, including the famous *J. M. White* in 1878.

Half the 208 staterooms offer a private veranda. All the cabins are named after river towns, old riverboats, and historic Civil War sites.

The *Mississippi Queen*'s calliope, with forty-four whistles, is the world's largest. The two-story Paddlewheel Lounge, decorated as an 1890s saloon, offers ragtime, Dixieland, and banjo music. In the Forward Cabin Lounge is a grand silver water cooler of the style of the Reed and Barton cooler that adorned the *J. M. White*. At midship, the grand staircase is topped with a trompe l'oeil ceiling of cherubs frolicking among the clouds.

Historians, "riverlorians," and naturalists accompany most cruises. In recent years theme cruises have included Big Band, Mardi Gras, Spring Pilgrimage,

Kentucky Derby, Korean War Years, the Great Steamboat Race, Old-Fashioned Thanksgiving, and Southern Christmas holidays. There are no childrens' programs on the steamboats.

GLACIER BAY CRUISE LINE

Address: 107 West Denny Way, Suite 303
Seattle, WA 98119
Information: (800) 451–5952, (206) 623–7110
www.glacierbaytours.com

The Glacier Bay Fleet

Wilderness Adventurer	1983	72 passengers	98 tons
Wilderness Discoverer	1993	88 passengers	95 tons
Wilderness Explorer	1969	36 passengers	98 tons

With a small fleet of intimate soft-adventure ships owned by an Alaskan company, Glacier Bay makes the most of its shallow-draft vessels to explore some of the more remote inlets of our most isolated state. The ships visit Alaska's Inside Passage, Glacier Bay National Park, Tracy Arm fjord, and Admiralty Island National Monument. All voyages include the option for sea kayaking and onshore hiking.

The company, which had been owned by Alaska native corporation Goldbelt, Inc., received new ownership in 2004, with the sale to three travel industry veterans. Among the immediate changes was the launching of a series of week-long adventure cruises featuring Oregon's Columbia, Willamette, and Snake Rivers, with kayaking, hiking, mountain biking, and whitewater rafting available, as well as an included jet boat ride into Hell's Canyon. Cruises depart in April and May or September and October.

■ WEB SITE

Glacier Bay's Web site presents basic information about the cruise line and itineraries. There is no on-line provision to check availability. Visitors must call the cruise line to book a cruise or go through a travel agent. *Ease of use: good.*

Wilderness Adventurer

Econoguide rating:	★★ 52 points
Ship size:	Small
Category:	Adventure
Price range:	Premium $$$
Registry:	United States

Year built:	1983 (formerly *Caribbean Prince*)
Information:	(800) 451–5952
Web site:	www.glacierbaytours.com
Passenger capacity:	72 (double occupancy)
Crew:	19
Passenger-to-crew ratio:	3.8:1
Tonnage:	89
Length:	156.6 feet
Beam:	38 feet
Draft:	6.5 feet
Cruising speed:	10 knots
Guest decks:	4
Total cabins:	34
Outside:	34 (B cabins have no windows)
Inside:	0
Suites:	0
Cuisine:	Alaskan
Style:	Casual
Price notes:	Single supplement, 175 percent of cabin category chosen; triple rates (three in a room) on request
Tipping suggestions:	$10 pp/pd

The **Wilderness Adventurer** carries a fleet of stable two-person sea kayaks for up-close exploration of southeast Alaska's spectacular shoreline. The ship also has a bow ramp for easy access to the shore.

The vessel was given a makeover for the 2001 season. Four new suites were added to the observation deck, and all of the cabins were refurbished. Glacier Bay also brought aboard twenty two-person sea kayaks and a launching platform. Other important work included updates to the vessel to meet strict new emission requirements, and improved fire protection systems throughout the vessel.

The ship had a minor mishap in June 1999 in Glacier Bay National Park and Reserve, going aground and spilling some of its fuel.

Wilderness Discoverer

Econoguide rating:	★★ 52 points
Ship size:	Small
Category:	Adventure
Price range:	Premium $$$
Registry:	United States
Year built:	1993 (formerly *Mayan Prince*)
Information:	(800) 451–5952
Web site:	www.glacierbaytours.com
Passenger capacity:	88 (double occupancy)

Crew:	19
Passenger-to-crew ratio:	4.6:1
Tonnage:	95
Draft:	6.6 feet
Length:	169 feet
Beam:	38 feet
Cruising speed:	12 knots
Guest decks:	4
Total cabins:	44
Outside:	44 (category B staterooms have no windows)
Inside:	0
Suites:	0
Cuisine:	Alaskan specialties
Style:	Casual
Price notes:	Single supplement, 175 percent; triple rate (three in a room) on request
Tipping suggestions:	$10 pp/pd

The largest ship in the Glacier Bay fleet, **Wilderness Discoverer** is still intimate, with just forty-four cabins on four decks. She sails one-way between Juneau and Sitka or reverse.

Wilderness Explorer

Econoguide rating:	★★ 50 points
Ship size:	Small
Category:	Adventure
Price range:	Premium $$$
Registry:	United States
Year built:	1969
Information:	(800) 451–5952
Web site:	www.glacierbaytours.com
Passenger capacity:	34 (double occupancy)
Crew:	13
Passenger-to-crew ratio:	2.6:1
Tonnage:	98
Draft:	6.6 feet
Length:	112 feet
Beam:	22 feet
Cruising speed:	9 knots
Guest decks:	3
Total cabins:	17
Outside:	17
Inside:	0

Suites:	0
Cuisine:	Alaskan
Style:	Casual
Price notes:	Single supplement, 175 percent
Tipping suggestions:	$10 pp/pd

Luxury lies beyond the windows of the **Wilderness Explorer,** not in the small but comfortable cabins and public rooms. The vessel is the only cruise to regularly begin and end in Glacier Bay National Park.

Wilderness Explorer ran aground in an inlet 70 miles west of Juneau in 1999; there were no injuries and the ship was repaired.

LINDBLAD SPECIAL EXPEDITIONS

Address: 720 Fifth Avenue
New York, NY 10019
Information: (800) 397–3348
www.expeditions.com

The Lindblad Special Expeditions Fleet

Endeavour	1966	110 passengers	3,132 tons
Polaris	1959	80 passengers	2,214 tons
Sea Voyager	1982	64 passengers	1,195 tons
Sea Bird	1981	70 passengers	100 tons
Sea Lion	1982	70 passengers	100 tons

The Lindblad family has been taking travelers to extraordinary destinations since 1979, visiting Alaska, the Pacific Northwest, Baja California, Central and South America, the Galapagos Islands, Western Europe, Egypt, the Baltics, Antarctica, the Mediterranean, Australia, and New Zealand.

The company traces its roots to Lars-Eric Lindblad, who began a travel agency in 1958, specializing in visits to far-flung places such as Antarctica, the Galapagos, China, Mongolia, Tibet, and Africa. Today the company is run by his son, Sven-Olof.

The company's fleet of oceangoing vessels carries between 64 and 110 passengers. The ships are equipped with Zodiac landing craft; some carry sea kayaks. These are tours for active travelers—swimmers, kayakers, snorkelers, hikers—and observers of all sorts. The onboard entertainment consists of naturalists and scientists who explain the views all around.

On these small ships, the accommodations and public areas can best be described as casual and intimate. There are open sundecks for observation, a dining room, and a lounge. Don't look for a casino, hydrotherapy pool, or a virtual-reality/multimedia entertainment center; the excitement is outside.

The line also offers a series of special photo expeditions conducted by naturalists and professional photographers who help guests record their journeys.

ITINERARIES

Sea Voyager is stationed year-round in Central America, sailing in the waters off Belize, Costa Rica, Guatemala, Honduras, Nicaragua, and Panama.

Sea Lion and *Sea Bird* sail in Alaska's coastal waters for the summer; in May and August the ships venture into Alaska, British Columbia, and the San Juan Islands. The same ships sail in Baja California and the Sea of Cortés from January through April.

Polaris sails year-round in the Galapagos Islands, with excurions to Peru and Ecuador.

Endeavour sails the world, visiting South America in October, and moving on to the Falkland Islands and Antarctica from November through February. Crossing the Atlantic in March, the ship sails in Europe from April through September, including visits to Scandinavia and the Mediterranean.

WEB SITE

The Lindblad Web site presents basic information about the cruise line and itineraries. There is no online provision to check availability. Visitors must call the cruise line to book a cruise or go through a travel agent. *Ease of use: fair.*

Sea Bird

Econoguide rating:	★★ 52 points
Ship size:	Small
Category:	Adventure
Price range:	Premium $$$
Registry:	United States
Year built:	1982 (formerly *Majestic Explorer;* refurbished 1995)
Information:	(800) 397–3348
Web site:	www.expeditions.com
Passenger capacity:	70 (double occupancy)
Crew:	21
Passenger-to-crew ratio:	2.5:1
Tonnage:	100
Length:	152 feet
Beam:	31 feet
Draft:	8 feet
Cruising speed:	12 knots
Guest decks:	4
Total cabins:	35
Outside:	35
Inside:	0

Suites:	0
Wheelchair cabins:	Main deck, category 3 cabins; no elevators onboard
Cuisine:	American
Style:	Informal
Price notes:	Single-occupancy premium, about 150 percent
Tipping suggestions:	$9.00 pp/pd

Sea Bird is a comfortable transport to some of the most remote places on earth. Guests venture out in Zodiac landing craft to view whales and explore onshore happenings. Most voyages carry naturalists and other lecturers.

Sea Lion

Econoguide rating:	★★ 52 points
Ship size:	Small
Category:	Adventure
Price range:	Premium $$$
Registry:	United States
Year built:	1981 (formerly *Great Rivers Explorer*; refurbished 1995)
Information:	(800) 397–3348
Web site:	www.expeditions.com
Passenger capacity:	70 (double occupancy)
Crew:	21
Passenger-to-crew ratio:	3.3:1
Tonnage:	100
Length:	152 feet
Beam:	31 feet
Draft:	8 feet
Cruising speed:	12 knots
Guest decks:	4
Total cabins:	37
Outside:	37
Inside:	0
Suites:	0
Wheelchair cabins:	Main deck, category 3 cabins; no elevators onboard
Cuisine:	American
Style:	Informal
Price notes:	Single-occupancy premium, about 150 percent
Tipping suggestions:	$9.00 pp/pd

Sea Lion is designed top to bottom for her role as an expedition vessel to exotic and remote ports in search of wildlife in the sea, the sky, and shore; much of her public areas are geared to serve as observation platforms.

Sea Voyager

Econoguide rating:	★★ 52 points
Ship size:	Small
Category:	Adventure
Price range:	Premium $$$
Registry:	United States
Year built:	1982 (formerly *Temptress Voyager;* refurbished 2001)
Information:	(800) 397–3348
Web site:	www.expeditions.com
Passenger capacity:	64 (double occupancy)
Crew:	25
Passenger-to-crew ratio:	2.6:1
Tonnage:	1,195
Length:	175 feet
Beam:	40 feet
Draft:	12 feet
Cruising speed:	12 knots
Guest decks:	3
Total cabins:	33
Outside:	33
Inside:	0
Suites:	0
Cuisine:	Regional
Style:	Informal
Tipping suggestions:	$9.00 pp/pd

The **Sea Voyager** was added to the Lindblad fleet in 2001 after a major refitting. Stationed full-time in Central America, the ship includes a full-time undersea specialist and carries a variety of equipment for exploring the area waters, including underwater cameras and video microscopes. A fleet of Zodiacs, inflatable kayaks, and snorkeling gear are offered to guests.

Endeavour

Econoguide rating:	★★★ 68 points
Ship size:	Small
Category:	Adventure
Price range:	Premium $$$
Registry:	Bahamas
Year built:	1966 (formerly *Caledonian Star,* renamed in 2001; refurbished 1998)

Information:	(800) 397–3348
Web site:	www.expeditions.com
Passenger capacity:	110 (double occupancy)
Crew:	45
Passenger-to-crew ratio:	2.4:1
Tonnage:	3,132
Length:	295 feet
Beam:	46 feet
Draft:	21 feet
Cruising speed:	12 knots
Guest decks:	5
Total cabins:	61
Outside:	61
Inside:	0
Cuisine:	International
Style:	Informal
Tipping suggestions:	$9.00 pp/pd

Lindblad Expeditions renamed the *Caledonian Star* as **Endeavour** in honor of famed explorer Captain James Cook's ship at a ceremony in Whitby, England, in 2001. Three of Cook's ships—*Endeavour, Resolution,* and *Adventure*—were built in Whitby in the second half of the eighteenth century.

Cook made discoveries and charted coastlines from the Arctic to the Antarctic, gaining Australia and New Zealand for Britain. The original *Endeavour* was built to transport coal; the *Caledonian Star* first went to sea as a trawler.

The modern ship includes an array of scientific equipment for exploration above and below the water, including a remotely operated vehicle with a video camera that can be piloted from the surface in areas not suitable for a diver, such as under unstable icebergs. Diving and underwater filming by a naturalist take place when conditions permit. Hydrophones allow guests to hear vocalizations from marine mammals such as whales and dolphins. The ship is also equipped with sea kayaks to allow guests of all skill levels to explore the Arctic and Antarctic.

Polaris

Econoguide rating:	★★ 61 points
Ship size:	Small
Category:	Adventure
Price range:	Premium $$$
Registry:	Ecuador
Year built:	1959 (formerly *Oresund;* refurbished 1987)
Information:	(800) 397–3348
Web site:	www.expeditions.com
Passenger capacity:	80 (double occupancy)

Crew:	34
Passenger-to-crew ratio:	2.3:1
Tonnage:	2,214
Length:	238 feet
Beam:	42.7 feet
Draft:	20 feet
Cruising speed:	12 knots
Guest decks:	3
Total cabins:	41
Outside:	41
Inside:	0
Cuisine:	International
Style:	Informal
Tipping suggestions:	$9.00 pp/pd

Polaris was built as a small ferry but was refurbished by Lindblad to serve as an expedition vessel. The Lookout Point on the Sky Deck is a favorite spot, along with the bridge, which is open to guests.

RIVERBARGE EXCURSIONS LINE

RiverBarge Excursions

Address: 201 Opelousas Avenue
New Orleans, LA 70114
Information: (888) 462–2743
www.riverbarge.com

The RiverBarge Fleet

River Explorer	1998	198 passengers	8,864 tons

River Explorer is the only hotel barge traveling America's rivers and inland waterways. The vessel is made up of two 295-foot-long river barges, pushed along by the *Miss Nari,* a 3,000-horsepower towboat.

The company is the brainchild of Eddie Conrad, a native of New Orleans who has devoted his life to the rivers; he founded a successful towing company in Louisiana. In 1990 he began carrying recreational vehicles along the bayous and backwaters of Southern Louisiana and the Mississippi River, expanding his offerings in 1998 with the launch of the *River Explorer*.

■ ITINERARIES

The company offers four- to ten-day excursions on the lower and upper Mississippi River, the Cumberland River Valley, the Atchafalaya River Basin, Ohio River Valley, Missouri River, and along the Texas-Louisiana Gulf Intracoastal Waterway.

Ports of embarkation include New Orleans, Memphis, Saint Louis, Kansas City, Nashville, Cincinnati, and Galveston. Fares include all scheduled shore excursions.

A sampling of recent cruises includes: Delta South, from New Orleans to Memphis, featuring Dixieland jazz, Memphis blues, and gastronomic delights ranging from BBQ, southern fried chicken, pecan pralines, and gumbo; The Arch and the Pyramid, from Saint Charles to Memphis on the Upper and Lower Mississippi Rivers, including the old Spanish settlement of New Madrid, Missouri, where North America's largest earthquake took place in 1811; Expanding Frontiers from Cincinnati or Saint Louis to Nashville or the reverse; and The Big Muddy from Kansas City to Sioux City or Saint Louis, tracing part of the paths of Lewis & Clark, Jesse James, and early westward pioneers.

On selected cruises that begin and end in different ports, the company offers free bus transportation to bring guests back to their point of origin.

■ WEB SITE

The Web site presents basic information about the cruise line and itineraries. There is no on-line provision to check availability. Visitors must call the cruise line to book a cruise or go through a travel agent. *Ease of use: good.*

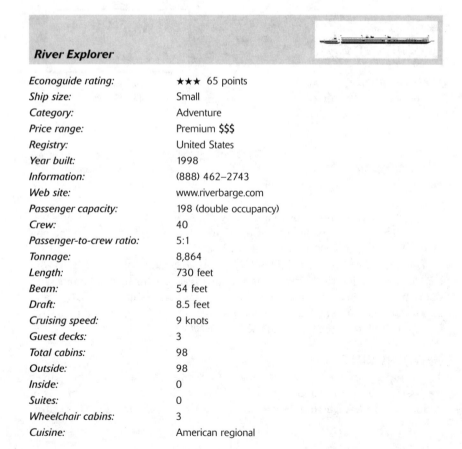

River Explorer

Econoguide rating:	★★★ 65 points
Ship size:	Small
Category:	Adventure
Price range:	Premium $$$
Registry:	United States
Year built:	1998
Information:	(888) 462–2743
Web site:	www.riverbarge.com
Passenger capacity:	198 (double occupancy)
Crew:	40
Passenger-to-crew ratio:	5:1
Tonnage:	8,864
Length:	730 feet
Beam:	54 feet
Draft:	8.5 feet
Cruising speed:	9 knots
Guest decks:	3
Total cabins:	98
Outside:	98
Inside:	0
Suites:	0
Wheelchair cabins:	3
Cuisine:	American regional

Style:	Casual
Tipping suggestions:	Included
Best deal:	Advance-booking onboard credits; discounts for active or retired teachers

The **River Explorer**'s forward barge, DeSoto, holds public rooms; the aft barge, LaSalle, is home to ninety-eight identical staterooms. Cabins on the upper Platinum Deck include verandas; Royal Deck staterooms have a picture window.

The Galley features home-style cooking and is able to accommodate all passengers in a single open seating. Just like at home, the kitchen is always open, allowing guests to raid the fridge anytime.

The Guest Pilot House is a replica of the real pilot house; open to guests, it features radar displays and radios with actual transmissions from the bridge.

SOCIETY EXPEDITIONS

Society Expeditions

Address: 2001 Western Avenue, Suite 300
Seattle, WA 98121
Information: (800) 548–8669
www.societyexpeditions.com

The Society Expeditions Fleet

World Discoverer	1989	160 passengers	6,000 tons

Society Expeditions was one of the pioneers of expedition-style cruising. The company was founded in 1974 as the Society for the Preservation of Archaeological Monuments to escort five small groups of adventurers to Easter Island. The profits were donated to aid the restoration of the gigantic stone moai statues. The company's name was changed to Society Expeditions in 1976 when more destinations were added. It is now owned by a German firm.

The original *World Discoverer* was chartered in 1980 to conduct a series of Amazon expedition cruises. One of only two of the world's expedition cruise ships, the vessel embarked on a long career of explorations to Indonesia, Myanmar, Singapore, Seychelles, Iceland, Greenland, West Africa, Saudi Arabia, Yemen, Polynesia, Melanesia, Micronesia, Korea, Japan, Alaska, the Northwest Passage, Hudson Bay, the Saint Lawrence Seaway, and the Galapagos Islands. The ship went aground in the Solomon Islands in 2000, ending its service.

Society Expeditions' "new" ship replaced the company's original vessel. The new *World Discoverer* was built in 1989 in Finland as a Baltic ferry; it was later purchased by Samsung Industries and refitted for educational seminars.

ITINERARIES

The *World Discoverer* lives up to its name with an eclectic collection of cruises mostly in the South Pacific, with summer forays north into Russia and Alaska.

From March through early June of 2004, the ship was scheduled to sail in the South Pacific with trips to Easter Island, the Society Islands, Western Samoa, Guam, and Tinian. From June through mid-August, the ship moves on to the Russian Far East and remote Alaska, with visits to the Kamchatka Peninsula, the Bering Sea, and Nome.

From late August through October, *World Discoverer* was due to move back to the South Pacific, with itineraries including "In the Wake of the Bounty," which calls at Papeete, Bora Bora, Tuamotus, Marquesas, Gambier Islands, Pitcairn Island, and Easter Island.

From November 2004 through March of 2005, the ship sails in Antarctica, departing from Ushuaia to the Falklands and the Drake Passage.

■ WEB SITE

The Society Expeditions Web site presents basic information about the cruise line and itineraries. There is no on-line provision to check availability. Visitors must call the cruise line to book a cruise or go through a travel agent. *Ease of use: good.*

World Discoverer

Econoguide rating:	★★★ 69 points
Ship size:	Small
Category:	Adventure
Price range:	Opulent $$$$
Registry:	Bahamas
Year built:	1989 (formerly *Delphin Star, Dream 21*)
Information:	(800) 548–8669
Web site:	www.societyexpeditions.com
Passenger capacity:	160 (double occupancy)
Crew:	90
Passenger-to-crew ratio:	1.8:1
Tonnage:	6,000
Length:	354 feet
Beam:	52 feet
Draft:	14 feet
Cruising speed:	16 knots
Guest decks:	5
Total cabins:	86
Outside:	86
Inside:	0
Suites:	2
Wheelchair cabins:	2

Cuisine:	Continental
Style:	Casual
Price notes:	Single-occupancy premium, 175 percent of cabin category chosen; triple and quad rates upon request
Tipping suggestions:	Included

Built specifically for expedition cruising, **World Discoverer** features an ice-hardened hull and is fully equipped for kayaking, scuba diving, snorkeling, and other sports and transport.

Econoguide Ship Classifications

Gargantuan	130,000 or more tons
Colossus	100,000 to 130,000 tons
Megaship	70,000 to 100,000 tons
Large	40,000 to 70,000 tons
Medium	10,000 to 40,000 tons
Small	Less than 10,000 tons

CHAPTER SEVENTEEN

SAILING VESSELS

🎖🎖🎖🎖🎖	Sea Cloud Cruises	🎖🎖🎖	Windjammer Barefoot Cruises
🎖🎖🎖	Star Clippers	🎖🎖🎖🎖	Windstar Cruises

SEA CLOUD CRUISES

Address: 32-40 North Dean Street
 Englewood Cliffs, NJ 07631
Information: (888) 732–2568, (201) 227–9404
 www.seacloud.com
Econoguide's Best Luxury Cruise Lines
Econoguide's Best Dining at Sea

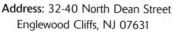

The Sea Cloud Cruises Fleet

Sea Cloud II	2000	96 passengers	3,000 tons
Sea Cloud	1931	69 passengers	2,532 tons

The four-masted bark *Sea Cloud* was built in 1931 for cereal food heiress Marjorie Merriweather Post by her husband, Wall Street broker Edward F. Hutton. Post, famous for her parties and social events, turned the ship into a gathering place for royalty, heads of state, and society hobnobbers.

After a half century of various adventures, including a stint as a weather observation and submarine spotting ship during World War II and as a notorious party boat for a Panamanian dictator and his son, *Sea Cloud* was restored to her former glory within and without.

More than a football field long, the ship is a place of marble and teak and gold-plated fixtures; several of the original owners' cabins have fireplaces. Dining includes fine wine and beer at lunch, often served beneath a canopy on deck, and dinner in the elegant dining parlor.

The ship was rescued from oblivion by a group of German businessmen who bankrolled her restoration. Modern updates include air-conditioning, some additional cabins, and the latest radar, satellite, and communications gear. But lucky guests are very much at sea in a classic with the feel of the 1930s and earlier. (You can read about a cruise on the *Sea Cloud* in Chapter 11.)

Sea Cloud II, built in 2001, has all of the romance of the original without the history. You will, though, find many modern touches within.

■ ITINERARIES

Sea Cloud winters in the Caribbean, sailing mostly fron Antigua. In spring she repositions across the Atlantic to sail in the western Mediterranean from Civitavecchia, Italy, and other ports, and in the eastern Mediterranean from Turkey. In late November she usually makes a two-week repositioning crossing from Las Palmas in the Canary Islands to Barbados in the Caribbean.

Sea Cloud II follows a similar schedule, sailing mostly in the western Mediterranean from Lisbon and Barcelona and in Northern European ports in the United Kingdom, Denmark, Russia, and Germany in the summer. She crosses over to the Caribbean in late November to sail from Barbados, returning to Europe in the spring.

Both ships are regularly chartered by large companies for floating conventions or as sales incentives, resulting in gaps in the schedule when one vessel or the other may not be available for booking by the public.

■ WEB SITE

The company Web site provides basic information about the ships and itineraries. There is no way to check availability of cabins on specific trips. Reservations must be made by telephone or through a travel agent; visitors can also request a callback from the line. *Ease of use: good.*

Sea Cloud	
Econoguide rating:	★★★★★ 94 points
Ship size:	Small
Category:	Adventure
Price range:	Opulent $$$$
Registry:	Malta
Year built:	1931 (formerly SV *Hussar;* refurbished 1979, 1993)
Information:	(888) 732–2568
Web site:	www.seacloud.com
Passenger capacity:	69
Crew:	60
Passenger-to-crew ratio:	1.15:1
Tonnage:	2,532
Length:	360 feet

Beam:	50 feet
Draft:	17 feet
Cruising speed:	12 knots under power
Guest decks:	3
Total cabins:	34
Outside:	34
Inside:	0
Suites:	8
Wheelchair cabins:	0
Cuisine:	Nouvelle; wines included
Style:	Informal
Tipping suggestions:	$10–$12 pp/pd
Best deal:	Various promotions posted on the Web site through the year

If you're very lucky, you'll find yourself in **Sea Cloud**'s Cabin 1, Marjorie Post's own cabin, a seagoing palace complete with a fireplace and bathroom of Carrara marble, mahogany furniture, Louis Philippe chairs, and an antique French bed. But even most of the lesser cabins are rather grand, outfitted in marble and fine furniture. (A few newer cabins, up top, are attractive but simple.) The restaurant, created from the ship's original saloon, is like a fine private club. Passengers receive rotating invitations to sit at the captain's table.

Sea Cloud II

Econoguide rating:	★★★★★ 94 points
Ship size:	Small
Category:	Adventure
Price range:	Opulent $$$$
Registry:	Malta
Year built:	2000
Information:	(888) 732–2568
Web site:	www.seacloud.com
Passenger capacity:	96
Crew:	60
Passenger-to-crew ratio:	1.6:1
Tonnage:	3,000
Length:	384
Beam:	53 feet
Draft:	18 feet
Cruising speed:	14 knots under power
Guest decks:	4
Total cabins:	48
Outside:	48

Inside:	0
Suites:	0
Wheelchair cabins:	0
Cuisine:	Nouvelle; wines included
Style:	Informal
Tipping suggestions:	$10–$12 pp/pd

The *Sea Cloud* gained a new cousin, the ***Sea Cloud II,*** in 2001. The new ship offers forty-eight cabins under a set of rigging with twenty-four sails on masts reaching 174 feet into the sky. Public rooms include an elegant restaurant, lounge, fitness room, and sauna. *Sea Cloud II* also has a water sports platform.

STAR CLIPPERS

STAR CLIPPERS

Address: 4101 Salzedo Street
　　Coral Gables, FL 33146
Information: (800) 442–0551
　　www.starclippers.com
Econoguide's Best Adventure Cruise Lines

The Star Clippers Fleet

Royal Clipper	2000	228 passengers	5,000 tons
Star Clipper	1992	170 passengers	2,298 tons
Star Flyer	1991	170 passengers	2,298 tons

The ships in the Star Clippers fleet are modern re-creations of the classic clipper sailing ships that were the wonders of the nineteenth century. The clippers were called the greyhounds of the sea in their heyday; the largest of the ships was the *Great Republic,* built in 1853, at 308 feet. Many of the ships sailed from Great Britain or the United States to Asia; the end of the clipper age arrived with the opening of the Suez Canal in 1869, which made the steamboat more cost-effective.

Swedish businessman Mikael Krafft brought the clipper ship back from extinction in 1991 when construction began in Belgium on what would be the largest clipper ship in history, the 360-foot-long *Star Flyer,* later joined by an identical twin, *Star Clipper.* In 2000 the even larger and more opulent 439-foot *Royal Clipper* joined the fleet.

Royal Clipper is the world's largest fully rigged true sailing ship, outsizing the Russian *Sedov* by about 39 feet. Her 226-foot-high mainmast is taller than almost any cruise liner on the seas, holding a suit of forty-two sails. The first five-masted sailing ship constructed in nearly a century, *Royal Clipper* is based on the classic German five-master *Preussen.* (Windstar's *Wind Surf* and sister ship *Club*

Med 2 are larger, but by some judgments they represent motorized cruise ships with sails, rather than sailing vessels with auxiliary engines.)

Although the ships are quite modern in their appointments, these are not computerized cruise ships with a sail on top for old-time's sake. The crew—and the passengers—are pressed into service to handle 40,000 square feet of sails on four masts on the *Star Clipper* and *Star Flyer* and 56,000 square feet on five masts on the *Royal Clipper.* Under a strong wind astern, the ships have reached speeds of as much as 17 knots, about the same as a modern cruise ship.

Rooms are attractive and tidy, most with small portholes; a few of the upper deck cabins have doors that open directly onto the main deck. The best views are found up on the large sundecks of the ships, outfitted with deck chairs and lounging spaces alongside several pools. The captain meets with guests every morning to discuss the day's schedule and tell stories of sailing lore and technique.

One of the real treats of these ships is posing for pictures for passengers along the rails of modern Megaships in the harbor; the Star Clippers are among the prettiest sights they're likely to find at sea.

ITINERARIES

Royal Clipper sailed out of Barbados from January through April 2004, cruising to the Windward Islands (Saint Lucia, Îles des Saintes, Antigua, Saint Kitts, Dominica, and Martinique) and the Grenadines (Grenada, Tobago Cays, Saint Vincent, and Bequia). The ship crossed the Atlantic to Italy to sail in the western Mediterranean for the summer, returning to the Caribbean in mid-October and resuming Caribbean cruises through the spring of 2005. From May through September *Royal Clipper* sailed from Civitavecchia (Rome) to Sicily and Malta, with longer trips at the end of the summer that visit Greece, Croatia, and Venice, Italy.

Star Clipper sailed from January through April 2004 from Saint Martin to the Leeward (Saint Barts, Nevis, Guadeloupe, Dominica, Îles des Saintes, and Antigua) and Treasure Islands (Anguilla, Virgin Gorda, and Norman Island) of the Caribbean. At the end of April, the ship crossed over to Cannes, France, to sail trips in the Tyrrhenian Sea (Hyeres Islands, Sardinia, and Corsica) and the Ligurian Sea (Corsica, Elba, Portofino, and Monte Carlo.) In October she is due to cross the Atlantic back to Saint Martin.

In 2004 *Star Flyer* sailed in the eastern Mediterranean from Athens to other ports in Greece and Turkey from May through September. From November 2004 through March of 2005, the ship was due to sail from Phuket, Thailand, to other ports in that country and in Malaysia.

WEB SITE

The Star Clippers Web site provides basic information about the ships and itineraries. There is no way to check availability of cabins on specific trips. Reservations must be made by telephone or through a travel agent; visitors can also request a callback from the line. ***Ease of use: very good.***

Royal Clipper

Econoguide rating:	★★★★ 83 points
Ship size:	Small
Category:	Adventure
Price range:	Moderate $$
Registry:	Luxembourg
Year built:	2000
Information:	(800) 442–0551
Web site:	www.star-clippers.com
Passenger capacity:	227
Crew:	105
Passenger-to-crew ratio:	2.2:1
Tonnage:	5,000
Length:	439 feet
Beam:	54 feet
Draft:	18.5 feet
Cruising speed:	Approximately 11 knots under sail
Guest decks:	5
Total cabins:	114
Outside:	108
Inside:	6
Suites:	16
Wheelchair cabins:	0
Cuisine:	International and regional
Style:	Informal
Price notes:	Single-occupancy premium, 150 percent
Tipping suggestions:	$8.00 pp/pd

This is not your basic little sailboat. In fact, *Royal Clipper* is the world's largest sailing ship. Her dimensions follow those of the famed clipper ship *Preussen,* which dominated the world's sail cargo routes from 1902 to 1908. Five steel masts hold forty-two sails aloft, a total area of 56,000 square feet, more than an acre of sail. (For the record, there are twenty-six square sails, eleven staysails, four jibs, and one gaff-rigged spanker.) Under full sail, the *Royal Clipper* is capable of speeds of as much as 20 knots.

The 197-foot-tall mainmast includes a 19-foot hinged top section that can be folded down to allow passage under bridges and other obstructions.

The ship is under sail most of the time, with twin 2,500-horsepower diesel engines in reserve when necessary. Stabilizing tanks are used to reduce roll, and heeling is usually held to less than 6 percent.

Cabins are trimmed in mahogany and brass, with marble bathrooms and color televisions. The three-level dining room is a step back into the Edwardian age. The ceiling above the Piano Bar is the glass bottom of the largest of three swimming pools. The lounge also offers submarine portholes, illuminated after dusk by underwater floodlights.

Each of the five masts includes a passenger lookout platform part of the way up; there's a settee in place, and stewards will deliver refreshments to the perch on call.

A small fleet of boats is available to passengers from the water sports platform that is lowered into the sea from the stern.

Star Clipper, Star Flyer

Econoguide rating:	★★★ 77 points
Ship size:	Small
Category:	Adventure
Price range:	Moderate $$
Registry:	Luxembourg
Year built:	Star Clipper, 1992; Star Flyer, 1991
Information:	(800) 442–0551
Web site:	www.star-clippers.com
Passenger capacity:	170
Crew:	72
Passenger-to-crew ratio:	2.4:1
Tonnage:	2,298
Length:	360 feet
Beam:	50 feet
Draft:	18.5 feet
Cruising speed:	11 knots under sail
Guest decks:	4
Total cabins:	85
Outside:	81
Inside:	4
Suites:	0
Wheelchair cabins:	0
Cuisine:	International and regional
Style:	Informal
Price notes:	Single-occupancy premium, 150 percent
Tipping suggestions:	$8.00 pp/pd

Launched in Ghent, Belgium, the **Star Clipper** and **Star Flyer** are four-masted, square-rigged barkentines with 36,000 square feet of sail. Although they are shorter in length than the *Royal Clipper,* the ships hold the record for the tallest mast in the world, at 226 feet above the waterline.

There are teak decks and a pair of swimming pools. Passenger amenities include an indoor-outdoor bar with a piano lounge and an Edwardian-style library with fireplace.

WINDJAMMER
BAREFOOT CRUISES

Address: P.O. Box 190-200
Miami, FL 33119-0120
Information: (800) 327–2601
www.windjammer.com

The Windjammer Barefoot Cruises Fleet

Legacy	1959	122 passengers	1,740 tons
Mandalay	1923	72 passengers	420 tons
Polynesia	1938	126 passengers	430 tons
Yankee Clipper	1927	64 passengers	327 tons
Amazing Grace	1955	94 passengers	1,585 tons (motorship)

Windjammer is the largest operator of Tall Ships in the world. The four sailing vessel in its fleet have passenger capacities of 64 to 126, sailing year-round in the Caribbean.

According to company lore, Mike Burke woke up in Miami in 1947 with a headache and a 19-foot sloop, purchased sometime during the night with $600 in Navy pay. The boat, christened *Hangover,* became the basis for the Windjammer empire.

Each of the ships has an interesting story of its own, the oldest dating back more than seventy-five years. The vessels have been refurbished and accommodations brought up to modern standards.

The fleet includes some true classics. *Mandalay* was considered one of the most luxurious yachts in the world when she was built in 1923 as a three-masted barkentine for financier E. F. Hutton and his wife, Marjorie Merriweather Post. (The ship was a predecessor to the even more opulent *Sea Cloud,* covered earlier in this chapter.)

Legacy, the flagship of the fleet, was built in 1959 as a meteorological research and exploration ship for the French government.

Polynesia, a four-masted schooner, was built in Holland in 1938 for the Portuguese Grand Banks cod fishing fleet. *Yankee Clipper,* the only armor-plated private yacht in the world, was built in 1927 for German arms maker Alfred Krupp. She was confiscated by the United States after World War II and later acquired by the Vanderbilt family and raced off California.

Amazing Grace is a former Scottish service ship, built in 1955, that provided supplies to North Sea lighthouses. The motorized vessel today supplies the five sailing vessels in the Windjammer fleet, carrying passengers on a full itinerary of Caribbean stops.

Windjammer suffered a major loss in 1998 with the destruction of the *Fantome* during Hurricane Mitch off Central America; the ship's passengers had been safely deposited in port, but the crew of thirty-one perished when the ship headed out to sea to attempt to outrun the storm. The handsome ship was built in 1927 as a destroyer for the Italian navy and was later reconstructed as a private floating palace for the Duke of Westminster.

In early 2003 the venerable *Flying Cloud* was pulled from the fleet, with its future uncertain. Built in 1935 as a cadet training ship for the French navy, it later served as a decoy and spy ship for the Allied Forces, participating in the sinking of two Japanese submarines during World War II.

In 2001 Windjammer purchased *Discover,* a 303-foot former oceanographic research vessel, and began converting it to carry 160 to 180 passengers. No plans have been announced for addition of the ship to the Windjammer fleet.

■ THE WINDJAMMER EXPERIENCE

None of the Windjammer ships could qualify as a luxury liner, and cabins and public rooms are small and simple. The atmosphere is decidedly relaxed, sometimes verging on nonstop partying. Some cruises have lifestyle themes, such as nudism, singles, swingers, and gays. Be sure to inquire whether any such gathering is planned on the cruise you might select.

Windjammer has been experiencing increasing bookings in recent years, and before the loss of the *Fantome* had announced plans to add three ships in the next decade and as many as five during the next fifteen years.

One interesting offering is a "stowaway" onboard the ship the night before departure. For a reasonable fee, guests can spend the night onboard the ship and partake of dinner, rum swizzles, a steel drum band party, and breakfast.

■ ITINERARIES

In recent years *Legacy* sailed in the winter from Saint Thomas in the U.S. Virgin Islands to nearby less-visited places including Jost Van Dyke, Saint John, Norman, Tortola, and Virgin Gorda. In summer, itineraries leave from Miami and Nassau to Bimini, Great Abaco, the Barry Islands, and New Providence. In fall she sails from Aruba to Bonaire, Curaçao, and Klein Curaçao.

Mandalay typically sails in June from the Caribbean coast of Panama to Playa Francis, Isla Grande, Isla Verde, Cayos Hollandes, Porvenir, and Portobello. In winter and spring the ship alternates between departures from Grenada or Antigua, sailing the Windward and Leeward Islands.

Polynesia sailed in summer and fall from Saint Lucia to Grenada, Saint Vincent, and Union Island in the Grenadines. In winter and spring Polynesia's home port was Saint Martin, sailing to Anguilla, Nevis, Saba, Saint Bart's, Tintamarre, and Saint Eustasius (Statia).

Yankee Clipper sails year-round from Grenada to Carriacou, Bequia, Saint Vincent, Union Island, and Tobago Cays.

The motor vessel *Amazing Grace* makes provisioning trips among the Caribbean islands to meet up with the company's fleet of sailing vessels. The home port alternates every two weeks between Grand Bahama and Trinidad, with calls to Antigua, Barbados, Bequia, Cooper, Dominica, the Dominican Republic, Grand Turk, Great Iguana, Grenada, Guadeloupe, Îles des Saintes, Jost

Van Dyke, Marie-Galante, Martinique, Nevis, Norman, Saint Bart's, Saint Kitts, Saint Lucia, Saint Martin, Tobago, Tortola, and Virgin Gorda.

■ WEB SITE

The Windjammer Web site provides basic information about the ships and itineraries. There is no way to check availability of cabins on specific trips. Reservations must be made by telephone or through a travel agent; visitors can also fill out a reservation request on-line and receive a callback from the line. *Ease of use: very good.*

Legacy

Econoguide rating:	★★ 57 points
Ship size:	Small
Category:	Adventure
Price range:	Moderate $$
Registry:	Equatorial Guinea
Year built:	1959 (refurbished 1989)
Information:	(800) 327–2601
Web site:	www.windjammer.com
Passenger capacity:	122 (double occupancy)
Crew:	43
Passenger-to-crew ratio:	2.8:1
Tonnage:	1,740
Length:	294 feet
Beam:	40 feet
Draft:	23 feet
Cruising speed:	12 knots
Guest decks:	4
Total cabins:	61
Outside:	61
Inside:	0
Suites:	0
Wheelchair cabins:	0
Cuisine:	Island/continental, served family-style
Style:	Informal
Price notes:	Single-occupancy, premium 175 percent; reduced rates for children younger than twelve sharing cabin; stowaway aboard ship the night before sailing for $55 pp including meals
Tipping suggestions:	$8.50 pp/pd

The youngest antique in the Windjammer fleet, **Legacy** is a four-masted barkentine built in 1959. Originally named *France II,* she served as a meteoro-

Windjammer *Legacy*. *Photo by Corey Sandler*

logical research and exploration vessel for the French government. The ship was acquired in 1989 by Windjammer and converted into a traditional Tall Ship. She spends the year in the Caribbean.

Mandalay

Econoguide rating:	★★ 50 points
Ship size:	Small
Category:	Adventure
Price range:	Budget $
Registry:	Equatorial Guinea
Year built:	1923 (formerly *Hussar, Vema*; refurbished 1982)
Information:	(800) 327–2601
Web site:	www.windjammer.com
Passenger capacity:	72 (double occupancy)
Crew:	28
Passenger-to-crew ratio:	2.6:1
Tonnage:	420
Length:	236 feet

Beam:	33 feet
Draft:	15 feet
Cruising speed:	10 knots
Guest decks:	3
Total cabins:	36
Outside:	30
Inside:	0
Suites:	6
Wheelchair cabins:	0
Cuisine:	Island/continental; family-style
Style:	Informal
Price notes:	Single occupancy, premium 175 percent; reduced rates for children under twelve sharing cabin; stowaway aboard ship the night before sailing for $55 pp including meals
Tipping suggestions:	$8.50 pp/pd

Mandalay was built in 1923 as *Hussar,* a three-masted barkentine, for financier E. F. Hutton and his wife, Marjorie Merriweather Post. The wealthy couple traded up to a new vessel, now sailing for Sea Cloud Cruises as *Sea Cloud.*

In the 1930s the ship was sold to shipping magnate George Vettlesen and renamed *Vema.* Beginning in 1953 she took on a new role as a floating laboratory for Columbia University's Lamont-Doherty Geological Observatory, sailing more than a million miles while studying the ocean floor and gathering important research in confirmation of the continental drift theory.

The ship joined the Windjammer fleet in 1982; it was renamed *Mandalay* and renovated throughout. All cabins are outside and have a porthole or window; two deck cabins have private verandas.

Polynesia

Econoguide rating:	★★ 50 points
Ship size:	Small
Category:	Adventure
Price range:	Budget $
Registry:	Equatorial Guinea
Year built:	1938 (formerly *Argus,* refurbished 1975)
Information:	(800) 327–2601
Web site:	www.windjammer.com
Passenger capacity:	126 (double occupancy)
Crew:	45
Passenger-to-crew ratio:	2.8:1
Tonnage:	430
Length:	248 feet
Beam:	36 feet

Draft:	18 feet
Cruising speed:	8 knots
Guest decks:	4
Total cabins:	57
Outside:	55
Inside:	0
Suites:	2
Wheelchair cabins:	0
Cuisine:	Island/continental; usually family-style, occasionally buffet
Style:	Informal
Price notes:	Single occupancy, premium 175 percent; reduced rates for children under twelve sharing cabin; stowaway aboard ship the night before sailing for $55 pp including meals
Tipping suggestions:	$8.50 pp/pd

Built in Holland in 1938, **Polynesia** is a four-masted schooner. Originally named *Argus*, she was at one time the swiftest and most profitable of the Portuguese cod fishing fleet on the Grand Banks. The ship was purchased and brought out of retirement in 1975. Renamed *Polynesia*, renovations have included the installation of a teak deck, exotic wood paneling, and a dining salon with each table depicting one of the islands on the ship's itinerary.

Polynesia is one of Windjammer's most popular vessels, hosting special singles' and theme cruises.

Yankee Clipper

Econoguide rating:	★★ 50 points
Ship size:	Small
Category:	Adventure
Price range:	Budget $
Registry:	Equatorial Guinea
Year built:	1927 (formerly *Cressida, Pioneer*; refurbished 1965)
Information:	(800) 327–2601
Web site:	www.windjammer.com
Passenger capacity:	64 (double occupancy)
Crew:	24
Passenger-to-crew ratio:	2.7:1
Tonnage:	327
Length:	197 feet
Beam:	30 feet
Draft:	17 feet
Cruising speed:	14 knots
Guest decks:	3
Total cabins:	32

Outside:	32
Inside:	0
Suites:	0
Wheelchair cabins:	0
Cuisine:	Island/continental; usually family-style
Style:	Informal
Price notes:	Single occupancy, premium 175 percent; reduced rates for children under twelve sharing cabin; stowaway aboard ship the night before sailing for $55 pp including meals
Tipping suggestions:	$8.50 pp/pd

The **Yankee Clipper** is an updated antique, one of the fastest Tall Ships at sea, often sailing at 14 knots. The only armor-plated private yacht in the world, the former *Cressida* was built in Kiel, Germany, in 1927 by German industrialist and manufacturer Alfred Krupp. After World War II the U.S. Coast Guard confiscated the schooner as a war prize.

Acquired by the Vanderbilts and renamed *Pioneer,* she was raced off Newport Beach, California, where she was considered one of the fastest Tall Ships on the West Coast. *Pioneer* was purchased by Windjammer's Mike Burke in 1965 and, following extensive renovations, renamed *Yankee Clipper.* In 1984 she was completely restored to her former majesty, with refurbishments totaling $4 million. The work included a new set of three masts and a new engine room with custom-designed navigation, communication, and weather-monitoring devices.

Amazing Grace

Econoguide rating:	★★ 55 points
Ship size:	Small
Category:	Adventure
Price range:	Budget $
Registry:	Equatorial Guinea
Year built:	1955 (formerly *Pharos,* a British navy motor vessel)
Information:	(800) 327–2601
Web site:	www.windjammer.com
Passenger capacity:	94 (double occupancy)
Crew:	40
Passenger-to-crew ratio:	2.3:1
Tonnage:	1,585
Length:	257 feet
Beam:	40 feet
Draft:	17 feet
Cruising speed:	14 knots
Guest decks:	5

Total cabins:	48
Outside:	46
Inside:	1
Suites:	1
Wheelchair cabins:	0
Cuisine:	Island/continental; usually family-style, occasionally buffet
Style:	Very informal
Price notes:	Single occupancy, premium 175 percent
Tipping suggestions:	$8.50 pp/pd

The motorized supply ship for the Windjammer fleet, **Amazing Grace** permits passengers to hitch a ride on her circuit through the Caribbean and the Bahamas. She sails from Trinidad to Grand Bahama, reversing course every two weeks.

Built in 1955 as the Scottish lighthouse service ship *Pharos,* she has hosted Queen Elizabeth II and other members of the Royal Family. Acquired by Windjammer in 1985, *Amazing Grace* delivers provisions to the four Tall Ships in the fleet on thirteen-day tours.

Restored to her original British charm, the ship has a smoking lounge, antique fireplaces, and a piano room. Only the top-priced cabins have private bathrooms; other cabins share facilities on the same level. The owner's suite, named Burke's Berth, has a large sitting room separated from the stateroom by a set of aquariums. The bath, which includes a hot tub, is built with marble and teak.

WINDSTAR CRUISES

Address: 300 Elliott Avenue West
Seattle, WA 98119
Information: (800) 258–7245, (206) 281–3535
www.windstarcruises.com
Econoguide's Best Adventure Cruise Lines

The Windstar Cruises Fleet

Wind Surf	1990	312 passengers	14,745 tons
Wind Spirit	1988	148 passengers	5,350 tons
Wind Star	1986	148 passengers	5,350 tons

In November 1986 the first commercial sailing vessel built in sixty years left the dock in Le Havre, France. Although the *Wind Star* had the appearance of a classic sailing schooner, the ship, along with the two others in the Windstar fleet, is a decidedly modern-day creation. Computers control the rigging; the huge booms are motor-controlled, with high-tech sensors to trim the angle of the sail. Some 21,000 square feet of white sail unfurls at the push of a button. The angle of heel is kept at a maximum of 6 degrees by a computerized stabilizing system that pumps thousands of gallons of water from side to side with changes in the wind.

Today the *Wind Star* is joined by sister *Wind Spirit* and the larger *Wind Surf,* a five-masted cruise ship. Originally the *Club Med I,* it was rebuilt for Windstar in mid-1998. (You can read a cruise diary about a trip on *Wind Surf* in Chapter 11.)

The ships have auxiliary engines that are used when wind conditions are not favorable and for maneuvering in some harbors. Windstar says, though, that almost half the time at sea is spent under sail.

In late 2002 *Wind Song*—another sister to *Wind Star*—suffered a serious fire while sailing 10 miles off the coast of Tahaa, French Polynesia. All 127 passengers and 92 crew were safely evacuated to the nearby island of Raiatea by a passenger ferry, but the ship was destroyed.

■ ITINERARIES

Wind Star left Tahiti at the end of 2004 to sail new itineraries in Costa Rica, the Panama Canal, the Mediterranean, and the Greek Islands. Windstar had a ship based year-round in Tahiti for more than a decade; the company said its long-term plans include an eventual return to Tahiti. *Wind Star* had been sent to Tahiti in 2003 after the loss of *Wind Song.*

Wind Star is sailing week-long cruises in Costa Rica through the end of March and then returns for two more sailings in December. The ship will also pass through the Panama Canal four times in 2005, with a fourteen-day voyage between Puerto Caldera, Costa Rica, and Bridgetown, Barbados, in March and again in November. A pair of holiday sailings take guests through the canal between Puerto Caldera and Puerto Limon, Costa Rica, in December.

The flagship *Wind Surf* will embark on twelve seven-night cruises round-trip from Cozumel, Mexico, along the Mayan Riviera from January until April in 2005. Ports of call include Cochino Grande, Honduras; West End Roatan, Honduras; Puerto Cortez, Honduras; Omoa, Honduras; Belize City, Belize; and Costa Maya, Mexico.

Wind Spirit will sail round-trip from Saint Thomas for part of the winter, while *Wind Surf* will sail from Saint Thomas and Barbados.

In April 2005 all three ships will embark on fourteen-day transatlantic cruises to Lisbon, Portugal. *Wind Surf* departs from Fort Lauderdale, *Wind Spirit* from Saint Thomas, and *Wind Star* from Barbados. In November 2005, *Wind Star* will make a fourteen-day return voyage from Lisbon to Barbados and *Wind Surf* will sail from Lisbon to Saint Thomas.

The ships will sail forty-eight trips in Europe in 2005, with home ports including Lisbon, Barcelona, Rome, Nice, Marseille, Venice, Monte Carlo, and Malta.

Wind Star is due to sail Mediterranean cruises from June through October. *Wind Spirit* will sail in the Mediterranean in April and again in October and November. *Wind Surf* has plans to sail six- to eleven-day itineraries in the Mediterranean from April through November.

Wind Star and *Wind Spirit* will offer thirty-four cruises in the Greek Islands in the spring and fall of 2005, sailing from Athens and Istanbul with ports of call including Kusadasi, Turkey; Rhodes, Greece; Bodrum, Turkey; Santorini, Greece; and Mykonos, Greece.

■ THE WINDSTAR EXPERIENCE

These are not the ships that Charles Dickens or Herman Melville wrote about. Cabin amenities include a color television and video player, CD player, refrigerator, and direct-dial telephones. Cuisine onboard the ships is directed by Joachim Splichal, chef and owner of Patina Restaurant in Los Angeles, with regional specialties and fine wines. Splichal created 180 signature dishes for Windstar vessels, ranging from rich continental fare to light menus.

Windstar shops local markets for native foods, including cheeses, fruits, spices, and fish. Ambience is casual, with no assigned seating or dress codes.

The ships offer waterskiing, sailboarding, kayaking, and snorkeling from a marina platform built into the stern. Scuba diving is available for an additional charge.

Windstar cruises include a wide range of shore excursions, from the ordinary to the extraordinary, including an exploration of Costa Rica's rain forests where guests will "zip-line" on a pulley and cable from tree to tree way above the forest floor. Other onshore activities include sea kayaking, cultural odysseys, and river float expeditions.

Children—especially infants and toddlers—are not encouraged aboard the cruises.

Windstar was purchased by Holland America in 1988; Holland America was in turn purchased by Carnival Corporation in 1989.

■ WEB SITE

Windstar's Web site provides basic information about the ships and itineraries. There is no way to check availability of cabins on specific trips. Reservations must be made by telephone or through a travel agent; visitors can also request a callback from the line. *Ease of use: very good.*

Wind Spirit, Wind Star

Econoguide rating:	★★★★ 84 points
Ship size:	Small
Category:	Adventure
Price range:	Opulent $$$$
Registry:	Bahamas
Year built:	*Wind Spirit,* 1988; *Wind Star,* 1986 (ships refurbished 1999)
Information:	(800) 258–7245
Web site:	www.windstarcruises.com

Passenger capacity:	148 (double occupancy)
Crew:	88
Passenger-to-crew ratio:	1.7:1
Tonnage:	5,350
Passenger-space ratio:	36.1
Length:	360 feet (waterline); 440 including bowsprit
Beam:	52.1 feet
Draft:	14 feet
Cruising speed:	8.5 to 14 knots, depending on wind; 8.5 to 10 knots with engines only
Guest decks:	4, plus flying bridge
Total cabins:	74
Outside:	74
Inside:	0
Suites:	1 owner's suite
Wheelchair cabins:	0
Cuisine:	Includes Sail Light and vegetarian menus
Style:	Casually elegant
Price notes:	Single-occupancy premium, 175 to 200 percent
Tipping suggestions:	Tipping not required
Best deals:	As much as 50 percent discount through A.S.A.P. early-booking program

A pair of football-field-size sailboats, **Wind Spirit** and **Wind Star** have four 204-foot-tall masts and six self-furling, computer-operated Dacron sails. Modern amenities include a restaurant that accommodates all passengers at one seating, a disco, CD and video libraries, a water sports platform, a saltwater pool, a hot tub, a casino, and a fitness center.

Wind Spirit broke its own record on a transatlantic crossing in December 2001 when it completed 103 consecutive hours under sail propulsion, covering 690 nautical miles at an average speed of 6.7 knots, with northeast winds ranging from 10 to 25 knots.

Sister ship *Wind Song* caught fire and was destroyed in a December 2001 fire in Polynesia; all passengers and crew were successfully evacuated.

Wind Surf

Econoguide rating:	★★★★ 84 points
Ship size:	Medium
Category:	Adventure
Price range:	Opulent $$$$
Registry:	Bahamas
Year built:	1990 (formerly *Club Med I*; refurbished 1999)
Information:	(800) 258–7245

Wind Surf at anchor at Îles des Saintes. *Photo by Corey Sandler*

Web site:	www.windstarcruises.com
Passenger capacity:	312 (double occupancy)
Crew:	163
Passenger-to-crew ratio:	1.9:1
Tonnage:	14,745
Passenger space ratio:	47.3
Length:	535 feet; 617 feet including bowsprit
Beam:	66 feet
Draft:	16.5 feet
Cruising speed:	10 to 15 knots, depending on wind; 12 knots under power
Guest decks:	7
Total cabins:	156
Outside:	125
Inside:	0
Suites:	31
Wheelchair cabins:	0
Cuisine:	Sail Light and vegetarian menus
Style:	Casually elegant

Price notes:	Single-occupancy premium, 175 to 200 percent
Tipping suggestions:	Tipping not required
Best deals:	As much as 50 percent discount through A.S.A.P. early-booking program

The seven-deck **Wind Surf** was born as the *Club Med I,* a thoroughly modern sailing and party vessel. The ship includes two restaurants, able to accommodate all passengers at one seating without assigned tables. Windstar refurbished the *Club Med* to reduce the number of cabins, adding a deck of 400-square-foot suites.

Seven self-furling, computer-operated triangular Dacron sails offer 26,881 square feet of surface area. Depending on destination and wind conditions, the ship is typically under sail about half the time.

CHAPTER EIGHTEEN

A HISTORY OF CRUISING

TODAY'S CRUISE INDUSTRY can trace its lineage back to the nineteenth century, when passenger ships were a means of transportation, primarily from Europe to the United States and between Europe and its far-flung colonies in Asia and Africa.

The arrival of commercial jet airplanes in the late 1950s marked the beginning of the end for the transatlantic and transpacific liners. Many of the big ships went to the breakers to be cut up for salvage. But not that long afterward, a new concept took hold: the cruise ship. Here the ship itself took center stage as a floating resort hotel.

THE ATLANTIC FERRY

By the middle of the nineteenth century, the traffic from Europe to America (and to a lesser extent, the other direction) was so steady that the route across the North Atlantic became known as the "Atlantic Ferry."

The race was on, literally, as shipbuilders pushed for larger and faster ships. The queens of the line also became more and more opulent within, at least for the relatively few wealthy first-class passengers; at the same time, builders crammed more and more low-fare travelers into "steerage" areas, which were often more like bunkhouses than staterooms. (Steerage, though, was the source of much of the shipping lines' profits because of the sheer number of those passengers.)

The first commercial steamship to cross the Atlantic was the *Savannah*, an American coastal packet ship designed as a sailing vessel in 1818 but refitted with an engine during construction. The ship made its first crossing in 1819, a twenty-eight-day voyage from Savannah, Georgia, to Ireland and Liverpool; the ship was never a commercial success.

The real beginnings of the Atlantic Ferry can be traced to Isambard Kingdom Brunel, chief engineer of the Great Western Railway in Great Britain. The rail line between Bristol and London was nearly finished in the 1830s, and Brunel decided to extend his company's reach across the pond. The ship he designed, the *Great Western*, left England for New York on April 8, 1838.

THE EARLY CUNARD LINERS

In 1840 the Cunard Line began mail service across the Atlantic with a quartet of paddle-wheel steamers that had auxiliary sails: the *Britannia, Acadia, Columbia,* and *Caledonia.* In 1858 Brunel's company launched the *Great Eastern,* an iron-hulled vessel that approached in size many of today's cruise ships, with a length of 692 feet.

For the next two decades, British and American interests competed for supremacy as merchant marine powers. During the U.S. Civil War, however, much of the American fleet was destroyed, and Britain regained its leading role, a position it held for the rest of the nineteenth century.

German shipping lines held size and speed records near the end of the nineteenth century, with vessels such as the 1,749-passenger *Kaiser Wilhelm der Grosse.* By 1898 the North German Lloyd line was carrying 28 percent of the passengers from Europe to New York.

The speed of the liners was limited because of the piston design of the steam engines. But by the 1890s, new technology using steam turbine engines began to be used. These systems were more powerful and reliable.

The British, led by the Cunard Line, sought to recapture preeminence with a set of superliners of the day. Cunard's *Lusitania* and *Mauretania* were launched in 1906. The *Mauretania* captured the Blue Riband for the fastest crossing in 1907, holding on to the honor until 1929. The *Lusitania* was sunk by a German submarine in 1915, an action that helped lead to the United States' entry into World War I.

THE *TITANIC* AND THE GREAT WAR

About this same time, the White Star Line, direct competitor of Cunard, also commissioned a pair of superliners. The 45,324-ton *Olympic,* launched in 1911, was for a short period of time the largest ship ever built. That title was taken over by White Star's slightly larger *Titanic* in 1912. The *Titanic,* of course, came to an unhappy end on her maiden voyage in 1912.

After the end of World War I, Germany was removed from competition, with the three surviving German liners confiscated as war reparations. In the postwar boom of the early 1920s, tourism grew markedly. Leaders included the French Line's *Île de France* and the return of the German lines. The Great Depression, though, slowed most new construction, but not all of it.

In 1930 the French Line planned and launched the gigantic *Normandie,* considered one of the most beautiful ships ever built. She was also the first large ship to be built in accordance with the 1929 Convention for Safety of Life at Sea rules. The *Normandie,* which included 1,975 berths, used turboelectric engines that reached a speed of 32.1 knots during trials in 1935. The ship caught fire and sank at a New York dock in 1942 while being refitted as a troopship.

Cunard struck back with the *Queen Mary,* a 975-foot-long classic that was launched in 1934. A sister ship, the 83,673-ton *Queen Elizabeth*, was launched in 1938 but served first as a troopship during World War II, along with most other civilian liners. After the war, it was completed as a luxury liner.

THE TRUE TALE OF THE *TITANIC*

The *Titanic* was big, all right . . . although in today's terms she would merely be one of many large ships, not exactly a Colossus. The *Titanic* was the new flagship of the White Star Line. Work began in 1909, with the launch of the uncompleted hull two years later.

Titanic was 883 feet long, 92 feet wide, and 104 feet tall from keel to bridge. Her gross tonnage was 46,328 tons. She was, at the time, the largest movable object ever made, standing taller than most buildings of the time.

The ship's construction featured a double hull of inch-thick steel plates. Below the waterline, the ship was divided into sixteen supposedly watertight compartments that could be sealed off with massive doors by the closing of a switch on the bridge. The *Titanic* also included an early Marconi radio system, allowing communication with other ships similarly equipped, as well as occasional connection with land-based stations.

Within, the *Titanic*'s accommodations were among the most luxurious afloat, at least for those passengers booked into first class. She was among the first ships with electric lighting in every room, as well as an indoor swimming pool, a squash court, and a gymnasium that had a mechanical horse and camel for exercise.

In an example of how everything old is someday considered a new idea, the *Titanic* offered two alternative restaurants in addition to the formal first-class dining salon.

Down below, hundreds of immigrants were packed into steerage-class accommodations, which were nevertheless described as being of better quality than full-rate cabins on some other ships of the time.

The ship's designers had specified thirty-two lifeboats, which was probably not adequate for the ship's total capacity of 3,500 passengers and crew. White Star made the situation even worse by reducing the number of lifeboats to twenty for appearance's sake. As the *Titanic* left on her maiden voyage, her lifeboats had a capacity of just 1,178 persons.

Titanic departed Southampton, England, on April 10, 1912, stopping across the channel in Cherbourg, France, to pick up some additional passengers and calling the next day in Queenstown, Ireland, for one more group. She headed out into the Atlantic on April 11, reaching her top speed of 22 knots; the *Titanic* was among the fastest ships of her time, but not expected to be the record holder.

The weather on the crossing was good. The winter of 1912 had been unusually moderate, making for good conditions at sea but also contributing to an unusually large amount of icebergs and floes breaking off the Arctic pack. In fact, the *Titanic* may have received a half dozen or more warnings of ice in the North

Atlantic. The captain, perhaps under pressure by executives of the ship line, continued to travel under full steam through the night of April 14.

At 11:40 that night, lookouts spotted a large iceberg ahead of the ship. The first officer ordered the ship hard to port and the engines put into reverse, but the big ship was moving too fast and was too slow to turn; she struck a glancing blow against the side of the berg.

Five of the ship's watertight compartments were ruptured, and water spilled over the top of the other compartment doors—the *Titanic* was doomed.

Investigations claimed that the liner *Californian* was less than 20 miles away from the disaster and could have been on the scene in less than an hour, but its radio cabin was not staffed during the night. Cunard's *Carpathia* finally arrived more than an hour after the ship went down, picking up most of the survivors in lifeboats.

In 1985 the wreck of the *Titanic* was located, split into two large pieces at a depth of about 13,000 feet. Surprisingly, no sign of the expected lengthwise gash in the side of the ship was found; scientists now believe the glancing blow against the iceberg popped open seams in the riveted hull plates of the ship and made a series of smaller gashes.

THE LAST HURRAH OF THE LINERS

The last great American liner was the *United States,* launched in 1952; the ship had a top speed of 35.6 knots and captured the coveted Blue Riband from the *Queen Mary.*

Not long afterward, the arrival of commercial air traffic across the Atlantic spelled the beginning of the end of the great liners. The propeller-driven DC-7 made the crossing at approximately 300 miles per hour, with a range of nearly 3,000 miles. By 1957 there were more passengers crossing the Atlantic by air than by sea. About 1958, commercial jet planes began regular service, and regular transatlantic traffic by liner was entering its final days.

Of course, today the industry is booming. The difference is that nearly all passenger vessels are cruise ships rather than liners.

The increasingly more fabulous ships and their ports of call are the lures, not mere transportation across an ocean or from continent to continent. On some cruises a significant number of passengers don't get off the ship when it ties up at the dock: Their entertainment, dining, and sports activities all take place on board.

GLOSSARY OF CRUISING

━━━━━━

OK, LET'S GET ONE THING STRAIGHT: It's a ship, not a boat. A boat is something you row across the pond or sail across the river. A ship is a big vessel that has lots of cabins, many levels, a bingo parlor, a health club, and a rotating disco at the top of its massive funnel. You get the idea: Boat is little, ship is big.

If you really want to sound like a swabbie (the opposite of a landlubber), here is a guide to some nautical terms for the cruise vacationer.

Abeam. To the side of the ship, at a right angle to the keel that runs the length of the vessel.

Aft. At the stern (rear) of the ship, or rearward from your present location.

Amidships. At or near the middle of the ship.

Astern. Behind the stern of the ship.

Beam. The width of the ship at its broadest point, usually amidships.

Bearing. The compass direction of the ship in motion, or the direction toward a specified point.

Below. Any area beneath the main deck of the ship.

Berth. A dock or pier for the ship, or a bed for a passenger or crewman.

Bilge. The lowest interior space of the ship.

Boat station. The assigned assembly place for passengers and crew in a lifeboat drill or a true emergency.

Bow. The front of the ship.

Bridge. The principal navigation and control station.

Bulkhead. A vertical wall used to divide sections of the ship into waterproof and fire-resistant compartments.

Bunkers. Fuel storage areas.

Colors. The national flag or emblem flown by a particular vessel.

Companionway. An interior stairway.

Course. The bearing of the ship as underway, expressed in degrees.

Davit. The rope and pulley or motor system used to lower and raise lifeboats.

Draft. The distance from the ship's waterline to the lowest part of the keel; a ship cannot safely enter waters shallower than its draft.

Fantail. An overhang at the stern of the ship.

Fathom. A measurement of water depth equal to 6 feet. The measure was derived from the average distance from fingertip to fingertip of the outstretched arms of a man.

Galley. The ship's kitchen.

Gangway. A walkway extended to connect the ship to shore.

Gross registered tons (GRT). A measurement of the total permanently enclosed spaces of the ship, excluding certain essential areas such as the bridge and galleys, developed as a means of taxing vessels based on their cargo-carrying capacity; 1 GRT = 100 cubic feet of enclosed space.

Helm. The steering mechanism. As a verb, to take the control of the steering mechanism.

Hull. The body of the ship.

Knot. One nautical mile. This is based on a measure of one-sixtieth of a degree of the earth's circumference, which works out to 6,080.2 feet, or about 800 feet longer than a land-based mile. The term knot as a measure of speed refers to distance per hour; 20 knots means 20 knots per hour. (Only a landlubber says "per hour.") To convert knots to miles per hour, add about 15 percent. For example, 20 knots is equal to just over 23 miles per hour.

Leeward. The side of the ship or a body of land that is sheltered from the wind. The opposite is windward.

Nautical mile. A measurement of distance equal to one-sixtieth of a degree of the circumference of the earth, or about 6,080.2 feet.

Pilot. A specially trained guide to local waters sometimes taken aboard when a ship enters an unfamiliar or tricky harbor or area.

Pitch. The rise and fall of the ship's bow when it is under way.

Plimsoll mark. A set of marks on the side of a vessel that shows at least three depths indicating the maximum safe draft (the lowest the ship can safely sit in the water). One line is for summer when seas are generally calm in most parts of the world, another for winter when seas are usually rougher, and a third is a freshwater line to account for the fact that fresh water is significantly less buoyant than salt water. The mark was named for nineteenth-century social reformer Samuel Plimsoll, who was concerned about ship disasters blamed on overloading by greedy owners.

Port. The left side of the ship when facing forward. On old Viking ships, the steering board was on the right side, so the left side was used as the side to tie up in port.

Quay. A berth or dock.

Rudder. A movable part of the ship that extends into the water and is used to steer the vessel.

Screw. A ship's propeller.

Stabilizer. An adjustable finlike structure that extends from the side of a ship to minimize roll.

Starboard. The right side of the ship when facing forward. On Viking ships, the steering board (the star board) was placed on the right side.

Stern. The rearmost part of the ship.

Tender. A small boat used to transport passengers or crew to shore when the ship is anchored away from a dock.

Veranda. A private balcony for a passenger cabin, a feature of some of the most modern and luxurious vessels and generally located on the upper decks.

Wake. The track of disturbed water left behind a ship in motion.

Watches. Assigned duties for the crew. On a naval ship, the twenty-four-hour day was divided into seven watches: the midwatch from midnight to 4:00 A.M., the morning watch from 4:00 to 8:00 A.M., the forenoon watch from 8:00 A.M. to noon, the afternoon watch from noon to 4:00 P.M., the first dog watch from 4:00 to 6:00 P.M., the second dog watch from 6:00 to 8:00 P.M., and the evening watch from 8:00 P.M. to midnight. Traditionally, because few sailors could afford a timepiece, the passage of time aboard Navy ships was indicated by the striking of bells during each four-hour watch. One bell was struck after the first half hour, two bells after one hour, three bells after an hour and a half, four bells after two hours, and so on up to eight bells at the completion of the four-hour watch.

Windward. The side of the ship or a body of land that is exposed to the wind.

And while I'm on the subject, here are a few terms from nautical sources that have become part of our common language.

Between the devil and the deep blue sea. On an old wooden ship, the longest seam, which ran from the bow to the stern, was called the "devil." The seam needed to be caulked regularly to keep it watertight, and to do so a sailor was suspended in a boatswain's chair—between the devil and the deep blue sea. The caulking was an asphalt pitch, also known as "pay." Sailors were sometimes assigned to this unpleasant task as punishment for infractions of the rules. The threat was to behave, or there would be the "devil to pay."

The cat is out of the bag. The cat-o'-nine-tails was used to whip sailors as punishment; when it was removed from its cloth bag, everyone knew what came next.

Chewing the fat. Salted beef was one of the staples aboard nineteenth-century ships, not much more edible than shoe leather. It sometimes required hours of chewing to make it soft enough to swallow.

Crow's nest. Vikings carried ravens or crows as part of their navigation equipment. In poor weather, the birds—carried in a cage at the top of the mast—were released. Sailors observed the direction the birds headed and plotted a course toward land. The platform at the top of the mast, or the uppermost place on a motor ship, is now known as the crow's nest.

Cup of Joe. Josephus Daniels, the U.S. Secretary of the Navy under President Woodrow Wilson, introduced a number of changes in the early part of the twentieth century, among them the end of the wine mess for officers; thereafter, the strongest available drink aboard Navy ships was coffee, which became known as a "cup of Joe."

Feeling blue. A ship that lost its captain or principal officer during a voyage would paint a blue band around the hull and fly blue flags from the rigging.

Hunky-dory. Derived from the name of a street in the port of Yokohama, Japan, where residents catered to the carnal pleasures of sailors, the term means that everything is satisfactory.

Jury-rig. Meaning to put something together in a makeshift way, the term comes from "jury mast," a temporary mast constructed from any available spar.

Log book. Early ship's records were kept on shingles cut from logs, hinged into a log book.

Mayday. The international radio phrase for ships in trouble is an anglicized version of the French phrase *m'aidez,* meaning "help me." It was officially adopted as a signal in 1948.

Minding your p's and q's. The careful and neat sailor took care that his pigtail, or queue, which was kept in shape with a mousse of tar, did not soil his pea jacket.

Portholes. Ships were equipped with large cannons in the fifteenth century held behind large doors that could be opened when needed; the French word for door is *porte.*

S.O.S. The letters S.O.S. were selected for a Morse code signal of distress because the combination of sounds—dot-dot-dot, dash-dash-dash, dot-dot-dot—was easily recognized. It is not an acronym for "save our ship" or "save our souls," a mere coincidence.

Three sheets to the wind. On a small sailing vessel, three sheets (ropes) controlled the sails; if the sheets were loose, the sails were out of control. Today we apply the term to a sailor or a landlubber who is out of control with the assistance of drink.

The whole nine yards. A square-rigger sailing vessel had three masts with three yards (or sails) on each; if the captain was sailing hard, he was giving the vessel the whole nine yards.

CRUISE LINES IN THIS BOOK

American Canadian Caribbean Line ♀♀♀
(800) 556–7450; www.accl-small ships.com
American Cruise Lines ♀♀♀
(860) 345–3311; www.americancruiselines.com
Carnival Cruise Lines ♀♀♀
(800) 227–6482, (305) 599–2600; www.carnival.com
Celebrity Cruises ♀♀♀♀
(800) 437–3111, (305) 262–6677; www.celebrity-cruises.com
Clipper Cruise Line ♀♀♀
(800) 325–0010, (314) 727–2929; www.clippercruise.com
Costa Cruise Lines ♀♀♀
(800) 332–6782, (305) 358–7325; www. costacruises.com
Cruise West ♀♀♀
(800) 888–9378, (206) 441–8687; www.cruisewest.com
Crystal Cruises ♀♀♀♀♀♀
(800) 820–6663, (310) 785–9300; www.crystalcruises.com
Cunard Line ♀♀♀♀♀
(800) 528–6273, (305) 463–3000; www.cunard.com
Delta Queen Steamboat Company
(800) 543–7637; www.deltaqueen.com
Discovery World Cruises ♀♀♀
(866) 623–2689; (954) 761–7878; www.discoveryworldcruises.com
Disney Cruise Line ♀♀♀♀
(800) 326–0620; www.disneycruise.com
Glacier Bay Cruiseline ♀♀♀
(800) 451–5952, (206) 623–7110; www.glacierbaytours.com
Holland America Line ♀♀♀♀
(800) 227–6482, (800) 426–0327; www.hollandamerica.com
Imperial Majesty Cruise Line ♀♀
(800) 511–5737; www.oceanbreezecruise.com
Lindblad Special Expeditions ♀♀♀
(800) 397–3348; www.expeditions.com
MSC Italian Cruises ♀♀♀
(800) 666–9333; www.msccruisesusa.com

Norwegian Cruise Line ✿✿✿✿
(800) 327–7030; www.ncl.com

Oceania Cruises ✿✿✿
(800) 531–5658, (305) 514–2300; www.oceaniacruises.com

Princess Cruises ✿✿✿✿
(800) 421–0522, (800) 774–6237; www.princess.com

Radisson Seven Seas Cruises ✿✿✿✿✿
(800) 333–3333, (800) 285–1835; www.rssc.com

RiverBarge Excursion Lines ✿✿✿
(888) 462–2743; www.riverbarge.com

Royal Caribbean International ✿✿✿
(800) 327–6700; www.royalcaribbean.com

Seabourn Cruise Line ✿✿✿✿✿✿
(800) 929–9391; www.seabourn.com

Sea Cloud Cruises ✿✿✿✿✿
(888) 732–2568, (201) 227–9404; www.seacloud.com

Silversea Cruises ✿✿✿✿✿✿
(800) 722–9955, (954) 522–4477; www.silversea.com

Society Expeditions ✿✿✿
(800) 548–8669; www.societyexpeditions.com

Star Clippers ✿✿✿
(800) 442–0551; www.star-clippers.com

Windjammer Barefoot Cruises ✿✿✿
(800) 327–2601; www.windjammer.com

Windstar Cruises ✿✿✿✿
(800) 258–7245, (206) 281–3535; www.windstarcruises.com

OTHER CRUISE LINES AND PACKAGERS

Abercrombie and Kent International
(800) 323–7308; www.abercrombiekent.com

Club Med
(800) 258–2633, (305) 925–9000; www.clubmed.com

Norwegian Coastal Voyages
(800) 666–2374, (212) 319–1300; www.coastalvoyage.com

Peter Deilmann Cruises
(800) 348–8287, (703) 549–1741; www.deilmann-cruises.com

Star Cruises
(305) 436 4694; www.starcruises.com

Swan Hellenic
(877) 219–4239; www.swanhellenic.com

INDEX

Cruise ships

ABOUT THE AUTHOR

Corey Sandler is a former newsman and editor for the Associated Press, Gannett Newspapers, Ziff-Davis Publishing, and IDG. He has written more than 160 books on travel, video games, and computers; his titles have been translated into French, Spanish, German, Italian, Portuguese, Polish, Bulgarian, Hebrew, and Chinese. When he's not traveling, he hides out with his wife and two children on Nantucket, an island 30 miles off the coast of Massachusetts.

EXPERIENCE THE QUEEN MARY

SPEND THE DAY, SPEND THE NIGHT

QUEEN MARY TOURS

THE HAUNTED SHIP
GHOSTS AND LEGENDS SPECIAL
EFFECTS ADVENTURE

SEE MORE OF THE SHIP
ALL NEW SELF-GUIDED OR
GUIDED TOURS OF THE SHIP

COLD WAR
RUSSIAN SUBMARINE

ART DECO
OBSERVATION BAR

ALL NEW TOURS

Come explore the elegance and adventure that is the Queen Mary. Tour this magnificent floating palace and discover its secrets. Your tour will take you through the entire ship from its impressive engine room to its newly restored decks. Stroll through Art Deco ballrooms, be captivated by the treasures from the Queen Mary archive. Your admission also includes the new Ghosts & Legends show and our new WWII exhibit that brings the Queen's rich history to life. So bring the entire family for a fun-filled, affordable adventure to the past.

THE QUEEN MARY.

HOTEL QUEEN MARY

365-STATEROOM
ART DECO HOTEL

AWARD-WINNING
CASUAL TO ELEGANT
RESTAURANTS

SIXTEEN ORIGINAL
SALONS FOR
MEETINGS AND BANQUETS

ELEGANT
CHAMPAGNE SUNDAY BRUNCH

For information or reservations call 562.435.3511. www.queenmary.com

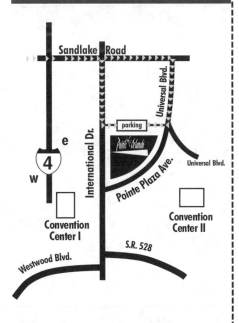

PRICELESS CAR RENTAL
Los Angeles International Airport
(800) 770–0606

$6 Off Rentals 1 to 4 Days

$12 Off Rentals 5 Days or More

Our car rental rates start at $19.95/day
• Under 25 years OK • Free airport pick-up/drop-off
• Low weekly/monthly rates

Expires 12/31/05

PRICELESS
CAR RENTAL

**4831 W. Century Boulevard,
Los Angeles, CA 90304
Outside USA/Canada,
call (310) 673–9899;
fax (310) 680–9797**